THE
FORGOTTEN PEOPLE

Seymour Freidin

CHARLES SCRIBNER'S SONS New York

PICTURE CREDITS

BLACK STAR: 8 (Peter Burchett); 9 (Friedrich Rauch); 13 (Hulton
Press); 16 (Curirpost Press and Photo Agency); 21 (Charles
Bonnay); 22 (Wanda Gawronska); 23 (Kosti Ruohomaa); 25
(Werner Forman)

MAGNUM: 1 (Robert Capa); 18 (Erich Lessing); 31 (Dan Budnik)

PICTORIAL PARADE: 2 (Paris Match); 4; 15 (Paris Match); 20 (London
Daily Express); 29

UNITED PRESS INTERNATIONAL: 3; 5; 6; 10; 12; 14; 17; 19; 24; 26; 27

WIDE WORLD: 7; 11; 28; 30

For Stiva

Preface

Through years of casual usage the word "satellite" has taken on double meaning. Today it stirs up an image of herculean Soviet spacemen and mighty rocketry against an uneasy, uncomfortable background of countries in Europe under Soviet subjugation. Eastern Europe, we must remember, was where the phrase, "Soviet satellite," first applied.

It was commonly used that way before the first sputnik blasted its way into our consciousness and sense of self-indulgence. The Russians used their scientific advance into outer space as a lever to compel us to recognize their Communized conquests of Eastern Europe. We have, rightly, refused to accept these conditions of the Communist version of the status quo in Eastern Europe. While we still lag in the spectacular thrust into space, the United States, we should remember, retains an awesome quantity of nuclear weapons. They are far more varied and more lethal than those in the Soviet armory. Moreover, our (scientific-propaganda) quests into outer space have not been made at the expense of neglecting the human factor on earth.

The power that launched a Gagarin and a Titov, makes—to many people—a satellite right here on earth seem rather unimportant. That is what the Russians would like the world to believe. But the massive strength concentrated behind Titov's feat is still small change, compared with the enormous effort, expense and planning the Soviet Union applies in keeping satellites on earth within its own orbit.

The advent of an actual Communist threat in our own Western hemisphere jolted our complacent society. We obviously never thought it could happen to us. In the United States government, planners and statesmen, including President Kennedy, talk soberly of meeting the Communists at their own game: Guerrilla warfare, psychological warfare and the ideological conflict for men's minds.

Through conditioning of power politics, too many of us in the West, have come to conclude that the Soviet satellites in Eastern Europe are here to stay. Many of us consider it immoral to write off 100,000,000 people and vast stretches of territory with ancient European cultures. But many of us—too many—shrug hopelessly and say that it may be tragic, or even criminal but after all what can we do about it?

Great events, like the Hungarian Revolution, shattered us. True, we always hoped for an expression against tyranny. When it exploded in our faces, we did not know what to do. We did not act. A clarion call for "Rollback"—in effect, liberation of Eastern Europe—had long before been buried as a political fraud. Thus, when the opportunity arose to come to grips with liberation of Eastern Europe, we recoiled. We had, you see, done little besides mention the sacrifices and aspirations such an aim could produce.

As we now know, "Rollback" was a cynical and chimerical campaign slogan—good for home consumption only. We never meant it. Yet we were ashamed. So, we helped refugees, spent some money and protested. The power that launched Titov, sputniks and luniks is, after all, something we must respect. That is known as political realism.

But, must we also respect the kind of power that keeps a large chunk of the world locked in its suffocating grasp? Is it realistic, moreover, to think that the satellites on earth are incapable even now of murmurs of protests or ferments of discontent? That is a convenient way out. Worse, it is wrong, which is the point. In the years of Soviet consolidation over

Eastern Europe, we came to believe that the satellite peoples could not speak. Uprisings stunned us. We somehow were gripped by the complacent logic that these hapless millions were being recreated in an iron mold, made in the Soviet Union.

We have been wrong for, basically, the same reasons the Russians constantly miscalculate in Eastern and Southeastern Europe. There may be satellite states but the people are not satellites. They speak out in myriad ways—in defiance, in death, in resistance—active and passive. The people of Eastern Europe spoke before there were any uprisings against Soviet rule by proconsul. They will continue to speak to us in the future. It is not up to us to "liberate" anybody. This is egoism misplaced for a country like ours that came into being by liberating itself. Oppressed people, in time, can only be liberated by themselves. We, for our part, can only help with pressure against the common enemy—political and economic.

The United States must realize that such action will require not only sacrifice, disappointment and frustration, but vast risk. In time, the compulsion for liberation begins to bedevil the occupier. Eastern Europe, we must always keep in mind, is in the grip of Soviet military occupation. A trumped-up Warsaw military pact gives the Russians free entry into Eastern Europe. Unlike the North Atlantic Treaty Alliance, no satellite member can freely opt to leave the alliance. Hungary, with tragic results, tried to leave.

It remains our responsibility to listen when the people of the satellites have something to say. Their messages, in everyday life of the West, may seem humdrum. They don't usually come in the form of dramatic outbursts, uprisings or secret messages smuggled over tightly guarded frontiers. It may be a whispered goodbye near a collective, a handshake at a tenement with the appeal, "Remember us because *we* do not forget," or the barbed jokes, honed sharp to remind the given regime of the repression that keeps it in power. Or it may even be a wee, parting gift that cost four days' pay. The messages are endless; the resistance is as inflexible as the ruling regimes are single-minded.

For years, the West mistook stillness in Eastern Europe for acquiescent silence. After the first courageous voices were throttled, the leaderless had to learn to talk again. It took time, courage and ingenuity to do it. Moreover it had to be done repeatedly. The underground torrent of expression sometimes burst without warning, as, for example, in Pilsen, Czechoslovakia. That was only a few days before the riots in East Berlin. Then it eddied into a turbulent pool, overflowing later into Poznan. In floodwater strength, it engulfed Budapest. The Russians, with vengeful cruelty, damned up the floods. These are temporary barriers. Soviet dikes are leaky all over Eastern Europe from the Elbe to the Iron Gates of the Danube.

Along with puppet governments, the Soviet Union has insisted on imposing its own mistakes on subject lands. Soviet power has never considered the human factor, the single most incalculable element in making plans for the rulers and the ruled. In Eastern Europe, there are, as noted earlier, about 100,000,000 people. The vast majority are unhappy, bitter, overworked and underprivileged. We talk today in lofty terms of the aspirations of underdeveloped countries. Eastern Europe, we frequently forget, also is maldeveloped because of Soviet colonial rule grafted tenaciously on alien peoples.

Planners, politicians and commissars, going by the book as inscribed by Marx and interpreted by Lenin, Stalin and Khrushchev, have tried to convert foreigners into the basic Soviet concept of men and women. They have always been a minority, backed by great armies or militant guerrilla forces. In Eastern Europe, with the exception of Marshal Tito's partisans, satellite regimes came in with the Red army. Nowhere have the Communists sponsored or won a genuine parliamentary election.

In their blinkered determination, the Russians ignored the fact that nearly all the subject populations had for centuries lived under foreign, and usually, tyrannical rule. Yet all survived oppression, partition and submission to emerge as nations and identifiable nationalities.

Few of these downtrodden nations and their people ever had a chance to savor principles of parliamentary democracy we so automatically invoke in our own defense. They have been groping interminably for the promised land where expression is free and human dignity is protected. This, to them, is the image of America rather than the legend that streets are paved with gold. We may never have had it so good and they, never quite so bad. They do not begrudge us our well-being; they are only disappointed that we have apparently turned a deaf ear to their aspirations. Conflicting great power interests often betrayed their quest for real self-determination. Frequently, their own leaders subverted them. But the compulsive attachment to liberation is constant. It often happens to be concealed; never extinguished.

As a reporter I have had a unique and mournful assignment—something like a death-watch. I was one of the handful of Westerners who witnessed the first phase, the consolidation of power through almost all of Eastern Europe. It started with the fall of Berlin in 1945, which I witnessed as I went with the Red army under the Brandenburg Gate to an arch of Soviet triumph. That was the beginning that led me to the Black Sea outposts of Soviet Europe, the coldblooded power play in Greece and back into middle Europe.

I saw political coalitions callously chopped up; men of goodwill executed; and countries terrorized. The macabre circuit took me to the Communist *putsch* in Czechoslovakia and the great rift in the Communist world between Tito's Yugoslavia and Stalin's Soviet empire.

For nearly seven years thereafter time stood still for us in the West. We were on the outside looking in except for our militant, well-intentioned, sometimes bungling participation in Greece. It was virtually impossible to report from Eastern Europe with the exception of Yugoslavia, at bay against Stalin. Why? One could not get visas. Soviet authority wanted no outside witnesses to the law of the midnight-knock-on-the-door. Still the voices of the satellite people could be heard.

In those seven years in the wilderness, so to speak, men and women went on defying, dying or holding their breath so they could speak again. There were hair-raising escapes under harrowing conditions. Men pretended to work to preserve themselves and their kin. They bowed but they did not surrender. The way they hoped, lived, loved and died was heroic, if not dramatic, in a world grown accustomed to cynicism.

Meanwhile, the Communist apparatus also hungrily devoured its own engineers. A permanent purge gave the world a nightmarish insight into the Soviet "monolith" in Eastern Europe. I knew many of the Communist proconsuls fed into Stalin's "liquidator." Pity had never been their strong point and they were pitilessly destroyed. In this jungle, a phenomenal man, a Communist and a dictator, alone held out. He was Josip Broz Tito, as tough as Stalin, as egocentric but craftier. Tito rejected full-blown Sovietization, second-rate comradely citizenship under Stalin. His country, anti-Communist in the main, rallied behind him. It was a fight for survival and Yugoslavs knew how to fight.

Tito also had—and has even broadened outside Europe today—his own ambitions. What is more, he made them stick in the teeth of Russian-imposed economic blockades, threats of invasion and provocation. The

Soviet world will never again be the same for the Tito-Stalin break. It smashed the unquestioned infallibility of the mother church of Communism in Moscow.

After Stalin's death, the seal of oppression and isolation in Eastern Europe began to melt slowly. Flights to the outside world became more numerous. Ferment among the new governing cliques became more apparent. A policy of controlled "relaxation" was attempted from Moscow, epitomized by the hurly-burly technique of Nikita Khrushchev.

The curtain that was iron parted a little in what has since become known as the "Thaw." Some of us could again travel in Eastern Europe— I was the first American back into Bulgaria, for example—and there was opportunity to assess at first hand what had gone before in the seven frozen years. Life was dirty gray, like trampled winter snow on which a city's soot had fallen. Men and women in countless number lay in unmarked tombs. But they were not forgotten. Nosegays were strewn on their graves. Word gets around even among gravediggers. There also were the brainwashed. Once-defiant leaders, local and national, gave up. From jails and torture chambers, they went to regime sinecures where they performed like automatons.

A new generation had come into maturity. All the indoctrination and care of the state had been lavished on these boys and girls coming of age. It was not a generation of which Soviet Europe could be proud. Embers of hope for a better future and repudiation of regime teaching glowed in the ashes of deliberate human indignity.

This younger generation experienced the bitterness of betrayal and false doctrine in its teens. Rejection of doctrine and dogma took many forms. There was, for instance, jazz, so long assailed as a poisonous export from the United States that special police details for years in Eastern Europe had no other assignment but to root out jazz clubs.

Shifting Soviet policies and Russian groping to insure succession rule to Stalin let in currents of fresh air. Circumstances, as a reporter, gave me a ringside seat to what followed. Khrushchev with his goat-bearded outside man, Nikolai Bulganin, went to apologize to Tito. The Yugoslav dictator—as vain as he is a relentless practitioner of power—was pleased to get the Soviet leadership's apologies. But his own Communist independence of Moscow, which brought him world renown, made Tito implacably opposed to returning to Moscow's fold.

Satellite regimes, built on police terror, were uniformly instructed to let up a little. Communist victims of their own parties' terror were publicly rehabilitated in grisly ceremonies. Khrushchev went further to help himself at home and abroad and denounced Stalin's years of terror. "Stalinist" became a dirty word in most regime councils of Eastern Europe. It was, I am convinced, also an outlet for pent-up passion over years of privation and injustice.

A little truth, however, is a dangerous thing in the tangled, murky undergrowth of totalitarian society. It places heinous crimes in much sharper perspective. Men, grown desperate, become audacious. Youth, disillusioned, turns into fearless reformers. Even in his tightly held, heretical preserve, Tito faced demands for a change from two of his most esteemed protégés—Milovan Djilas, party theoretician, and Vladimir Dedijer, Tito's own biographer.

The fever of ferment infected party and non-party members alike.

The voice of discontent in Eastern Europe was heard throughout the world—in the bloody riots in Poznan and at the turbulent meetings of writers, students and intellectuals at the Petofi Club in Budapest in the late spring and summer of 1956. Then, in its furious majesty the revolution in Hungary exploded to shake the Communist world "even to the mainland of China," as Mao Tse-tung has admitted.

I was a bystander at these upheavals. But being a reporter does not endow one automatically with the dispassionate qualities and scholarly perspectives of the historian. Above all, I am interested in people and what impact they have on events and vice versa no matter their meanness of station in life. I do not believe any historian could have forecast Poland's October nor the Hungarian Revolution from a mass of documentation or research. Even today it would be, I think, presumptuous to offer an all-definitive assessment of how and why Eastern Europe is in periodic ferment. I say so because I also have traveled extensively in Soviet Europe since the great events in Poland and Hungary.

In the great power quest for accommodation—East and West—coexistence is held up as the goal for peace, plenty and justice. Yet the meaning of coexistence is not the same in the Soviet Union as it is in the West. Khrushchev, for example, wants us to renounce forever our interest in the plight of the satellite people and their incessant struggles. He is determinedly unwilling and incapable of admitting that Soviet hegemony over Eastern Europe is totally contrary to self-determination. He wants us to underwrite a status quo, which approves lasting Soviet domination. This is a form of coexistence but certainly not peace with justice. We cannot, with our heritage, cynically barter away anyone else's right to life, liberty and the pursuit of happiness.

Through situations, case histories and actions of Eastern Europeans— the rulers and the ruled—I want to show aspiration and acquiescence, resistance and betrayal, flaming hope or brutal terror. As an American, I have lived in many Eastern European countries and with Eastern Europeans. I have also watched a good number fight and defy, each in his or her own way. I have seen too many die, even if they continued to live. I do not believe in what is still sometimes described as "objective reporting." To me this is an all too simple solution of trying to reflect man's fate by accepting none of the responsibility for it. A Hungarian Freedom Fighter did not try to listen to the Soviet side. He knew it. So, he took up arms where he could find them, or grabbed a bottle of gasoline and charged a thirty-ton tank.

These are the actions that give tone and volume to the voice of Eastern Europe. To purists, it may not be history in the classic manner. But it is from and about people who make and have made history. I prefer it because it is experience, not theory. You cannot write off, for reasons of policy, fear or selfishness, other people and how they may want to live.

The most vivid statement of aims I remember came not from any venerable statesman but from a twenty-year-old boy in Budapest in 1956 who was a rifleman from the Revolutionary Students' Committee:

"Some day the world will realize that Eastern Europe is simply people who want to live like decent people," he said. "For us and for you it is a search that never ends. It is a journey without time."

In this I believe. A space shot always will be complicated and spectacular. But the search for a life of freedom and human dignity also will always be complicated, sometimes even more spectacular and always more worthwhile.

CHAPTER 1

THE sodden Red flag, flapping high above the Brandenburg Gate, was fanned into a streaming banner by gusts of a chilling wind. You could not mistake the hammer and sickle, embroidered in yellow, that glowed with a phosphorescent light in the premature darkness of the afternoon. Rain slanted over the smoking ruins of a dying capital. This was the heart of Berlin, opposite Unter den Linden, where there were no more trees. It was May, 1945.

Wind and rain, raging so bitterly for early spring, tore the shouts of men at deadly work—killing—out of their mouths. Their cries and curses blended into the Götterdämmerung of total war. Heavy artillery was the booming bass; automatic weapons the sharp soprano. Round-the-clock bombardment created grotesque scenic effects. In the background was the constant crunch of buildings in collapse. Tongues of flame darted from the shells of homes. Even shards of walls were riddled as if an epidemic infected every standing thing with the sign of the plague.

1

Corpses, frozen in sudden death, were strewn like worn-out machinery dumped in junkyards.

"It is about all over, Mr. America," the chunky Russian said to me quietly in German. He shook himself and seemed to shudder. He wore a captain's insignia on his beat-up uniform. His name was Alexandre Malokovsky, a man of thirty-five who looked fifty. We were on a nickname basis and I called him Sascha.

"No more Hitler," he went on. "The Battle of Berlin is finished. A few snipers. A few crazy people. Maybe we can really start to think about going home."

We stood there, staring at the Brandenburg Gate. It had been the German symbol of military glory. Three red flags entwined the driver of the victory chariot. The archway was blocked by concrete, a feeble effort to keep foreign visitors from marching through. Russian soldiers were scrambling all over the arch. Names in Cyrillic script were scrawled at the base.

"What's the Russian for 'Kilroy was here'?" I asked him.

"What do you mean?" he asked back in surprise.

I told him to forget it and we strolled the Tiergarten, once Berlin's famed Central Park. It had become a shell-shredded no-man's land. Germans had built bunkers, now blasted. Paths were chewed by fire and trees were interlaced with toppled statuary. Colored posters of Stalin, in a marshal's uniform, were plastered all around. I pointed to them and Sascha shrugged.

"Agit-prop," he muttered.

A tattered group of elderly men and women were grubbing near a bunker. They were oblivious to occasional bursts of fire nearby.

"It doesn't matter for them any more," he said.

The old Berliners looked back at us. Just a hasty glance. They went on digging with their hands and putting things in their pockets. Only blackened potatoes from a cache they remembered. Finders keepers seemed to be the rule of war here.

Two open trucks, Studebakers, clattered up to us and braked. Men in Russian uniform leaped down. Under their arms they carried large rolls of what looked like newsprint. Some hauled pails sloshing over with paste. They also wore armbands.

"Who are they?" I asked Sascha.

"Anti-Fa; anti-Fascist Germans," he replied.

"Achtung," bawled a uniformed German to the potato grubbers who straightened up slowly. The German was big and beefy, in his late twenties and obviously enjoyed authority.

"This is a forbidden zone," he said to the dazed Berliners. "Empty your pockets and get out."

"Only potatoes," an old man began.

"Raus," said the anti-Fa leader. He grabbed the old man roughly, turned out his pockets and ripped one that dangled loosely. One by one, the elderly Berliners emptied their pockets. They trudged away. Two women looked back, not at us, but at the little heap of charred potatoes.

To his two truckloads of comrades, their leader gave instructions. They split up, slapping more circulars and posters on tree stumps and overturned statuary. The Russian and I stepped over to look at one.

"We come as liberators to help you into a democratic future," the poster read.

Up to us strode the anti-Fa leader. Stiffly, he saluted my companion and spoke to him in Russian.

"He wants to know who you are," said Sascha.

I replied in German. The "anti-Fa" said he was surprised, that he had heard all Western allies were excluded from the area. For their own safety under such conditions, he explained. Then, questions rolled out in a torrent. How many of us were there? Did we have propaganda teams with us?

The captain stopped him. He said that I had been with him, on and off, for the past few days. I asked the next question. How did he, the anti-Fa man, get that way? The answer was smooth. It must have been given many times before.

"I was a soldier in the Wehrmacht," he said. "I was taken prisoner on the Western front. I have been re-educated. It is my opportunity to re-educate others. We will have a people's democracy, not what you say yours is in America."

Two of his poster-pasting comrades who paused to listen beamed approval at the spiel. The big anti-Fa man raised his arm melodramatically, pointing in the direction of the Brandenburg Gate.

"You will see one day not too far from now what the Soviet will build," he said oratorically. "From the Brandenburg Gate you will see people building socialism all the way to Asia."

Strange, I remarked to the captain, that it was a German who made

the first direct propaganda speech to me while I was with the Red Army.
"Marx and Engels were Germans," he replied.

"They have been followed by Lenin and Stalin," chimed in the anti-Fa
soldier.

By the way, could he have the name of the comrade captain? He certainly could not, the Russian replied tersely. The anti-Fa man saluted
impassively and rejoined his detail. We retraced our way slowly to the
Brandenburg Gate in silence and walked around to Unter den Linden.
There were more busy paste parties, some Russian. A huge color poster
of Stalin had been unrolled on the façade of the gutted Reichstag. In
foot-high letters, on ruined buildings, was the legend: "The future belongs to socialism, thanks to dear Comrade Stalin."

The painters didn't waste time the last few hours, I told Sascha.

"Politics, politics," he replied wearily and shrugged.

Did he also believe, as the anti-Fa man claimed, about a whole new
world, starting at the Brandenburg Gate?

"I am not an agit-prop," was the answer. "It is too complicated. Who
knows what will happen? We talked about the world back there. Remember?"

That was a few days before, in a different world, when East met West
through a link-up of American and Russian soldiers. We were on the
heady brink of victory and the end of the war in Europe.

Every American army in hailing distance raced to be the first to meet
the Russians. I was with the Ninth Army, commanded by brass-bound
Lt. Gen. William (Baldy) Simpson. Before we started looking for Russians who never answered our radio signals, Simpson briefed staff officers
and correspondents attached to his army.

For a few days our objective had been to try to find a hole through
which we might rush into Berlin. That was finished, said Simpson. Why?
Direct orders from Eisenhower, he replied. A colonel piped up, "General,
we won't have any trouble. Practically no opposition. An armored team
could do the job. A couple of days."

"It's out. Orders," said Simpson.

That was only a few days after President Roosevelt died. We chatted
in the briefing room with some of the officers. They were disconsolate
but only about being held back. A victorious army cannot check its mo-
mentum easily. A corps commander re-entered the room.

"Gentlemen," he announced off-handedly, "we have orders to contact
the Russians. That's our next objective."

In the field that was the way in which politico-strategic policy was handed out to us. Competition began. Nobody questioned change of objective. So off we went to the banks of the Elbe and fanned out to find our allies in combat.

A rush call was sent to collect Russian-speaking radio operators or interpreters. Some of us spent the afternoon in a smelly, low-ceilinged German farm. We amused ourselves by decimating the poultry and cooking chicken and turkey over a wood stove.

"Well, we lost this one," a division commander observed disgustedly the next morning.

How come? Third Army made the first contact with the Russians at Torgau. Big doings, parties and plenty of headlines back home. The whole report was at corps headquarters. Anyone want to look at it? No answer.

"Do we sit around and suck our thumbs, General?" an infantry major asked of his two-star boss.

"Nope," he replied. "Let's get moving and find the bastards today. The guys from Third Army made us look sick."

We made it the day after through pure chance. We never did get a reply from the Russians directly in front of us. Our reconnaissance team spotted strange uniforms across a sun-dappled field. "Not krauts," remarked a moon-faced officer after unslinging a pair of "liberated" German field glasses to look things over. "Must be Russians. Anyway, nobody's shooting at us. Let's go."

The lead jeep bucked over the field. Seconds later it catapulted into the air. Two of the three occupants lay where they landed, killed by a land mine. The third crawled and scratched the ground. He moaned low and horribly. The jeeps halted. We got out and someone bent over the wounded man.

"On foot around the field," commanded the field-glasses-toting officer excitedly. "Rest of you stay back."

We spread and minced our way across to a gathering crowd. "Amerikanski?" The question was hurled at us. "Russky?" was the question in reply. Then chattering soldiers in some of the most bedraggled uniforms we'd ever seen, rushed to meet us. In no time, there were embraces, even kisses for the Americans.

One bitter remark passed. "Why didn't you warn us about those mines, you sons of bitches?" a young lieutenant demanded of a Russian who clung happily to his right arm.

The Russian was puzzled. He spoke no English but it was obvious the American was furious. The lieutenant pulled out of his grasp. He pointed to the blown-up jeep a few hundred yards back. The Russian nodded eagerly, made signs for the lieutenant to stay where he was. In a couple of minutes he was back with a strapping young man of about twenty-five, with blond hair cascading down his forehead. He wore shoulderboards on which were stars. Medals bounced on his chest when he walked. A machine pistol was holstered on his right side.

"Sprechen sie deutsche?" was his first question.

The angry American lieutenant simply stretched out his arm to point to the wreckage of the jeep and the dead men. All around us, Russians were piling into American jeeps and roaring into the streets of the village whose sign read, "Apollensdorf." GIs and Russians were already busy trading souvenirs. They were firing each others' weapons into the air. If a German working party had been lurking in ambush it would have had a field day.

In pidgin German, the Russian officer explained that he, too, was a lieutenant, senior grade. Too bad about the mines. Why didn't the Russians sweep the field? The senior lieutenant looked surprised. The Russians laid the mines there themselves. His face clouded with anger, the American began to swear. The crowd around us swelled. Into the circle burst an American colonel. He had an interpreter with him and a Russian officer who rated a salute from the senior lieutenant.

"What's all this about?" asked the colonel. The American explained.

"Can't be helped," retorted the colonel. He had a nicely creased uniform, right out of the headquarters pipeline. His mustache was in military toothbrush style.

"Break it up here," he added. "I'm taking over to report back to headquarters. The Russians are inviting us to a party as a kind of celebration. I've got to get the general."

The lieutenant, a slender young man with snapping black eyes, saluted.

"Yes, sir," he said with great emphasis. He strode away muttering as he went. The only audible word was "party."

The reconnaissance team were already celebrating the encounter—from jugs of cherry brandy. A few were peering and leering at Russian women soldiers, booted to the knees and wearing blouses that miraculously stayed buttoned. Pidgin German was the lingua franca. The girls, on the husky and sawed-off side, intrigued the GIs.

"Man, oh man," one of them summed up. "How do they carry them knockers?"

Some Russian enlisted men chugged up with a Rube Goldberg contraption. It was a big stove on wheels. They ladled out food to the GIs on regular plates. I turned one over and a Meissen mark stared up at me. The Russians were serving kasha (buckwheat).

"Naw, we don't eat cereal in the afternoon," said a GI. He went back to tinkering with a motorcycle a Russian had lent him.

The American lieutenant suddenly shouted orders. A couple of sergeants went around hauling GIs off motorcycles, out of captured German sedans and away from the Russian Wacs. The lieutenant restored discipline while the Russians watched attentively. A couple of GIs tried, surreptitiously, to wave to the women soldiers. The lieutenant chewed them out.

"The general's coming and lots of other brass," he warned. "Remember who you are and where you are. Otherwise I'll eat you out good. The general's coming to a party. Remember, a party."

I moved out and went along with the Russian lieutenant who kept asking me my rank. "Bigger than a general," I explained. "Civilian rank of field marshal. It counts a lot in the U.S."

We walked through ankle-deep mud from Apollensdorf to the town close by, Wittenberg. Red flags festooned the biggest building. It was a German-Victorian stone structure that had once been the city hall.

Four Russian soldiers, in much sharper uniforms than their comrades, flanked the entrance. They wore blue hats. What did the blue indicate, I asked the lieutenant. Special unit, he said. I remember seeing those blue hats all over Eastern Europe later. They belonged to the MVD, or special security. In the entry-ways, soldiers were hauling heavy wooden cartons along the floor. Bottles of vodka were jammed inside.

Tables had already been set up in the biggest room of the *Rathaus*. Colored prints of Stalin looked down from all the walls. Cloths were spread on the tables. Some were bedsheets but they looked festive. Women and men soldiers were arrayed behind the tables, ready to serve. Fresh bread, cut in hunks, were centerpieces. Vodka was stacked up like small glass thickets. Piles of meat pies were passed to the guests from the assembly line of soldier-waiters. A group of Soviet officers gathered along a big table in self-conscious expectancy. A soldier orchestra, half a dozen pieces, including an accordion, sat in the anteroom.

The American staff arrived to the reedy tune of "Stars and Stripes

Forever." Three, two and one-star U.S. generals were introduced around to their opposite numbers. Another song blared—it was the Soviet anthem. Speeches of welcome began. An egg-bald Soviet general, his tunic covered with medals down to his pockets, hailed us this way:

"To our American comrades, we bring greetings from the Soviet army, the Soviet peoples and our great leader, Joseph Vissarionovich Stalin. May we march together in peace and reconstruction as we do in the war against Hitlerite Germany."

Not a bad mouthful, everyone thought. The Americans replied politely. Vodka was poured into glasses and we jostled our way into seats, catch-as-catch-can, except for the big brass. I found myself next to a tubby little captain who spoke good German. That was when I first met Sascha Malokovsky.

Opposite us sat a bemedalled Russian colonel—a tankman, Sascha said. The colonel drained his vodka glass about every thirty seconds and asked the captain to translate everything that was said, toasts or table talk. At the other end, John Groth, the artist, was busy sketching. The colonel was pleased to pose but Groth wanted him to be natural. Three GIs, Signal Corps photographers, table-hopped and came to rest beside us as mounds of food were heaped on the table.

The buzz of conversation droned higher as vodka bottles emptied. A Russian started a song. Toasts began to tumble out. Malokovsky, who drank sparingly, asked what I generally did for a living. I told him and also told him where I came from. He was from Minsk, he said, a piano teacher before the war. As a soldier he had been in the infantry and was now in the supply corps. His family? He didn't know exactly. His brother, he thought, was alive. His own wife and young son, he knew, were dead.

"I'll go back to Minsk," he continued pensively. "Once you are alive you have to keep living. It won't be easy. It never has been for us, as far as I can remember."

He asked about America—the all-inclusive word for the U.S. that I found almost every Russian used. Did people live pretty well? What was an average apartment like? Does the American wife work? Had Roosevelt been such a good man? I replied briefly to all his questions. The colonel, from time to time, asked what we were discussing. He proposed toasts to practically every subject.

"We have to make a future," the captain said thoughtfully. "Who knows what we will do. We must hope for the best."

He didn't sound optimistic, I observed. Optimism, he replied, was not particularly realistic. At least he didn't believe so. Was he happy with the way of life as he knew it in his country?

He froze into a brief silence. He glanced at the colonel, jabbering at Groth's sketch. Sascha shrugged. Politics and system, he replied, were really too much for any average man's ken or control.

"You may say you have good things," he added. "Ours is still a young country. You talk about optimism. All I want is peace and to be left alone. Do you understand?"

I nodded, but it was the vodka replying. I didn't really understand until a long time later. The colonel held up his glass in a toast to Groth. Great artist, Sascha translated. Around the room everyone, or so it seemed, was toasting his neighbor as a fine fellow and a courageous comrade in arms. Someone, at the big table, was chanting "On Wisconsin" and the orchestra tried to follow. It missed.

"To the last battle, Berlin," toasted the colonel solemnly.

We drank. One of the GI photographers asked if he'd been up around Berlin yet. The colonel, through Sascha, said yes. Ask him if he can show us the way, the GI told me. Sure, said Groth. Ask him. I relayed the question. The colonel said he could but we would have to take him to his headquarters first. If we wanted to wait, said Sascha, we could also tag along with his supply convoy. He was heading for a suburb near Berlin.

We didn't want to wait. The photographers grabbed their equipment and told us they'd be waiting in their jeep outside. I shook hands with Sascha, saying that we'd meet on the road.

"My best wishes for your happiness," he said.

We tore out of the dining hall. It was a bedlam with Russian and American songs and the out-of-tune orchestra. The colonel planted himself between Groth, at the wheel of the jeep, and me. He pointed straight ahead. The photographers came right behind us.

Informality was the word for the trip. We had no orders, from either the Allied Supreme Command or the Russians, to pass through Red Army lines. Actually, General Eisenhower had agreed that there would be no on-the-spot observers unless the Russians approved first. But we had a Soviet colonel in our jeep and were on the road. Front-line indifference always overcomes headquarters paperwork.

In less than an hour we ran into a huge concentration of Russian

troops on the march. They were riding, driving and shooting. Captured
German cars hurtled alongside horse cavalry. Old nags hauled carts
filled with soldiers. Huge tanks, officers in the turrets, rumbled in the
fields. Tommy-guns slung over their shoulders, some soldiers pedalled
furiously on German bicycles they had grabbed on the way forward.
Little open carts mounting light machine guns, drawn by sheep dogs,
carried two and three men each.

Afoot, slogged endless columns of infantry. Many munched hunks
of bread and some amused themselves by shooting at occasional low-
flying Russian planes. The faces of the men and women, in stained uniforms and dusty boots, were the map of the Soviet Union. Some were
strapping specimens from the wind-swept regions around Finland. Short,
swarthy soldiers from places like Baku plodded along quietly. Mon-
golians streaked past on small, powerful ponies. Soldiers from central
Asia puttered with captured cars that stalled. Without the vehicles it
might almost have been a canvas painted from "War and Peace." Transportation was whatever you could get your hands on.

I wondered about supplies. There were no gasoline trucks or dumps
in sight. We never did see any. The soldiers looked like Sad Sacks come
to life until you saw them field strip a weapon. They knew their business as soldiers. Everyone travelled light. The uniforms on their backs,
weapons at hand and a few crusts in pockets that also bulged with spare
ammunition. It would have made an American Quartermaster officer
freeze in horror, especially if he could see—as we did—horses slaughtered in their traces for the next meal of meat.

Most of the soldiers paid little attention to us. They waved when a
photographer GI shouted, "Amerikanski." Traffic was directed by women
military police. They held up little red or yellow flags, turned smartly
in the direction they wanted you to go, and everyone obeyed without
any wisecracks.

As we got farther forward, because our jeeps were faster than most
vehicles around us, we hit a traffic jam. Trucks that had the mark
"Chevrolet" or "Studebaker" were clogged together. The jeeps marked
"Willys" were scudding like bugs about huge Stalin tanks, bigger than
any tanks we had on the line.

At a crossroads, our colonel came alive. He gesticulated and shouted.
We got the idea and headed where he pointed. Up a fork in the road
we went. Two female MPs stood before a roadblock beyond which was

a farmhouse with a company of soldiers sprawled in front. The colonel jabbed a forefinger at himself. That was his command post, we gathered. He embraced Groth and me, shook hands with the GIs and went past the barrier into the farmhouse. Our travel orders, personified in his rank, went with him.

"Where do you think we are?" asked Groth.

Nobody could say for sure. The Germans, in retreat, demolished most of the road signs. Those the Russians put up were in Cyrillic script. We turned around and went back to the crossroads. Groth and I stopped a couple of officers. "Berlin?" we asked, pointing towards the moving columns. They replied, "Da," looked at us a little puzzled as we headed right along beside a line of jeeps that honked at us. We honked back, a couple of soldiers jumped into the back seat, grinning and relaxed. It was getting dark and we knew no password—even if the Russians had any. Groth narrowly missed colliding with a horse. He explained it had been five years since he had done any driving worth mentioning. Our Russian passengers hopped off a few miles down the line, shouting goodbye at us, I guess. Gunfire crackled off to our right. We were alone in the middle of the Russian army.

Groth drew up to a collection of Studebaker trucks parked on the side of the road. Some soldiers, we noticed, were making a little fire. They were cooking slabs of meat. Nobody paid any attention to the kind of black-out security about which we always fussed. Here and there, in the surrounding fields, flames shot up from other campfires. We walked up to the soldiers and introduced ourselves, "Amerikanski."

From the deepening shadows in the circles of trucks, someone approached. He wore the shoulderboards of an officer. In the light of the fire he peered at our faces.

"Sprechen sie deutsch?" he asked.

In peculiar German we made ourselves known. The Russian, a lieutenant named Vladimir Emelyanov, offered us a meal. He also asked for an American "papyrusse." We handed out K-ration cigarettes all around.

At the campfire we took stock. The Russians had half-a-dozen of their women in uniform. They were shy although the GI photographers with us tried to thaw them out.

As we sat and ate stewed meat that defied identification, we asked about getting to Berlin. The lieutenant, dark of complexion and intense in expression, thought it would take some time. We were not, he said, more than fifty miles away. The only trouble was that pockets of German resistance still held out all along the way. His unit, he explained, was part of the army commanded by Marshal Georgi Zhukov.

Had he heard of Eisenhower? Yes, but he was a little vague. Roosevelt's name he knew but he did not know he was dead. Was the new U.S. president a good man? Certainly, we replied. Had he ever seen Stalin himself? No, he was from the Caucasus and had never been to Moscow. What did he think of Stalin?

"He is our leader," was the reply.

That was the extent of our political discussion. The Russian women soldiers, less reserved by now, said something to the lieutenant. He translated, saying they wanted to know if the Americans had women in the army and if so, what they did. We told them. They giggled, which sounded strange coming from such robust creatures.

"Our women fight," Emelyanov said proudly. "Many of them better than men. They know how to use guns and tanks. You may see for yourself."

We did later on. The meal finished, the lieutenant asked us if we wanted to follow his truck convoy. It was probably the best idea for us anyway, he added. It was already night and we might, alone, run into difficulties we could not handle. We agreed gratefully. The soldiers stamped out the fire, wiped their hands on their uniforms and piled into the trucks. Medals they wore on their tunics gleamed in the dark. The heavy-gaited tread of infantry beat out its monotonous obbligato above the warming motors of the trucks. Horses, inches away from us, neighed. Tank treads crunched in the fields and self-propelled guns clattered in the highway. It was the cacophony of men and arms in motion. It was like nothing we ever heard before.

The rear tail-light of the last truck was our convoy signal. We kept within inches of it, preventing anything else from separating us. Occasionally, a soldier or an officer would pass a lantern over our faces and shout. In the eerie light you could see massed humanity, wagons, cows, tethered carts, parked tanks and rolling batteries of big guns. You couldn't help but wonder how this chaotic mass got organized for combat. For a couple of hours we cruised in convoy, sometimes just creeping, occasionally at reckless speed. When the last truck turned off the main highway we hurtled after it.

Over a dirt road we jounced. The trucks pulled up to a cluster of farmhouses. There were lights in all of them. Someone was singing, a voice that was lusty if not tuneful. Emelyanov approached our jeeps. Come in, he invited us. We followed him into the farmhouse of the singer. A dozen or so officers and soldiers were around a table. Three were women, stacking dishes. We were introduced as Americans. A babble of excitement broke out. One of the women ran out and returned quickly with a soldier who spoke English. His name was Anton Samborsky and he had lived in Milwaukee in the 1920's and early 1930's, he explained reticently. In the depression he returned to Leningrad with his parents. He still had relatives in Milwaukee. Model-A Fords and department stores were what Samborsky remembered best.

The women produced steaming hot meat patties. An officer asked us to sit down. Another dug around in a burlap bag and came up with a couple of jugs of cherry brandy. They had been stamped "For the Wehrmacht Only." Someone else placed bottles of German white wine on the table. More officers crowded into the farmhouse.

A young woman entered and everyone greeted her demonstratively. She was an officer and by far the best looking Russian girl we had seen. Cap in hand, her tiger-tawny hair tumbled about her ears. Her skirt was below knee length and boots came up to the hem. Emelyanov escorted the girl to our table.

She also was a lieutenant, he explained, in command of some light tanks. Her name was Maria Dononyeva and she was in her early twenties. She spoke excellent French and told us she had been a school teacher. Her eyes were large and violet and she walked and talked with natural grace. The holstered pistol at her right hip didn't seem out of place.

We talked—all night. The Russians spoke of the war, of the ruined communities they retook in the Soviet Union. They talked of their shattered families and of ruined lives. Once we brought up the subject of the Hitler-Stalin Pact. Nobody answered or explained. The war against the Nazis took full precedence, they said. It was about over. What next?

"We will go home," said Lieutenant Dononyeva. Her voice was low pitched. "I will go back to my school—if there still is one."

What did we, Americans, plan to do? Go home, too, was the reply. Questions flew. They all dealt with life and living. We talked about bathrooms and cars; about movies and books; shoes and tractors and even sports. American football was too complicated for them. Not a mention did they make of political systems. We toasted each other, person-to-person. They asked for some of our insignia marked "U.S."

Lieutenant Dononyeva snapped one on her tunic, next to a medal for heroism. She wore it in combat the next morning.

Pale spring light washing the cracked farmhouse windows broke up the party. Emelyanov told us to follow his trucks. Lieutenant Dononyeva's tank would escort us. She said I could ride with her if I wanted to.

Nobody asked why we were up there. Nobody ever did until the end, in Berlin. Dononyeva's invitation to ride in her tank in these circumstances seemed quite normal. She stood in the turret and I clung to the side. Some Russian infantrymen squatted on the tail end. The day cleared rapidly under a determined sun to uncover a bizarre combat deployment.

Interminable columns of armor, wagons, carriages, horses, foot-soldiers, trucks, captured vehicles and cows sprawled over the highways, dirt roads and meadowland. How, I asked my lady lieutenant, did all these people make liaison with their units? They always do, she said. I never found out how. We kept going, bunched up, even after German shells —from 88's—whistled overhead. Horses pawed the ground uneasily. The soldiers paid no attention. Some of them dropped their bicycles casually on the ground and continued forward. Dononyeva was busy with her radio operator. She swung binoculars in a sweep of the fields beyond us.

"Get off or sit with them," she said, indicating the soldiers seated on the back of the tank.

We passed a built-up place that had a name-plate, "Zahna." Some walking wounded were dragging themselves along. Infantry units were being formed. It was easy to see why. A series of concrete bunkers on the brow of the hill, visible to the eye, were in flame. Bundles were strewn on the approaches. They were dead soldiers. I watched one unit go into action. Nobody wore helmets. Medals bounced on their chests as they charged, shouting. Their tommy-guns chattered and coughed. It was a pure human-sea attack. The Russians used about a battalion to take a position against which we would have sent a company. A lot of people got hurt, or killed. I never saw any medics on the field. I asked Dononyeva about it when she halted her lead tank and fanned the others out in a skirmish line. She never thought about it, she said. Dressing stations were down the line.

She went to work. Her tanks pumped shells into the smoking bunkers and the thickets beyond.

When the guns let up, more massed infantry tore up the hill, tommy-guns blazing. The soldiers were heedless of cover. Last-ditch Germans, dug-in, swept the slopes with rifle and machine-gun fire. There were, I noticed, no prisoners nor surrenders that morning around Zahna.

Dononyeva's tank started up again. Her skirmish line, guns elevated, drew into a wide arc around the bunker area. She held out her hand to me. It was small but the grip was unexpectedly strong. She said I had better rejoin the truck-jeep convoy which she thought was about a mile back of us. "Au revoir, monsieur," she said. "Bonne chance." For a moment I thought about kissing or embracing her, just as in the movies. The idea passed as quickly as it came. Dononyeva had her binoculars to her eyes. She was back in business. I dropped off the tank and walked slowly towards the rear. For a while, I looked back every few yards. She never did.

In the disembodied atmosphere of total war, it never occurred to me or any of my companions that we could get lost. We had split up, as I did by going with Dononyeva, without thinking twice. I ran into the GI photographers on the way back. They had been with other Russian troops. We returned to the highway, dodging trucks, cars and lines of infantry. In the jumble of men and machines, we spotted our jeeps by the white star painted on them.

Lieutenant Emelyanov was smoking casually. His soldiers sat in the trucks or watched Groth sketching on the shoulder of the road. Emelyanov didn't ask what I had seen. He seemed to take it for granted we would all return. We sat around another couple of hours. Emelyanov spoke to one of his drivers. We could go forward now, he said. How he decided this, we never learned.

Bumper to bumper we crawled along the highway. Open wagons carted wounded, lying on straw. They headed in the opposite direction. There was only desultory firing around Zahna. The women MPs were already there, wig-wagging their little flags. Houses we passed on the road had open roofs and caved-in sides. The only civilians we saw were some old men and women with chickens under their arms. A few others tried to drive cows out of the path of the Soviet army.

The ribbon of highway parted a large stretch of woodland—thick fir trees and old poplars. The clearings were littered with burned-out German vehicles still holding the ghastly remains of their crews.

Emelyanov got out of his truck to stretch his legs. We asked about the corpses in the woods. A German counter-attack that tried to cut the highway two or three days before, he explained. Emelyanov's trucks had been caught in the assault. They took cover in the woods for the day. "I lost five trucks," he said.

The slow trek got up a little speed. Emelyanov's driver called to him as a gap opened between us and the cars ahead. He ran forward and swung himself into the cab. We began to drive at a crisp clip of about 35 miles an hour. For a period we seemed to lose track of time and battle when only traffic and buzzing planes were heard. Then we would be rudely jolted by heavy artillery firing from nearby fields at regular time-on-target intervals. We stopped once more so that Emelyanov could test a plank bridge. He nodded and the trucks rolled, although the flooring clattered shakily.

Villages, gray and silent, slipped by. Here and there Russian soldiers looked around with detached curiosity. Some tried to break into shuttered little shops with signs that said, "Tabak." Armored cars and tanks idled at corners that gave them a clear field of fire. Our convoy slowed at the corners, honked, and went on unchallenged. There were more signs in German around now. The retreating Wehrmacht apparently didn't have time to get rid of them. Our convoy paused briefly before a sign that read, "Blankenfelde," then rolled forward. Houses were a little bigger here than in the country.

The streets were wider, although cobbled. There were several churches instead of the lone spire that dominates a community in farm country. Cars and motorbikes flashed through the streets. Trucks stripped of canvas tops were jammed with Russian soldiers. An anti-aircraft battery was emplaced in the biggest square.

Emelyanov got out near the square. He signalled his driver, who backed up to a building and parked. The others followed suit. From the parked trucks, soldiers leaped and strolled down the street. They seemed to know their way around. Emelyanov got into our jeep explaining we were about to have some supper. He took us through narrow, winding back streets. Glancing up, you could see Russians, rifles in their arms, watching the street below. From darkened interiors, a few radios squawked.

In front of a two-family house, with an ornate bay window, Emelyanov told us to stop. Some trucks and jeeps, guarded by nonchalant soldiers, were scattered around the house.

"You will eat with my comrades," said Emelyanov. He led the way up the buckled stone steps.

Russian army overcoats were hanging on the clothes pegs in the vestibule. An umbrella, its seams split, was on a chair. From the next room came the rattle of dishes and occasional laughter. Light flickered through the curtained door. When we entered we saw sputtering candles on a massive dining table. Emelyanov greeted his fellow officers. They shouted back to him. Turning his head slightly our way, he introduced us, "Amerikanski." Room was made for us at the table.

"I see you got here all right," one of the Russians at the far end of the room said in German.

It was Sascha Malokovsky, the little captain from the celebration in Wittenberg. He had arrived hours before us, he said, because he had not stopped anywhere overnight. The question period to which we had by now become accustomed, began with examination of our uniforms. The Russians thought it was funny we didn't wear boots. We looked at the boots and asked to try them on. An officer pulled off his boots. He wore no socks; just rag wrappings. The boots didn't fit any of us. They were too tight.

We asked Malokovsky how far Blankenfelde was from Berlin. He chuckled. Very close to it, he replied. Blankenfelde was a suburb of Berlin. We'd all be going there in the morning. Everyone was going to sleep early. He said he would have someone look after our jeeps. We were shown a couple of rooms. They were bedrooms, I suppose, because there were night-tables with thunder-mugs in them. No beds, however, so we slept in our trench coats on the floor.

It was still dark when Malokovsky woke us. Bleary-eyed and bedraggled, we followed him to the dining room. Nobody looked much better than we. Still, they sounded more cheerful. Breakfast was a shot of schnapps, a hunk of bread and some raw bacon. We skipped the bacon.

In a few minutes we were outside. A couple of Russian soldiers wrapped in carpets were asleep in our jeeps. Captain Malokovsky shook them. They opened their eyes, got to their feet slowly and saluted in an offhand way. As they stepped out of the jeeps we entered and they saluted us, too. Emelyanov came over to say he would not be going so far as Malokovsky. He shook hands with us all and asked for and received a "U.S." insignia. Malokovsky placed our jeeps behind his lead truck. As it turned out we were almost within Berlin. Malokovsky's convoy drove along at a fast clip. Traffic was sparse on the outskirts. In town the only congestion was caused by tanks and weapons' carriers that became snarled with dangling trolley wire.

We passed Tempelhof Airport, ripped by mammoth bomb craters. Rain poured through gaping hangar roofs. Burned-out German and Soviet tanks blocked the entrances to the airfield. Ammunition lay loose in the streets. Corpses were everywhere. Abandoned German equipment—even issue socks and underwear—was scattered like a trail through the streets.

Gunfire could be heard in every direction. Despite the heavy downpour, flames licked in blocks of devastation and ruin. Buildings shook and toppled, burying beneath them people and horses. One soldier, unmindful of the action, sat on a sign that indicated Dr. Paul Hentsche once practiced medicine there. The soldier was trying to divine the complexities of a German-made accordion. We parked our jeeps near the ruined Reichschancellery.

Once again, Groth, the GIs and I split up to prowl. Gunfire drummed in bursts at Russian soldiers who were piling bits of furniture in a cart. A big tank wheeled up, lobbed a single shell at the sniper's nest. It didn't shoot again.

Malokovsky was chatting with another Soviet officer.

"The news is that Hitler is supposed to have killed himself," he told us. "Who knows?" I said we ought to poke around the Reichschancellery to see if we could find any evidences. The Russian captain looked doubtful. He came along though. We asked some Russian soldiers, souvenir-hunting in the debris, to help us look around a little. It was useless in that mountain of devastation to uncover anything momentous. A blackened portrait of Hitler was found. Sascha placed it deliberately at the south end of a dead horse.

It was, I think, the second longest day of my life. We stumbled into the beginning or end of a half-dozen small street battles. I kept my helmet in my hand because the Russians didn't wear any and someone might mistake mine for a German's. We had to flatten ourselves to the ground so often for a while that it became difficult to rise. The next time I was to have such an experience was during the Hungarian Revolution in 1956.

Towards early afternoon, the shooting in Berlin slackened perceptibly. We could walk around upright and take in the battered view. With a group of Russian soldiers we watched the slogan painters under the Brandenburg Gate. Nobody said anything. Two big Mercedes roared up to the Gate with a motorcycle escort.

Out of the cars stepped men in uniforms, some of which I had never seen before. The military police escort formed a protective belt under the arch of triumph. Who were they?

"They are Polish officers, Czechs, anti-Fas, Bulgars, a Hungarian and some Rumanians with our people," explained Sascha. "I know the uniforms. I have seen them for some months. They are comrades with our army."

The important visitors lined up below the Brandenburg Gate a little stiffly. They were posing for still and movie cameras. At either end an officer held a portrait of Stalin and a placard hailing the "unconquerable forces of socialism." They posed in positions of triumph for about fifteen minutes. Strangely, none of the soldiers cheered. The only sound accompaniment was a sporadic rifle shot or a busy tommy-gun.

The posing over, the visitors returned to their cars and drove out of sight eastward over Unter den Linden. I walked back with Malokovsky to the place near the Chancellery, where the trucks and jeeps were parked. Groth and the GIs were there, impatient to start. For the second, and last, time I said goodbye to Sascha Malokovsky. His handclasp was warm but I thought something was out of place.

I asked if he had lost the "U.S." insignia we had given him. No, it was in his pocket. I didn't particularly blame him. It was just that it happened so quickly. The war was over and politics had taken supreme command.

We got the jeeps rolling and headed away from Unter den Linden westward. On the way we passed Belle Alliance Platz. Groth called to my attention that the statue dedicated to the Beautiful Alliance was in ruins. It didn't take long for the symbolism to become reality.

CHAPTER 2

In the wake of war, all Europe seemed ravaged and pitted with defeat and misery. But the two halves, Western and Eastern, already showed different faces to the future. Different determinations, too. Large Communist parties, organized and disciplined, fought for power in France and Italy. In Eastern Europe small, often tiny, professional cadres were grafted on to the sullen, stubborn non-Communist populations.

In good time and with indigenous effort and through awakened support in the U.S., anti-Communist parties were able to meet and blunt Communist penetration (to power) in the West. Not so in Eastern Europe. There, actively aided by the Soviet Union and the occupying Red Army, the opposition was terrorized and suborned, kidnapped and liquidated, rendered speechless or forced to flee. The Soviet Union began to impose an alien system on the nearly 100 million hapless people of Eastern Europe; and attempt to cast a new generation in its own mold.

The Nazis and their inhuman policies, in distorted peace and all-out war, made the Russians popular; or so it seemed to the West. Stalin, however, and his troubleshooters and proconsuls were hated in Eastern Europe. It was a deep-rooted factor the West was either unaware of or conveniently overlooked. The Russians did not, which was why they sent overwhelming power in to Eastern Europe. With the Red Army came men and women devoted to the extension of Soviet power and dogma.

Only in a very few cases did the Russians permit Communists who had not been trained in the Soviet Union to rise to positions of power. Men like Wladyslaw Gomulka, austere and parochial, were welcomed into the Polish party fold. There wasn't much choice, in this case. Stalin himself liquidated the highest echelons of the Polish party shortly before Hitler made his pact with the Soviet dictator and unleashed the Second World War.

The triumphant comrades who swept into their native lands with the Red Army already had assignments. They were dressed in the uniforms of high-ranking Russian officers and their limitless amounts of money were in dual citizenship—Soviet. Where it was necessary, to placate suspicion at home and abroad and to buy time to build and extend the party apparatus, Communist organizations entered into coalition governments.

These coalitions lasted from a few months to a few years. The Russians and their local associates took over, from the beginning, key posts. First, was the police. Communists ran the ministries of interior throughout Eastern Europe. They were actively assisted by seasoned secret policemen from Moscow's own dread department, run by Lavrenti Beria. Soviet security troops, the feared and loathed "blue hats," helped keep the subjugated countries safe for the incubating "People's Democracies."

The political-economic apparatus of the U.S.S.R. was transferred, in microcosm, to territories where Communists held the upper hand. Czechoslovakia, whose coalition government prattled happily of being a bridge between East and West, was an exception for a couple of years. Another, more notable exception to the Soviet rule of power and the permanent purge, was Yugoslavia.

There, a partisan army led by a chunky ex-sergeant in the Austro-Hungarian forces of the First World War, owed nothing to Stalin nor to Russian support. Josip Broz Tito, a vain but ambitious dictator in his own right, fought several wars at once in his own country. He fought the Germans and the Italians; the Chetniks under the tragic figure of Gen. Draja Mihailovitch; German collaborators from his native Croatia, the Ustachi, led by Ante Pavelic, and the occupation forces sent into Yugoslavia by Hungary and Bulgaria.

The Yugoslav partisans fought alone. Their aid came from U.S. and British sources. I remember one of Tito's chief aides, little Mosa Pjade, at the airfield on a spring day in 1955. He was watching the Ilyushin transport, carrying Nikita Khrushchev and Nikolai Bulganin, about to land.

"I suppose," murmured Pjade with a mocking twinkle, "that those are the planes the Russians promised us back in 1943."

The fierce independence and asceticism of the partisan spirit and the vast experience of Tito as an international Communist apparatus agent, made the Yugoslav Communists suspicious of Soviet aims. From the beginning, after the Germans were expelled, Tito's men kept an eye on Soviet agents. The Yugoslavs had undergone their own training, in illegality and conspiracy as well as in active warfare. They all would have preferred to belong to the "great" Soviet camp. But they refused to be subject camp followers. Tito and the men around him by no means enjoyed massive support and popularity in Yugoslavia. They knew, however, how to extend and consolidate their own power. Moreover, they refused to adapt Yugoslavia to the pattern Stalin cut for other Eastern European countries.

Not so fortunate were other nations, with longer and shorter histories of independence. Take a look at the list: East Germany, part of a truncated, defeated Germany. Goat-bearded, slavishly pro-Stalin Walther Ulbricht turned up with the Red Army to take a permanent position as first secretary of the Communist party in the Russian zone. He had helped prepare, with Soviet planners, territorial distribution of East Germany to Russia and Poland. That has become known commonly as the "Oder-Niesse Line."

In Poland, Gomulka, more of a Polish nationalist than the party imports from the chopped-up Polish apparatus, went along with the transfer of East Poland to the Russians. Watching over Gomulka constantly was Boleslaw Beirut, mustachioed and saturnine, who chose to fly to

Moscow whenever a tough decision had to be made. The Poles, having suffered so much during the war, had no choice afterwards. They were given German provinces. They had to take them because their regime said there was no other way. Poles detest the Germans about as much as they loathe the Russians. Territorial readjustment, unilaterally, affected their *amour propre*. They thought nostalgically of communities like ancient Vilna and Lwow. Still, having former German territory, fairly rich compared with what was lost to Russia in East Poland, eased the pain.

Their hatred of the Russians, the Poles tell strangers, is something traditional. When they speak of it, their eyes glisten and their voices take on a razor's edge. Poles are also deeply religious and fervently Roman Catholic. In times of deep difficulty, Poles turn to the church for solace. They also turn to their priests and lately, to one of the Twentieth Century's most astute prelates, Stefan Cardinal Wyszyński. His predecessor, August Cardinal Hlond, was not so intelligently agile. He tried frontal attacks on the hated regime. The assaults were blunted by Communist power on the spot.

Most Polish political sentiment was massed behind the bulky peasant personality of Stanislaw Mikolacjczyk. He hadn't much chance despite the feelings of the Poles. Communists have never won a normal parliamentary election like those held in the West. Mikolacjczyk, originally in a postwar coalition government, was driven out. Then he was forced out of the country. Power was in the calloused hands of Polish Communists and their Russian advisers, who were determined to bring the country as rapidly as possible into the Soviet orbit.

There were in the tumultuous postwar days a disproportionately large number of Communists of Jewish origin high in the Polish party. Despite the decimation of Poland's Jews by the Nazis and the grisly but glorious episode of the Ghetto uprising in Warsaw, the average Pole doesn't like Jews. The presence of Jews in high Communist places—men like Jakub Berman and Hillary Minc—enraged the Poles. The fact that non-Jews such as Gomulka and Beirut held top spots merited little consideration. I recall a Polish Socialist who opposed the shotgun wedding of the Communists and his party speculating that Stalin deliberately sent Jews into Poland with the party cadres.

"He believed that he could trust them because they would be scrupulously anti-Fascist," the Socialist observed. "He also knew that he could use them one day as scapegoats in Poland. The Poles, my countrymen, have three obsessions: They are anti-Russian, anti-German and anti-Semitic."

The man, now in Britain, was not a Jew. On the cinders of the old Ghetto, however, it was hard to reconcile anti-Semitic feelings with the Polish plight. Under the Germans, they had both suffered as inferior peoples. There also was the concentration camp, Auschwitz, in Poland, which will live forever infamous in man's memories. At the same time, Poles, even the younger ones, never forget that their officer corps was liquidated in the Katyn Forest during the war.

"The Russians did it, of course," Polish students have told me repeatedly.

"It was the Nazis, but they left a suspicion of doubt," was the way a Polish central committee member described the episode to me.

There was never that kind of dubious foreboding, south of Poland, in Czechoslovakia. Most people blamed the West for selling them out to Hitler at Munich. They had, even the majority who voted against the Communists, a certain enthusiasm for the Soviet Union. Of all Middle and Eastern Europe, Czechoslovakia enjoyed the only Western-type parliamentary democracy that existed between the wars. The Communist party, while fairly large, was in the shadow of a *mystique* and personality much larger: Thomas Garrigue Masaryk, founder of the republic. His political heir, Eduard Beneš, a small, neat man with a well-groomed mustache, was legalistic to the core. He also was unimaginative and hoped, almost to the broken end, that Czechoslovakia could become an East-West window.

Jan Masaryk, large, fluent and popular, had the misfortune to be a great father's son. He had no illusions. In his own way, he was a patriot and tried to serve as the "new" Czechoslovakia's Foreign Minister. He chided other Americans and me for our "myopic policies." Masaryk could be bitter without sounding ferocious or complaining. He also had profound doubts about his own people's capacities to do anything but survive.

"We served the Hapsburgs 300 years," he once told me in a reflective mood. "We tried to serve the West. Britain and France sold us out. Now we're trying to serve East and West. It probably won't work."

Masaryk wasn't being especially clairvoyant. He knew his people, his political peers and the pressures. In a curious way, so did his deputy, a veteran Communist, Vlado Clementis. Western-educated, Clementis enjoyed puffing on a pipe as he expounded his views. He was a far cry from the hardened, dedicated men who were weaned in the Moscow school. Clementis wasn't the kind of Communist the party wanted or needed in the formalistic, no-nonsense regime it wanted to install in Czechoslovakia.

For a nation that enjoyed far more political liberties than any other that came under Communist hegemony, Czechoslovakia also let the most blood. It was committed for a while under the hate-the-German days. From the Sudetenland, original root of Hitler's expansionist ambitions eastward, many Germans were either packed off or shot. Elsewhere under the highly organized SNB (police) of the Ministry of Interior, influential anti-Communists were shooed out of the country or shot. Non-Communists, who were less vocal, were cowed into economic and political silence.

Lidice, the village not far from Prague, became a national symbol. Quite rightly, up to a point. It was where the Nazis razed a community, exterminated nearly all adults and carted off the children to be raised as "Aryans." The Czechoslovaks, at the urging of the large and disciplined Communist party, began to hold up Lidice as a symbol of national resistance. Unfortunately, that is not the case. Lidice was a prime example of Nazi bestiality, wreaked upon a helpless and unsuspecting community. Czechoslovakia, though, was in fair shape for a postwar country that had been under German occupation. People managed to eat better there than they did elsewhere. War factories under German management were in operation to the end.

"You cannot judge a nation by some menus," Rudolf Slansky, First Secretary of the Czechoslovakian Communist party, once roared at me.

His hierarchical superior, in name only, was more amiable. Prime Minister, later President, Klement Gottwald, said the Czechs needed more of a sense of direction and more discipline.

"Only the Communists can really do that," Gottwald confided to me. "You will see. Come, now, have a drink."

Gottwald was a great believer in taking the curse off disagreeable subjects with a large amount of alcohol. At a reception, I once saw him single out a uniform stiffly at attention at a reception line. Bleary-eyed, Gottwald made a beeline for the uniform. He hugged the startled figure, saying, "Together, your nation and mine will be so powerful, my dear comrade." The officer was an American military attaché.

American officers in Hungary never got that kind of treatment, even briefly. An old toper, sharp in the ways of political infighting, ran Soviet interests in the country. He was Marshal Klementi Voroshilov. Voroshilov, an old Bolshevik, set up shop in Budapest as commander of nearly 1,000,000 Soviet troops who lived off the ravaged land. With them arrived a small but power-minded force of veteran Communists. Matyas Rakosi, as short and broad as a human being could get, ran the party. He had been a big-time commissar as far back as Bela Kun's short-lived regime after World War I. Soviet troops bolted into Hungary, "a-shootin', a-lootin' and a-rapin'." They stayed around a long time, while Rakosi was guiding Hungary straight into the Communist fold.

In Budapest, as in Rumania and Bulgaria, there were Allied military missions. They were there as a symbolic occupation. Hungary and the other two had been Nazi satellites. Voroshilov usually ran the occasional military mission councils. British and American officers could barely protest. The rest of the time they had little to do but try to enjoy themselves in the ruins of Budapest.

Our military delegates there despised the Soviet authorities but didn't quite know why. They fumed at their inability to get anything done. When time hung heavy on their hands, they posed for homeric busts of themselves. The currency was being inflated to kill off whoever was solvent. The Hungarian pengo got a lugubrious name from wandering Americans. We call it the kropnick, a term which became the label for all Eastern European currency. They were all equally valueless.

To the locals, in this case the Hungarians, having worthless money was worse than nothing. Theirs was in the class of a defeated nation and one that was occupied by the Russians. Even shattered Austria looked greener across the frontier, the eastern half of which was also occupied by the Red Army. In Hungary, Rakosi had a team of experienced party cadre members. His chief policeman, Lazslo Rajk, was a flinty man who punctuated staccato outbursts of orders by pointing to a large portrait of Stalin for emphasis. Ernoe Geroe, later a Rakosi successor, was an unsmiling, middle-aged man who sucked his teeth audibly when he talked. Imre Nagy, with pince-nez and mustache, looked like a Hungarian rural school teacher. He stated his views quietly and steadfastly, and never gave an outsider any reason to believe that he was anything but a devoted Communist.

Zoltan Vas, the economic czar of the country, was a fast talker with good clothes—the only ones seen on a professional Communist outside Yugoslavia. He was not above being a five-percenter, or even a fiftypercenter, depending on who was being milked. Vas put his shakedown money in a safe place, outside the country. These funds were the subject of recurrent investigations, from which Vas always seemed to emerge more firmly secured on top than ever. Rakosi's wife, a Yakut from Asiatic Russia, loomed importantly in the early days. To show her contempt for finery, Mrs. Rakosi went around for a time in a brassiere, made-in-Budapest, over her Russian uniform.

Aligned with the Communists in a "Popular Front" amalgamation were the Social Democrats. Quite a few balked at the prospect. They were the men and women who remembered too vividly what Communists had done to Social Democrats in the past. But the Social Democratic leadership forced the alliance through. It was the only way out, they argued. That was the argument given to me by a volatile man with the name of Arpad Szakasitz. He was a voluble apologist for the unholy political alliance. Into it he dragged, more or less willingly, Istvan Reiss and Ana Kethly. Miss Kethly, a lady of great courage, mistrusted the Communists then but also had graver doubts about the non-Communist opposition of the time.

Actually, the non-Communists were a confederation drawn together to stave off Communist domination. The aim was brave, with the country prostrate and under Soviet occupation. There was also an active Communist organization, expanding in power. Belonging to it meant that younger people, disillusioned by war and defeat, could get jobs. Not belonging meant unemployment or worse. The opposition called themselves the "Smallholders." It was intended to convey that while many had some property, they weren't the big land barons of old.

Into the Smallholders poured the spectrum of anti-Communist opposition. There were brave and good men, like Bela Kovacs. He was so good that the Russian army eventually abducted him and sent him to a Soviet prison. Bela Kovacs had been a genuine anti-Nazi and would have been a decent liberal voice in any Western land. He also had the affection and respect of the Hungarian peasantry, a commanding voice in politics in those days. Kovacs built up an organization that beat the Communists in the only free election they ever permitted in an occupied area. His Smallholders won a handsome national majority in 1945 despite Rakosi's smug predictions to Voroshilov and Moscow that the Popular Front would win hands down.

The story is that Voroshilov received the news of the resounding defeat in his guarded villa. Rakosi personally told him about it. Voroshilov reflectively patted his Hungarian mistress, who, a year before, had been the girl friend of a German general.

"You know better than that," Voroshilov said mildly to Rakosi. He patted the girl, without missing a stroke. "Just love them to death—soon."

In his fashion, Rakosi did just that. The Smallholders, Kovacs notwithstanding, permitted the Communists to control the police. Ferenc Nagy became Prime Minister. A man of peasant stock, an anti-Nazi but loath to do more than to compromise when in office, Nagy Ferenc slipped into the slicer that Rakosi called "salami tactics." Without Bela Kovacs, after his abduction, the Smallholders descended into leaderless factionalism.

Joszef Cardinal Mindszenty, Primate of Hungary, sought to support the Smallholders publicly, from the pulpit. But Mindszenty was by no means the careful, adroit politician such as was Wyszyński in Poland or Josef Cardinal Beran in Czechoslovakia. These clerics also were pilloried by the regime. Yet they chose to speak out on important, human issues, not just on the mountain of domestic problems the regimes created.

Once, in the drafty castle at Esztergom, hard by the Slovak frontier, I talked lengthily with Cardinal Mindszenty. We were alone and we spoke in German.

"You Americans are at fault," said the Cardinal, his steely eyes glaring at me. "They are at fault, too," he said, pointing at the river and beyond where stretched Slovakia. The Cardinal, symbolically, was reminding me of the slide toward Communist domination of the Czechoslovaks. He lectured me about the faults of the United States—our lack of knowledge and insight of the Russians and of Communist intentions. One thing struck me in our conversation. Not once did the Cardinal ever admit that there might also have been Hungarian faults.

It was much different in Yugoslavia. Tito and his partisan politicians took over a country shorn of resources, blackened with occupation and still reeking of hundreds of thousands of dead. The difference was that the Tito army and its military commissars assumed control of a divided nation without the assistance of the armed forces of any other power. They claimed, in the Communist style, to have fought their own revolution and to have "liberated" their own country. In all Eastern Europe Tito's partisans comprised the only Communist striking force of any consequence that didn't ride to power on the guns of the Red Army.

The Yugoslavs were largely responsible for creating a partisan army in the mysterious mountain enclave on the Adriatic, Albania. The fact that the Albanian party hierarchy remained faithful to Stalin and subsequently shied from Nikita Khrushchev to Mao Tse-tung cannot alter the fact of the helping hand Yugoslav Communists provided. Stalin actually offered Tito the wild stretches of Albania as a satellite. In the big-power vision of Stalin, a Yugoslav satellite would be convenient in the Soviet scheme of interlocking control. After all, Yugoslavia figured as a bold and militant Moscow satellite. Therefore, Albania could easily fit the groove as an appendage of Tito.

From war-time, though, it seemed that French-speaking Enver Hoxha, the pudgy ex-tobacconist who ran Albania's party, couldn't get along with Tito's field operators. Neither could his No. 2 man, the handsome and dark Mehmet Shehu. Before the war, Shehu learned Italian in a Mussolini-operated Fascist school. He is a cruel man who thrives on the role of police chief. Yugoslavs who worked with the Albanians during the war, in hindsight, attribute all sorts of intrigue to the Albanians who attack them so much today. They also worry constantly that the Albanian minority in Yugoslavia is still unstable. It numbers nearly a million—only a couple of hundred thousand less than in all Albania.

Old-time Balkan intrigue figured—and still does—in the conflicting Communist approaches of the Yugoslavs, the Albanians, the Russians and even inside Yugoslavia itself. You cannot, even with planned and harsh determination, wipe out devotion to conspiracy that existed for 500 years under Turkish occupation. Tito actually took over a hodgepodge country. The Serbs, brave and imaginative, exploited their victory after World War I. They absorbed, at least geographically, western approaches like Slovenia, Croatia and the Dalmatian coast, all of which were once part of the Austro-Hungarian empire.

Serbs sought to dominate non-Serbs between the wars under a combination of regal authoritarians. They were hated by Croats, who were

Catholic while the Serbs were Orthodox. The nation showed itself as
an entity to the world. Within, however, regional loyalties remained
fierce. When war came, plotters against the Serbs went over to Hitler
and Mussolini. Nazi policy made of Croatia a separate state. This also
added to the mutual hatred and distrust that exists between Croats and
Serbs even today. In Croatia, then Archbishop, later Cardinal, Alois
Stepinac, is regarded as a hero and martyr. Serbs and Tito's regime, not
necessarily of the same political conviction, regard Stepinac as a monstrous traitor. Tito felt strong enough to imprison Stepinac and try him
publicly. The Cardinal died not long ago, after having been alternately
in jail and house confinement.

His name still means much in Croatia. Arguable as it may be, Stepinac
in the local sentiment probably means a lot more than Tito, also born
in Croatia. The Titoist police, nevertheless, ubiquitous and highly efficient as they are, have managed one positive result: they keep Croats
and Serbs from flying at each other's throats. Serbs and Montenegrins,
fighting people by tradition, frankly admire Tito. Their loyalties to the
Karageorgevich monarchy are dimmed today. They don't like Communism. But these men, from Tito down, did fight. What's more, the
country didn't become anyone's satellite.

The Yugoslav Communists started, after the war, in rather orthodox
fashion. They had plans for collectivization and nationalization of all
property. Their party theoreticians and economic planners foresaw, for its
size, a mighty Communist Yugoslavia rising in the Balkans. It would be,
in a manner of speaking, a Communist showplace of balanced new industry and thriving agriculture. They began to rebuild on the aid from the
United States-supported UNRRA. You could see locomotives, "made in
the U.S.A." and trucks, too. Basic Yugoslav plans, however, didn't fit in
with Stalin's. He wanted to keep the Yugoslavs more or less a pastoral
people, a breadbasket for his own Communist world in Europe.

Yugoslavs quite early balked at dictation from Moscow. They were
rudely and bitterly anti-American. But they still could not grasp, as Communists forged in fire, why the Russians should treat them as backward
Balkan people. "Who do they think they are?" Vladimir Dedijer once
grumbled to me about the Russians. Dedijer, once Tito's biographer and
protégé, has since broken with the regime. He sided with Milovan Djilas,
coiner of the "New Class," and once as fierce a Communist militant as
ever existed.

"If I could have my way, I'd hang people like you on the Teraszje," Djilas told a couple of us in his office. (The Teraszje is the main street of Belgrade.)

He wasn't emotional about it. To Djilas, partisan and plotter, oppositionists were best out of the way. The others in the top party structure felt the same. But they didn't say it to visitors' faces. Edvard Kardelj, who looked enough like him to be a younger brother, was once called "Little Molotov." Except for Tito and Pjade, all the Yugoslav Communists of importance were young men, then at most in their thirties. Partisans, who came out of the forests, shaggy and hot-eyed with fervor, were much younger, so their chances for rapid advancement in such a regime weren't rosy. Everyone else was young, too.

The situation was reversed in Rumania, where there had never been a Communist movement worthy of the name. The country had been ruled by an oligarchy and dictatorship. Opera-bouffe kings, like Ferdinand and his son, Carol, let the police keep Rumania safe for them. It was a country rich in agriculture, oil and other resources. Educated people preferred to speak French. Bucharest was known as "Little Paris" but Rumanians abroad had a highly unsavory reputation. Everyone cracked jokes about their corruption. As a matter of fact, so did Rumanians. As dubious sharers of the spoils after World War I, Rumania had received the heavily Hungarian speaking province of Transylvania from the dead Hapsburg empire and the region of Dobrudja from Bulgaria. The territory added something to the country's natural wealth. Bessarabia was taken from the new U.S.S.R.

A Fascist dictatorship run by Marshal Ion Antonescu permitted the boy king, Mihai, to keep his title after Carol was run out of the country with his mistress, Magda Lupescu. Antonescu's Iron Guard organization set up authority in the countryside, complete with district cells. When the tiny Communist cadres came out in the open with the arrival of the Red Army, the old Iron Guard organization was highly useful. Iron Guardists became Communists virtually overnight. They were badly needed. Before the war, the party had not more than a few hundred members.

Walking along the broad Boulevard Bratianu, as it was called then, I asked Ana Pauker about the party number. A big, brass-bound figure,

Mme. Pauker for a few post-war years as deputy Party Secretary was one of the most powerful women in the world. She later became Foreign Minister. Would, I asked, 400 Communists be about right for the "pre-liberated" Rumania?

"Fairly accurate," she replied. "Numbers, please remember, mean little. Applying numbers is much more interesting."

The Russians brought Mme. Pauker into Rumania with them. It was the first country the Red Army "liberated." Under Antonescu, Rumania fought on Hitler's side. Its armies had units in Stalingrad and had taken Sevastopol. As booty, Rumanian forces sent back trolley cars from Sevastopol to Bucharest. They also settled down in areas of the Ukraine with Russian mistresses, permitted peasants to leave collective farms, and tried to think their work for their Nazi superiors was finished.

When the Germans began to reel out of the Soviet Union, Rumanians around the king sought to interest the Western allies in a separate peace. The Russians, getting wind of prospective talks, quickly moved into the country. Helping them in a show of defiance was, strangely, King Mihai. He locked up the dictator, Marshal Antonescu, in the vault housing the royal stamp collection. Antonescu was to be tried later when the Red Army moved into Bucharest. Overt Soviet occupation was necessary there.

The Communist party was hated and defied in the country. Only a handful of Communists could even pretend to administer so large a territory—a couple of Rumanian Communists were known in the country. Gheorghe Gheorgiu-dej, who once led a railway strike was best known. Lucretiu Patrascanu, of a middle-class family, who studied in France, had been considered a black sheep of good people. He never had the iron required of a Communist. Patrascanu could not tolerate liquidating old schoolmates and friends, no matter their political beliefs. He was a handsome man, and almost idealistic. I once asked him to intercede for a merchant whose son fought bravely in the U.S. Army.

"The man's in jail, you know," said Patrascanu. "His son fought with your people. That doesn't help a great deal now. I'll get him released anyhow."

Patrascanu did. He couldn't last long by being so sentimental. He didn't. Under the pattern, another Communist was assigned the top police job as the Minister of Interior. He was a short, swarthy man with the arms of a gorilla. His name? Teohari Georgescu. Many of the policemen under his command had been officers who interrogated him when they served the fallen dictatorship.

"It doesn't matter, I tell you," he said, when a few of us taxed Georgescu with his list of oldtime policemen. "You can't ruin a good organization overnight. There was lots of good in it, you realize."

That kind of "good" also extended high in the regime. Andrei Vyshinsky, who came to Bucharest to fix up the first coalition, brought Gheorghe Tatarescu into the government as Foreign Minister. As wartime Premier, Tatarescu had been a flaming disciple of the Axis. The province of Bessarabia, grabbed by the Russians in an earlier Stalin deal with Hitler, was acclaimed again by Tatarescu as part of Rumánia. At the time he proclaimed that "Rumania would never falter in the holy war against Bolshevism." Quite a politician, Tatarescu. Apparently Vyshinsky thought so, too.

At a glittering reception in Bucharest—glittering only in comparison with the rich countryside that had been despoiled—I asked Vyshinsky about his concept of the law and his feelings towards Tatarescu.

"What matters, young man," tersely declared Russia's purge-trial prosecutor and later international troubleshooter, "is the letter of the law, not the spirit."

He never talked about Tatarescu, though. In the Rumanian regime Tatarescu was part of a motley collection paving the way for Russian-type "People's Rule." Ex-Fascists administered alongside Communists. A one-time deserter from the Rumanian army, Emil Bodnaras, returned with the Russians. He took over the Defense Ministry. The politicians who tried to run the opposition, supported by most Rumanians, were old and often compromised. Juliu Maniu was probably as close to a national politician as there was in Rumania. His peasant party was organized loosely all over the country. Against Soviet iron-fisted occupation and growing Communist organization, Maniu could fight only a delaying action.

Against him, as self-appointed defender of the peasants, was a Russian favorite, a man who was a wealthy landowner from Transylvania. He was Petru Groza, the sponsor of the "Ploughman's Front," a vain man, bubbling over with ambition and vitality. He wanted to be a big personality in Rumania. Being pro-Communist helped a lot. Groza loved to talk of student days in Vienna, his amours and the good life Rumania would have under his rule. Travelling with him was illuminating. To answer sticky questions, Groza would seek out the nearest Soviet diplomat. He'd repeat the question to the Russian. The Russian would shake his head, call Groza off into a corner, and then Groza would return beaming with the proper answer.

Besides Maniu, two other politicians opposed the take-over. One was ancient Constantin (Dinu) Bratianu. He had graceful manners and spoke near-flawless French. Bratianu represented the Liberal feeling of the Rumanian cities. His ideas must have been considered quite liberal, even radical, before World War I. But they had not changed since. Flanking Maniu and Bratianu was a sad, small man, Titel Petrescu. His had been a Social Democratic Party. It never amounted to very much in prewar Rumania. Still, it was much bigger and much more important than the nation's Communist Party ever had been. Petrescu, small in body, was large in heart. He didn't like his allies but he feared and hated his Communist enemies.

"We have in Rumania a living paradox, for the moment," Petrescu once told me. "Here, there is a king, tolerated by Communists who really run the country. For the first time, I think, you can say, 'His Majesty's Communist government.'"

South of the Rumanian border, in Bulgaria, there was ambivalence. For a small Balkan country, the Bulgars used to entertain big ideas for themselves. They turned out, in wars they usually lost, to be good soldiers. They also were ferocious occupiers, as the Greeks and Yugoslavs will attest. But Bulgaria never had really big landowners as once flourished in Hungary, Poland, Rumania and to a smaller extent, in Czechoslavakia. They also were quite pro-Russian, although not necessarily pro-Soviet. Russian Tsars had helped liberate them from the Turks. Russian names of pre-Revolutionary times still adorned streets. Farms, for generations, had been linked together on a cooperative basis. It was by no means a collective society, but an association of agrarian communities.

A fairly strong and highly disciplined Communist party had existed for years in Bulgaria. Shining Communist names like Georgi Dimitrov, Vassily Kolarov, longtime party boss Vulko Chervenkov, and his successor, Todor Zhivkov, had been part of the Soviet international apparatus. There also had been a radical peasant movement, infinitely more reformist in nature than almost anywhere else in Eastern Europe. They were radicals but not Communist. The monarchy, with firm equality, persecuted both. King Boris, who played with toy trains for relaxation, had been poisoned by the Germans in 1943 after they became worried about his state of vassalage.

An infant son, Simeon, was installed in what probably was the ugliest royal palace in Europe. It was low, strung along the main boulevard, and seemed to have been built in early Hamburg dock style. Although Nazi satellites, the Bulgars refused to enter the war against the Soviet Union. That was for payment, they said, for earlier Russian help to them. When their emissaries went to Cairo to ask the West about an armistice, the Russians promptly declared war against Bulgaria. Without opposition, the Red Army entered the country in September, 1944. It was the second "liberation." A few weeks earlier, Rumania had been first.

Another coalition, again fused by Vyshinsky, began the process of bringing Bulgaria into the Soviet orbit. Dimitrov didn't show up in the rickety capital, Sofia, for some time. He kept sending cables from Moscow that were read at all rallies. Soon Dimitrov was called, even by comrades, "Georgi the Telegram." Despite his absence, the administration of the police, as was to become customary in these unhappy countries, was assigned immediately to the Communists. The coalition included some men who previously worked for King Boris. A figure-head Prime Minister, Kimon Georgiev, had served so many previous governments he couldn't remember them all. Georgiev had an owl-eyed look and the wisdom of self-survival. His Foreign Minister was a pretentious man, who confided that he could outwit Vyshinsky and anyone in the Balkans. Petko Stainov was his name and he could quote from memory passages from Machiavelli's "The Prince." In Italian, too, if you cared to listen.

Far superior to them was Nikola Petkov, with a fullback's build and the heart of a lion. He was neither frivolous nor arrogantly ambitious. Petkov, in a way, inherited agrarian leadership in Bulgaria. His father, in the reform cabinet of Alexander Stamboulisky in the Twenties, had been torn to pieces by Balkan assassins, as had his elder brother. Petkov fought totalitarianism in whatever form it showed itself. He fought the Nazis uncompromisingly. In the same way, he devoted himself to opposing the Communists. They offered him a rigged union with them. He refused. It would have been easy to take, after his own long struggle for the justice he believed Bulgaria should enjoy.

"Sometimes, I even think about what might have been," he told me in his house one night in 1945. "When I talk it over with myself, I know that I behaved the right way. So, I go on. How long? You tell me."

A long-bearded elder, Kosta Lulchev, joined forces with Petkov. He ran the small Social Democratic Party. As in Rumania, the Socialists didn't count for much politically. But they had members devoted to democratic change and reform. Lulchev, who had long known Dimitrov, had no illusions.

"I fought for him and his kind when they were in trouble here," remarked Lulchev. "I didn't do it because I thought I could change them. I did it because I believed intellectuals should not become, in this part of the world, captivated only by the Dimitrovs."

Throughout Eastern Europe, in their search for some tangible aim, many worn-out intellectuals sought the paternally despotic arm of the Communist party. Their ranks were swelled by young returning prisoners in search of careers and some kind of future. Once, not long before, they had seen members of another totalitarian party enjoy the fruits of belonging. Disillusionment made the newly visited brutality seem primitive but manageable. It was not a mass movement, mind you, but it seemed to quite a few the path of least resistance. In an astonishingly short time they changed their minds, these products of the wartime generation in Eastern Europe. They had been suspect from the beginning. The "new society" would build its own generation, faithful to principles uttered by, or for, Stalin and the motherland of "socialism," the U.S.S.R.

A new alphabetical language came into use. Men and women spoke the letters in whispers. They stood for the police organizations, the hard-eyed security men who took people away at night. More often than not the victims never returned. It was in Rumania the Siguranza; in Czechoslovakia, the SNB; in Yugoslavia, OZNA, later the UDBA; UB, in Poland; AVH, or "Avos," in Hungary. The alphabet sometimes changed with shifting personnel and purges. The job was always the same— buttoning up lips and battening down criticism.

Lawlessness and crime washed like a tidal wave over Eastern Europe in those postwar days. Red armies of occupation lived off the land. They looted and they raped. Soviet monuments to "liberation" quickly acquired different names among the subject peoples. "Statue to the Unknown

Plunderer," Eastern Europeans would say as they saw another concrete monument erected in a central plaza. The peasants, defending their own countryside, resisted the incursions of the commissars more violently than their city kin. They refused to deliver harvests, slaughtered what little livestock remained and hailed land reform much differently from what the Communist planners expected. Formerly, landless peasants fell upon redistributed farms as their very own. They reacted as violently, as neighboring landed peasants. The land, they declared, was now theirs. How could the government dare give orders about it? But the government, following Soviet practice faithfully, did.

It was somewhat easier to cow the townsfolk. But terror only planted deeply the seeds of doubt, distrust and mass confusion in a generation the Communists set about to nurture as their own. Eastern Europe was in the throes of a revolution and didn't realize it.

"You can't do it the way you did in the Soviet Union," cried Nikola Petkov.

The Russians and their East European proconsuls paid the warning no heed. What mattered, as Vyshinsky said, was the letter of the law. Soviet law, then, became rapidly applied the length and breadth of Eastern Europe.

CHAPTER 3

Like a jig-saw puzzle, fitted so the pieces could suit Soviet expansion and control, the geography of Eastern Europe was rapidly carved up and rearranged. When it fell into place, Russia had common borders with Poland, Germany, Czechoslovakia, Rumania and Hungary. Pieces and provinces of all the redrawn countries had been taken by the Russians without consultation with the West. For Stalin, it was a matter of straight politico-strategic consideration. The Russians were either in direct control or could bend a shakily nervous regime's decision, as in Czechoslovakia, to a demand from Moscow.

Populations shifted across the land mass affected. Worn horses, beat-up carts, piled high with household goods, milled across the pocked landscape. Local Communist commissars saw to it however, that houses remained untouched. The grapevine is lightning-fast about impending change in Eastern Europe. Peasants, particularly, have almost extra-sensory perception. They began to depart to be with their own countrymen. Behind them, they left farms worked by generations of their own folk. Into the new territories assigned them or into the countryside still technically part of their own nation, they started new lives. Suspicion greeted them at every door and in each office.

"It may not mean much today," a young Polish peasant said. (He wore Russian army boots and a Wehrmacht tunic.) "We were supposed to be on the winning side. What happens? I find myself in an old German village. It's supposed to be better here. Maybe. But I will never forget the village in East Poland that was supposed to be bad. It's Russian now."

Looking at the map, the Russians appeared to be firmly in control. Before them they saw contiguous borders with Germany and most Eastern European countries. Bulgaria was not tied to the U.S.S.R. by a land-line. But it lay just below Rumania, straddled by a huge Soviet army of occupation. Russia's own Black Sea port of Odessa was a quick destroyer run to the Bulgarian coast. Only one putative satellite was cut off from Russia and isolated. That was little Albania, bounded by Yugoslavia and hemmed in on the south by non-Communist Greece. The Adriatic Sea was an outlet and inlet. Still, Soviet planners felt Albania was safe in the hands of Hoxha and Shehu. There also was Marshal Tito, so reliable then, to watch over Albania.

Our military control commissions could do little but protest. There was no Western force worthy of the name left in Europe, even if we intended to use it to back up policy. The U.S. had gone into quasi-isolation after a big war. Congress, seeking votes, was determined to bring back the GIs. Our armies were broken up. Policy for the outside world generally was played by ear. We became somewhat alarmed by Soviet power plays in Eastern Europe but preferred to forget about people we normally thought of as underdogs. Looming bigger than any man's hand, so we believed, was our monopoly of the atomic bomb. We believed that was enough and looked smugly inside the U.S. to get rid of the wartime taste. Americans did not fully realize that they had gone from a flamingly hot war into something perhaps more dangerous and unfathomable until they were already in it.

Under the circumstances, American military missions and diplomatic installations in Eastern Europe mostly tried to convey a feeling of urgency to the men who make policy in Washington. To be sure, we had eight-balls, dewy-eyed dreamers and simple time-servers around. Our military mission in Budapest, so absorbed in buying knick-knacks, once sent a heavily-laden C-47 out with baroque bric-a-brac to outfit a couple of bars in the southwest United States. This mission was a classic study in self-made mediocrity. In Bucharest and Sofia, on the other hand, both the military and political missions were ably administered. Unfortunately they never got much of a hearing back home. Why? A Congressional fact-finding group, if you forgive the expression, once went whirling on visits to all our military missions. I was on the plane, from Vienna to Budapest, with the group. A Congressman, still a loud voice in Washington, summoned the conducting officer to him as we approached the capital on the short flight.

"Major, son," intoned the Congressman importantly, "why do they sometimes call this Budapest, sometimes Bucharest and sometimes Belgrade?"

Ironically, the Soviet diplomat or secret policeman, posing as an administrator, was deeply suspicious of visitors like the Congressman. For a long time the Russians thought this ignorance was an act we were putting on, to bewilder them while we went after something else.

"Some of your people put on a nice, innocent face," the Soviet Ambassador to Hungary, beetle-browed Georgi Pushkin, remarked to me at a reception. "Don't try to fool us that way. We know better."

In that respect, the Russians didn't know and perhaps never really will. But they never permitted their confusion over our innocence in Eastern Europe to block their own plans. On the gaping ruins of cities and in the desolated countryside, the new class of Communist rulers and administrators introduced industrialization and collectivization programs tailored in Moscow. Monarchies, of course, were relics. One after another, they were swept out of existence—Albania's, whose King Zog long before had fled into exile; Yugoslavia's, whose young King Peter served the war also in exile rather than in the mountains; and the paradoxical Regency of Admiral Horthy in Hungary, which was ended with little mourning. Horthy, who helped draw Hungary into the war on the Nazi side, was taken off by the Germans. He had been king in fact, if not in name, since he never did permit a monarch to ascend the throne. The child-king of Bulgaria, Simeon, was sent packing with his family. Only Mihai, who had been awarded the Order of Victory by the Russians, remained.

His was a sullen, somewhat mulish attitude against the Russian masters of his monarchy. Talking to him once at the summer castle of Sinaia, deep in the green-forested slopes of Transylvania, King Mihai gloomily fore-saw the end of his rule. He indicated that he wanted to buy time for his country. The monarchy was in poor repute in Rumania. Mihai, though, was a popular personality. His popularity was probably compounded of anti-Communist feeling and the fact that a king could not really be a party member.

Mihai's Soviet decoration was something of a source of embarrassment to him. After all, a king with a comrade's medal! Marshal Tito had been awarded the same decoration. It made them, after a fashion, equals. The citation from Stalin, in Mihai's case, read: "For heroism displayed in the Allied cause when the balance was not yet in our favor." Apparently Ana Pauker didn't set much store in Mihai's decoration.

Less than a year before Mihai was given his walking papers, Mme. Pauker, her nylons snagged in the limousine that brought her, stood before her sovereign and droned: "I swear faith to my King. I swear to respect the laws of our country. I swear not to divulge state secrets." An interesting oath for a Communist to take. It didn't last long. Mme. Pauker, once called Madame Marx, soon became foreign minister. Mihai went into the relative oblivion of exile, surrounded by a retinue that thought he had big money hidden away. When it turned out he didn't, they left.

The days of rouged and corseted Balkan kings and Eastern European potentates gave way to the privileged commissars. A classless society that was supposed to be in the making really never developed. Higher-up Communists had cars, apartments and villas at their disposal. Top ones also had bodyguards. Getting into a party headquarters was as difficult as infiltrating a fortress. In Eastern Europe, commissars ruled by the book. It was the sacrosanct book of planning and dividing by terror. Police, as sadistic as the Nazis in interrogating their victims, ruled. Secret police officers were among the most privileged of the highly placed. Their terror also cut across party lines. Few, if any, run-of-the-mill Communists could say which comrade had police contacts.

Within this jungle, Soviet operatives threaded their way. Their command was above the law of the given land. Besides, they had come from Beria in Moscow. Thus, when leading opposition politicians were causing more trouble than a regime bargained for, Russians usually arranged to abduct them in haste and liquidate them at leisure. That was the case with courageous Bela Kovacs, the brains of the Smallholders Party in

Hungary. Over coffee one late afternoon in 1946 Kovacs said that neither he nor his party must give any "provocation" to the Russians or to Rakosi, his sworn enemy.

"What is provocation?" asked Kovacs sadly. "In the language used by the Soviet Union, it could be anything—anything to get rid of you."

A few hours later Soviet secret policemen seized Kovacs on the street. They bundled him off to the Soviet Union. The Russians made no secret of it, that time, that they were responsible. Kovacs, they said with finality, had been working against the occupation authority. Kovacs remained in Soviet jails and labor camps for ten years, returning home a broken man, just before the revolution exploded in Budapest.

The West, in Kovacs' case, issued another strong, but empty protest. In Soviet Europe, the climbers to total power would not be bothered by the frustrated utterances of the United States or Britain. The British, taking a more leisurely and historical view of conditions, told us to keep our shirts on. They were being run by a Labor Party back home that was bogged down in social adjustment. Getting involved in Eastern Europe was more than its resources could stand, even in a propaganda-political conflict. Unlike crude but shrewd Ernie Bevin, then Foreign Secretary, a small but vocal group of Labor M.P.s were away off to the "Left." This wing always had ready-made excuses for the disappearance of the non-Communist Left in Eastern Europe. Not so Bevin, or the British Prime Minister, Clement Attlee. They saw the forced marriages of Socialists with Communists as a monstrous tragedy.

"Ours will never again be the same party," a Polish Socialist explained sadly. "We were confronted with the choice of being incorporated with the Communists or being liquidated. As simple as that. Better if the party had accepted liquidation. It will be a miracle if a new generation ever again believes in us and what we did."

As a reward for collaboration, the Polish Socialists took over various regime posts. Egg-bald Joszef Cyrankiewicz vaulted into the office of Prime Minister. He had been for years in a Nazi concentration camp. He also was a long-time Socialist. While a leading Socialist, he had close associations before the war with the Comintern. Enemies in his own party insisted that Cyrankiewicz had always been a Soviet agent. Some of them have since died. Others remained silent and went along with the fusion. Cyrankiewicz, always a fun-loving fellow, lived well in ruined Warsaw, where he drove his imported automobile fast along deserted streets.

Even when Gomulka, austere and parochial almost alone of the Moscow-appointed group in power, went to jail as a Titoist, Cyrankiewicz flourished. His retinue of young girl friends did, too, in the ballet and the theater.

"Who else is there to help build up the country?" Cyrankiewicz reportedly once demanded of a British Laborite. "Stalin, for reasons of his own, liquidated the whole Communist party hierarchy before the war."

Using the wretched political clichés of their time—many still do—Social Democrats elsewhere sold out their own parties. In Czechoslovakia, Zdenek Fierlinger had a leading role. Fierlinger, a professional diplomat, had been wartime and postwar ambassador to Moscow. He also belabored his own political party to make a workable union with Czechoslovakia's Communists. Vaclav Majer, broad and blunt as befitted an ex-miner, fought Fierlinger all the ways he could. On and off, Fierlinger fought Majer for party leadership. Majer won all the battles but the last.

"I should have broken his (Fierlinger's) neck," Majer burst out once when I was in his office shortly after the war. "That would have given us something, anyway."

Instead, other necks were broken and minds were trained away from opposition to Communist party drives. Color and black-and-white photos of Stalin were even more ubiquitous than in the Soviet Union. Public display was always considered by party propagandists as not only signs of loyalty but good insurance of their devotion. Once in Debrecen, in eastern Hungary, I found a Communist official in tears. His photo of Stalin had fallen from its place of honor in his shop window. The frame broke and had to be taken away to be repaired. A more important bureaucrat spotted the empty place in the window. He accused his underling of "deliberate vandalism."

"I will have to face my comrades at a party meeting tonight," sobbed the poor man. "It will be self-criticism. What does that mean?"

It was not that way in Tito's Yugoslavia. Few photos of Stalin showed around the country. Tito's was everywhere. In other Communist countries, the local pro-consul often had his photo run up alongside Stalin's. In Yugoslavia, it was the other way around. Tito's picture, certainly;

Stalin's, very occasionally, and then next to Tito's. The immediate post-war Yugoslav partisan regime was frank in admiration for the Soviet Union. It copied plans from Moscow faithfully and racked back the peasants early. People's courts flourished as they did all over Eastern Europe. The Yugoslavs, however, had more experience.They held people's courts during the partisan war. Nobody had to impart a code to them.

"We know how to handle criminals," Pjade told me.

"They do, but by their standards," was the laconic explanation of a Royalist officer who spent the war years in a German P.O.W. camp.

Before repatriation, he never saw or knew a Communist. The fact that he had been in the Royal Yugoslav forces before the Germans overran the country, automatically made him suspect. It was the case with thousands of others, despite the fact that Tito, from a cellar, urged the partisans on to war against the invader after the Germans knifed into Yugoslavia. This was even before the Nazi attack on the Soviet Union. Before that, the line was that the Hitler-Stalin pact stood; that good Communists must ignore an "imperialists'" war. Timing of the partisan entry into war was another irritant the Russians remembered. But they had no cause to fret over looseness or benevolence of the Titoists towards the opposition or outsiders from the West in the formative years.

Travel from the flat plains of Hungary to the outer recesses of Communist Europe was an exercise in developing ulcers. It was also a good way, done by jeep, to see for yourself the physical changes made in the stricken territories by their new political look. Once when I reached the Hungarian border, after driving from Vienna, a couple of Red Army sentries stopped me. Papers seemed all right to them but the most important was one for the jeep. That required approval from an officer. They went to fetch one. A young Hungarian soldier, who spoke some German, waited with me.

"Do you really want to go there?" he asked unbelievingly, pointing to the road that led to Budapest.

I said, yes; that I also planned to go much further east.

"Most people try to go the other way," he answered.

Why didn't he? There were parents in a suburb of Budapest. He had a job in the open and could send back eggs and chickens from the countryside. What had he done before? He had gone to grade school and then was a tinsmith's apprentice. His class had just been summoned to the Hungarian army when the Russians besieged Budapest.

"We all stayed in the cellars," he recalled. "It was awful."

His army class had been recalled so he served. How was it now? Any change?

"It's still awful," he murmured and looked away.

The Russian soldiers, accompanied by a lieutenant, returned. The officer barely glanced at the travel papers. He scanned the form putting the jeep in my custody. It was stamped by "Order of Gen. Mark W. Clark." The Russian and I spoke pidgin German together. The tongue of the vanquished was the lingua franca between Russians and Americans. The rubber stamp meant more than my documents. I was waved through, but I also had to take a passenger to Budapest—the Russian lieutenant. Soviet installations dotted the fields and were installed in the larger houses in the villages. Honking geese marched precisely through muddy streets. Villagers and country folk began to wave at me, then dropped their hands. They saw the lieutenant in his Red Army uniform beside me. Signs in Russian and Hungarian festooned walls, some of them only the ruins of buildings. They hailed the "liberation" and the "joint march to socialism."

About every twenty-five miles, we were stopped by roadblocks. Russian soldiers and uniformed Hungarians checked us out. I asked the Hungarians who they were. One, a cigarette in the corner of his mouth, replied: "Police, of course." What was surprising was that he spoke English. The fields behind him had an unkempt look; corn stalks smashed and wheat trampled. A woman gathered up a snorting sow in her arms as we started up again and drove slowly past.

Banners and slogans became more profuse as we approached the military bridge that was the only one then spanning the Danube from Buda to Pest. The old castles on the Buda hills had been demolished in the siege some time before. War and occupation, however, could not diminish the real beauty of the city. Bisected by the Danube, there was an old grandeur that sprang up among the ruins. The huge and gloomy Parliament loomed on the Pest side of the Danube. Somehow, it had not been badly damaged.

The Russian knew where he was going. We turned off in a maze of narrow cobbled streets. Passers-by stopped and stared. There was the American flag to identify me on the jeep, a strange license plate and a

Russian officer. Almost everyone carried a briefcase. Some munched slices of dark bread as they stood and stared. Total drabness and the stench of defeat, even death, was in the street. Corpses were still in the ruins of houses.

Beckoning to me to follow, the Russian officer went to the door of a large office building. It was pockmarked with gunfire. I went back, then, and locked the jeep wheel. When I finished, I noticed two women in old slacks, carrying hods. Women were already at work in a city once re-nowned as middle Europe's gathering place for amusement, indolence, sparkling wit and perfumed chatter. To take women from the home and even the beauty parlor and put them to work cleaning up streets was something of a wrench, for the women. One of the hod-carriers, I noticed, had her hair tucked in a net. The other wore a thin trace of lipstick. They were in their mid-thirties. They were not Nazis rounded up for mass mop-ups because they were unguarded. They seemed to sense a kind of permanence in their new roles. Loitering on a job to help pass time starts early in the Communist program to "build socialism."

In the guarded office building, I was ushered into the presence of a Soviet colonel. He was short and had a mop of unruly hair. A junior officer stood beside his desk. He spoke fair English. My own escort, leaving me in the office, vanished. What, demanded the young officer, did I want in Hungary? A newspaper man. The colonel reflected on the answer briefly. He spoke, the words cascading heavily.

"You are all spies and propagandists for reaction," he declared. "I want to tell you this: Do not try to incite people against us. Try to re-educate yourself in what is being done here."

He waved me out to launch my own "re-education program." In East-ern Europe, re-education as devised by Communist parties with the active assistance of Soviet political officers was as much in vogue as paying public homage to Stalin and everything attributed to him. Rakosi, squat and bald, smilingly explained to me why he believed re-education was so vital. I talked to him in his panelled office. He was a Vice Premier then. Before the war, after having been jailed for life, the Horthy regime traded him to the Russians. The price? Some Hungarian battle-flags seized by Tsarist troops that came to the rescue of the Hapsburg Empire in the great revolt of 1848. The standards were Louis Kossuth's, fighter for Hungarian freedom. Why Horthy should have been interested in the banners is a mystery.

"It will be nice to be free soon," Rakosi said, his teeth flashing in a half-golden smile. "Re-education is absolutely vital. Hungary and her people have been held back so long. It will not be your way of education. You will be annoyed. But it cannot be helped."

Rakosi and his Moscow-trained associates in Eastern Europe were confident of their own power. They had the Russians behind them. Only the people opposed them. Who, after all were the people?

"They must be led and they must be shown." Those were words from Laszlo Rajk, an intense and devoted party man, who variously ran state security and the Foreign Ministry in the postwar days. A lifelong devotion to the party did not spare him from the purge later. When comrades, even high-ranking ones, balked at a project or argued difficulties in carrying out a Draconian measure, they could be accused of left or right-wing deviation. The gabble of doctrine to suit a policy had begun in earnest. At Czepel Island in the Danube, the industrial stronghold of the country and traditionally radical, the workers balked at the demands imposed on them.

"I've been a worker all my life," a horny-handed machinist told me, while a knot of co-workers nodded agreement. "But I'll be damned if I'll take orders from a man who is a director because he has been a member of the party. He doesn't know a lathe from a drill. All he does is to post quotas for us to follow. If we don't meet them, no money. Or worse, they call it sabotage. Sabotage, my foot. We had big hopes. These characters, with their fine paper plans, are planning us right out of work."

Another overalled worker slipped beside the machinist and whispered to him. The machinist shrugged angrily.

"Sure, someone is listening," he said. "Someone always is listening and informing. We're used to it. We lived with it in the old days, too."

A young man in a blue smock broke away from the crowd. The others watched him, resignedly, I thought.

"He lectures us on our glorious road to socialism five nights a week," the machinist said. "Floor managers also get his comments on us. You know what? Our little lecturer never worked in a plant before. How do I know? I can see right away if a man knows his job or not."

"We should be more careful," a co-worker observed. "Especially you."

"Careful, careful," roared the machinist. "We should keep quiet, I suppose and just accept. Well, I won't."

A middle-aged man, lean and lanky, with a cloth cap on the back of

his head, came up to the group. The men fell silent. He spoke to me and
his voice had authority. It was the director.

"You were supposed to be here as a guest—to look," he said. "Instead,
you have started a discussion, a very bad and dangerous one. We will
not permit that. You will leave at once. There will be no more of this
idiotic grumbling."

He stopped and looked at the machinist. The machinist stared back
at him, defiantly. "Come to my office," commanded the director. The
machinist followed. What will happen, I asked the others. They shook
their heads. At my elbow, stood the young man in the smock. "I will
show you the way out," he said coldly. He led me to the exit. Nobody
said goodbye.

Having a factory job was the next best thing to being a peasant. A
worker got special rations and could eat meals in the canteen. He also
could pilfer a tool or some other salable item, here and there. The black
market was starved for goods of any kind. It was not only the postwar
conditions, but strict Communist planning that made any consumer com-
modity scarce. No incentive, as a former small shop-keeper observed, to
make consumer goods for the regime. Stealing had become a way of life
in the war. Stealing and outwitting authorities became a fine art in
Soviet Europe. It is today the biggest most extensive form of private
enterprise in all Communist-dominated countries. The death penalty,
introduced to curb the practice, has been revoked and re-introduced
several times. A regime revokes it to ease police pressure and then re-
introduces the law in desperation to try and protect production, stock-
piling and distribution.

Another Communist-sponsored law compels youngsters to parade in
large groups. I saw thousands of school children, red banners held high,
march slugglishly through Budapest. Leaders or activists, usually many
years older than the kids they commanded, boomed out slogans and
songs. Their charges were supposed to echo them. "Glory to the Soviet
Union," or "Glory to Stalin," were some of the chanted mottoes. These
were the Communist youth groups, organized and carefully nurtured by
the party. They existed everywhere in Eastern Europe. In countries like
Hungary, where the party had been fairly no-account before, youth
leaders tried to show, with more marchers and by making more noise,
that they were building fast.

"Children should be given children's development," the ill-fated Bela

Kovacs said to me as we watched a parade from his window. "A child can resent discipline if he wants to play. You cannot cram his little head full of doctrine. In the end, he usually does just the opposite of what you want him to do."

Marching children, marching workers and "spontaneous" demonstrations were prevalent as I travelled from Budapest into the rich countryside to the Yugoslav frontier. District party officials would call for "spontaneous" demonstrations in the morning, afternoon or early evening. Every act had to be spontaneous. So, the orators and printed appeals demanded. In their mass formations, chanted slogans and ringing shouts to Stalin, the youngsters rolled back the very recent years. A world had torn itself inside out to finish off that same contrived spontaneity and discipline of the Hitler Jugend. Apologists for Soviet programs in Europe claimed this was totally different. The "people" were doing it all voluntarily. They were determined to make a better life, the regime contended. The Soviet Union said so, too. There could be no arguments.

That was just the point—no arguments. Conformity and acceptance were laid down as the daily rules of life. Only the state, through its appointed leaders, had the will, wisdom and experience to guide and to teach. Propaganda and blind obedience were something that most people knew only too well. Those and drabness. Drabness was etched on every town and village. It would not have stretched the meager resources of any community to brighten a public building with whitewash or to touch a little paint to some houses, but grayness and ruin was all there was to see.

"The Fascists did that," a country commissar said as he pointed out a crumbling farmhouse to me outside Budapest.

They were very old ruins, it turned out. Plenty of other shambles were to be seen from the war. But the theme was that all that was ghostly and grisly was the fault of the old regime. People had to bear with it and with whatever the government decreed to help build the "New Hungary." Personal services were almost totally neglected. Restaurants and inns served, if they served anything, drinks and food at under-the-counter prices. Money went into an inflationary spiral. Barter was much better. Cunning and contacts paid off. To try to live halfway decently, you started by being corrupted.

"Never mind your papers," said the guards at the no-man's land between Hungary and Yugoslavia. "Cigarettes are documents."

A couple of packs lifted the road barriers. Strange, I thought, that there should be such heavily manned roadblocks between the new "People's Yugoslavia" and comradely Hungary. On the Yugoslav side, sentries were much different. They were correct and hawk-eyed. Papers had to be stamped and routes were carefully described.

"Zivio Tito," were slogans crisscrossing an archway leading to Yugoslavia proper. Hammer-and-sickle drawings and photos of Tito, like paper creepers, were strung along the road. Outwardly nothing looked like praise for the Soviet Union. Indeed, Yugoslavia was Communist-run but devotion to Stalin was almost ignored. The Yugoslav partisans, as Vlado Dedijer told me later, felt so mighty that they thought they could turn back the sea. Just like Communist Canutes. They fought the war pretty much against all comers by themselves. That, they really believed. In the blazing sun and the chilling mountain nights you could hear songs of the "Youth Brigades" marching, working and camping. Partisan veterans, scarcely older than their detachments, led the work units. "Tito, Our Little White Violet," was the way one paean of praise opened.

It reverberated in the shattered villages and on mountainsides so recently scorched by war. Teenagers hefted tommyguns and watched prisoners working in the open fields. Everyone was supposed to be working at something. War and civil war cost the country dearly. The regime's new leadership demanded activity. So, off to work people went. They went pretty hungry as well. Factory managers were dismissed or arrested. In the past, they might have worked for the original owner. Or they were denounced. Denunciation was a way of trying to get on with the new regime. Plans for everything required in the country were boundless. A labor supply? Somewhat cut by the losses of war but it looked huge. There were partisans, prisoners and just everyone around.

"We'll make everything grow, just like a paradise," a brigade leader with whom I spent the night swore to me.

Hadn't things grown pretty well before? Yugoslavia, like virtually all East European countries, had been an agricultural surplus territory in prewar days. The brigade commander, all of twenty, answered disgustedly.

"How could you really understand?" he demanded. "We'll do it."

Some of the ex-partisans crowded around. How many had been farmers and worked the land before? Maybe two or three. It was a group of twenty, not perhaps typical. They peppered me with questions. Why was the United States so imperialist-minded? Were we really going to use the atom bomb on the Communist countries? Wasn't Tito a great man? The line of questioning was right out of the Communist mold. The brigade leader nodded with satisfaction at every question. Indoctrination was an important part of every partisan's training, like knowing how to use a gun properly.

Then came questions about the United States and its customs. They were naïve, in the main, and were about the concentration of wealth because so many in that camp had relatives who had a house and car in America. Some of the relatives had even sent packages. Under a British battle-jacket, one boy showed me a gaily colored shirt he wore. It came from Uncle Dusan in Florida.

"Tell us a little more about your music," asked a boy. "It's jazz. We know. The tunes are very catching."

Jazz among ex-partisans sounded strange. It wasn't exactly forbidden but it was frowned on, by culture commissars who spoke in terms of symphonies and ballets. The new Yugoslavia should not, Tito himself said, be tainted by poisonous infiltration from the West. Yet there, in a huge Croatian farm now transformed into a collective, we talked about Benny Goodman, Louis Armstrong and Isham Jones. Those were names the partisans remembered. How? From tuning in on the American Forces Network. The brigade commander broke up the discussion.

"Your music is good propaganda, it seems," he said solemnly.

I wondered how many young Americans would have thought about jazz in terms of propaganda. The word is all-important in Communist jargon. It cropped up in every talk I had in Belgrade with the men who were in the saddle of the new government. Tito, bronzed from the outdoor life of the war and well-uniformed, spoke to me caustically of American "propaganda" against him. He is short and stocky and his hair then was what we'd call dirty blond. In facial appearance he bears a striking resemblance to Goering. Nobody around him dared make the comparison.

"We want good relations with you," Tito said. He had an English interpreter beside him. But his German, with a harsh Slavic accent, is very fluent. He worked once, in the days of the Austro-Hungarian empire, as a mechanic in Wiener-Neustadt.

"But the Americans do everything they can to injure us," Tito continued in a matter-of-fact voice. "Of course, you give aid. That is probably your conscience bothering you. We are and will remain a country governed by the Party."

Milovan Djilas was even more unbending. Hair unkempt and pipe in mouth, he told me that Yugoslavia would show the way in Eastern Europe. In a way, he was prophetic. It wasn't the meaning he meant to convey at the time. Djilas talked of "crushing the class enemy without mercy." The Americans wanted to help the enemy, he declaimed, but it would not help us or them.

"They are doomed," he said, and tore a strip of paper in half to emphasize his point.

In those days Djilas had one extra-curricular obsession. A bamboo fishing rod stood in a corner of his office. He was a passionate fisherman. It seemed strange to talk trout and salmon, in terms of pure sport, to so dedicated a Communist. As a boy in Montenegro, he said, he learned to fish in the wild mountain streams. When he spoke of Montenegro and of fishing, Djilas appeared positively sentimental.

The elder of the party, Pjade, was regarded by his comrades as an intellectual of high order. He was from a Sephardic Jewish family and had studied in France and Germany. Pjade also was a painter. He was a round-shouldered gnome of a man who looked hunchbacked. His tongue was sharp and so was his wit. He told me a story in answer to a question I asked about Yugoslav programs for land collectivization and industrialization. He had led a delegation to Paris after the war. (Communist-ruled nations, by the way, bank heavily on delegations. They travel at the host's expense, live on the host and even get presents. In between, business is done. Travel for a Communist ordinarily means getting on a delegation.) Pjade's delegation stopped over in Geneva. They had a few bodyguards along, a normal procedure for them. In opulent Geneva, the group peered in the tastefully decorated shops. The windows were adorned with watches and consumer goods. Pjade's own bodyguard, a Montenegrin partisan, whistled in wonderment.

"Chica (Uncle) Moshe, look," exclaimed the bodyguard. "How do you account for so much in a capitalist country?"

"Son, when it becomes socialist," replied Pjade, "there will be nothing in the windows."

That was Pjade's answer to me, through illustration. He left it for me to interpret: Cynicism, or his view of equality? Certainly, the ranking Yugoslav Communists began their careers as administrators by moving into the Dedinje district of Belgrade. That is a tree-shaded suburb above the popular park, called Topcider. Prewar, the best people of the time and the richest had villas in Dedinje. Tito took over the White Palace, used by the royal family. He acquired other homes away from home. The island of Brioni, where Europe's royalty played before World War I, became Tito's exclusively. All year round, the weather is mild and the Adriatic sounds a pleasant obbligato against the coastline. He also took over hunting lodges and had a lovely old castle in Slovenia near the Austrian border.

Belgrade itself had a worn-out, Balkan look. Translated, that means many Turkish-cobbled streets, beat-up buildings, open spots where German bombing razed landmarks, scraggly trees on the main avenue, sleazy restaurants, one-story tenements that stretched half-a-block and mammoth photos of Tito. The atmosphere was stifling. In your hotel, a porter would disappear. If you stayed long enough, he might reappear. His appearance had altered, meanwhile. His head had been shaved in prison. He had been arrested on a denunciation or even a trumped-up currency charge. In the main, Serbs were not so much anti-Tito as they were anti-Communist. Belgrade, after all, had been Serbia's capital and then the capital of all Yugoslavia. It remained that way even after the Communists made a Federal Republic of the country, giving six provinces nominal autonomy under Communist secretaries.

The policeman's midnight knock on the door—so usual in Communist-ruled countries—sounded long and loud in Belgrade. I asked Aleksander Rankovich, a tallish, dark, ex-tailor's assistant, why terror was so necessary. He had been a partisan chief with Tito and was Vice Premier in charge of the Ministry of Interior. Rankovich bristled at the word "terror."

"You have the wrong idea," he replied. "These are necessary precautions in our young state. We still round up Chetniks who stupidly believe in Mihailovitch. They are enemies. There are plenty of other enemies. We dare not, we cannot, relax our vigilance."

Even after Mihailovitch was tried by a "People's Court," Chetniks remained a term of opprobrium. Watching Mihailovitch in the prisoner's dock, much of the tragedy of Yugoslav against Yugoslav came into bitter focus. He was a wan figure, with rimless glasses shining, dressed in nondescript clothes. His little beard waggled as he defended himself. He never tried to leave Yugoslavia. Deep in the mountains, from which he launched the first Yugoslav guerrilla attacks against the Germans and became a household name, Mihailovitch had been seized. He had been hunted day and night. He vehemently denied collaboration with the Germans. Conflict with Tito? Yes. He had been caught up, observed Mihailovitch sadly, in forces and counterforces of history. How could he understand what happened if more important men didn't or wouldn't. He was taken out after this fair trial, by local standards, and secretly executed. This was the way of solving the Chetnik question. Today, nobody knows where Mihailovitch is buried.

CHAPTER | 4

Barriers and roadblocks had been installed all over
Eastern Europe within a year after the war's end. You couldn't go as
far as, say, from New York to an outlying suburb, without being stopped
and checked. Going into and leaving a town brought on all the trappings
of a major border incident. The few foreign travellers, patience exhausted and tempers frayed, could only wait under guard for papers to
be cleared. Local people soon found ways of moving around check-
posts. It was simple if you had goods or money to exchange. A check-post
evader got in touch with the "underground." It meant crossing fields at
night or hiding in a Soviet Army truck. The Russians were in on the
racket. Otherwise, it couldn't have operated.

Most people couldn't pay, and official papers were almost impossible
to get. In Bulgaria, I spoke to a peasant woman at one check-post. She
had been at the Soviet-Bulgar command center for three days, calmly
waiting her turn. She was calmer and more resigned than the city folk,

which made her more noticeable. She explained her calmness to me: "I have food with me for a week," indicating a loaf-filled basket in which there were also six eggs and some sausage.

"The whole procedure is intended to break you and make you submit to authority," an intense and emaciated Bulgar journalist explained to me.

His first name was Victor and that will do for here. During the war he had been tortured by the Gestapo and their Bulgar collaborators. Later, he served a sentence meted out to him by Bulgar Communist authority. Victor had been out of prison only a couple of years. He later went back. I have heard that he is now out again, toothless, uncommunicative and coughing blood.

"The old regime was cruel, backward and stupid to people like me," Victor said one night in Sofia.

We sat over glasses of watery rosé wine in the room a family friend let him have. The apartment building, like nearly all in Sofia, was old and the façade flaked. There was little war damage in Sofia itself. But the city was an architect's nightmare. Small Turkish-style one-room cottages jumbled against three-story houses and office buildings. Scrawny trees stood in unmanicured parks. People's clothes were old and often patched. Disbanded soldiers still wore uniforms without insignia. Peasants in their thonged, home-made leather slippers wandered around town. They carried big loads on their backs. Peasant women, in home-loomed skirts covering layers of petticoats, staggered under bigger loads. Everyone came to town, either to stay or to look for work. Despite traditional enmity, the Bulgars, especially the peasants, looked strikingly like Serbs in Belgrade. •

"Our German monarchy," he continued, "which never had anything in common with the country, pushed us into this war as it did in the first one. This was an authoritarian state. The natural-born right for civil liberty was not respected.

"We, who came out of schools in the 20's and 30's, fought for what I suppose people in the West consider is inalienable to them. Most of us, I might tell you, also come from peasant stock. Our peasants love the land. We have had a system of cooperatives here almost as long as they have existed in the States.

"We worked for a chance to have people say what might be on their minds. We wanted some genuine social justice. In the old days, we were all lumped as Communists. There were quite a few Communists, and though they were not in the majority we still had plenty of opportunity to see how they tried to push us around. You can't be pushed around by both right and left indefinitely, and, after the war we thought we had a future. Now people like me know. Everyone has forgotten us except the Russians. My generation—the hopeful ones—is finished. It's up to the next, and the next."

Victor filled my glass. "Long speech," he remarked wryly. He talked so long, he added, because a man in his position never knew how much he could get off his chest when he wanted to. Men like Victor always had premonitory sensations. He disappeared one day. I left him notes at his newspaper and apartment. At the end of a week, Victor called me. His explanation was simple.

"The police wanted to know why I had you, a foreigner, in my room," he said. "It usually takes them a week to go over us."

Without mentioning Victor's name, I talked about harassment with Vladimir Topencharov, then a big man in the Bulgar regime. He was a veteran Communist. Unsympathetic eyes peered out from behind horn-rimmed glasses. He was short, stocky and with his mustache looked like a bulkier Georgi Dimitrov. Topencharov, through marriage, was lucky and unlucky. His brother-in-law, Traicho Kostov, was then the most important man, after Dimitrov. Topencharov was Minister of Information, a chief censor and regime spokesman. A short time afterwards, in the wave of purges of people charged with the crime of "Titoism," Kostov was executed. Topencharov went to jail, was "rehabilitated" in the cynical conditioning of the party and given odd jobs. He is still an odd-man out.

The first time I talked to him, though, Topencharov was a very influential party man. He saw defiance in men like Victor as a hold-over, of "mushy, bourgeois beliefs in what they call liberty."

"These people are unwanted museum pieces here in Bulgaria," said Topencharov coldly. "They will either learn to understand what we are building or they will vanish. We have no time to argue sentiment with you. We are in a hurry."

Haste was a factor that Dimitrov also impressed on me. The man who was probably best known in the operative days of Russia's international apparatus, the Comintern, and hero of the Reichstag fire trial in Germany, Dimitrov obviously enjoyed his power position in Bulgaria. His mustache and hair shone with so much black luster that I remembered stories—from Communists—that he was vain enough to use blacking to hide the gray. I intervened at one point in our talk to ask him about the black dye reports circulated by his foreign comrades.

"Vicious gossip," snorted Dimitrov. "Don't you people have better things to talk about?"

I reminded him, casually, that Communists in Prague, Budapest and Vienna talked about his personal habits. He shook his head in annoyance. Personal habits and private lives, he said to me sternly, should not be of interest to any outsider. It was a peculiarity of the non-Communist world that personal affairs attracted so much eavesdropping and so many busybodies.

"Just abandon any morbid interest you may have in personal habits in this country," Dimitrov declared. "Programs and the will to accomplish them are what matter most."

Trying to get details of such projects in Communist-ruled countries was easier said than obtained. It was a violation the then Interior Minister, Anton Yugov, told me, to go after information which would be normal procedure in the West. Yugov, who has been the professional survivor of the Bulgarian regime, has served in top and bottom jobs and makes himself studiously unpleasant to foreign visitors.

After saying hello, he demanded: "What do you want out of Bulgaria?"

When I said I wanted to see and talk to people like him and to get information, Yugov said I had better skirt the lines of anti-espionage laws carefully.

"We know what Western journalists want," he said. "They are interested in putting out lies and to make as much mischief as possible. You are all *agents provocateurs*."

That was the way in which Yugov also considered many Bulgars who had Western educations, especially those who had attended the American College in Sofia. As part of the Near East Foundation, the American College brought a little bit of Kansas deep into the Balkans for nearly fifty years. Its faithful teachers were now out. Students, some of them even budding basketball stars, were under deep suspicion. They were on trial to prove their loyalty to the "People's Regime."

"In the short run, a number will give up and do Dimitrov's bidding," Nikola Petkov told me. "I don't blame them. Don't most people try to think of themselves and their own first? To defy means you can also die. Too many people want to live, even under terrible circumstances. They believe they can outlive what harms them."

Petkov had a boy of about nine or ten in his arms as he spoke. The boy had been weeping. His mother was dead—executed by the Gestapo when he was an infant. After being in hiding, his father emerged to take care of him. Now the father, a lieutenant of Petkov's, was under arrest. The lad was frightened. His father had been taken into custody by police agents who burst into the room where his father had been reading to him. The housekeeper delivered him to Petkov.

That was the last time I saw Petkov. He had been personally denounced in Parliament by Dimitrov. His arrest, summary trial and execution soon followed. Eastern Europe and the world lost an unflagging champion of liberty and democratic idealism when Petkov was murdered. In desperation young Bulgars tried to keep spirits up and morale high. They could not organize street demonstrations. The police arrested too many of them and would not allow large groups to assemble. They walked the streets, singing songs which puzzled the authorities but had meaning to them and a few others. The songs, in a way, were pitiful. One was the old jazz favorite, "I'm Beginning to See the Light," and another, to the tune of "Barney Google," began, "I love Bulgarians with their big Bulgarian eyes." Sound offbeat and maybe a little foolish? Maybe to American ears. It took real courage to do that little act, in English. You could be arrested for less.

On the small, neat farms on the way north to the Danube and Rumania, you could find peasants talking and arguing in groups. At mid-day that isn't usual. There, the peasant should be in the fields working when the weather is good. They were, however, aroused and not at work now. City folk, I found generally, are more easily coerced by authority than the peasant. He is usually brusquely independent, suspicious of orders from the big town. He is profoundly dubious about the official, with little or no farm background, who comes out to say what must be done. Through work-worn generations, East Europe's peasantry love their land. They are wedded to it and don't give up what they hold without a stiff fight.

It turned out that these peasants in the enclaves running north and south had been given government instructions. Prepare for state cooperatives and collectives, ran the edict. The peasants were furious. They were arguing, near Pleven, famous for a Russo-Turkish battle seventy-odd years before, with a city-suited man who shouted back at them. He was a party organizer who had come out to tell the peasants what faced

them. Besides, he wanted to lecture to them. They would not stand still
and listen.

"Can I help you?" an American-English voice asked me.

A tiny old lady in rusty black smiled at me. Her thin gray hair was
tied in a neat bun at the nape of her neck. Her skirt and jacket seemed
to have been taken from a horse-opera costumer. She voluntarily quenched
my astonishment.

"More than fifty years ago my husband and I came to Bulgaria," she
explained. "He was a pastor, a missionary. I just stayed on when he died.
I don't feel there's any other place for me."

Peasants in this district, the old lady said, fought regime requisitioning
during the war. They became partisans. Some even swore they were
Communists.

"They became very different when Communist programs were applied
to them and to their land," she remarked. "Just look."

The party official, face contorted with rage, flung his arms out and
swept through the angry peasants. He stopped once to shake his fist at
the crowd. Into a waiting chauffeur-driven German Opel he stepped.
The car accelerated and roared down the road, kicking up clouds of dust
in everyone's face.

"The administration will get its way," said the old lady. "It will be at
a terrible cost. I know these people. Back home, they don't."

She wanted nothing, not even a chat on Nebraska, from where she
had come. This was her life and she would stay put for what was left of
it. She helped me out with road instructions. I'd be met, she predicted,
by a big crowd as I reached the outskirts of Ruse, the last big Bulgar
community on the Danube. How did she know?

"In the country, in this part of the world, you hear everything that
affects it," she replied. "Everyone is related or associated with someone
in the administration. It keeps them going, as it will even in bad times."

She was dead right, on all counts. At least 2,000 people—men, women
and children—were massed at the main road entering Ruse when I arrived. They bore dozens of photos of men, whose names they clamored:
"Stalin, Truman, Attlee!" Some threw nosegays of flowers at me. Children
were put in my arms. Photographers carefully took pictures. A self-
conscious official, in white shirt and red-figured necktie, came up to greet
me. He read, laboriously, a prepared speech, first in English, then in
Bulgarian. There were at least three references to understanding "the
new Bulgaria and the building of socialism."

Then came a march. It was a mass demonstration, spontaneously sparked. So the official greeter told me with a beaming smile. I never knew how so many people could be spontaneously assembled for a complete stranger. My welcomer never tried to explain. A Bulgar soldier, in his early twenties, did. "Your picture will be in the papers tomorrow," he said. "It's good to have an American in a demonstration." As an afterthought, he said, "When you get to the Rumanian side, you'll see another big reception. Demonstrations of solidarity are important."

I looked at him sharply. He never indicated as he escorted me with the crowd to the Danube ferry whether he was being ironic or solemn. He didn't say another word on the quick trip across to the Rumanian side on an old rust-coated boat. We arrived on the banks of Gheorghiu, where not only as big a crowd was massed but a brass band played. The song was "Tipperary." With a stiff salute, the Bulgar soldier said goodbye. It was only then that I noticed his bloused tunic and shoulder-boards. The Red Army influence was already showing.

Besides "Tipperary" nothing else but a visit to a military cemetery was remotely English or American. The mayor, a tall and ebullient man, greeted me in the name of Rumania. "Marching steadfastly with the Soviet Union," he added hastily. Cheers went up from the crowd. I noticed that in front of the crowd, a row of men and women bawled lustily. Two young men and a girl ran up and down, waving their arms like cheer-leaders. In French, the mayor, tugging self-consciously at his pearl-gray necktie because few others wore one, said he would be proud to show me the graveyard. We walked through, noticing headstones with names of British and American airmen who fell in raids when Rumania was a Nazi satellite.

"Why," asked the mayor, "should your country be so prejudiced against what we are trying to do in a new Rumania?"

That was a good question, I replied. Why? The mayor, translating to a short, dark-complexioned man, repeated what I said. He was puzzled and so was the man beside him. Who was he? I was then introduced to the Soviet equivalent of our military government administrators. The Russian, though, was called "Comrade." Around the crowd, shouting itself hoarse after the graveyard visit, I noticed details of Soviet soldiers. All had their tommyguns slung across their backs. In Bulgaria, Russian troops were kept out of public sight in conveniently located cantonments. These soldiers, the mayor informed me, were to help as guides.

"They will escort you to Bucharest," he announced.

It was only about an hour's ride and there seemed no need for a military escort. I said so to the mayor. He looked worried and consulted the Russian. They spoke for a few minutes.

"It's for your protection," said the mayor. "You can never tell these days who will stop you on the road."

I was "protected," in close-convoy formation, to the farewell chant of "Stalin, Truman, Attlee" when I left Gheorghiu. Red and white banners were strung above the highway. "Long live Soviet-Rumanian friendship," they read. There were plenty of photos, too—Stalin's and King Mihai's— an anachronistic study in comradely togetherness. The Russian soldiers knew their way, and their orders. When I slowed down to have a better look at some buildings or at peasants waving to me from the fields, the soldiers said dead-pan: "Nyet," and pointed straight ahead. Obviously, I would be protected if it killed me.

They led me straight to the Athenée Palace Hotel, famed and notorious for riotous living in pre-war Rumania. It is on the main boulevard, a short walk from the royal palace. In the more rococo Balkan style, the palace is large, low-slung and gloomy. Its fascination lies in its studied ugliness. This is true of Bucharest generally. A few broad streets pretended ostentatiously to resemble the charm and worldliness of Paris. There was even a "Calla Victoria," although the Rumanians never won anything except what other powers gave them. A miniature *Arc de Triomphe* was easily reached. Rumanian troops who supported Germany in the invasion of the Soviet Union marched up to the arch with tokens of booty. After them, the Red Army marched to the memorial and collected the booty.

Some of the streets had now been renamed for Stalin and victorious Red Army generals. This was an obsessive habit with the Russians wherever they took over a country. They immediately renamed streets that had just a short while before been called "Hitler Square" or "Ribbentrop Avenue." Once the décor had been changed the Russians didn't waste much time showing their hand and objectives in Rumania. Their sponsored Communist Party, too small to take control, quickly organized a coalition. Vyshinsky provided terms of reference and Groza was installed as a "national" Prime Minister.

Once, to give the Western Powers a stopgap sop, the Russians agreed to include two men from Maniu's and Bratianu's parties in the regime. W. Averell Harriman, then ambassador to Moscow, worked that grudging concession out with Vyshinsky. It didn't last long. The Russians were bent on breaking the anti-Communist influence. Demonstrations were, hourly and spontaneously, held in the square before the palace and the Athenée Palace Hotel. Cries of "Traiasca (Long Live) Groza," rang out in the streets. Counter-demonstrations were smashed. The pro-regime demonstrators had police protection. Many also had been accustomed to Iron Guard demonstrations. On one minority group both factions frequently had tacit agreement. They beat up Jews, an act that seemed to come naturally to them. Communists of Jewish origin, like Ana Pauker and Josif Chishinevski of the Politburo, were universally hated. The average Rumanian Jew, usually a returnee from concentration camps, frequently was mauled.

At night, there was often rifle and pistol fire. Pro-regime demonstrators would be attacked by anti-regime groups. Calls would go out for help. In rushed Soviet army detachments, flanked by Rumanian security police. Anti-Communists, recoiling or fleeing, were fired upon. Corpses were photographed and shown in the censored newspapers the following day as martyrs to enemies of the new state. The fact that yesterday the victims were anti-Communists didn't move the propagandists. In the villages and provincial cities, it was different.

The Communists and their Soviet advisers held the countryside in the daytime. At night, however, the activists had to barricade themselves, protected by local security police and the Red Army. The peasants and the peasant-bred townsfolk, in defiant roving bands, smashed party headquarters and brought retribution to Communist sympathizers. It was guerrilla warfare of a sort, mainly political, that riddled the Rumanian countryside. There were some shootings and ambushes. But it was never the no-quarter guerrilla warfare that the Poles carried out against the commissars in the country and the villages. There, small armies made a habit, for a couple of years, of eliminating Communist Party district leaders. A commissar in a Polish town frequently had a forty-eight-hour life span.

In Rumania, the crisscross and jumble of nationalities often stopped at regional loyalties. The Saxons, of German origin, hated Rumanians more than they did the new masters. Their neat farms and flaxen-haired families preferred to watch from the sidelines as Rumanians were chopped up by Communist police. Only when the Saxons were directly threatened, as next on the list, did they respond.

"We burn our crops and slaughter our animals," was the way a Saxon peasant stolidly explained his resistance to collectivization. "Rumanians? They are as bad as the others. Maybe worse."

So, they stuck to speaking German among themselves, just as Hungarians in the dappled valleys and rust-colored hills of Transylvania spoke Hungarian to one another. They disliked the Saxons only less than they did the Rumanians. Their children's colored school caps proudly showed their Hungarian origin. To weld a common front among Saxon, Hungarian and Rumanian was a wild dream no Rumanian politician tried to translate into practical terms. Within this division, the Russians and their puppet regime moved with trial by terror. They split communities and drove one ethnic group against another. Ambuscados and resistance were easier to smash by isolating groups and factions.

Soviet-sponsored land reform and the turbulence of farm and village resistance to Communist control, swiftly made a have-not food country out of Rumania. With more than a million Russian troops spread over the country, foraging for local supplies, famine loomed menacingly. Farm machinery had been seized as war booty by the Russians. I saw it in great piles near railheads. The old tractors and harrows rusted in the open. Sometimes freight cars, bound for the Soviet Union, stopped to load the machines. Bath-tubs and splintered grandfather clocks peeped out from above the groaning cars.

Distribution of food supplies was haphazard. Once a rich land with a large agricultural surplus, Rumania quickly became a nation of potato grubbers. Everywhere food black markets mushroomed. Groza grumbled, back in Bucharest, about speculators. He desisted when Maniu, worn with age and frustration, documented the cases of Russian soldiers busy with their own free enterprise in confiscating and selling food. The lei, the national currency, began to have a tennis-ball bounce. Deliberate inflation, to debase all traces of the old economy, was begun by the regime, as it had been in all Eastern Europe.

The sensibilities of the West, highly offended by grinding Soviet tactics, were even more outraged by the prospects of hunger on a rampage in Rumania. At the time, only the U.S. had an overflowing cornucopia. We sent food ships to the Black Sea port of Constanza. The Communist Party, after consultation with the Russians, struck on a cynical and, for them, highly pragmatic scheme. They would call for national elections, with the arrival of the food, to "legalize" the Groza regime.

It was a prototype of all Eastern European elections. Soviet garrisons were conveniently close to all big communities. Local Communist and pro-Communist parties and organizations had money, and better yet, food baskets and job lists. They had the control of gasoline, printing presses and, most important, the police and security. Barnstorming and electioneering with Premier Groza was an instructive exercise.

In Bucharest, police and party workers assembled by thousands to listen to their candidate. "If you don't show up, no job," was the way two factory workers explained. "No appearance, out of the university," students said. Names were checked at street assembly points. When the unwilling demonstrators tried to show their hearts belonged to the opposition, they were beaten by thugs. When some of us asked Groza how come, he replied: "Those men are there for the protection of city people and peasants."

Travelling with Groza then were always at least two Russians from the Soviet Embassy. There may have been more but the two were known to some of us. One was a ham-handed, outsized man who spoke only to Groza. The other was English and Rumanian-speaking, Sava Dangulov. He was known to the writing trade as "Strangulov." Cheery in appearance and stocky of build, Dangulov had been a spokesman in the Soviet Foreign Office in Moscow. He looked over all of Groza's prepared speeches before a whistle stop. Groza would thrust papers into his hand and say:

"Look at this dear friend. You will agree I am sure. The reactionaries hate me for this. Don't you?"

Then, Groza, landowner and choice of Vyshinsky, would leer at those few Western correspondents with him. Crowds, assembled as in Bucharest, were always waiting for Groza at the station. A couple of times he was loudly booed. A short scuffle would mar the docility of the crowd. Struggling figures, frog-walked by Rumanian security and Soviet officers in uniform, were taken out. There were always trucks waiting at the edge of the station to haul prisoners away. At this point, Groza would hold up a well-manicured hand for emphasis:

"You can see for yourselves," he thundered. "Our elections are much freer than those in the United States."

That remark brought stormy applause from the rear and front ranks of party workers. They also cheered lustily when Groza voted on election day. Opposition ballots, Rumanian regime officials reported all day, were being spoiled. How? Not properly marked, they answered blandly. To vote opposition, you also had to drop your ballot in a clearly observed separate urn.

Naturally, the voting resulted in a landslide for Soviet policies. The Russians could now reveal that the Rumanians approved of a secret deal made to provide the Soviet Union with an iron-clad hold on the local economy. Groza, almost forthwith, disclosed terms of a "fifty-fifty" deal. The agreement gave the Russians equality in numbers on boards set up to exploit oil, shipping, aviation, industry and agriculture. In case of a tie vote, the decision was up to the director. In every instance, he was a Russian. These companies for "co-operation" were quickly set up throughout Soviet Europe except in Tito's Yugoslavia.

The elections, fifty-fifty companies and police terror in Eastern Europe evoked futile protests from the West. But the Russians were in armed control and paid no attention. And the United States never went beyond protest. In times of desperate need, as in the Rumanian famine, the United States shipped food. There was no policy or project the United States administration had evolved to curb wilful violation of human rights. We thought differently and interpreted agreements with the Russians in two totally different languages.

I remember how morose a young student friend felt in Bucharest after the elections. We went to dinner at a popular restaurant, thronged that night with mournful oppositionists and Rumanian officials and Soviet officers, toasting their success. The floor show was limited to versions of popular folk dances. It opened in a swirl of skirts with girls dancing the can-can, for the French. It was greeted with a patter of polite applause. A British dance, a moody two-step, got perfunctory handclapping. So did an American jitterbug number and a wild Cossack dance for the Russians. Most diners seemed to be sitting on their hands. In the grand finale, one girl appeared in Rumanian national costume. To Rumanian gypsy music, she whirled and pirouetted. Most of the crowd went wild, standing on chairs, shouting and applauding.

"There goes our national resistance," said my young friend, gloomily pointing to the cheering audience and the taciturn Russians.

Plunged in the despair of the moment, he was premature. His generation was being squeezed. The regime's intention was to remodel and weed out dissidents. They would crush and recreate, they firmly believed. The young and new generations belonged to them. So they boasted. Our diplomatic representatives in Eastern Europe, fighting whatever delaying and rearguard actions they could muster, began to believe in the Soviet consolidation themselves.

All our representatives were followed, right into their bedrooms. Security agents dogged their walks and limited trips into the countryside. When they sought the asylum of rented apartments and houses, they had to be careful. Microphones were concealed everywhere. One of our ministers had one under his night-table. Young women who went out with unattached Americans were called in to report to the police. Attached, but lonely, diplomats found themselves targets of blackmail if they looked for local company. They were offered a simple tit-for-tat. All they had to do was to turn over papers from the embassy or legation to a police agent or the girl who went out with them.

"You learn to distrust almost everyone just after you get here," an American Foreign Service officer, now an ambassador, said to me ruefully. "It's a conspiratorial atmosphere that closes in."

Bad as it was in Rumania, a certain inefficiency for a time made the continuous surveillance a bit Graustarkian. A tired diplomat came home to his apartment one afternoon looking forward to a drink and playing records. He was dumbfounded to find a stranger asleep on the sofa, with a mechanic's bag open on the floor containing two microphones. Awakened rudely, the visitor seemed more annoyed than chagrined.

"You weren't supposed to be home until tonight," he said indignantly. Then, he gathered up microphones and tools and stalked off.

But the sloppiness never existed, except for mechanical deficiencies, in the vast cemetery that was Poland. From the beginning Russians were installed on all echelons of the Polish state apparatus. They were planted in the police, called the "UB," and in the retreaded Polish army that had fought at the side of the Russians. The first sight of postwar Warsaw was a nightmare. Frames of buildings gaped openly. Many still do. Big streets were impassable, so high was the rubble piled. A habitable spot had long been a challenge to find. Like strands of loose spaghetti, twisted building steel dangled on the skyline, or curled into cratered streets. Children in tatters played among the ruins.

They had never known anything else. Weaned on war, the lullabies they heard were the roar of guns, the anguished cries of the wounded and the rattle of death. Over the desolate streets hung the swamp-like smell of moldering corpses. Thousands lay beneath the rubble. In place of Warsaw's ghetto, only a vast tract of rubble and cinders was left.

The Polish home underground army, the "A.K.," rose against the Nazis towards the end of the war. It was probably the biggest underground combat army in all occupied Europe. The anti-German, anti-Communist forces fought for sixty-three days. The Red Army was halted on the opposite bank of the Vistula River. It waited until the Germans crushed the rebellion and destroyed Warsaw, virtually block by block.

The Home Army was forced to capitulate. It was precisely what the Russians and the Germans wanted, a mid-war Hitler-Stalin pact with the Poles as their target. Neither the Nazis nor the Russians have ever been forgotten or forgiven by the Poles for this. Sharply aware of Polish feeling and bitter enmity, the Russians took no chances. They partitioned Poland again, grabbing eastern provinces for themselves. As compensation, they turned over German territories to Poland. Russian troops were installed astride main Polish lines of communications. Remnants of the Polish Communist Party, regathered during the war, formed a provisional government in Lublin, south of Warsaw. It was created with the announced approval of Stalin.

The "liberators," as the Russians and their Polish collaborators described themselves marched into devastated Warsaw, proclaiming in tracts and banners a new future and life for the country. The organization and apparatus of post-war government were taken over by Communists and Russians. Peasants took up where they left off sniping at Germans. They fought pitched battles with Soviet troops. In the villages, they waylaid Communist security units. Unorganized civil war was waged against the Communists and the Russians as, once organized, it had been fought against the German invader. The war had already cost Poland 6,000,000 dead. Nobody dared estimate what postwar casualties were.

Even among the devoutly religious Poles, factionalism was introduced. A Polish Fascist, Boleslaw Piasecki, offered his services to the Russians. Piasecki proposed to organize a pro-Moscow Catholic organization, which he called Pax. He had worked out all the details while he had been in league with the Nazis. Piasecki claimed he would subvert the influence of the church and bring the clergy to its knees. That accomplished, the Polish people would submit to Communist rule. Piasecki was given control of the sale of religious articles, newsprint and various properties.

It was—and remains—the biggest single private enterprise permitted between Berlin and the Yellow Sea.

On paper, Piasecki's plan looked unbeatable. Translated into action, like so many Communist-supported plans, it enraged Polish feeling. They succumbed to Pax infiltration in buying things that couldn't be gotten elsewhere. But Poles, above all the clergy, condemned Piasecki and his operations.

"We have all made mistakes," Piasecki confided to me. "There is no other way to go but the Soviet way today. I have even lost my son for that belief."

Piasecki's boy, then sixteen, was kidnapped. Nobody can say for sure today whether it was the work of anti-Piasecki people or Communist agents who wanted to remind him of their own power. Communists in Warsaw still privately talk of both possibilities. The lad was found dead months after the abduction. Sympathy is confined only to the unfortunate boy. Piasecki is openly despised and his pious reference to his son has brought him only more hatred. He is useful to the Russians so he stays.

"Anyone who will work with the 'potato faces' has a job for a while," a Polish Socialist explained to me. But the Russians were leery of all Poles, including the Communists. They held meetings with local party higher-ups in a villa, just outside Warsaw, called Natolin. The site gave rise, later, to the name "Natolin" group. These were the pro-Stalin diehards prepared to carry out every order and whim issued from Moscow. The permanent purge, arrests and torture under interrogation became routine. Why did even party members acquiesce so quietly?

"We were afraid," a central committee member told me.

"You must understand party mentalities," an embittered veteran who has since given up her membership explained. "Today, it may be your turn to tear out my fingernails. Tomorrow, it's my turn."

In freezing weather, General Marian Spychalski was lowered in his underwear into a well. He had sided with party secretary, Gomulka, who was sent into custodial disgrace. After the secret police gave their Salem treatment to Spychalski, the general was never again the same. With the terror came the forced industrialization of Poland. Torn by war and impoverished by Soviet occupation, the country had one accountable surplus—misery. Stealing had become practically an honorable profession. It deprived the state of something. The shops offered only the barest necessities at high prices. Everyone, including wives and mothers, had to work. Prices couldn't be met otherwise. Absenteeism became the smart thing. Doctors could be bribed. Poles evaded, dodged, wriggled and clawed. Their infuriated rulers, requiring something to show, cooked up figures and programs.

"You may think it's all a vast fraud," a Polish member of the Sejm (Parliament) observed to me once. "Poles don't. This is how they must live. What can you do about it."

It was tragic and humiliating for an American, without a Polish background, to see Americans assigned to the spot think in terms of how soon they'd get another spot. They could not be blamed. The United States clucked sympathy but tried to avoid the subject. Everyone knew, or said he did, that the Communists and the Russians would find themselves ultimately in an impossible fix. Give them enough rope, was the cliché applied to the masters of Soviet Europe. They got it, and hanged their enemies. In their narrowing frame of reference, British and United States diplomats railed at the regime and asked frayed remnants of the former ruling class to tea. Workers and students became untouchables. The regime said the same thing about our observers. The gulf widened.

"Nearly every Pole you see is a walking tragedy."

A boy named Stefan Nowak, then just seventeen, told me that. He was scrawny and dressed in cast-off army bits. Big gaps showed between teeth that hadn't been examined by a dentist probably since early childhood. He had seen me drive to Communist Party headquarters in a car with American insignia. He was curious why an American should go there. So he pretended to polish the headlights until I emerged. It was the usual way of getting a few cents on the side.

"Want to know about a good restaurant?" the boy asked.

Why?

"All the foreigners go there," he replied. "Them, too."

He pointed his head at the party building. Where did he eat?

"Where I can get it," Stefan said. "Poles can't afford to go to restaurants."

The emphasis was on the word "Poles." On the reverse of his worn lapel buttonhole was a metal symbol.

"Polish eagle," said Stefan. "From *our* resistance."

I offered him a ride back.

"No, thanks," the boy replied somberly. "I have something to do. I'll walk back later. It's all the way uphill. But you can't wait."

CHAPTER 5

THE Soviet pattern for power in Eastern Europe showed clearly within two years of the end of World War II. A peace conference in Paris a year after V.E. day even caught the Russians with their plans down. Still, Stalin and his proconsuls had plans: substantive, active and totally oppressive. The Western world was shocked. Winston Churchill's "Iron Curtain" speech at Fulton, Missouri, confirmed to the public what the few on-the-spot observers had learned. Their protests fell on deaf ears or on a public-at-large absorbed with personal day-to-day problems.

Therefore, we played it by ear. That technique never gives rise to bold, imaginative or even preservative responses. Only the mass populations under Soviet occupation in Eastern Europe sought to preserve an identity of their own, to defy and even to dam up Communist control that washed like an unreceding tide over them. Looking at the map, as Russians and their Communist comrades-in-power often did, they could speak out with confident delight.

71

"Look at 'progress,'" Rakosi chortled at me in his office in Budapest. "There it is for you to see. East Germany, Poland, Rumania, Bulgaria, Yugoslavia, Albania and my own country. In Czechoslovakia their hearts are really with us, you know."

His pudgy finger, still wet from coffee that slopped over our cups, left a smudge on the map to which he directed my attention. To the Western world, the suspicious, proud and hard-bitten do-it-yourself Communist program of Tito and his partisans was still an intramural party squabble. No Westerner really knew about it or if he did he did not know what it meant. The Yugoslavs had shot down unarmed American transport planes that strayed into their air corridors. Tito's fierce reprisals, incidentally, caused Stalin through his trusted henchman, V. M. Molotov, to rebuke the Yugoslavs.

"Don't you understand," Molotov told Tito and his entourage, "the Americans have the atomic bomb. Don't arouse them."

We didn't understand what a monopoly over such a fantastic weapon meant to the Russians. Since the U.S. reacted only sympathetically towards the plight of Eastern Europe, the Russians pressed quickly to make the area safe for themselves. Take a look once more at the map and the populations within them: East Germany, 17,500,000; Poland, around 23,000,000; Rumania, 17,000,000; Bulgaria, 7,500,000; Hungary, 9,500,000; Yugoslavia, 16,000,000 and Albania, 1,400,000. To tidy up the bulge represented by Czechoslovakia and its 14,000,000, only a fully oriented Communist regime was required.

The Sovietization process was underway in Czechoslovakia, with pressures from the Communist Party. Plots against the "neutral" hopes of the government were in the works. Czechoslovakia was, indeed, a big prize. Its basic economy was well-balanced between agriculture and industry. Czech factories and workmen were among the finest in Europe. The technical know-how of the country was better and more advanced than anything that existed in the part of Europe that had come under Moscow's stern direction. Besides, there had been little war damage to Czech industry. Under Nazi supervision, it had worked for Hitler's regime until the last.

Czechoslovakia and her political directors believed that the world— East and West—owed them a living. The crass sellout at Munich was always cited as the reason. What the world seems to forget is that a capitulation also had been in the cards for poor and embattled Greece, when Mussolini attacked from Albania. The Greeks were supposed to show token resistance in the face of overwhelming odds: fire a few rounds and surrender. Dictator General John Metaxas, whose totalitarian ideas weren't far away from Hitler's or Mussolini's, thought so. He was wrong and so was Mussolini. The world knows how Greece fought and bled. When Hitler came to Mussolini's rescue, the Greeks fought on in the battlefields and later underground. When I once cited this example to Fierlinger in Czechoslovakia who had been haranguing me with an attack on Western perfidy, he replied, "That is no comparison. The Greeks are primitive people."

Apparently, Greeks have remained steadfastly "primitive." They also fought a ghastly civil war. From the borders of Albania, Yugoslavia and Bulgaria, Greek Communist guerrillas began launching hit-and-run raids on half-ruined Greek villages and shattered towns. The domain of Soviet-run Eastern Europe was to have incorporated Greece. Therefore, active assistance and sanctuary was provided for Greek Communist leader, Markov Vafiades, and his forces. Source for this assessment? A Yugoslav former partisan leader still high in Tito's regime.

Greece, however, was regarded as a nation that needed the "liberating" stimulus of Communist rule. No regime followed this line more ferociously than did Dimitrov-led Bulgaria. He adamantly ignored wartime Bulgar occupation of portions of Greece and the rightful claims of the Greeks for reparations. Instead, Dimitrov occupied himself with settling his own political scores at home. Following Petkov's execution and the smashing of the Bulgarian Agrarian Party, other political executions churned up Eastern Europe. The accelerated tempo seemed to indicate Soviet impatience. In Rumania, beguiled and bewildered King Mihai was given his walking papers into exile. The anomaly of a monarch in a Communist-run state puzzled the Russians for a time, too. They had managed, with party connivance, to rocket the cost of living to nearly ten times what it had been before the war. Scarcity was the law in the cities and near-hunger in the once-rich countryside.

"We'll starve those bastards into believing in us," party boss Gheorghiu-dej told visiting Yugoslava.

Gheorghiu-dej was on the ragged edge at the time. Marshal Tito paid a state visit to Rumania. His quarrel with Moscow had already filtered through compartmentalized secrecy that governed Soviet relations with satellites. It was in Bucharest that the first sign there was something wrong in having Tito as a comrade appeared. His photos, which had a place of honor in various government buildings, came down. After he departed, of course. Removing someone's photo was the traditional Soviet way of telling the world that he was in deep disgrace.

Rumania may have been chosen as the first place for an outward demonstration because the country's last shreds of defiance were summoned in support of Mihai. Rumanian Communists and Soviet diplomats seriously thought of finding a stopgap king to succeed Mihai. It was in the best Graustarkian tradition of the Balkans. Archduke Anton of Hapsburg interested the Communists. He was married to Princess Ileana, Mihai's aunt. The Russians said no to Anton. A monarchy might still be useful, they believed, but a Hapsburg could cause ex-Austro-Hungarian territories to be outraged. Maybe Mihai's father, Carol, the Russians suggested; could be interested in the job. That was out, too, because the regime wanted someone of relative popularity to do a façade job for them. An appearance by Carol might well have led to short-lived but great violence among the peasants who hated Mihai's father. In the end, the decision came to a republic straightaway because there was no suitable kingly candidate.

Meanwhile, the Russians anchored their hold in Hungary. Peace treaties had been concluded. Only a few weeks were required before the stipulated departure of military missions. There was not even the myopic scrutiny of our mission in Budapest to hold the Communists in check. Rakosi still smarted under his big defeat when the Smallholders' Party had gotten more than 60 percent of the vote in the only free elections the Russians have ever permitted in an occupied zone. Presence of the Red Army, abduction of Bela Kovacs and Rakosi's fearsome influence on Smallholder leaders watered down the magnitude of the Smallholders' victory and Communists still ran police and security, even after the elections.

Before their military mission withdrew, the Russians wanted to leave something solid besides their occupation army behind. They were entitled by peace treaty to keep troops in Rumania and Hungary as lines-of-communications forces to their units in occupied Austria. Rakosi and his party staged a brazen coup, down to a child hostage. Premier Nagy hastily went to Switzerland. Once there, Rakosi announced that the police had discovered a plot against the state by Nagy and top Smallholders. If Nagy didn't resign, threatened Rakosi blandly, he ought to remember that his youngest son was still in Hungary. His son delivered, Nagy resigned. A wave of arrests in Hungary followed. Cardinal Mindszenty was closely watched. In his exuberance, Rakosi told the world, "We brought this off successfully before the U.S. could rub its eyes."

He followed up this lilt of triumph with his succinct doctrine of "salami" techniques. It should have been a lesson to remember for all politicians who think about coalitions or popular fronts with the Communist Party.

"You slice them, link by link," exulted Rakosi, "like a salami."

A good case in point was Bela Havas. He had been a young prisoner of war, returned to Hungary with a bursting desire to create a democracy in his homeland. Havas thought in terms of a Hungarian "Sweden." He had worked in the Foreign Office.

"I'd get letters from abroad," he reminisced. "They'd be opened. The AVH (police) would ask me about the senders. I was in touch with abroad. Bad. I got bad marks in my dossier."

Why did he keep writing abroad? Havas smoked a cigarette furiously for a minute.

"I'll tell you why," he said. "It never pays to be more afraid than you have to be. Remember that."

Havas told me that he planned to escape. He delayed because he wanted to have his say in an election Rakosi staged to stamp legality on his coup. During the brief campaign, Havas was arrested. Later on, his death was announced in a one-line message to his mother. She could never even claim his body. Rakosi and the Russians required more sacrifices for approval of the Communist drive to power in Hungary. Before the elections, they forced remaining national oppositionists into exile or arrested them. One of the most lamentable cases was that of Viktor Csornoky.

He had been the son-in-law of Zoltan Tildy, an ex-Premier and ex-President of post-war Hungary. Tildy, a little, tubby man who was a Protestant pastor and thought of himself as a progressive, tried to please where he could. His trouble was that he tried to please Westerners whom he knew and Russians whom he didn't. Csornoky tried to save the family political fortunes.

"I know all the mistakes the others made," he told me in a hotel room in Budapest. "I'll be more careful. I won't give the Rakosis a chance to make wild charges against me and make them stick."

Csornoky went around in a sports shirt without a necktie. Don't try to put on unnecessary airs, he suggested to skeptical followers. Csornoky was temporarily useful to the regime led by Rakosi. Then he was hanged. The Communists had no use whatever for Smallholder politicians of note or for any of their relatives. Salami tactics were applied again and again. The Socialists, who had been driven by ambitious and avaricious leaders into a political fusion with Rakosi, felt his knife, too. Before the elections, Rakosi disfranchised nearly 200,000 Socialists. He already had deprived many more Smallholders of the vote. They were the opposition. In a last ditch show of opposition, the Socialists, split in leadership, threatened to withdraw from their coalition with the Communists.

The threat sent Szakasits, Socialist advocate of close ties with Rakosi, to the Communists to ask for advice. They gave it by summoning Col. Gen. V. P. Sviridov, Soviet commander and successor to Marshal Voroshilov. Sviridov, a few weeks earlier, also offered his counsel on how to keep Ferenc Nagy out of the country. A busy general was Sviridov, a brass-bound man who not only inherited Voroshilov's mantle but the Hungarian mistress, too. Sviridov's advice to the supine Szakasits and rampaging Socialists was to take things as they stood. There would be jobs for Socialists in the next regime.

"Otherwise, there will be nothing—and none of you," Sviridov told a Socialist delegation.

A Socialist at the meeting reported the gist of it to me later. What was the reaction?

"Szakasits said he had warned us," my informant answered. "He thanked Sviridov for his interest and help. The rest of us, I suppose, were stunned. It was the first time I ever saw actual Soviet interference in the flesh. I never believed it before."

Szakasits was eminently pleased. He brought the Socialists, sullen and serried, into line as he saw it. That fact alone, he said, made him co-equal with Rakosi. Besides, his reward would be promotion to President of Hungary. Not bad for a smalltime local politician at whom intellectuals of the party once sneered. He recalled his humble political jobs one afternoon to the late John MacCormac of *The New York Times* and me. Reminiscences over, we asked him how he could account for the fact that in a couple of years the Smallholders could be driven from a national majority to a small minority.

"The first thing, their majority was nothing, you know," said Szakasits. "It was just an arithmetical illusion."

Not far away, across one of Hungary's western borders, Czechoslovakia was wondering nervously about the merits of being free. The coalition government, including some Communists like Vlado Clementis, saw merit in the Marshall Plan. Their economic recovery was limping mainly because trade was lopsided with the barter system of Soviet Europe. On international affairs, they were neutral in favor of Soviet proposals. The Czechoslovak position, between East and West, produced only one tangible result. Soviet army units had been withdrawn as had American forces that came into Pilsen. The Russians, in a friendly and allied country, managed, nevertheless, to take home souvenirs with them—furniture, statuary and machinery. Jan Masaryk once told me that he had seen them even load bidets on a truck.

On their own, the Czechs cleaned up the Sudetenland. That was the first outside source for Hitler's nationalization claims. Sudetenlanders, who actually had been German speaking under the Austro-Hungarian monarchy, either fled before the fall of the Third Reich or were driven out to Germany and Austria by Czechoslovaks. The Sudetenland was barren ground. Slovakia sent off sparks in Czech-dominated Bohemia and Moravia. It was mainly agricultural and had been given puppet status by Hitler under a priest named Father Josef Tiso. He had been tried and executed for collaboration with the Germans.

In the splendid, almost unspoiled capital of Prague with magnificent baroque buildings and monuments etched above the Vltava River, crosscurrents were swirling over politicians. The Communists had, in a free election, been installed as the single strongest party in the country. They crowed about it and made constant demands on the government. Remember, though, that two-thirds of the country's voters were non-Communist. They were divided, however, into several parties and often, cliques.

Prospects of sharing in the Marshall Plan gave Communist and non-Communist a chance to be tempted together. It was the last chance. The Russian ambassador, Valerian Zorin, rushed back to Moscow to report on the unorthodox behavior of Czech comrades and Czechoslovak government people who vowed to be neutral. A delegation of Czechoslovaks was summoned to the Soviet Union. When they returned, their tentative acceptance was annulled.

"The biggest reason was two-way," Vaclav Majer explained. "The Marshall Plan exposed Soviet selfishness and determination to run things where they could their own way. To help counteract the Marshall Plan, you must never forget that the Russians launched the Cominform organization."

All Communist-governed countries and representatives from other European parties assigned delegates and officers to the Cominform. Ironically, its headquarters were installed for a while from the beginning, in Tito's Belgrade. The Czech Communists thought, or as an afterthought, believed the Cominform was a true beacon to guide them.

"We can learn a good deal from organizations like that," Vaclav Kopecky, the Czechoslovak Information Minister told me.

Czechoslovak Communists actually spent lots of time talking to founders of the Cominform. It brought them into constant touch with Bulgars, Rumanians, Poles and Hungarians, whose coups had been so recent and so successful. Whether association with Cominformist elements spurred Czechoslovak party decisions or prior commitments set a time-table, nobody but party men now dead can say. In any case, a rash of plots was uncovered. Police, ordered out by the Communist-directed Ministry of Interior, arrested 200 people in Slovakia. They were accused of trying to re-establish a "Fascist state." Then bombs in packages were sent to, among others, Jan Masaryk. They were discovered and de-fused. The Communists immediately claimed anti-Communists were behind the hatched-up outrage.

Suspicion stalked the Communist protests and accusing fingers. Many Czechoslovak forward-looking, non-Communists through the campaign, unleashed in the Communist press and in Parliament itself needed more investigation. Prokop Drtina, the Minister of Justice, said he thought the bomb plot stories sounded as contrived as anti-Russian conspiracies in Hungary.

"This is a very fishy and very delicate affair," Drtina said to me at his modest home, over thin wafer cakes and coffee.

Led by men like Drtina and Prague's basso-voiced and lion-hearted Mayor, Peter Zerkl, a separate inquiry into the bomb conspiracy was launched. It had to be more or less unofficial. The official investigation was carried out by the Communist-held Ministry of Interior. Investigators found themselves looking into the fact-finding mission of other investigators. Rudolf Slansky, Moscow-trained party whip, didn't hesitate to hurl menaces and warnings against the extra-curricular investigation.

"Munichites (a favorite epithet in Prague) are trying to disturb the country's tranquility and progress," thundered Slansky.

He was a strange man to talk of appeasement. During the grim purge days of the thirties in Moscow, Slansky's wife wheeled her infant up to a newspaper kiosk. She parked the carriage and went to buy her paper. When she returned the carriage was empty. The woman, sobbing and hysterical, ran to the police. They were laboriously sorting out her story when her husband burst into the police station. He took her by the arm, apologized momentarily to the police officers, and led her aside. Slansky talked to his wife, fast and furiously. Then, he turned to the waiting policemen.

"There are no complaints," he told them, his face white with anxiety. There never were. Slansky had heard that the Soviet secret police simply picked up his baby as a hostage, for future reference. Those were purge times and an international Communist trainee like Rudolf Slansky dared not complain against actions of the Soviet state apparatus. He had to believe and accept any and all decisions. Nobody ever knew what happened to the child. The story reflects the mentality of the man. It was first told to me by his brother, Richard, a political ne'er-do-well. He found it useful to join the party, use his relationship and get sinecures. Richard Slansky also loved a life of luxury and flashy but expensive girls. His brother's only show of personal weakness was towards the erratic career of Richard.

Otherwise, Rudolf Slansky displayed no sentiment, no personal peccadilloes. His office contained a huge portrait of Stalin and a somewhat smaller picture of Lenin. Slansky's associates included a man who called himself Andre Simon. His real name was Katz, an old hand in the Comintern network and in global Soviet espionage. He spent a lot of time in Mexico, in close touch with conspirators who worked on the plot to kill Leon Trotsky. Slansky and Simon, some years later, died in the purges that swept Soviet Europe. Before, they stood supreme among many Czechoslovaks as dirty names referred to only as "S & S."

This pair sparked a campaign to discredit Thomas Masaryk as the founder-liberator of the Czechoslovak state. Their views were made known privately, to other Communists. The country was not yet ready for the notion that Masaryk was not a national hero. Jan Masaryk, the son, moreover, was still alive. His personality and his name aroused massive affection. Slansky was contemptuous of Jan Masaryk.

"His fine manners cover up a lard barrel," Slansky told a Social Democrat one afternoon. "Jan Masaryk is nothing to us. Not even this."

He cracked a wooden pencil in half and threw the pieces on the floor. The Socialist, who had been invited by Slansky to discuss the "academic" possibilities of full cooperation between the two parties, returned with a report to his comrades. Top Socialists like Majer, hearing every detail, confirmed their own opinions. They wanted no part of a popular-front deal with the Communists. Fierlinger strove for it and sought to show advantages in fusion tactics.

"It's like putting your life at the disposition of cannibals," roared Majer at Fierlinger. "We know, on real workers' level, how Communists behave."

The Czech Social Democrats, with an old tradition, tried to keep their influence with the workers. Their organizers were being beaten by Communist agitators and strong-arm squads. When Majer's men tried to protect themselves and when they pitted their own youth organization against the Communist youth, they suffered heavy casualties. The reason was not hard to find.

"The Communists have action committees," a badly mauled young Socialist told Majer in my presence. "They also have guns."

In every factory in Prague and the outskirts, action committees existed. A table of organization just as you would find in any army, listed men, their roles in an emergency and their arms and equipment. They were headed by activists, who held officer rank. It was a separate military organization within a state that supported a national army. Action committees, less numerous but well-indoctrinated, existed in cells in government ministries. They met regularly and only semi-secretly. Their operations were known to most politicians and government figures. The Ministry of Interior said the action committees were simply a political group. They represented only a guarantee of democratic organization within the nation, Klement Gottwald claimed.

President Beneš, the wiry little professor who aspired to continue in changed circumstances the work of his mentor, Thomas Garrigue Masaryk, was not up to the monumental challenge. He spoke of constitutionality as if the Communists would accept the Western book of law. Munich, of course, helped reduce Western values for him. He talked to me about memoirs that he was publishing. We sat opposite each other in the magnificent baroque background of Hradcany Castle. The Battle of the White Mountain, where the Czech nobility was overwhelmed by the Hapsburgs, was probably the only feat of arms ever accomplished by the Austro-Hungarians. It happened in 1620, but for 300 years thereafter the Czechs kept the Hapsburg administration in working order.

Beneš' lecture to me on that point took us far from the leaden scene in Prague. I suppose it was a no-decision argument, just as were his views about Czechoslovakia in the mid-Twentieth Century. Czechoslovakia, insisted Benes, was the crossroads between East and West. He wanted each side to tolerate and trust each other. Then came some ideas, which were generally put across in his memoirs.

"There are times when revolution by force is necessary in national development," Benes said, in his mild, professorial way. "At certain times I also know that revolution by force can mean the worst way of bringing about actual reaction."

Communists, added Beneš, must be patient and must understand how to exercise reserve. His Prime Minister, Gottwald, would have smiled indulgently at the lesson in Communist behavior. Slansky, across the river in downtown Prague, paid no attention whatever. He was busy haranguing his subordinates and terrifying the opposition. Not only were the security police at Slansky's call but he had the active advice of Soviet ambassador Zorin. At the Russian residence Slansky was a frequent visitor and guest at meals with Zorin. It was a cosy political arrangement in comradely togetherness.

In talks with foreigners and in public declarations, Slansky never failed to raise the specter of Lidice. Whenever he chided some Czech politician for an anti-Communist remark, Slansky demanded: "Do you want to prepare another Lidice?" The Communists never had any active role in the reasons that led to the massacre and razing of Lidice or in the district's resistance against the Nazis. Yet it was so ghastly an episode that the Communists found it convenient to recall it constantly for the shock effect on the public. I went one morning to the scorched earth where Lidice once stood. The world knows the story of how Czech agents, parachuted by the British, assassinated the Nazi gauleiter, Heydrich. In revenge, the Nazis wiped Lidice and most of its population off the map. The agents slipped through the little community. All over Europe, in France, Yugoslavia and Greece, I had seen Lidices. Bigger ones. The world hardly heard of them. Their people lived with their bitter memories and mourned their dead. In silence, true, but they refused to attract sympathy and penitence. Maybe they were wrong. The murder of Lidice proved the Czechs right, not in their defiance which was miniscule at Lidice, but in what they felt to be their due.

Meanwhile investigations of the bomb plot continued and all the opposition, from the Catholics, Liberals, Centrists, Beneš Socialists and Social Democrats, was alarmed by the implications. Separate investigations undertaken proved to them that the Communists organized the whole affair. They banded together, often bickering among themselves and sometimes aghast at the formidable opposition they had raised against the Communists. The non-Communist majority wanted to end Communist police controls. They wanted to start with police chiefs, in and around Prague. Instead of being a flank diversion, it was a direct attack. The Communists saw it that way and joined battle. The outcome was not a long way off.

A fight for Communist survival *against* Communists, however, was even then being contested every step in a country Czechoslovak Communist officials regarded with amused indifference. Of all the Eastern European regimes, the Yugoslav seemed to the outside world the most determined to go the Russians one better. The partisans who ran the state were militant, often crude and generally rude to Westerners and everything Western. They saw their devastated country as highly underdeveloped. They thought they spotted unfriendliness and hatching enmity everywhere in the West. But they had supreme confidence, close to arrogance, in what they could do themselves.

"Tito thinks that a sneeze in Belgrade is a bugle blast heard round the world," an annoyed diplomat once observed.

Having fought their own war, which no other Communist regime in Eastern Europe did, Tito's partisans genuinely believed they should control their own destinies. After they took over Yugoslavia, they thought of the Russians only as advisers and consultants in technical matters. Their own structure of governmental organization was totally Communist, from their all-pervasive police force down to peasant collectives. They had learned their Marx while resting on rifles. On organization the Russians had nothing to teach Tito and his partisans.

The Russians, accustomed to others tugging at their comradely forelocks, were shocked. They also were angered when they found that the Yugoslav secret police was keeping tabs on them, too. That was not the way in which Stalin thought regimes should be consolidated. The Russians attitude was that Yugoslav behavior was not just an affront to Soviet policy but to Stalin personally. In the locked room, closed society atmosphere of Communist politics, Russians and Yugoslavs talked to each other. Mostly in Moscow; only occasionally in Belgrade. For a long time, as their differences widened, secrecy increased.

"Think of the fight in terms of religions, which you must," an old Cominform hand, since totally disillusioned, explained. "There was the mother religion in Moscow. It was being defied. By whom? A Communist Martin Luther, in the form of Tito."

Tito and the men around him, as we learned later, held their own conferences. Some balked at defying Soviet might. There were two in Tito's own Politburo: Zujevic and Hebrang. The army chief of staff, Arso Jovanovic, a man with opaque brown eyes and a flinty disposition, was horrified at the idea of challenging Moscow. Any time a partisan or party comrade showed signs of weakening on behalf of Stalin, he became a police target. Pro-Soviet Yugoslavs in the administration were watched as carefully and as calculatedly as known anti-Communists. Still, the secret was kept while the fight between Tito and Stalin flared higher. People disappeared suddenly in Belgrade. Two men with whom I frequently dealt in the Foreign Office vanished the day I had appointments with them. They had been partisans. They boasted of what good Communists they were.

When I appeared punctually for the first appointment, two secretaries were in chin-to-chin conversation. Gossip can go on even in Communist society. I waited a bit and then broke in to ask about my meeting. One of the girls asked me to take a seat. I did and stared at a photo of Tito, in a marshal's winter uniform. One girl went out and the other returned to her desk, fumbling at her German-made typewriter. About twenty minutes later, the other secretary returned.

"I am sorry but your appointment has been cancelled," she said. "He is sick, very sick."

Broken appointments aren't unusual in Communist-governed countries. I tried to be briefly pleasant and left. Two hours later I returned to the Foreign Office for my second appointment. I went down a red-carpeted hall, opposite where I had been earlier. A man I had never seen before was at the secretary's desk. Who was I? he asked. He had a thick mustache, wore a sack suit and a Communist emblem in his buttonhole. The official I wanted to see, he said promptly, was not around. When would he be back? A shrug.

"Sorry you are inconvenienced," he added. He didn't smile.

It turned out that the two officials had been arrested in their homes the night before. Their offense was in being "Cominformists," a word that was just beginning to be heard to describe pro-Soviet Yugoslavs. The Cominform headquarters had just been set up in Belgrade but was already inoperative. Later it was transferred to Bucharest.

"We were very good and very exacting Communists," Djilas told me, speaking of that early fight with Stalin. "I negotiated with Russians. They were simply wild with fury that I talked to them the way I did. I said we were nobody's errand boys. We wanted to patch up the quarrel. It would be on the understanding that we all had equality."

"In the U.S.S.R. itself, there is no equality," Kardelj told me after the break with Moscow. "How could Stalin stay equal with us? He didn't even permit it in his own Politburo."

The Yugoslavs not only stuck to their guns, they oiled them and moved them into place. High staff officers were sounded out about defense. When told why, many were shaken. Once the surprise wore off, the vast majority rallied to Tito. Nevertheless, the population was not prepared for what broke on them and the world later.

A supreme contempt for people in the mass exists among Communists already in power. People are to be led, herded or guided. They normally are never to be let in, when conditions look bleak, on what may be in store for them. Sometimes, they are, in the jargon of the party or by buried announcements, "informed" that something strange is going on. That is known as preparing public opinion for something of cataclysmic proportions.

"The procedure is a distortion of what Abraham Lincoln said," a former Polish Communist said. "By the people, for the people, fleece the people."

He actually said something stronger than fleece. Embattled as Tito and his partisan government were, they kept their growing differences and concern from the Yugoslavs. Only a few weeks before the Soviet Union rejected the last round of correspondence from Belgrade, a Yugoslav official asserted that relations could not be smoother. Why, I asked, had Tito's picture been taken down, not only in Rumania but in all other Communist states?

"They all asked us for new ones," he replied.

Perhaps more than anything else, Tito's regime wanted to prove to the world—the Eastern world—that it was Communist to the core. Defenses were planned against actual attack from the East, but real action was shown on the Western frontiers. The Yugoslavs sent new protests and demanded a one-sided settlement of the Trieste with Italy. There were provocations against Anglo-U.S. forces in Trieste, a bus ride from the Yugoslav border. Titoists kept the fight for their lives under wraps and used their harshest manners where it least concerned them, in the West. The technique still holds true for them.

CHAPTER | 6

WASHINGTON's birthday, 1948, is a day to remember and reckon with in Czechoslovakia. Dusk fell early and snow flurries embroidered the majestic spires and gleaming towers of Prague. Bundled inside serviceable overcoats, men and women hastened homewards past bright shop windows rimmed with frost. Meanwhile booted men trod in disciplined measure along the Vaclavske Namestic, St. Wenceslas' Square. Action committees were on the march, summoned by the Communist titular leader, bulbous-nosed Klement Gottwald.

As Prime Minister of a state pledged to parliamentary democracy, Gottwald publicly demanded an illegal show of strength. He appealed to Communist-trained-and-armed shock troops to demonstrate their power in Prague's streets. They were a paramilitary force existing within a state. Action committees were tolerated in Czechoslovakia because the Communists extorted the special privilege from their non-Communist coalition partners. They had, in 1946, chalked up around 38 percent of the national vote. It made them the strongest single part in Czechoslovakia. As Rudolf Slansky said in mass meetings, Communist power deserved and intended to preserve a special position.

The party, through Slansky and Gottwald, ignored the nearly two-thirds non-Communist vote in the country. President Beneš strove to keep coalition arguments from becoming a Communist vs. non-Communist test of strength. He wanted, as he claimed during the crisis, to settle problems through constitutional methods. He meant the kind of constitutional democracy he advocated and which Communists interpreted as a lever they could use whenever it suited their purposes. The time for action had now arrived.

Soviet Europe had been rapidly consolidated. The quarrel with Tito was sharp, but still secret. In East Germany the Russians were busy finishing the division of Berlin and building their apparatus. Only Czechoslovakia still had not produced a "people's democracy." Stalin gave the task to Valerian Zorin. Then non-Communists challenged the Communist-run Ministry of Interior. They wanted to replace eight police chiefs.

"A shameful sabotage of democracy," was the way an eager-to-please, wizened department head in the Foreign Office described the demand for police changes. "Don't they realize they cannot have changes without the approval of the Communists?"

They could not, as it turned out. The Social Democrats held the balance of power. They argued, in caucus. Fierlinger and a strangely ambivalent man, Bohumil Lausman, advocated solidarity with the Communists. A bigger group, led by Vaclav Majer, wanted to join the non-Communists. The time for agonizing decision had arrived. Fierlinger and Lausman filibustered. In the streets, the boots of action committees crunched noisily in the snow.

"Red Fascists," cried an American with me as we watched the units stride precisely and purposefully in the main street.

His own world was shattered with the appearance of the units, armed and at the ready, egged on by the Prime Minister. He had believed that in Czechoslovakia the Communists would be content to live and let live. He had not been anywhere else in Soviet Europe. Here, for him had been the real window, looking in on East and West. The image was shattered under foot by armed action committees.

"Red Fascists," he shouted again. Then he wept unashamedly. Czechs, hurrying along, looked briefly and curiously at the angry American. They stared at him longer than they did at the marchers trampling out their independence for the second time in ten years. Theirs had been the only practicing parliamentary democracy in central and Eastern Europe. Protecting and preserving it required leadership in the face of force. It also demanded sacrifice that could be demanded only by a national leader prepared to sacrifice himself.

"Our people made sacrifices later," Hubert Ripka, the Socialist Minister of Foreign Trade recalled dolefully. "They made them individually, when they were easy prey. We argued too much among ourselves while the Communists acted."

Ripka has since died in exile. He was one of the lucky ones who got away. The all-talk, no-action which he mentioned was as blustery and chilling in the non-Communist conference rooms as the weather outside. It was up to the Socialists, or Social Democrats, to make up their minds. The Czech Socialists, as they were known, were Beneš' own party and were not part of the Social Democratic organization. Their program was basic democratic socialism and they had once been known as National Socialists, a name the Nazis used and was, therefore, opprobrious to Beneš Socialists.

Beneš, as President of the Republic, held to parliamentary tradition. He stayed above political infighting. His own party, however, had decided with other coalition non-Communists to go along with replacing the police chiefs. In decent, normal politics, all the opposition waited for the Social Democrats—Socialists, as they were called—to give their word. Fierlinger and Lausmann stalled and refused to accept a clear-cut party decision.

"Let's wait," Fierlinger cynically told the weary caucus "for a constitutional settlement."

Outside marched action committees. Gottwald had publicly urged them to prepare to "fight for our inevitable victory." Communist flying squads sped around the city, mustering reinforcements. Arms were distributed. The Communists had mobilized while their opposition argued. Police, directed by the Communist-held Ministry of Interior, quietly set up blocks at the entrances to opposition political headquarters. A machine gun was pointed from the sidewalk level straight at the Beneš' Socialists offices. This was too much for loyal army officers, some of whom had served with Western wartime forces. I spoke to one of them, alive today and a broken, ailing, aged man. He said he had hurriedly gone with others to inform President Beneš of the imminent threat against the country and its people.

"We pointed out that the Communists were staging a coup," said the officer. "In anybody's language that is illegal. We asked him, as commander-in-chief, to permit us to decree martial law. That way we could have summoned the country to its senses, arrested Gottwald and have fought for our freedom."

The Russians had given active support to the coup-makers. When action committees were marching, *Pravda* already had an article supporting them. It was spontaneous in the way that arson touches off a fire. Beneš, weary and bedevilled, said he could not bear to see Czechoslovak blood spilled. There must be, he is reported to have told my informant, a legal solution to the crisis. There was, but it was Communist legality. Police and action committees, supported by police, were in street battle positions. By the time heavy-hearted oppositionists roused themselves early the next day, Czechoslovakia was in the grip of its second totalitarian occupation.

Communists stormed into the stronghold of the opposition, the offices held for the Social Democrats by the ex-miner Majer. He had been a government minister, up from the working class. Hoodlums of an action committee burst into his room. Thumbs flicked back, they demanded he go. Majer doubled a huge fist.

"I was elected to this post," he thundered. "Get out."

They withdrew. But they returned with reinforcements. Five of them approached Majer's desk menacingly. Majer did not hesitate. He knocked down two of them. The fight was uneven. Majer was in the hospital for ten days afterwards. He was able to slip out of the country, though. His party associates risked their lives to help Majer escape.

"They are the people worth fighting for," Majer told me much later in Paris.

Once his massive defiance was removed, Fierlinger stampeded the rest of the party leadership. He took control of the Social Democrats and told Czechoslovakia the party would be delighted to cooperate with the Communists. Action committees went off to occupy government buildings, radio stations and even monuments with Fierlinger's blessing. Those same committees, a little earlier, pledged allegiance to Gottwald. I saw activists lead them in roaring cheers in streets covered again with a new mantle of snow. In forty-eight hours of action, the Communists for all practical purposes seized control of Czechoslovakia.

For good measure, their action committees marched triumphantly past the house of Archbishop Joseph Beran. Later a cardinal and for many years under arrest, Archbishop Beran had been an heroic resistance figure under the Nazi occupation. When the Germans goosestepped into Prague, seminarians he was lecturing fell silent. Beran went to the window.

"They are the symbol of the anti-Christ," the Archbishop said as he faced his class again. "We must pray."

Nazi humiliation and concentration camps had not dimmed Archbishop Beran's flame of resistance. Now he looked down on marchers waving the red flag.

"The anti-Christ, my friends, has returned to us in another form," said the Archbishop. "We must pray."

Communists didn't go after Beran then. They turned on more accessible and vulnerable quarry. Opposition leaders were rounded up quickly. A nation-wide manhunt was launched by Interior Minister Nosek. He demanded "absolute vigilance" after a long talk with Slansky.

"Now, we are on the road to real democracy," Slansky shouted at some of us he received in his office.

He offered export slivovitz all around. There were only a few takers. Slansky's party organization and action committee didn't take time out for impromptu celebrations. It was a Communist plan that fulfilled its quota for once. Action committees hurdled into control of every possible function of normal life, everything political, cultural. Not even ping-pong was spared. An action committee leader took over the ping-pong association in Prague. He had been second worst player in the past. Committees called meetings and had everyone present swear allegiance. The Communists had publicly instructed action committees to take over all community life.

Offer of negotiation, of constitutionality, had become ancient history in two days. Beneš was inaccessible in the Hradcany Castle, where he brooded over the death of the republic. He alone was the only public personality spared the humiliation of pledging fealty to an action committee. Beneš was still the highest ranking public figure in the country. At least on paper. Hulking, jovial Jan Masaryk was not spared, although he never joined a party. Down with a bad cold or depression, or both, he was summoned to a meeting of the action committee in the Foreign Office. He attended, head bent in thought, in a bathrobe. Gottwald was charmed with the image of Masaryk at such a meeting. He was so elated that he worked himself, with a bottle at hand, into a state of magnanimous euphoria.

"We even have room for him in the new Czechoslovakia," Gottwald said of Masaryk. "Everybody is welcome."

Neither Slansky nor outraged young Czechoslovak students agreed. Without wasting time, the Communists demanded that Beneš accept their new cabinet. All the outspoken oppositionists from the previous government had been eliminated from the new list. It was only Feb. 25, but the critical days seemed like years to students who tried to reach Beneš before he accepted the Communist-dictated cabinet.

Determinedly, they formed in a line of march, four abreast. They were all young, seventeen to twenty-two, serious of mien except for excitement that shone in their eyes. "Long Live the Republic of Thomas Garrigue Masaryk," some shouted. The cry was taken up and floated over the old city section, where they assembled. Action committees started at them but fell back. The students were packed solid. As they marched spectators wept. There was nothing jaunty in the youngsters' gait, only the determination to be seen and, perhaps, heard.

Off to Hradcany Castle, over the ancient and magnificent Charles Bridge, they strode. Their ranks were swelling and the beat of the chant was, in its way, catching.

"London is calling at nine o'clock," they shouted. During the Nazi occupation, that was a favorite and banned program beamed to Czechoslovakia. "Remember November 17," was another cry they took up lustily. It was a date in 1939 when other Czechoslovak students were executed for defiance. Before the chanting marchers could get near Castle Square where Beneš was accepting Gottwald's regime, police rushed up to block them.

"Break it up, you stupid bastards," shouted a police officer, waving a pistol. His men cradled rifles in their arms.

The students did not falter. They tried to ward off the blows of the rifle butts as they ran a gauntlet for nearly a mile. Some fell but others surged ahead. Finally they confronted police and militia units shoulder to shoulder, barring their way with guns leveled.

An officer gripping a cocked revolver ordered the demonstrators to step back ten paces. The front ranks teetered, prodded by the guns, and fell back.

"Ten paces more," shouted the officer. The ranks stepped back again. Hoarsely, the officer demanded: "Twenty paces."

Nobody moved. Butts of rifles thudded on unprotected heads. Gun muzzles raked strained young faces. "Get them," shouted the officer. In went the Communist riot squads. They smashed at students who twisted guns out of their hands and fought with their fists. The young demonstrators were unorganized. Police hammered them into smaller groups. On a little rise near Hradcany Castle, a group of about fifty university undergraduates pushed and tugged at their tormentors.

"Fire," was the order that rang out as cold as the bitter day. Boys fell, at least two of them dead. Another volley rang out and bullets ricocheted from stone walls and trees. The students broke and ran for their lives. Dozens were seized by pursuing police. Authorities later admitted that "100 or so" had been taken in for questioning. They were roughhoused in jails for their flare-up. It was a brief but searing footnote in Czechoslovak history.

"We can never forget it, no matter what they do," two students, bleeding from skull gashes, told a few of us.

While their demonstration was being wrecked, other manifestations were organized under the benevolent eyes of Communist hand-picked police. Bands played songs and women with tommyguns slung across their backs hauled passers-by into street dances. Action committees led the cheering when Gottwald, victorious with his cabinet list in hand, announced Beneš formally accepted what the Communists demanded.

"The attack on the new Czech democracy has been quite beaten now," enthused Gottwald.

He had reason to be enthusiastic. The cabinet his party picked contained twelve Communists, seven pro-Communists and two non-party officials, of whom Jan Masaryk was the most prominent at home and abroad. Men who had been government ministers only a couple of days before were squeezed into house arrest or brought right to the Ministry of Interior. Benes, sick physically and in spirit, sat in Hradcany Castle after Gottwald left him, contemplating resignation. Many of his old and trusted friends had, overnight, been labelled "enemies." Beneš himself couldn't move without being watched by a detachment of elite Communist security policemen.

"Poor Beneš signed on the dotted line to avoid bloodshed." That was the only comment after the coup I ever got from Jan Masaryk, who took his own thoughts with him to his office and apartment. It was extremely difficult to see him. He had known some of us correspondents for years. It had always been the easiest thing to call on Masaryk if he had known you before. In business at the Czernin Palace, the Foreign Office, with a splendid view of the hills and Prague from on high, I caught Masaryk for fleeting minutes in the corridor.

He had nothing else to say except that he was bothered by a bad throat. "You can't really talk with a bad throat," he said to me solemnly. I wondered if that was a ghost of a grin on his face. The police, on instructions, worked overtime to make Czechoslovakia secure for the new regime. Professors, described as "unreliable" were summarily dismissed. The student body, which voted 75 percent anti-Communist in electing their own officers, had themselves been run through action committee purges. Anti-Communists, who had been in the underground against the Nazis, were thrown out of jobs.

"We will have a new educational system shortly," Gottwald promised party workers.

Unanimity was the order of the day. It was all, of course, attributed to the supreme genius of Stalin. Czechoslovak Communists could, with reason thank him. Stalin had given his formal approval by sending in a top trouble-shooter, Valerian Zorin to assist and report to Moscow from the spot. The Communist pattern for power was so deliberately drawn and run off that the West was totally befuddled.

President Truman and Prime Minister Attlee were shocked and said so. The brief history of Czechoslovak parliamentary democracy and the name Thomas Garrigue Masaryk ran through Western man's consciousness. Communist action, with Soviet support, caught us flatfooted in Prague. We could have done little anyway. There was no policy that pretended to thwart Communist aspiration even after what had happened in the rest of Eastern Europe. Our late ambassador, Laurence Steinhardt, even gave the Communists a sly excuse to put in a dig at the United States.

He turned up, from consultations in Washington, just as the crisis got rolling in Prague. So did Zorin. His appearance was a friendly act, in Slansky's own words. But Steinhardt was assailed as a messenger just returned with anti-regime orders. Steinhardt never knew what was being

cooked up until the lid blew. A political appointee, with experience in
Moscow and Ankara, Steinhardt was unloved by his staff. He was not
naïve nor was he generous. Moreover, despite face-to-face dealings with
Stalin, Steinhardt never knew how to break up Soviet lock-step tactics,
even in diplomacy. He had not really done his homework.

In his office one afternoon, some of us were "post-morteming" the
coup. Steinhardt's professional staff was also there. He talked most of
the time, until one reporter asked him if he knew what, indeed, he was
talking about. Dead silence washed over the office. Steinhardt began to
splutter indignantly. Some of us began to rise and make motions to leave.
The telephone rang on his desk, just as in heavy movie scenes. Steinhardt
covered the mouthpiece and announced importantly: "Wait, it's Jan
Masaryk."

The conversation from Steinhardt's end went like this: "Yes, Jan; I
quite understand, Jan," and "I'll do it, Jan." Masaryk had called to say
that the blistering comment of President Truman over the Communist
coup, set up in the U.S. Information show window, was bothering the
new regime. It attracted too many people. Masaryk said he had been
instructed to relay the government's displeasure and its demand to remove Truman's declaration. Steinhardt apparently equated Masaryk's instructions with a Masaryk desire. He removed the declaration of the
American President.

"You'll understand why I will do it," he called after us as the handful
of American reporters walked out of the room without another word.

A man of probity and courage who did not understand such a gesture
was already in the hospital, hovering between life and death. He had
been Minister of Justice Drtina. He had been a Beneš Socialist. His me-
ticulous sense of honesty uncovered the main evidence that the bomb
plot against Masaryk and others was Communist-contrived. Under the
most mysterious circumstances, Drtina was found unconscious on the
sidewalk outside his apartment house. Suicide attempt, said the new
regime. He had flung himself, Interior Minister Nosek told me, from an
upstairs window.

"Drtina has a very bad conscience," Nosek said.

Conscience had nothing whatever to do with Drtina's brush with death.
He was found on the pavement, at least forty feet from the entrance to
the house. To have landed there, he would need more than fancy-diving
experience. Drtina had to clear a garden before landing where he was

found. He had been tossed out of the window by police agents. They dragged him to the outside street and left him there. This is what Drtina told me when I walked into the hospital where he was staying under guard.

Another plunge from a high window reverberated sickeningly around the world. Another American reporter and I got anonymous dawn telephone calls that Jan Masaryk was dead.

"His body is in the courtyard," said the male voice, choked with emotion. "We might as well all be dead."

The receiver went on the hook. Our own telephone calls to ministries got no information. The city was beginning to stir. Nothing on the local radio. We telephoned a man who accompanied Masaryk three days earlier, on a Sunday, to the Masaryk family plot. His father, founder of modern Czechoslovakia, is buried there. Jan, the son, went out to mourn him and his country.

"We waited for him while he stood alone for half an hour beside the grave," said our informant.

He knew nothing else. Masaryk lived in the Czernin Palace, seat of the Foreign Office. He had an apartment above his working quarters. A taxi ride to the Foreign Office indicated something unusual. Police barred the way to only certain cars. Even charwomen were standing at the roadblocks. They hadn't been able to enter the gate. Police refused to admit any outsider, or to say anything. There was nothing to do but return to downtown Prague and try to check people who might still talk.

Gradually, the paralysis that had gripped Prague since the coup began to disappear. Rumor of a misfortune spreads quickly. Sealing off the Czernin Palace kept people out. It also kept people whose job it was to work nights, strictly inside. They had, it seems, access to telephones for some time. That was stopped. So were, suddenly, some communication lines that made connections possible with the West. Finally, the announcement from the government came through. It had been withheld at least six hours from the time Masaryk's body had been found officially. There had been a sixty-foot drop from his apartment to the paved courtyard below.

Masaryk's death stunned the nation and even made the Communists briefly defensive. His is a much-revered name, even if today the regime tries to make of his father an agent of imperialism and of Jan Masaryk a no-account functionary. The regime was alarmed then, on March 10, 1948, that the Foreign Minister had died violently. He had committed suicide, announced the government. Why? A combination of insomnia and gibes at him by the Western press drove Masaryk to the little bathroom window from which he plunged. The tragedy, however, did not cause Communists to postpone their first meeting between the new cabinet and the purged Parliament. A large bouquet of tulips and lilies covered Masaryk's desk before an empty chair. Interior Minister Nosek, a macabre figure, pronounced the eulogy.

Details leading to the death plunge began to come out, some from the regime, some from those around Masaryk. Minor surgery had been performed on his left arm and the heavy strain of work induced "a moment of nervous disorder." The government said so. From others, it was learned that lights of his five-room apartment on the third floor gleamed all night. Cigarette butts overflowed an ashtray on Masaryk's desk. He had been chain-smoking. Any suicide notes? Not a trace of one, was the regime's answer.

I remember going over to the house in which Dr. Alice Masaryk, his sister, lived. She had been the founder of the Czechoslovak Red Cross. Dr. Masaryk dearly loved her brother. Her little house was only 200 yards from the Foreign Office. To a knock, a maid answered, opening the door half way. Her cheeks glistened with tears. She shook her head.

"Please come some other time," she said. "Madame is crying for her brother."

Indeed, it seemed that most of Czechoslvakia was crying for Jan Masaryk, or the Czechoslovakia many people believed he represented in mind and outlook. So many felt that the pursuit of personal and national happiness they wanted would be buried with Masaryk. Masaryk's last day of life included an auto trip to Sezimovo Usti, sixty miles from Prague, where Beneš had gone to his country home. He went to see Beneš in formal dress; dark jacket and striped trousers. The two men talked alone.

When Masaryk returned to Czernin Palace, he changed into a worsted suit. He wrote some letters. They were, said Masaryk, to be sent to London. None of them ever turned up again. His steward, Vaclav Tolpinka, and valet, Bohumil Prihoda, brought him a lonely meal. They had been with the Masaryk family for years. Masaryk dined slowly on roast chicken, roast potatoes and a glass of Pilsener beer. The servants cleared the dishes away at 8:30 in the evening.

"I don't want to see you until 8:30 in the morning," he told them.

Masaryk stayed up late. There were some people he received in his apartment. Nobody can, with accuracy, pinpoint their names or their mission. The bathroom window from which he plunged contained a tub, a washstand and a small couch underneath the window. To reach the window, you would have to stand on the couch, climb up and open the window which fronts on the parapet. It is not hard to do, either alone or with unwanted help.

The regime gauged the impact of the tragedy in Czechoslovakia and elsewhere. It tried to take the funeral over as its very own stage management. But this was no time for theater. Newly Communist-dominated Czechoslovakia could make the arrangements and order a state funeral. It could not, however, control the emotions that swept the nation. With one voice, the regime ordered deep mourning, with another it approved unanimously the Communist structure, making it a "People's Democracy." In a show of hands, the step was taken even as Masaryk's corpse was embalmed.

Weeping throngs, nearly a quarter of a million, passed through the Czernin Palace in their last tearful goodbye to Masaryk. They walked silently through the great hall. Almost everyone had flowers to place at the bier. City women clutching nosegays took their places beside peasant girls holding field flowers. Trolley conductors waited patiently with dispossessed shop keepers. Mothers said farewell, babies in their arms.

Jan Masaryk lay in state, reposing in a simple black coffin that had been placed on a raised dais. To be seen was only a swelling of the right temple and some discoloration of the face. Candles burned in four silver sticks around the coffin. Stiffly erect, lips trembling, Foreign Ministry employees stood vigil in two-hour shifts. Uncontrollable crying crashed through the funeral silence. One look at Masaryk was enough to unseal cautious spirits. A cab driver told a stranger that he went on strike when the Communists called for a no-work protest a couple of weeks before. "If I knew this would be the result," he said bitterly, "I would have smashed my taxi against the wall."

A peasant grandmother, all in the rusty black of country people, cried out: "Dear God, this is our fate, too!" Others nodded assent. Three students said Masaryk died for them—for the country. "We are all in a concentration camp now," one exclaimed. Communist security agents noted the outbursts. There was little they could do in the great hall. The crush was too overwhelming. In the government, orders for an ever-widening purge net were given. One of the organizations "cleansed" was the Masaryk League for Tuberculosis Prevention. A close friend of Masaryk's, mentioning the grimy little purge of the association, talked briefly of the return from his father's burial ground.

"Jan only said when I talked to him: 'For me nothing matters now. If only I could do something to help the nation!'"

Beneš had retreated into total silence when he received the news of Masaryk's death. This was the son of his sponsor, Thomas Garrigue Masaryk, who worked with him in exile and again in postwar Czechoslovakia. Had Beneš counted on his fingers his remaining loyal and influential co-workers, he could not have gone far. From his country house, Beneš drove to the National Museum in Prague. The state funeral was being held there. Tremendous crowds overflowed the sidewalks. Three out of four, it seemed, wore black or a mark of mourning. Public demand, by workers who left jobs late, forced the regime to keep doors open all night so latecomers could pay their last respects to Masaryk.

When the time came for the funeral procession, people stood on swaying chairs and rickety stools. They held up their children to see—"to remember," one man put it—the coffin trundled along on a gun carriage in St. Wenceslas Square, Prague's main street. Through loudspeakers, the service was heard outdoors. Inside, Gottwald, pink-cheeked, spoke into a microphone near the coffin. His theme was that Masaryk's death was caused by "reaction."

"I can prove," he declared, "that Masaryk fully agreed with the action program of the new government."

He never did because he could not.

An old Czech legionnaire of World War I followed Gottwald. He was brief but pointed. He remembered Masaryk saying: "By the name I bear, we shall win. The fight for truth will prevail."

Beneš ran his right hand across his eyes. In the packed streets outside, men and women wept. Up rose the vibrant voices of a children's choir. "Plough Your Land, My Son," they sang. The resonance of the tone rolled through the museum. Beneš broke into tears. The song had been the favorite of the elder Masaryk. It ended the state service. Masaryk was borne to Lany, amid the rich farmland of western Bohemia, to the family cemetery, accompanied by only a small group of relatives, close friends and government officials.

Vlado Clementis, Communist successor to Masaryk, spoke softly and non-politically at the grave. Masaryk was much beloved, said Clementis, and turned away. A few years later nobody was around who dared speak for Clementis. He was dead—by Communist execution. The comrade who helped gather material to put Clementis away was already telling the nation to forget childish sentimentality. Don't, he said, make a pilgrimage of going to Masaryk's grave.

"We must face the future, not the past," said Alexj Cepicka. He was the new Minister of Justice, in Drtina's place. Cepicka was not only a devoted Communist but a son-in-law of Gottwald. It was a cosy arrangement in which both party and personal feelings were accommodated. For a while Cepicka liked to talk about how revolutionary he thought things were going in Czechoslovakia. "Do you realize," he said to me one day, "that we have more than 10,000 action committees in the country today?"

One of his new associates in government went much further. Antonin Gregor, Communist Minister of Foreign Trade, boasted how the Soviet Union should be thanked for Communist accession to power in Czechoslovakia.

"We must thank our Slav allies, especially the Soviet Union, for the fact that we succeeded in overcoming all obstacles in defeating reaction," Gregor crowed.

In the regime drive against what it called reaction, Slovakia, which had been a puppet state under the Nazis, became the main target. It was a stronghold of the peasantry and the Catholic church. There had been, through the years, ill feeling between the more dynamic Czech from Bohemia and Moravia and the taciturn, suspicious Slovak. In the past, Slovakia had a wide measure of home rule although it participated actively in the National Assembly.

"All we need are two generations of education and understanding between the two," Masaryk used to claim.

The Communist regime had other ideas for Slovakia. It launched investigations of Slovak political and church activity. Large-scale arrests were made and figures proudly published to show how intensely vigilant "new Czechoslovakia" was, compared with the old government. "Quisling" was the charge freely applied to anyone arrested in Slovakia because it had been a Nazi puppet state. Almost all the collaborators had already been tried; fled with the Germans or vanished. The reign of terror, in any case, was good practice for the security units wanting to show how efficient they could be without the restrictions of the past.

"They learned well in Slovakia," a girl whose Communist father led some of the raids told me a few years later. "They could put together a dossier faster than you could explain a case."

Her own father was himself a victim of such a dossier. He was an early target. He was one of the many who showed so much fervor and energy on behalf of the new regime that some of his comrades thought he had something to hide. The permanent purge process in Czechoslovakia got a head-start because the party was eager to show the Soviet bloc just how advanced it really was. A "Gottwald Week," for example, was used to try and increase party membership by eighty percent. A big job, even for single-minded Communists, in a week. Their aim was a neat figure of 2,000,000.

"There is a place in the party for every honest Czech," Richard Slansky observed heartily over a good dinner which he gave for some Western guests.

In factories, government offices and nationalized shops, the only way to keep a job or get ahead was to join the party. A man or woman who refused was often held up to public condemnation. Reasons were asked in front of co-workers. While the party drummed up trade for membership, with open threats against those who held out, old-time Communists became jealous of their prerogatives as veterans.

"How can you tell if an ex-Beneš man or an ex-Social Democrat is heart and soul with you?" an aggravated veteran asked me when I went to the Ministry of Food. "It's a good thing now. So everybody joins. Who knows what they think?"

The party got some idea when it demanded an extra day's free work to celebrate the Communist coup. Part of the day's pay went into a special fund, the regime announced, to aid Greek Communist guerrillas. The rest, in theory, went back to the state. Factories, government offices and farms were checked to see that people were at work. It was all voluntary labor, Gottwald had said.

"If you didn't go," a Czech office worker said afterwards, "you didn't know if you had a job when you returned to work. This was explained to us by the chairman of our action committee."

Labor for an unpaid day was not up to par, complained action committees in reports to the party. There was a singular lack of enthusiasm,

Minister Cepicka said with a frown. "There must be enthusiasm," he warned section chiefs. In ancient Charles University, where students protested about the professorial and curriculum changes, they were ordered to give a day free a month by the action committees. If students didn't go to work at farms in the country, they were blacklisted and threatened with expulsion. But the peasants on whose land they were dumped didn't like the idea.

"It's all nonsense," a rangy farmer explained one Sunday evening after the trucks went off from his farm, crammed with students. "None of the boys here ever worked with a horse or a cow before. Neither did their leaders who sang songs most of the day. Crazy songs. All about the glory of workers and peasants. They did less work than anybody."

It didn't take long for revulsion to express itself. Students played at haying in the fields on "voluntary" days. Sometimes, they figured out ways of dumping an action committee leader in a pile of fertilizer. In offices, security men reported on others who seemed to be shirking work. It turned out that they were noting the no-work habits of other security agents. Such information, a Foreign Ministry acquaintance noted, was one sure way of finding out who had been reporting on people in an office. These were fairly light-hearted reactions to a regime that took itself dead seriously. Arrests in many cases and forced unemployment in some instances took the lightness out of opposing a forced march to what the new ruling class said was socialism.

"Above all, be enthusiastic," Fierlinger told a meeting of former Social Democrats.

Their expressions did not change. Fierlinger saw why. Someone had forgotten to remove a photo of Masaryk right behind him.

CHAPTER 7

Frost comes early to the mountains that mark the long and jagged frontier between Yugoslavia and Albania. It stays late, mantling the mountains and choking the rough passes right through to a late spring thaw. On a bitter night early in 1948, when the cold cut sharply through the greatcoats of border patrols, Yugoslav soldiers, chins dug deep into upturned collars, slid behind giant boulders that brooded over the narrow path. Clasping tommyguns against their chests, they waited. A fleeting movement crossed the stony landscape in front of them. Shadows rose on the trail and gradually took the shape of men—three men in bulging civilian clothes, arms wrapped around their waists. Tito's soldiers waited until the intruders were well inside Yugoslav territory. Then they closed in, their tommyguns levelled. As the strangers raised their hands in the night, the bulges vanished from their clothes. Bundles of paper sheets, tied together with string, dropped to the trail.

A soldier pounced on them, making sure none was whipped away by the wind before the patrol marched off with its prisoners. Printed on the paper sheets in heavy black type, this warning ran: "Yugoslavs! Together we will show our solidarity with the Soviet Union. Stand fast and prepare." This was only the spring of 1948. None of the Yugoslav-Soviet exchange of recriminations had yet found its way to an unsuspecting public in the West or in Russia's Europe. Tito and Stalin, the Soviet Goliath, were still keeping their quarrel in the family, namely among high personalities of the Communist parties. One puzzling episode had just occurred. A bare brief announcement crept into the Yugoslav press that Zujevic, Tito's war-time assistant chief of staff and a Politburo member, had been removed. It was arrest. The same laconic announcement and the same treatment had been imposed on Hebrang, a short and corpulent Croat. He was an old Communist, who had served twelve years in pre-war Yugoslav prisons for illegal party work. Right after the war Hebrang had been boss of the Five-Year Plan. When he was thrown in jail, Hebrang was Minister of Industry.

"It's an internal matter of no concern to you," Djilas said when I asked him about the two arrests.

The case was, of course, a matter of interest for everyone in Yugoslavia, Eastern Europe and the outside world. To veteran Communists, able to plough through unexplained arrest items and jargon of party lexicography, removal of Zujevic and Hebrang rang alarm bells. They became uneasy. "Something strange is going on inside the Yugoslav party," an ex-Polish Socialist turned Communist diplomat in Belgrade tried to reason. Deliveries to Yugoslavia from Eastern European countries slowed down noticeably. A plant manager I knew just outside Belgrade was puzzled. A non-party man, he was put in the job as a "progressive" but mostly because he was a pre-war, trained technician and engineer.

"We are still building from the beginning," the engineer told me one evening over a meal of cevapcici, succulent finger-sized Serbian sausages. "We make allowances for delays in getting materials. Everyone in the East has troubles. But I haven't gotten anything for at least two months. We can't even produce our electric bulbs."

Tito and his hierarchical trouble-shooters in the party knew why Soviet agents tried to infiltrate with propaganda. They also kept a close count on freight trains diverted from reaching empty Yugoslav mills with raw materials and desperately-needed finished goods. The whole Yugoslav apparatus was put on a defense-in-depth position to tighten up against

either a Soviet-led economic blockade, an actual invasion and subversion
or a violent take-over version of all three. Troops moved into old partisan
hide-outs. Food and ammunition caches were restocked. Rankovich's
secret police kept a day-and-night vigil on Russians, East European Communists and suspected Yugoslav agents of the Soviet Union. Not only
were Westerners kept in total ignorance and at an untouchable arm's
length, but also the Yugoslav people had no idea of what was in store
for them. After nearly three years of Communist rule, they intensely disliked the regime, the swash-buckling ex-partisans who ran their lives,
forced marches to mass meetings extolling Tito and a guaranteed life of
penury.

"Let them take what they want from these fields," a disgruntled peasant
in South Serbia remarked. "We know what to do. They don't."

The fields his bony finger stretched to show were pretty fallow. Party
activists had been sent down to accelerate the pace of collectivization.
The peasants, who survived Turkish and other occupations, figured they
could outlast agricultural planners. If he didn't grow things, a visitor
asked, how did he eat? The peasant winked, accepted a cigarette which
he lit and inhaled gratefully.

"I've got enough put away," he replied. "Animals? I'll kill the pigs this
summer. I'll sell and eat them. I won't give them to the government. What
has the government done for me?"

The regime kept them all in the dark about the cataclysm that was
shaking the entire Communist world. It was not an oversight. The ruling
Communist party of Yugoslavia wanted to prove that it hadn't turned
its back or deviated in the slightest from ideology laid down by Marx
and Lenin. The big backslider was Stalin and this later was made clear
in the exchange of party-to-party correspondence between Belgrade and
Moscow. Such momentous issues, however, were not for the mass of the
people to digest and review. Having come to the top, Yugoslav Communists believed unquestioningly they could lead the people in the direction vital to their movement and the country.

"Grandma knows," Vlado Dedijer explained to me one time. "It's an
old Serbian story. Grandma knows what's best for everyone."

In this case, Grandma was the Yugoslav party and Tito her eldest and
most beloved son. Dedijer and his comrades swore by the "Old Man"—
Tito. Neither the party nor Tito could do wrong. How, then, could they?
Yugoslav partisans knew how to obtain power and how to hold it. There-

fore, the people, under any extremity, would accept without a murmur Tito's leadership. The late Boris Kidric, Viennese-born and the son of a professor, took pains to point this out to me in a long exposition of how entrenched the system was in Yugoslavia. Later on, hindsight brought home to me what Kidric meant. Only two months before the break with Moscow became public knowledge, he was arguing that the Yugoslav pattern for power did not intend to bend either before outside or inside influence.

"We have built a new society here in Yugoslavia," lectured Kidric, once a chemist and then chief of the planning commission. "Nobody is entitled to force us from that path and we will fight anybody who tries to do it."

When the great schism was finally made known to the Yugoslav people, and to the world generally, the "anybody" to them meant the Soviet system. Tito undoubtedly was able to rally the vast majority of Yugoslavs behind him in the crucial days that followed. The average Yugoslav felt that he was girding to repel the Russian Communists.

"We will get help from you and from other places," a miner named Fei Vojislan said complacently. "Tito? As long as he fights the Russians, everything is fine. This isn't a country of Communists. You will see. He will change, too."

That was precisely what Tito and the party had no intention of doing, at least in those early days of the break. The Russians forced the schism, they carefully pointed out. Yugoslav Communists were true to the doctrine of Marx and Lenin. It was Stalin who violated the principles of "socialist equality." The upper crust of the Yugoslav party continued to practice its own form of equality. It didn't budge from its recently sequestered villas. The country was pulling in a collective belt but the partisan leaders who took over the country scarcely drew a deep breath.

Tito's private life, like all other Communists of the time, was closely guarded from the public. But he had a son, Zharko, by his first wife. In Belgrade, Zharko got into a night club fight with some Russian officers. It was over a girl, not ideology. Zharko lost an arm as a result. He repeatedly got into hot water ever after, usually with girls. I remember Zharko, a most gregarious chap, holing up in a hotel strictly for foreign correspondents and business men. When Zharko went out one afternoon, agents from UDBA came in, rapped on his second-floor room and brusquely entered. Squeals of rage and hysteria burst forth. It seemed the girl wouldn't get dressed. The agents bundled her off in a blanket before the eyes of the amazed clientele.

When Zharko returned a few hours later, he found the room empty. He asked the terrified desk clerk some questions. The answers evoked from him: "My father did this. Damn him to hell. I'll get her back." He never did nor did he set foot again in the hotel. He kept to himself morosely except in his night club forays.

Generally speaking, the upper echelons kept to themselves. They planned and conspired together. A look at the table of organization in power gave you some sound insight into why Tito's partisans felt secure even though Stalin growled at them. About 3,000 pre-war party members survived to share in the fruits of power afterwards. Party members amounted to roughly a half-million in a country of 17,000,000. Being a member meant active soldiery in the partisans or the underground.

Tito's secret police were ubiquitous, well-paid and looked-after by the state, and highly organized as a paramilitary body. Most had been partisans. On all government levels, no matter how small the community, Communists were in control. They handled rationed food, distributed raw materials and tried to know what all their neighbors were doing. The Yugoslav army, huge in that it maintained 350,000 or so foot soldiers, was directly under command of partisan officers. The lines of power were in Tito's hands and he made them pliable to his own political needs. Because it was a Communist regime, the Russians believed that Communists would stand up for Moscow. Stalin never thought that anyone in a smaller country would talk back to him.

"They thought we would roll over and say please forgive us," Steve Dedijer, Vlado's brother said when the storm broke.

Steve is an interesting and mixed-up character. He went to Princeton, probably the only Ivy Leaguer in any Communist country in Europe. During the war, he was a paratrooper in the 82d Airborne. When Germany was crushed, Steve lit out for his Yugoslav homeland and service to Tito. When his brother, Vlado, sided with Djilas years later, Steve supported both of them. He is a harassed man today. His wife divorced him, with party approval, and Steve never sees her and hardly ever his children. Making a living is a real problem for him now. It was different then.

"It's an extension of our own revolution," Steve told me with real fervor brightening his eyes.

How many Yugoslav Communists felt so deeply and bitterly against the Russians is hard to say. Pro-Russians were packed off to jail immediately or lapsed into prudent silence. "We didn't give them a chance to make trouble," a Yugoslav editor related later with satisfaction. Most of the trouble-makers were the Russians themselves. Instead of behaving like big Slav brothers, the Russians demanded special privileges in higher pay as technical assistants than Yugoslavs earned; better housing and access to all information. It had worked everywhere else with comradely parties. Why not Yugoslavia, reasoned Russians aggrievedly.

"They behave very strangely very often," was all Vlado Dedijer would say to an outsider he knew before the break.

It turned out that the Yugoslavs thought it strange and even diabolical of the Russians to try and recruit locals for espionage, economic and political. The Russians apparently thought such a recruiting program came naturally. If the Yugoslavs were better comrades than any other, why object to Soviet proposals of fifty-fifty deals in which Russians would hold the veto power over the Yugoslav economy. Russians in Belgrade, before the break, would sometimes observe that the Yugoslavs were being most difficult. "It's the newness of their revolution," they said, by way of explanation to Westerners.

When the conspiratorial correspondence between Moscow and Belgrade grew more voluminous and inflamed, Russians stopped seeing Yugoslav contacts. They simply did not turn up for appointments, stayed among themselves and more faithful people of the bloc or were just recalled to the Soviet Union. Yugoslav Communists, so blasé about being late for appointments or not showing up at all, got offended. To the brink of the break they did what they could to stay on the best possible terms with the Soviet Union. Their terms were equality with the Soviet Communists. The very idea was an affront to Stalin's pursuit of acknowledged hegemony. What Tito demanded seemed in Moscow like narrow-minded local nationalism. After all, Tito did say, "No matter how much any of us may love the fatherland of socialism, the U.S.S.R., he can in no way love his own country, which is also building socialism, the less."

A "Pravda" correspondent commenting on these words later seemed shocked that any Communist would dare say so. Finger trembling with indignation for emphasis, the "Pravda" man said to me: "You managed to infiltrate us pretty well for a while. Tito and his crowd are, of course, your agents."

It never occurred to the Russians, with their doctrinaire blinders, that the Americans were caught totally dumbstruck and uninformed about what caused the schism. Our demonologists in Belgrade and Washington regarded the affair as either a plot to deceive the West or a local intra-mural quarrel of no serious interest to us. Only a handful, especially among the younger diplomats in our embassy, recognized the enormous earthquake that had ripped through the monolith that the Communist world tried to present. These hard-working, cool-thinking diplomats were fairly low on the diplomatic totem pole. They were anti-Communist and they found Tito's personal dictatorship distasteful. What they saw was something bigger than Tito and even more important than Stalin.

"National Communism will be a ghost running around Communism's house forever," a young and farsighted American diplomat told me over a bottle of Slovene Riesling late one night. "Communism is a religion. We must remember that even if we hate it. It has its church, its disciples and its bible. Along comes the Martin Luther of Communism, Tito, and nails up his declaration on the church wall. This is the first real split but there will be others."

That diplomat's early recommendation to enter into cautious negotia-tions with Tito were largely discounted in Washington. We were too busy running through the post-mortems of why a country with the solid traditions of Czechoslovakia went Communist. If Czechoslovakia could be taken over, what chance was there for Tito? He was a Communist and so was his whole regime. Besides, the new Cominform headquarters were ensconced in Belgrade. It all looked too fishy, at first.

"We tried not to be outcasts to the very last," explained Vlado Dedijer. "We were genuine Communists and we wanted to belong. We also knew how we had to defend ourselves to survive. We knew Russian practices. Of course, we excused them. That was the way things had to happen, we believed, in rotten countries. We were different. We fought our-selves."

Yugoslav Communists were different, although rank-and-file Yugoslavs would dispute that point. They had lived under varying dictatorships before. When they dared speak a little of their minds, which began after the break, they told how they were disapproved.

"Tito talks equality," a high-school teacher protested at supper one evening. "How about equality here at home. It's a different equality he talks about. Equality is for the big men."

What did he, the school-teacher, intend to do in case of real conflict with the Russians? "Support the regime, naturally," he snapped. The Russians obviously never believed Tito could get the support. The Yugoslavs would reach out gratefully, so Russians told me, and smash the structure Tito built inside the country. What made them so sure? It will happen, as certain as we were sitting in a restaurant. At the beginning, the Russians never thought it would go otherwise.

"A matter of time," a Czechoslovak diplomat recently arrived in Belgrade confidently predicted. "Look how long it took for a developed country like mine."

As a reward, Czechoslovakia's Communist regime was chosen towards the end of June, 1948, to spread the news that Tito was a pariah in the Soviet bloc. His party and he had been cast out of comradeship in Russia's Europe. The newest and most eager-to-please satellite, the Czechoslovak regime printed the news big in the party paper, "Rude Pravo." That article, castigating Tito and the men around him, was also the first word Yugoslavs generally got. Soviet and satellite radios beamed the text and gist of the expulsion order in Yugoslav-language programs on the offending nation.

"They expect the people to get aroused and to throw our government and party over with the news," said Vlado Dedijer calmly. "They probably don't realize how wrong they are."

Yugoslavs were stunned. Their own regime hadn't filled them in yet. That came soon afterwards but in the lacy language normally employed in theoretical addresses. What the Yugoslavs understood was that the Soviet bloc had Tito under a pitiless attack. Since loyalty was demanded of them under these circumstances, Yugoslavs responded positively. They still could not grasp why the Russians attacked Tito who was still arguing his case as a genuine Communist.

You could scarcely blame the average Yugoslav's confusion. In down-at-the-heels Belgrade, they could still walk past—but fast—the Cominform headquarters. They didn't know, because they were never told, that inside the building Tito's security agents had their eyes glued to former East European comrades who wriggled uncomfortably in their offices fiddling with meaningless papers.

"I suppose that the Cominform staff was months, even a year, getting properly organized," Djilas recalled much later with open satisfaction. "In Belgrade they were as much worried about us as we were about them."

To the world at large, however, Tito stuck fast to a pro-Soviet line-up in foreign affairs. He had his capital redecorated in the main streets, new bath-tubs installed in aged Balkan hotels and fresh signs painted for a big international conference. It was Yugoslavia's first and guests were countries which had an interest in using the Danube as a commercial river. In speeches across the conference table, Yugoslav delegates laced as merrily into Western representatives as did the Soviet bloc.

"We haven't changed our views about Western encroachment," a Yugoslav party theoretician said loudly enough in the corridors to be overheard by Soviet-bloc guests. "We are Communists and we will remain Communists."

The Russians and their faithful satellites were totally unimpressed. Tito's apostasy had been circulated in detail to all party cadres. It was too late to shift the scene of the Danube conference to some other locale. Besides, the Russians enjoyed turning their backs in public on Yugoslav reassurances that the Tito party remained loyal and persevering in the march towards Marxist-Leninist goals. By this time, the Yugoslavs ignored reference to Stalin entirely except to say something uncomplimentary. It was a curious conference, perhaps the strangest ever staged. The Russians, supported by the Yugoslavs, held physical control over most of the Danube. In voting, they could easily outnumber last-ditch U.S.-British-French objections to making the Danube a Communist waterway once past the American zone of Austria. Each Yugoslav attack on the West was fiercer than those of any other nation. The Russians paid no attention. Outside the conference hall and in whispered asides at the table, Soviet European delegates taunted the Yugoslavs.

"It's worse than the jungle," a Western delegate, sweating with bewilderment, observed after a session. "The Yugoslavs are renegades to the Russians. They are treated like intruders in their own home. The Yugoslavs support the Russians on the Danube. In between, they argue their case with the Soviet bloc. It's a nut house."

Foreign diplomats assigned to Belgrade contributed heavily to the confusion. One, from a small Western European country, got a bad case of jitters. He had been using his elevated position to sell, under the table, cheap diplomatic whiskey and cigarettes. The Belgrade job had been handed to him on the understanding that he stayed there and out of trouble. When the Tito-Stalin break burst on him, his government began to see the post in a much more important light.

The ambassador, stopped in mid-sale of black-market luxuries, had to start some serious reporting back home. He was totally out of his depth but had to report. So he started a rumor mill. With the glazed smile of a croupier, the ambassador announced to anyone who cared to listen that Yugoslavia would soon be invaded from the East. He even named a date. Then he told his staff to take off to less exposed places than Belgrade. Nobody would notice, he wrote in a confidential memo circulated in his embassy, if they filtered out while the Danube conference occupied attention. Some of the staff talked about the order and word got around. It was picked up, of course, and relayed all over the world.

To make it seem more logical, Soviet armor had been seen maneuvering close to the Rumanian-Yugoslav border. The Albanians skirmished with Yugoslav frontier guards. Their agents tried to make contact and trouble within the large Albanian minority just over the border. From the Hungarian side and from the Bulgar border, Soviet satellite forces flew, marched and demonstrated their ability to create a menace against Tito. They began the psychological war of nerves against Tito while they sat at the conference table in Belgrade. The overt pressure lasted five years.

Only the beginning of the menace was enough for the diplomat. He came out of his mink-lined lair to offer quotations on just where and when Soviet satellite forces would strike. His panic began to have some impact on the rather small Western foreign colony. The Yugoslavs remained imperturbable. They didn't think that Stalin would strike with open force but they were ready for it. Isolation, economic blockades and psychological warfare they fully expected.

"We can defend ourselves from actual attack," a Yugoslav with years of association with party higher-ups said to me one night while a gypsy orchestra drowned out our voices. "But you have to give the people more incentive than the possibility of fighting an invader. Suppose the invader doesn't come. You have to build houses, make shops and factories turn things out and get food from the country."

That was exactly the problem Tito and his planners mulled over at length while they smiled publicly for the benefit of the Danube conference. Since they proclaimed themselves as Communist purists, they would not think of exploring the possibilities of credits and aid from the West, above all the United States. Such a move, they feared, would point a condemning finger at them from Moscow. The Russians could say that they suspected Tito's treachery all along if he asked the West for help.

Even hard-core party ranks inside Yugoslavia shied away from the possibility. They claimed they'd get along somehow. Inside the bold exterior, they worried seriously. The Soviet bloc withheld deliveries for which contracts had long ago been signed. Yugoslav trade, staggering to its feet, was trussed up with Soviet economic plans and strategy. Nothing was coming into Yugoslavia, except anti-Tito propaganda stuffed in mailboxes and surreptitiously circulated in the provinces. Moreover, the disgruntled countryside was groaning under drought conditions.

Once the Danube conference was over, the name-calling began. Soviet Europe used every epithet to describe Tito and his henchmen. The nicer names were "Fascists," "traitors" and "agents of imperialism." Tito also became known as a "Balkan dwarf." In retaliation, the Yugoslav Communists made public the Soviet demands. They were akin to surrender terms imposed by victors on the vanquished, not socialist equality which Tito said was necessary. When the Russians swore at Tito, Yugoslavs at large began to believe that the quarrel was in dead earnest. They hadn't been told or been prepared for inter-Communist factionalism of such a vicious quality.

"Tito may be tough and bad but not what the Russians call him," a farmer in Sarajevo said, squinting along a fertilizer barrel. "We've called him worse. That's because we're not Communists. Tito is. I can tell you that. If Stalin is against Tito, I'm for him. You'll see. Other people will feel the same."

In trips through the Yugoslav republics, the farmer's pithy summation was borne out. When former partisans listened in, the peasant or factory worker became cautious and chose his words carefully. Most of what they wore was patched, darned and cannibalized from two pairs of pants to make one. They were poor, their expectations were low but their spirits glowed. Tito had his picture everywhere; in mess halls, town squares, coffee houses and country taverns. He gave the impression of real bigness. What could little people do?

"We won't let Stalin in here," a man seeing his family for the first time since the war remarked. We were just outside Srenska Mitrovitsa, which houses the sprawling, scabrous building that held many political prisoners. Before the war, it also held Tito, Pjade, Rankovic, Djilas and others. Pure, national patriotism retreaded itself quickly in the Yugoslav mind. Where once, not long before, Croats hated Serbs and vice-versa, and Slovenes looked down on Macedonians and Montenegrins and virtually everyone else, they made a common front in spite of themselves against the Soviet Union. Soviet contempt for smaller nations fused a nationalism in Yugoslavia which Stalin unwittingly said existed before it did.

Pride and defiance, however, couldn't sustain a nation that needed housing, feeding and employment at useful jobs. Yugoslavs were not going hungry but they were getting close to the borderline. The party tightened up in discipline at the same time. Everywhere you went, labor brigades of young people were on the march, mending roads, tilling farms and painting schoolhouses. They were not being given state circuses. The reason was simple. The state didn't have enough resources to take Yugoslav minds off the daily problem of defiance on the outside and nourishment on the inside. Work was bandied around as the watchword. The gospel of the new Yugoslavia, new again because of the Tito-Stalin quarrel, was that real progress begins with Tito. In some instances, it reached extraordinary lengths. Take museums, signs of cultural continuity in any Communist regime. In Yugoslavia, they had been looted, razed or left as empty shells. New staffs and old curators wanted to prove that they could do the best in a community even with the slenderest of resources. In Sarajevo at the time I met an energetic little man with a flair for local archeology and a student of the gypsy dialects in Eastern Europe. His name was Rade Uhliek.

"Under the Austrians and the old Yugoslavia something always came up to prevent us from putting together a proper museum," said Uhliek.

He paused in his fluent English, which he said he learned generally by reading books on archeology. He pointed to some packing cases stacked up in the dusty courtyard of the stonehewn museum done in Franz Josef provincial fussiness. Older workmen, wearing fezzes, ripped crates open with rusty hammers. Boys in undershirts and shorts with rope-soled slippers, staggered through the doorway with boxes on their backs. There wasn't a piece of machinery in sight.

"Now this is one of the finest museums in the Balkans," Uhliek said rapturously. "The government gives us every cooperation. By the way, I've been a member of the Gypsy Lore Society in Liverpool for many years. Do you know it?"

He didn't wait for an answer. A deeply tanned man, bare to the waist, came to greet us. He was stocky and muscles bulged in his arms. His hair was black shot with gray and close-cropped. "Here," Uhliek said happily, "is the best snake catcher in the Balkans. Meet Ljubo Tchoritc. He's been catching snakes for twenty-four years."

Tchoritc gravely acknowledged the introduction. Uhliek begged my pardon and asked Tchoritc something in a language I didn't understand. Arabic, explained the little curator. Tchoritc and he spoke Arabic for practice when they got the chance. In a long speech Tchoritc replied.

"He says that here in Bosnia-Herzegovina we have the most artful and the most poisonous snakes in the Balkans," Uhliek translated. It seemed that Tchoritc got all possible cooperation hunting snakes. Uhliek was most enthusiastic.

"He says that our snakes are becoming very much in demand abroad," he continued. "We are beginning to export them to zoos all over Europe. There is a big lack of snakes in zoos since the war, you know. But it isn't easy for Tchoritc. He is still waiting for some equipment. What he does now is to sneak up behind a snake and use forked sticks he makes himself. He puts them in a sugar bag."

We wandered out of the gateway with the snake-catcher and stood amid a group of Moslem women. Minarets dominated Sarajevo's skyline. The women were still veiled. But the veils were pretty transparent. The snake-catcher said something in a burst of words.

"He says the government will help him get new equipment," explained the curator. "Everybody will have an opportunity in the new Yugoslavia. Enthusiasm. That's all you have to have."

Leaders of youth brigades, party officials and regime leaders had only a surplus of enthusiasm. They had little else. In Belgrade I saw brigades of boys and girls passing home-made bricks from hand to hand in human chains for walls of a new building. At mine-shafts in more developed Slovenia, horse-carts hauled ore. On the Montenegrin roads, winding above the beautiful but desolate valleys, men crushed stone with hammers for highway gravel. In a city, queues lined up for bread, a very brown bread.

Tito needed our material help. It wouldn't bring him any closer to Western ideologies. He was a Communist and a dictator. In this respect, he has never changed. Tito remains a self-made cult of the individual. Through the years he has been able to let up a little on personal domination and relax a bit on dogmatic positions where clothes, jazz and the like are concerned. As long as it did not threaten to undermine his position and the party's local appetites were appeased. It was vastly the other way around in those immediate-break days. He was at the beginning of his fight with the Cominform, or "Inform Bureau," as the Yugoslav Communists liked to call it. Already his battle ate into the monolithic unity the Soviet world pointed to with so much chimerical pride. Tito's preservation, overnight, became of value to us. We hadn't planned on it. Neither had the Yugoslavs, as one of them still high in the regime, admitted to me years later. Still, a popular song was wailed out in open-air cafes that summer. "Stalin, you'll never rule us," was the first line.

Suspicion never left the mind of the wife of an influential Western ambassador. Her father had been an official in Croatia when the area was still under Hapsburg rule. She spoke fluent Serbo-Croat but would not use it unless she was addressing her servants. When her husband invited the Politburo to his country's national day celebration, a few weeks after the break, his lady was horrified. What if they turned up, she asked? Most of them did. It was the first time assigned diplomats had a chance to collar Yugoslav top brass and try to pump them on serious business. The invitations read, 6 P.M. to 8 P.M. At 8:01 promptly, we were all treated to the spectacle of Mrs. Ambassador marching purposefully on the lawn. Behind her were two servants, in starched jackets, and carrying a wooden chair between them. The lady firmly planted herself on the chair and deliberately unscrewed colored and white lights strewn across the lawn.

"I suppose that's the way it's done these days at capitalist parties," Pjade remarked owlishly as he watched the lady.

That little incident sent the Yugoslav Communist heretics back deeper into their shell. They announced they wouldn't cut back from their back-breaking Five-Year Plan. How they'd do it, they didn't explain. There was not only a desperate shortage of raw and finished materials but an austerity diet for the people that was really austere. Behind this gloomy picture stretched the biggest army in Europe outside Stalin's—Tito's. He didn't have investment capital for farms and factories but he was unable to replace used-up guns, broken tanks and airplanes for which the Russians refused to send in spare parts.

"If we ever dreamed of asking the West for military assistance," Vlado Dedijer said firmly, "we would outrage world leftist opinion." They took the risk a couple of years later, but only after a credit and commodities deal had been transacted to bail Yugoslavia out of the Soviet economic blockade.

The list of Tito's wants was already, so early after the break, pressing and long. You looked and you saw rolling stock in a state of critical disrepair. The vehicular roads were in dreadful, rutted and pot-holed condition. Traffic didn't matter, though, because the regime was pitifully short of trucks and cars. The shopping list for which Tito at the time didn't dare shop was longer than any revisionist's arm. Medical supplies were appallingly inadequate; safety appliances didn't exist in mines, machine tools were lent out on a factory-to-factory basis, and where, finally, was enough food going to come to feed people?

A distribution system, patterned faithfully on Russia's, was still operative. Farm planning, which ran into the pitfalls of collectivization, was right out of Moscow's book. To make alterations in the Philosophy governing a Communist-ruled state meant abandoning pet shibboleths. The Yugoslavs knew from experience that Stalin was having trouble in postwar Russia but at first they refused to change what they knew was inherently wrong. Doing that would make other Communists indignant. Tito has always been ultra-sensitive of such reaction. He still is today although much more cynical about it. The West didn't present any difficult ideological issues for the Yugoslav Communists to overcome. When they began their first tentative credit-aid talks they demanded sums and material we were not even making available to old friends and allies. Tito's negotiators probably asked for the capitalist moon because they knew they wouldn't get landing space. Refusal, in the purist beginning, was more important to them. They could say they tried and that we failed them. A gross distortion like that never faced Tito's advisers.

"They are quite capable of asking for $500,000,000 at one gulp," a sorely tried American expert explained. "A little grudgingly they might come down by $50,000,000. But they tell you they won't take a penny less."

It was senseless under those conditions to try. The West, led by the United States, simply had to wait for the Yugoslavs to come to them with more sensible proposals. Tito sized up conditions, probed and then held back. Meanwhile, the propaganda war between Soviet Europe and Yugoslavia was fanned into harsh tension. The UDBA was the busiest agency of all in Yugoslavia. It could show an overproduction in arrests. Almost all were anti-Soviet in tone. Former White Russians who settled in Yugoslavia after the Russian revolution had been urged by Tito to obtain Soviet citizenship in 1945. They had no real choice. Three years later, they were accused of plotting to overthrow the state with Moscow aid.

The prison population grew and vigilance was the order of the day.

In Belgrade a correspondent of Tass, the Soviet press agency, complained bitterly to me. "I can't even go into the country without permission," he protested. "What kind of a government is this?" If nothing else, it was a government determined to preserve its own Communist character. In midsummer, just after the break, came the terse announcement that Tito's wartime chief of staff, Gen. Arso Jovanovic, had been shot to death while trying to escape to Rumania.

"There are traitors on the left as there are traitors on the right," declared Kardelj. "We'll smash them all to pieces before they can put any of their evil plans into effect."

The next five years were absolute proof that Tito's men meant every word they said about keeping themselves in power.

CHAPTER 8

THE mighty break with Tito led the Russians and their faithful satellite regimes into fixed positions. They wanted to consolidate and to give the outside world the feeling that their control was impregnable. Behind the Draconian measures was the plan to make of the vast occupation zone of Soviet Europe a going concern running on Moscow time. Through Russia's mold, tens of millions of men, women and children were poured. They would come out Soviet beings. So believed the cold-eyed, power-compelled men who contrived the programs. They launched vast projects for outright terror, plotted subversion and looked even indifferently at sparing their own faithful. The process of the permanent purge roared terrifyingly into motion. Communists were put on trial and executed. The revolutions they hailed so proudly as their own devoured them. The Russians exerted full mastery. They had, after all, concocted these revolutions.

Tito was, of course, Target No. 1. His heresy had to be stamped out. The Russians stopped only at outright invasion. Why Stalin never did invade remains an unanswered riddle of contemporary history. One of Tito's aides asked me, out of curiosity, whether the West would come to Yugoslavia's help if there was invasion. The answer was that we probably would not; certainly not in those early days after the schisms between Belgrade and Moscow. Stalin may have felt that he could starve Tito into submission and he may have believed that his professional agents of subversion would do the job, too. At any rate, the Russians did not move on Tito. They pressed, they blockaded and they subverted. It only stiffened Yugoslav will to resist. When they finally made a deal with us for help, nearly two years after the break, their determination to resist became obsessive.

Yet the Yugoslav example was the one Stalin's purgers applied inside the satellite empire. Any Communist who opposed an economic plan proposed by Moscow became automatically a "Titoist." He didn't last long. Public trials of former party big-shots became commonplace circuses throughout Soviet Europe. There were veterans like Rudolf Slansky in Czechoslovakia and a rising, twisted gunsel of the party, Bedrich Geminder. They were accused of high treason, Titoism and for good measure, Zionism. The sophisticated Vlado Clementis deliberately returned to Czechoslovakia from a United Nations session in New York to go to his execution. Clementis had been warned. Death, he remarked, was preferable under these eat-your-sons devices. He was far from the last, though. Purges and trials went on for years. Westerners could rarely attend them. The dark system of justice meted out to Traicho Kostov in Bulgaria was one good reason for limiting Westerners.

Kostov was considered the No. 2 man in Bulgaria at least by Dimitrov, yet the steely arm of the purge reached out to grab him, nonetheless. The Yugoslavs always liked to speculate that had Dimitrov been alive it would not have happened. Ill, Dimitrov had gone to Moscow to die in a sanatorium there. A few months earlier, he met Tito on his way back to Bulgaria. "He told us to stick to our positions," Djilas once told me. Who knows? When Stalin thundered at the Tito-Dimitrov idea for a Balkan federation, Dimitrov repudiated at once his end of the bargain. It might be stretching the imagination too far to think of him opposing instructions from Moscow.

Kostov, tough and a true believer, regarded his arrest and trial as a

Titoist as a mistake. During the war he wrested his way out of the grasp of Gestapo interrogators. He dove out a window to escape his tormentors but didn't die, shattered though his bones were. In court he still blinked unbelievingly. His eyes roamed some of the front benches. Strangely, they lit and rested on a few Western correspondents. Kostov opened up. He repudiated a confession that he supposedly made. "I am not at all guilty," he cried. "I've been tortured, tortured by men who call themselves comrades." The trial was stopped in mid-sentence. Kostov, silent now, was led away. The following day he was brought to the stand. This time he agreed that he was "a traitor." His flash of defiance was unique. There is not a record of any other in the dozens of staged trials when any outside observer was around. Kostov's outburst made satellite inquisitors much more careful. Their future spectacles were confined to a minimum of trustworthy spectators. The trial of average non-regime, non-Communist citizens never hit the limelight.

"You were arrested as you might usually eat your supper," a Polish writer, who spent three separate stretches in jail, recounted. "Your interrogators loved beating you up. Charges? Spying for the West, pro-Tito, oh, anything. It didn't matter. Going to jail and arresting people was part of the whole system."

Threatening death also was an integral phase of the party apparatus. Slogans were shouted like "Death to the enemy," whomever that might mean, at the close of most meetings. It was echoed as a regular feature as were the hail Stalins that provoked stormy applause. Hearing the cries and seeing them on signs were chilling in themselves inside Eastern Europe. To listen to it outside seemed like darkness unlimited.

In Trieste, contested by Tito, the West and the Russians, I heard the death call urged on a crowd. A chunky man, his gray thinning hair standing on his head in wisps, shouted the slogan. "Death to the enemy," he called hoarsely. "Death to the Anglo-Americans." The addition was for the benefit of the U.S.–British forces stationed in controversial Trieste until a settlement could be arranged. Tito wanted the lovely, decaying Adriatic port but the Italians wanted to keep it. In Trieste, a few minutes' drive to the Yugoslav border, the Russians saw a splendid spot for making Tito uncomfortable. Their chief agitator was Vittorio Vidali. He had been born just outside Trieste proper. His adult years had been spent in the service of the Comintern, where he got to know Tito. He was a dangerous and slick agent, who left behind in his travels a litter of corpses.

"Wherever I happen to be, they always say I'm organizing agents to kill some anti-Soviet personality," Vidali said matter-of-factly. We were sitting in a littered room of his office in a trade union building on the waterfront. The only framed photo in the room was Stalin's. Then, in his early fifties, about Tito's age, Vidali had a thumbless right hand and a massive chest. He spoke good English, as he did half-a-dozen other languages. In days gone by, Vidali did lots of travelling. Police of many countries swear that he helped organize the assassination of Leon Trotsky in Mexico and of Carlo Tresca on lower Fifth Avenue in New York. Tresca was an articulate anti-Communist writer of the Left.

Offering me a cigarette, Vidali asked how things were going in the States. I said he might have had a bird's-eye view himself. He had been there often illegally, the American police have claimed. "How could I get back into the U.S.?" Vidali asked me, grinning. "Your government deported me in 1928." He travelled extensively after that, first to Moscow where he met Tito. During the civil war in Spain, Tresca was called Commandante Carlos Contreras. Names didn't mean a thing, Vidali said loftily. He used at least ten in his time. I asked him how he, an old comrade of Tito's, could be so violent now?

"Many of us could see it coming," replied Vidali coldly. "When Tito was finally unmasked, we were prepared for his attacks against us. I know Tito and I know his methods. His regime must go. It cannot remain as a place from which an imperialist invasion can be launched against the Soviet Union."

Vidali tried frantically slipping agents into Yugoslavia after the break. The Russians made no secret of wanting to get rid of Tito violently. Reason for haste at the time was an inglorious end to the Greek civil war. Tito closed his borders with Greece against its use by Communist-Greek guerrillas. The savage war, sponsored by the Soviet Union, had an unbroken fastness of asylum when Albania, Yugoslavia and Bulgaria were used to regroup and supply Greek guerrillas under an ex-tobacco worker, Markos Vafiades.

One of Tito's ace organizers, Svetozar Vukmanovic-Tempo, rangy and saturnine, arranged for Communist forces to base on common Yugoslav-Greek border areas. He also arranged to close the bases down. The guerrillas, denied the vast and friendly retreat to Yugoslavia, were pinned down at the corners, in Albanian and Bulgar pockets. Gen. James Van Fleet told me that closing the Yugoslav border was really the crusher for the Communists. Tito's motives were by no means anti-guerrilla then. He calculated, as Yugoslav government people told me later, that it was the most practical solution of an agonizing decision. The Yugoslav regime could not afford to keep foreign Communist armed forces and political commissars loyal to Moscow in Yugoslavia. Most of them chose to follow their leaders eastward.

Unfortunate Greek children were never given a choice. They were pawns swept up in war, revolution and selfish power ambitions. I shall never forget Maria Kirdides, a young mother who was typical of many in her anguish. I met her in the Greek border village of Chionades, a few miles from Albania. On the doorstep of her crumbling farmhouse, Maria and her husband sat in numbed anguish. They gazed every free hour at the mountain barrier that separated them from the Soviet world. Somewhere across that frontier Maria's children were living in camps. Her two sons had been abducted by Communist rebels.

"The Communist *capitanos* came down from the mountains and marched them away," Maria said. "I have written out a petition and given it to the Red Cross. Do you think it will do any good?"

Maria Kirdides' children were two of nearly 30,000 Greek youngsters uprooted from their homes. They were sent to Communist Europe, of which Yugoslavia was still a throbbing part. In the last few years some have been repatriated. In their villages, they are looked on with suspicion, even hate. Today, they are men and women who grew up in foreign lands.

Watchtowers on Eastern European frontiers became common sights after the Yugoslavia break. The Russians even have miles of wire, towers and patrol dogs on their borders with countries in the Soviet bloc. Hungary went all the satellite regimes one better. Not only were watchtowers built to brood on the frontier with Austria, but strips of farmland were plowed and mines sown in them. To escape, a refugee had to be prepared to be blown up. The unfathomable factor in the Hungarian Communist preoccupation with isolating the country was that a would-be refugee for ten years had to get past Hungary through a zone still occupied by the Red Army in Austria.

Still refugees poured out into Western Europe. They hid in tank cars, held up airplanes in flight or drove locomotives past the border, smashing down frontier blocks and patrols. There also were some modest mass escapes. The biggest I have ever known was a gypsy encampment in Czechoslovakia. After the Communist coup, party busybodies in the provinces wanted to make a good showing in their districts to obtain recognition from Prague. In the Sudetenland, denuded of the German population, the party found a large gypsy camp. Officials were delighted. Here was an opportunity to bring their form of socialist enlightenment to underdeveloped nomads. The gypsies, suspicious of all-embracing authority and remembering their wartime experiences, were perplexed.

Led by a triumphant party troupe, they were settled in an abandoned village. The houses were in good, sound shape. A couple of agricultural experts provided farm implements, some livestock and plenty of advice. Pictures were snapped for party papers. The act was hailed as proof of what a get-ahead movement like the Communist could do. A few weeks later, the same activists were summoned from district headquarters. They found the gypsies still living contentedly in their wagons camped out in the fields. Not a cow had been milked because there were no more cows. The houses still had a dismal abandoned look to them. They were stripped of electrical fixtures, bathtubs, window glass and in some cases, the flooring.

Explanations were simple. The gypsies, told that the farms were theirs, helped themselves to everything they could carry. In the markets they sold their wares. The items they had were almost impossible to buy in shops. For barter or cash, the gypsies could get what they wanted. Afterwards, they could continue to live in the way that came most naturally to them. Nothing in Marx, Lenin or Stalin ever discussed what to do in such an emergency. The party talked things over. Gypsies were so backward, officials decided, that they should be given another opportunity. Off to another village the gypsies were guided. On them were showered fresh farm implements, livestock and houses. Additional pictures were taken and roseate stories written.

The gypsies changed their tactics. They went to market on market days. Instead of selling or bartering livestock, they slaughtered it themselves. Household installations they sold piecemeal. One day, a young man came back from market. He was very excited. A group of satisfied party people had just come to town, he explained. They'd be all coming out to the gypsies' village unannounced the next morning. Around a campfire, gypsy elders held their council. They decided to break camp immediately. What was left in the houses, they loaded in the wagons. They also crated what was left of the chickens and ducks. In the dead of night they headed southwards towards the Austrian border. They crossed the frontier, wagons, families and loot. I talked to them at length just outside Salzburg. How did they get across? A shrug for an answer. Borders were still simply waiting rooms for these people. The same was true for farms thrust upon people by plan. But the gypsies' exodus was by no means concluded. Communist agents approached them, trying to convince the gypsies to return. A few days' harangue bored the listeners and angered them. They tossed the agents into the river while boys were dispatched to call American military police.

Theirs was a fortunate and unfettered release. It was far more complex and deadly a few hours away down the road in Vienna. The ancient and beautiful city, like Berlin, was carved into four sectors. Britain, France, the U.S. and Russia ran their sections. Vienna, also like Berlin, was surrounded by Soviet-held territory. Unlike Berlin it was never partitioned. It quickly became a magnet for attracting refugees from Eastern Europe, for intrigue, sordid espionage, daylight abduction, illegal trade and murder. By car, Vienna was less than an hour's drive from Czechoslovakia and Hungary. The East-West conflict overflowed the banks of the Danube there. A war was going on between Russians and Americans which was not the cold diplomatic skirmishing the papers talked about.

In one week, Austrian policemen found nine bodies floating in the beautiful blue Danube. They weren't swimmers sucked under by the swirling current. These bodies were corpses before they ever hit the water. Two were recognized as Soviet agents. One was a Tito triggerman. The others were too disfigured to be identified. They were all victims of an undercover war as hot as bullets that drilled a man named Benno Blum. Alias Nikolai Borrisov, Bulgar smuggler and hijacker, Blum was shot while resisting U.S. Army counter-intelligence agents. There were lots of other casualties. More than 1,800 men, women and children had been abducted from Vienna by the time the freeze was solid in the cold war. At least 380 members of the U.S. intelligence network—mostly Austrian citizens—had been killed or kidnapped. The count was appalling. A score of unsolved murders, an untold number of American soldiers corrupted by rackets, girls, spies and the lure of easy money. In those grim days, the West and Soviet Europe decided to go into the street brawl of politics in Vienna.

It was Europe's busiest political underworld and remained so for years until neutrality and the withdrawal of armies brought in more respectable spies and intriguers. Back then, however, you'd enter plush clubs or seamy joints and see the "trade." There were secret agents of almost every nation, watching each other and the clientele. It was just like the movies without the proxy thrills. Stateless fugitives could be bought or bullied into intelligence work. Soviet repatriation teams, acting on informers' tips, would try to shanghai refugees. Once they went into the main headquarters area of the Americans, in Salzburg. Their informer, however, also passed the tip on to the Americans. The Russians, a group of five going to a car with their captive, were surprised. A gunfight in the streets opened. Three Russians were taken alive. They were returned to the Soviet command and disappeared. Their rescued quarry was sent to a more secure hideout.

The Russian took cold-blooded action against anyone they suspected of engaging in anti-Soviet or anti-Soviet bloc activity. They didn't believe that love could be apolitical. Apparently still do not. There was the case of beautiful and talented Margarethe Ottilinger. She was a top official in the Austrian Ministry of Economic Planning. She fell in love with a Soviet officer who did liaison work with her department. He deserted. Miss Ottilinger, entitled to immunity because of her position, was arrested summarily by the Russians. In reply to Austrian government protests, Col. Gen. Alexei Zheltov said Miss Ottilinger had been sentenced to twenty-five years by a Soviet court.

Zheltov was an important man. He was counsellor to Marshal Konev and later became political director of the whole Red Army. His work in Austria provided experience for setting up and meshing all facets of his work that dealt with East and West. Once in a while, Zheltov's plans were exposed to the world. It happened in the "Heigh-ho Silver" case. An Austrian was tabbed to be arrested as a Titoist agent. He used to ride a white horse through a big park. When plainclothes men went after him, the fingered victim rode his horse down the main street, screaming for help. He got it. He was luckier than a chauffeur who worked for the Russian Kommandatura. The Russians accused him of persuading a Red Army officer to go west. They took him under guard for interrogation. The chauffeur tried to escape by jumping out of a fourth-floor window in the heart of downtown Vienna. Broken and bleeding, he was dragged back into the building.

There were plenty of similar incidents in Berlin. But the mid-Twentieth Century battle for Germany took precedence over intrigue, espionage and Soviet Europe trying to look bold. The Russians deliberately partitioned Germany and sought to create their part into a country attached to the Soviet bloc. I often travelled into East Berlin and sometimes into East Germany. The Soviet zone, so inflammatory in East-West relations, is a vital link with Eastern Europe. I did not spend as much time there as I did elsewhere east of it. Rightly or wrongly, I felt that it was the only large zone in Europe deliberately truncated from its own countrymen. Poland was partitioned, but Poles could still rejoin the heartland of the mother country. Not so with East Germany, which while the Russians claim is part of their bloc, deserves completely separate treatment. The story of Germany has an identity of its own.

Yet there are scenes I witnessed in Berlin through the years and people to whom I talked who should be chronicled as far as possible within the context of this book. German Communists who were evident at the Brandenburg Gate in the last great battle of the European war, worked overtime detaching the east zone. When the split was formally announced, a Communist regime and apparatus slid smoothly into assigned jobs. They had already been installed there by the Red Army administration in East Germany. Many had entered the zone with the Russians. Their wartime training was in the Soviet Union. Along with hard-core Communists, the Russians assigned captured German soldiers. Men who had gone through special Soviet-run schools and pledged allegiance to the dogma of Communism returned to East Germany as Moscow-approved "Antifas," or "Anti-fascists."

Among them were fanatical former Nazis. They knew where to search for their own ex-Brownshirt comrades and recruit them to the New Order, post-1945. The shattered apparatus of the Hitler Jugend became a new youth organization, "Freie Deutche Jugend." A new German army, Communist this time, began drilling as "new soldiers for socialism." Special elite units wore old black uniforms of the Nazi SS, with the death's head insignia removed. Organization and planning for East Germany, now called the "Deutsche Democratische Republik" (German Democratic Republic) was in the hands of Walther Ulbricht, the first secretary of the East German party. Ulbricht, a cold-eyed zealot, also has a strange vanity—his resemblance to Russia's greatest revolutionary, Vladimir Ilyich Vlianov Lenin. Ulbricht's one passion has been to create a Germany in the image of the Soviet Union. He forced a shotgun wedding in the Soviet zone of the strong Socialist party with his Communist cadres to create a "Socialist Unity Party" (SED).

With his secret police, so normal for a Communist state, Ulbricht forced political opponents into exile or silence. Berlin was cut in two; one-half under Western occupation, the other under the Russians and Ulbricht was their chosen pro-consul. The Brandenburg Gate was the symbolic demarcation gateway to the West, if one fled, or to Soviet Germany, if one believed as fervently as Ulbricht does. Once his rump regime was set up as a challenge to the united three-quarters of West Berlin, Ulbricht wasted no time showing what he had organized in a few years. He launched his first mass challenge to the West in the form of half-a-million youngsters on parade. It was a Whitsun holiday and the demonstration would pass close enough to Western sectors of Berlin to be seen. The propaganda and pressure implicit in the organized march were sharply seen by the then American commandant, Maj. Gen. Maxwell D. Taylor. Although Taylor carried only two stars on his shoulders then, he carried the responsibility of a field marshal in the field and a president in politics.

"If they start a fight," Taylor told me then in his office, "we'll finish it. I don't think they'll try it. They'll try to scare us. Berliners don't scare. Neither will we or should we."

Berliners had been through a gruelling blockade, imposed unilaterally and capriciously by the Soviet Union. A Western airlift brought them the means to subsist and to keep them at work. The late Lord Mayor of West Berlin, Ernst Reuter, had steel-nerved confidence in his people, in East and West Berlin.

"The Communists will never get anywhere with Berliners," he used to say. "They can pretend to lead them and make a big fuss. In the end, the Berliners will make a fuss that will ruin the Communists. The same is true, more or less, with Germans all over East Germany."

Reuter showed contempt, not concern, for joint Soviet-Communist German threats and pressures. As long as the West stood behind the Berliners, Reuter said there was nothing to worry about. "Only when you begin to worry about the necessity of helping us is it really time to worry," observed Reuter. "I know." He had first-hand experience with the Soviet system and with Berlin. Reuter had been in an early Soviet government, which he left in disgust and disillusion. "I was working with population minorities," he recalled to me. "It didn't take me long to find out that the Soviet Russians didn't care a damn about people or what made them tick."

The Communist German regime faithfully reflected the attitude. Right on the American-Soviet sector border I remember watching Gerhard Eisler try to provoke a riot. After jumping bail in the U.S., where he was undercover chief of the Communist party, Eisler was welcomed into East Germany by his comrades. In no time, he became their chief voice of Hate-America. His ups-and-downs have been many since. In the early days of Communist zone government, he rode high and explosively.

The street-corner demonstration he held was supposed to send angry youths pouring over into the West sector. "To show your strength," Eisler urged. A thin group of young men straggled over. Nobody followed. Eisler looked bewilderedly at the crowd. They broke up and headed back into downtown East Berlin. The militants were chased back by helmeted West Berlin police. Eisler dashed into a waiting car as soon as the first intruders drifted back. Sitting beside Reuter on a sofa, with a couple of cans of coffee between us on a table, I described the scene later to Reuter. Wearily he swept back his scraggly strands of gray hair.

"The Communists are always hoping to conquer Berlin," he mused aloud. "They will never stop trying. Your people must keep that in mind. We can defend ourselves. We can fight the Communists. We know that if Berlin is lost, we are lost too. So is all Europe."

"We are not going to let the city fall into the hands of those people beyond the Brandenburg Gate," said General Taylor. "We are prudent men but we are not stupid or cowardly men."

That first big scare stunt Ulbricht launched against West Berlin fizzled badly. He dragooned East German youth into a mass demonstration, all right. Except for the slender cadres of shouting activists, East German youth marched out of step and kept their lips well glued.

"What we need is more training," was the way Communist youth leaders explained their fiasco. They started getting it through an illegal army Ulbricht and his Soviet sponsors developed. Long before anyone in the

West even thought of suggesting a West German army, Soviet Germany was systematically rearmed. It was not given the name of an army, not then, anyhow. Ulbricht called it "Bereitschaften," meaning "alert units." It was equipped from the beginning for aggressive warfare with tanks and artillery and staffed with veteran Nazi generals to make things efficient. Gen. Vincenz Mueller was chief of staff. On the Eastern front, he had issued personal orders that for every Wehrmacht soldier shot by partisans, fifty Russians would be executed. As a prisoner, an Anti-fa course changed his perspective. The same was true of men like Marshal Paulus, captured at Stalingrad.

The Bereitschaften was different from the Volkspolizei (People's Police). Paramilitary police were on hand all over East Germany as guardians of Communist authority. The Soviet German army began clandestinely before the Korean war to learn the grim business of waging war. It started with a first class of 50,000, strictly volunteers. They were vetted by political commissars before rifles were ever placed in their hands. Bonuses, special housing and rations were the recruiting calls. In East Germany, people openly referred to the army as the "Red Wehrmacht." At the beginning there were plenty of deserters.

"The only difference I could find between Nazi and Communist propaganda," a deserter told me after he had been turned loose by Western interrogators, "is the size of Hitler's and Stalin's mustaches."

Only a few years after the collapse of Hitler's war machine, a truck carrying heavily armed, uniformed Germans was captured deep inside the American sector of Berlin. They had lost their way. All of them went to jail. But Judge John A. Sabo called them scapegoats of a system whereby the Soviet Union went into the bootleg business of rearming Communist Germany. On the basis of the testimony of the wayward East German soldiers, the United States, Britain and France indicted Russia in a protest. The West accused the Soviet Union of creating then a 50,000-man army in flagrant violation of Four-Power agreements. Neither Ulbricht nor the Russians paid any attention to the exposure. They went right ahead training young soldiers who would one day take over from older ex-Nazis. Chief political director for the new army was General Wilhelm Zaisser. He was a brawny Prussian-officer type who became converted to Bolshevism in 1917 when he served on the Russian front. Zaisser, known also to the espionage trade as "General Gomez," the name he used as 13th Brigade commander in the Spanish

Civil War, was an old Comintern hand. His headquarters in Berlin's Soviet sector were right next door to the old MVD offices. Later on Zaisser and his wife were snicked off in one of Ulbricht's purges.

Some of Zaisser's war-time protégés didn't wait that long or so fatalistically. One was an authentic count and a direct descendant of Otto von Bismarck, the Iron Chancellor and unifier of Germany. Count Heinrich von Einsiedl, young and impressionable, was a great-grand-nephew of Bismarck. As a pilot he was shot down near Stalingrad. He became a crusading Communist and a leading light of the Soviet-organized Free Germany Committee. Von Einsiedl's name and background had German Communists and Russians in rapturous thought of how his influence could spread. He worked for some years with German officer prisoners and then was sent to Berlin. He beat the drums for Communization of Germany and for a new German army. "A People's Army, of course," he told me with a wry grin.

"Zaisser himself taught me political history," reminisced von Einsiedl. "He tried to treat me like a father or a kind uncle. He knew, naturally, that my name meant something in propaganda. I helped organize propaganda teams that went out to the front during the war to induce German soldiers to surrender."

On his round in Berlin, von Einsiedl said that he noticed his pep talks to young East Germans drew sour looks. He overheard conversations. "I was astounded to hear my own countrymen, boys at that, say that I was a scoundrel," von Einsiedl added. "I even caught some making faces at me or gestures that show a man to be either crazy or that he's lost his manhood. My ardor cooled when I started questioning various orders.

"Then I got into a big argument with Zaisser. He wanted action. Plans called for more militancy, he used to tell me. I said you could only go as far as people wanted to go. Zaisser looked at me queerly. Our arguments continued and I went very carefully over each set of orders, always bringing them back for discussion.

"It may sound very naïve. But I began to realize that the Russians wanted to build up an elite as fanatically devoted to them as ever the Nazis had built up. I wanted no part of that any more. I refused to lecture at the Bereitschaften schools. I knew enough not to walk out after resigning. I fled."

Flights like von Einsiedl's only whetted Ulbricht's appetite to build himself a show satellite Germany. He had some accomplished triggermen and women, veterans of the international apparatus, to try anything out for the cause. They applied terror and set arbitrary work quotas. But as West Germany, after a currency reform, began to boom, Communist Germany fell far behind.

"You can't believe what the jails are like," a student formerly at East Berlin's Humboldt University explained. "Filthy, little food and degradation all the time. You're worse than an animal."

His crime? Upholding the right, in a classroom, of workers to strike. In the East zone, Ulbricht had declared, there was no need for workers and peasants to strike. It was the old story. You'd be striking against yourself and, therefore, that was a crime. Right after the war, he made cooing coalition noises. Ulbricht had arrived in a Russian airplane, dressed in a colonel's uniform of the Soviet Army. In a baggy black suit, however, he presented himself at Berlin's City Hall some weeks later. He was, he said with a toothy smile, a politician.

"We Communists are of the opinion that it would be wrong to force a Soviet system on Germany," asserted Ulbricht publicly. "Germany will get a democratic regime, a parliamentary democratic regime with all rights and freedoms for the people."

He soon disproved his own words. Ulbricht's ruthless methods and his implacable devotion to the Soviet Union have made him an unloved man even among East European comrades. Polish Communists, including those who held sway in the years of the deep freeze, loathed Ulbricht. They delighted passing stories around about him. They didn't spare personal habits. He had a lumpy mistress, Lotte, another German Communist he knew from Moscow days. She was a sort of mate. Ulbricht never displayed emotion about her or any other human.

"Lotte," a Yugoslav Communist once said, "looks like the mattress with the stuffing sprung open. Ulbricht looks like the same mattress except that it sprouted a goatee and the seams stay closed."

As front men Ulbricht got for Premier a renegade Socialist, sallow and slow-moving Otto Grotewohl. The "grand old man" of the party was ancient Wilhelm Pieck, who has since died. He was the President of the East zone, and looked fat and fatherly. Whenever an official needed official welcoming to East Berlin, Pieck would waddle out to do the honors. On one occasion, the old man was in bed, wheezing with a bad case of asthma. It didn't matter. Ulbricht personally called on Pieck, saw that he got dressed and helped escort him to the airport for the ceremonies. Ulbricht started early to compete for recognition in Europe, and then in the young uncommitted nations of the world. West Germany reacted coldly. Any country, with the exception of the U.S.S.R., that recognized East Germany lost its relations with the Federal Republic in Bonn. Except for Tito, who thought he rated the same deal as Russia, no other country has yet dared defy the West German declaration. And Tito lost.

The recognition fight came much later in the build-up for Germany between the Eastern regime and the Bonn government. But Ulbricht had a premonitory feeling about it years before. "We are as equal as the revenge-seeking Bonn regime, and more equal," he told a cheering meeting of the Volkskammer (Peoples' Chamber) that passed for a parliament in Communist Germany. About one-third of the members once held Nazi party cards. Ulbricht campaigned for national and international equality, upheld only by the Soviet Union. The satellites went along, approving unanimously. But officials in other countries under the Moscow thumb almost invariably had snide cracks to make about Ulbricht, however.

"He'll never be considered an equal with us," a disapproving Polish party official told me in a street café.

Chancellor Konrad Adenauer was the regular target of Communist Europe's attacks. But examine, if you will, all the declarations of support for Ulbricht and it is rare, indeed, to find any reference of personal sympathy for the man. For a while, he tried hard to be a folksy, man of the people. Fed up with party demands and strictures, Ulbricht became the regular butt of jokes instead. "He looks like a pancake strolling," was a favorite. Ulbricht retreated to his iron-guarded office. The comic was again the relentless commissar. West Berlin was a particular annoyance for him. Booming West German prosperity filtered through to West Berlin. The Federal government and the allies did all they could to show the marked difference between the two Berlins. Going from West to East Berlin was like passing a throbbing, gaudily decorated metropolis into pitch darkness at night.

In shattered East Berlin, which Communist Germany claims as her capital, no full-scale attempt has ever been made to put the blasted areas in a state of decent repair. Some streets, done in the ornate Stalin Gothic, were laid out amidst the debris. The whole enclave was appropriately called Stalin Allee. Only "worthwhile" citizens were housed in the apartments there. Average East Berliners live in dank and generally substandard housing. They haven't been given much to which they can even look forward. "If you live like an animal, maybe then one day the party can control you as animals are controlled," said a professor from Dresden when he got to Berlin. "Germans can be misled, abused, intrigued and excited. But when they get stubborn, something will break. I don't want to be there for that. The big party people don't or won't realize it. They live off the people's backs, anyway. How would they know about the people?"

Another big gulf that separated ruling Communists from the people they claimed as their own was the vast difference in standards of living. A new class, as Djilas subsequently so bitingly described the entrenched Communist power elite, was living it up in a style to which it had never been accustomed. Poverty, so standardized and planned for the masses, was deliberately eschewed by the aristocracy that tried to tell fellow-citizens how to work and live. East Germans had, if they were of rank, guarded villas. Official cars buzzed around and ferried children of the powerful. Money was never an object. Worthless outside the Soviet bloc, it was hard enough for a worker to earn. Party officials carried around gamblers' bankrolls.

Where a family lived was, still is, a rundown room. They ate and cooked in the same room unless the Soviet system of communal kitchens had been installed. Regimes preached how lucky the people were. They had socialized medicine and free vacations. Try a hospital or clinic sometime yourself in Eastern Europe. Not as a foreigner demanding emergency attention. Walk in with the crowd. Sure, you get free medical advice if you can wait your turn long enough. You pay for medicine, though, which can be very expensive for a working man or someone on a state pension. If you get tired of waiting, you see a doctor privately. Somehow, people always scrape up enough to see a doctor outside clinic hours. Free medical attention at home is only acquired in the biggest emergencies.

This is no welfare state system as you might find in Scandinavia or Britain. Doctors, driven to the wall by being underpaid and overworked, often try to do two jobs. "I'm also supposed to go to party meetings," a physician in Warsaw told me. "But if I fix up a party personality, I can manage to escape some meetings." The average patient is less lucky. About half his pay is docked for his board and treatment at the hospital. That hardly helps his family. None of these rules apply to the class elite.

Technicians of a high grade, artists, writers and top officials get special treatment. When necessary, they also enter special hospitals. They receive no bills. If the case is difficult and the patient is important enough, a physician from the West is brought to town. All expenses and fees are paid.

Visiting a convalescent ulcer case once in a Warsaw hospital, I asked the patient what happens to a machine-shop worker in the same health boat. The patient was a real wheel in the regime. He had an important job, a car of his own as well as an office auto, a five-room apartment and access to foreign currency. When he didn't answer me, I repeated the question. "For a sick man," he replied morosely, "that isn't the kind of subject I want to discuss. How the hell do I know what the machinist does and what hospital he attends? Who is more important, he or I?"

CHAPTER 9

In applying doctrine and plan, Communists quickly built up a have and have-not society in Eastern Europe. As the teacher, judge and confessor, the party lost touch with the masses so revered in regime speeches. The party apparatus became inviolable, except for party inquisitions. For seven lean years, from 1948 to 1955, party official-dom divorced itself from thought, hope and misery that were the daily rules of life and living. Hatred of officialdom spiralled like weeds in an untended garden when party higher-ups began to live in the lap of luxury; luxury by most standards and out of a Thousand and One Nights for the occupied populations.

In Hungary there were even special schools where the younger set of the party elite could learn what passed for good etiquette in Western society. There was an elderly lady I knew, who had been a life-long seamstress. She sewed for the rich from before World War I to mid-

World War II. All she had were strong fingers, growing arthritic, and a sense of style. But she also had a shrewd insight into people.

"I have made some dresses for important party ladies," she recounted to me over a glass of strong tea one evening. We were in her tiny flat, one room spotlessly clean but jammed with dressmaking figures. She was unafraid to receive a foreigner. She was past seventy and she wanted to hear how her daughter was doing in Paris. She was a seamstress, also.

"I don't think my Julishcka puts her hands on as fine materials as the ladies who have me fit them," continued the old lady, smiling. "Do you know what I handled today? Velvets and some silks. The best. From France and from Italy. Look what I wear."

She was dressed in a suit, dyed black, that had been made out of blanket material. If they had a contact, most people in Communist Europe wore such suits. That was for good wear. My old acquaintance said she could lay her hands on some squares of silk or velvet. "That's my tip," she explained. The women she served were very exacting in what they gave her as little presents. Only the remnants that they thought could not be used for some other purpose.

"When I get some goods," said the old lady, "I trade them. I can get tea like this, sometimes good coffee and a little meat from time to time. But you ought to see the looks of people when they see these important ladies in their new dresses." The seamstress shuddered.

Shuddering or quivering were not exclusively reserved for reactions of displeasure or sheer hatred. Any time of the year, early in the morning, you can see shivering lines waiting the turn in the shops. Queuing up for food, for milk, for clothes, or for a picture frame is part of the regimented life. When you finally get into a shop there is no guaranty that you can buy the meat you want or the coat on which you had your eyes. The queuing process, I have been told, started with wartime shortages. In Communist Europe it became a regularized system. There was too little to sell to too many. It hasn't changed much in the intervening years.

Many times I have stood in line with other would-be buyers. We'd stand in front of a supermarket, Communist-style. Smoked meat hung on hooks in one department, dried fish in another section, canned goods at a far end, all without easy access. The reason is simple. After each purchase, you pay the cashier and bring back your receipt. Sometimes, you can avoid returning to pay by paying first. You have to be pretty accurate on the size of your purchase.

"It doesn't really pay to do it that way," Polish housewives said grumpily. "Suppose, you have some extra money and you see something on sale suddenly. A piece of ham or some butter. You grab it and go back to pay for it."

Simple shopping often took hours. The women also had to get to work. To make ends meet in a family, women learned fast that they required salaries to make a household operate. The youngest children were sent to state-run kindergartens. Parents disapproved of them because children were exposed at tender and sensitive ages to Communist curricula. They saw in the kindergarten indoctrinations the first concentrated attempt to break through the family unit. In Eastern Europe, family life always has been a treasured thing. Even today, I hear aged mothers call their highly-placed sons in front of other people, "my son," or the equivalent of plain, "sonny." Young parents in lesser roles of Communist society tried carefully to disabuse their children of notions they picked up in kindergarten to be further exploited in elementary schools. They had to be very careful the way they did their home education with the young.

"A five or six-year-old might blurt out in kindergarten what his parents told him," a shoemaker explained cautiously in Bucharest. "You say just enough to give a child the idea that something else can be more important. Not enough to get you in trouble if he tells it. But enough to make him think a little extra."

Few children really ever wilfully and deliberately exposed their parents. Those who did, usually first at school and subsequently before party authorities, were promptly ostracized by their schoolmates. A boy whose father was an ordinary laborer in Warsaw described to me what happened in school to a classmate who turned informer on his parents. Maybe the informer wanted to be something like a teacher's pet. The reasons didn't matter. The parents, protecting their own son, agreed to all charges he made against them. They were sent to prison. The boy was placed in state charge as an only child.

"From the day he said his parents were bad because they talked against the state all of us in school stopped talking to him," his school comrade related. The boy doing the talking was a scrawny kid, like so many in postwar Warsaw. But his eyes, big and brown, were alive with intensity and young anger.

"We just would not have anything to do with him," he said. "When we played, he would be left out. He was bad, bad, bad."

The target complained apparently to school authorities. Other children were warned they were taking an unsocialistic attitude to the pariah. They were threatened with bad marks and even expulsion. Warnings left the class unmoved. A whole class of eleven-year-olds, after all, couldn't be expelled. In this case, the offending child was sent off to another town. Some others turned out differently after their comrades staged a strike of silence and no-contact with them. They recanted their own accusations.

"Children are often more courageous than adults," an ex-Polish woman Communist, a mother herself, remarked rather sadly. "They don't quibble on issues. They take the lead."

Feeding and caring for children was almost entirely in the parents' hands, though. Milk, when it could be bought, meant standing in long lines at the risk of losing other shopping. It was almost impossible to buy milk and meat by standing patiently on the same line. Buying a place in line from racketeers who saw a good profitable thing has long been part of the scene in a classless society. Sometimes the police break up the racket. Usually it comes back into vogue quite quickly. Rackets in a have-not society grow fast. If you want to buy a movie or theater ticket, chances are you'll buy it from a recognized scalper. He is recognized by the buyer, not by the regime, of course. Otherwise, you don't go to the movies. The same practice was started for stealing goods and commodities from state enterprises.

Pilferage is about the biggest form of private enterprise in any Communist-ruled country. On many occasions, I have watched government trucks back up to a loading site at a factory. The merchandise is checked off by assigned people. It is very business-like, much more efficient usually than the checking system in the factory. After loading, the trucks go to their destination. How do you know these are illegal deliveries? First, there are watchers who stand vigil. Also, you are usually told in advance by some friend that the goods are coming out "black." Then, you follow the truck and see the goods deposited either at someone's home or cellar. The next day, people in the know come around to buy. They can't get it elsewhere. Shops are bare. Distribution is uncertain. When a load of coats, for example, comes into a state store, the manager already has passed the word among friends. He will say to the public customers that he has only half or a quarter of the promised delivery. It's true to a point. He promised the rest in advance. He gets something, he pays the store staff a bonus for keeping quiet and the buyer gets what he desperately wants. It is a practice carried to virulent forms in Eastern Europe. By local standards, people can get rich quick by stealing from the state. They also equate it with a certain pride of patriotism; they are defeating regime production quotas and ruining all statistics. Many of the more affluent men involved are themselves responsible for cooking the books. That way their enterprise looks good in the central office of statistics, they wax richer and almost nobody cares if the state is defrauded regularly. There is police protection and party protection up and down the whole assembly belt of pilferage. The network sometimes begins to strangle the whole process of production and distribution. Then, the regime makes more plans and declarations.

They issue denunciations of theft. Penalties are invoked and the first victims are usually the former shopkeepers kept on as employes in their old stores. They are, before trial, guilty in the eyes of the regime as bourgeois holdovers. But no improvement results from these object lessons. Only then does the party move against its own. It uncovers huge fraud and mismanagement. Members are jailed. Some are executed. Severe penalties reduce thefts but do not stop them. The profits are too great and there is no social stigma attached. In Bucharest, a Foreign Office official went through a long explanation of how profiteers were uncovered and sent to jail. "We'll begin to have some socialist legality here now," he said emphatically. We left his office to go to another. The car which had called at my hotel disappeared.

"That damned fellow," my escort said of the driver. "He's probably picking up fares in town." He hailed a cruising car, which belonged to the Ministry of Agriculture. When we got out at our next stop, my escort paid off the driver. Not another word about legality.

It was a system that quickly corrupted the young. Hanging around the fringes of the rackets, running errands and picking up side money, was enormously attractive. It also led to heavy drinking by juveniles, particularly in Poland, Hungary and East Germany. Juvenile delinquency, as I have seen it in Eastern Europe, is a bigger problem than in the United States. The regime generally pretends it does not exist. When they do round up delinquents, the authorities say "Western influences" on the youngsters were responsible for the crimes.

But building "socialism" was supposed to turn children away from the pernicious impact of the West. Stealing from the state was not a Western innovation, like blue jeans and jazz. The creation of Communist regimes, promising heaven on earth for the new generation, produced the thieves, unbelievers and free-enterprise profiteers. What was good for the party brass, youngsters quickly decided, was good enough for them. They could not come by it legally. Who could? So they stole. Their own people scarcely blamed them for it. Nearly everyone was in on an illegal act at least once a week.

Courting and making love in the traditional style was also not for a progressive-minded "Peoples' Democracy." A girl met a boy in a factory. They were supposed to send off sparks to each other as they revelled in the glories of making a machine. To show their devotion, the boy and girl tacked up on the bulletin board their own accomplishments. I recall a notice in a factory in the Hungarian town of Gyor. It said romance had spurred Erzebet and her fiancé, Sandor, to double their production. "Let us all rejoice in their romance," was the written comment the factory manager had added.

Love in Soviet Europe started by having built-in hurdles to conquer and they get more difficult as time goes by. It does happen that foreigners, usually men, fall in love with a local girl. Invariably, she wants to go away with him, after marriage. The regime steps in, saying no; that no nice "socialist" girl can be escorted down the "capitalist" garden path. She is almost always forbidden to leave or even to marry the foreigner. An English student pressed me into impromptu service in Bulgaria as a best man. The girl, quite excited, was very willing. We went to the city hall in Sofia. One official passed us along to another. The answer was no. The young couple couldn't even get a license, let alone a passport for her exit. It was a romance with a tragic ending. The student was refused a visa extension. He was forced to leave. Immediately thereafter, the girl was arrested. How dare she, police asked, want to marry an Englishman? She was obviously a secret enemy of the state. Being young, she would learn her lesson. Released, the girl threw herself under a train.

Jazz was the music young people liked to hear and in Soviet Europe it got its start by being prohibited. Communist Party hacks, who censored what people read or heard, ruled out jazz. It was an American export, to begin with, and was cruelly caricatured as violent, vicious and maybe even an opiate of the young masses. Making jazz illegal guaranteed its popularity in the satellite states. The U.S. Armed Services programs from Germany that featured jazz had an avid audience. So did the "Voice of

America" with its "Music, U.S.A." Willis Conover, who directs the musical feature, is probably next to the American President the best known contemporary American name. Jazz has, in the last few years, been accorded grudging acceptance by the Communist regimes. Under Stalin's forced cultural feeding for the new generations, jazz was strictly taboo. Yet it expanded and flourished and the commissars could do little to stop the trend.

Youngsters listened to programs in groups. They learned songs by heart and those with the best knowledge of English wrote down the lyrics. Popular tunes were recorded on X-ray plates. Jazz clubs played to entranced audiences at secret jam sessions. In Cracow, the charming medieval city in southern Poland, a students' jazz club was broken up by the police. They made too much noise and got caught. At school, the musicians reformed and passed the word around. For several years afterwards, they played every Saturday night in ghoulish surroundings. They had their session in the city mortuary on the outskirts of town. Nobody ever went there on a Saturday night. The saxophonist's uncle was the caretaker. He stood watch outside and the students didn't mind the surroundings. They were that eager to have a place for jazz.

Bootlegging any idea or item was legitimate, however, if the Communist planners thought it would enhance their positions. They launched a big business venture that soon ran to a turnover of at least $250,000,000 a year. It dealt only with materials the U.S. banned for export sale into the Soviet bloc. To Budapest went ball-bearings, to Prague copper, to Warsaw machine tools, to Bucharest prohibited dies. The man behind the mammoth smuggling business was Anastas Mikoyan. He established it with offices in a district then occupied by the Russians in Vienna. It had an innocent-sounding name, The International Trading Corporation or "Intrac" for short.

Almost all of Intrac's agents were from Soviet Europe. They all spoke three or four languages, had wads of loose cash with which to entertain or bribe. On the side, the business agents also trafficked in human consignments when necessary.

Mikoyan demanded the most experienced and reliable men Soviet Europe could supply to handle bills of lading. These were men who knew how to make profitable cash advances and to protect, as long as it was convenient, the source of supply. Sometimes, the involved deals had a tragicomic conclusion.

On one occasion Intrac wanted some specially tempered steel that was in short supply. Its contact men although thinking hungrily of a huge profit, demurred. The order, they said, could be too easily detected. A devious system was worked out by a Polish agent (who later exposed the program) and approved directly by Mikoyan. A group of import licensees wanted Hungarian salami, a great delicacy and good for a quick and profitable turnover. A trade freeze with Budapest made the coveted sausage unobtainable. In stepped the agent, who also sweetened the bargain with a few tons of honey. Out went the salami to the persons holding the licenses. They in turn bought the steel and immediately transshipped it to Budapest.

Western experts were put on Intrac's trail. They fought, some still do, firms that dealt under the table from the banned goods' lists. Probably the most blazing fights and cloak-and-dagger competition brought Yugoslav commercial agents up against Mikoyan's troubleshooters. In those days, anything denied to the Yugoslavs was something for the Russians to gloat about openly. Whenever, by fair means or foul, the Yugoslavs could put one over on the Russians, they celebrated.

They tangled all over Europe, in business offices, with recrimination, and in darkened streets, by old Chicago hijacking methods. Soviet bloc agents had to keep their eyes and ears sharply attuned to all rumors and reports of where Yugoslavs were trying to do business. It was part of the economic warfare campaign against Tito. A Yugoslav agent, about to sign with an Italian business man in then "neutral" Vienna, was stopped when the hotel door burst open and three men bolted in before the startled Italian. One of the intruders reached out and calmly took the contract. He tore it to shreds. The Yugoslavs, glowering, didn't move. The other two intruders held pistols on him.

But the business man was mollified. He was offered a deal to do future business with the Soviet European agency. "It was the first time I was convinced to shift business at the point of a gun," he told me years later. "Still, the others were correct. They paid more for the same thing."

It wasn't by all means debit for Tito's rough-tough outside men. When East Europeans gave them the horse laugh by buying a badly needed shipment of tools under Yugoslav noses, retaliation came fast. Trucks and even freight cars were switched to Yugoslav destinations. Sometimes they were baldly hijacked, occasionally a big bribe did the trick. To Tito's agents economic warfare meant just plain warfare for survival.

Yugoslavia, at bay, was already committed to a fight to the end with the entire Soviet bloc. In those days, Hoxha, Albania's first secretary, and the number two man, Shehu, should have been utterly grateful to Tito. Instead, they hated him with a fierceness that more than matched the Kremlin's. Yugoslavs had trained Albanians in partisan warfare in the good old days. But now Yugoslavia spoke disparagingly of the courage of Hoxha and bitterly of the cruelty of Shehu.

"Hoxha used to tremble at the sound of a rifle," a veteran Yugoslav described his own former protégé. "Shehu just likes to kill. He is mad that way."

Just as violent was an Albanian named Koci Xoxe, who had been a special pet of the Yugoslavs. He ran the state security.

"We are opposed to mercy," declared Xoxe, opening Albania's first big trials. "We want blood."

That was about the only point on which Hoxha and Shehu agreed with Xoxe. Once Tito was cast out of the Soviet family circle, Xoxe's comradely enemies got their revenge. He was tried as a Titoist and executed. So were innumerable other Albanians, whether Communist or not.

In poor and mountainous Albania, terror became operative law. The country was geographically isolated from the Soviet Union. Only an occasional Russian plane could keep contact. But Soviet technicians were ferried into Albania by sea, through the Dardanelles, to keep the regime's back stiff and to refurbish the old German submarine pens. The bases, facing the Adriatic, were the Soviet answers to the U.S. Sixth Fleet.

Revanchism, which the Soviet bloc labels most things the West German government does, has always been smeared on Tito by Albania. His Albanian minority in the wild and lovely Kosmet area, flanking Albania's north, is almost as large as the whole Albanian population Hoxha and Shehu rule with an iron fist. For a Westerner, getting to Albania is almost impossible. Today, the same is true for a Russian now that the Hoxha-Shehu combine prefer Chinese Communist militant dogma to the Khrushchev "salami" technique.

The mountains permitted a large degree of loose exit and entry into each country. They could not be sealed off nor properly patrolled at every pass. Albanian agents slipped into Yugoslavia and tried to interest the minority in sabotage against Tito. Yugoslav agents tried to stir up Albanians in Albania. In the border areas, people still carried their own weapons, worshipped in a Moslem manner, and held the blood feud dear to their families. Communism was an ideology that just whipped up passions wilder than they had been before. In a Yugoslav border town I listened to Captain Lukai Deva, a young Albanian company commander who had defected. He had grown ill of sending in execution parties to keep mountain villages in a state of abject fright. The one that sent him over the hill was in the dilapidated town of Mirdita. Captain Deva could not find that extra spark of inhumanity in him that day to shoot. He was arrested. His judge was Shehu, gaunt and savage as he strode before Deva, flicking him with a pistol muzzle across the face.

"We will destroy your kind," Deva quoted the enraged Shehu shouting at him. "Your execution will be a lesson to cowards who think like you."

Out went Shehu on another foray. Deva was spared because his prison guards, listening fearfully to him, agreed to try to escape. They got away. If you know the mountains as most Albanians do, the trek into even a Yugoslav sanctuary isn't extremely difficult. Why, I once asked some French and Italian diplomats who are the only Westerners there, don't all Albanians try to flee? They are simple and rather stalwart people, I was told. The vast majority tend flocks in the mountains and prefer to stay—die, if necessary—where they feel at home. Today, their Vermont-sized country couldn't be more walled off from the outside world if it were in the Gobi Desert.

A quick review of Albania's real estate shows, though, why the wretched little nation is so important. It commands the forty-six-mile-wide Strait of Otranto. Mining the strait would seal off the Adriatic. Through centuries, occupation of Albania represented fulfillment of his-torical aims of varying foreign powers. The czars of Russia dreamed about it, so did Turks as well as the French and British. A late-starter in the imperial stakes has been Mao Tse-tung of Red China. In Tirana, the ramshackle Albanian capital, French and Italian diplomats are virtually blindfolded. They are the only missions remaining; the U.S. pulled out in 1946. The Italian and French can hardly stir outside town without per-mission. Shehu's security police openly follow them even when they go shopping. A big deal for a Westerner is to take a weekend, Albanian security willing, and live it up in Titograd. This is a renamed Montene-grin town hard by the Albanian frontier.

The Yugoslavs, less exacting in their back-to-the-wall fight against Soviet hegemony, had to exist in Albania by maintaining a silent war. Yugoslav diplomats were publicly humiliated, denounced, beaten up and expelled. Tito, whose picture had come down well before the break, was reviled in terms that even his Soviet bloc enemies hadn't thought about. One charming Albanian description of Tito was "an abortion conceived in a sheep by an ass." The horror of the regime even appalled more sophisticated comrades from the bloc. A Polish journalist, returned from a tour of Albania, said he really wanted to forget the experience. Pressed, he agreed reluctantly to present a brief picture. Uncomradely, it was, too. "It's not a country," he concluded. "The poor place is a bloody abbatoir."

The name of the security force is imposing enough: Divizion i Mbrojitjes se Popullit, or Division for the Protection of the People. The abbreviation, known to all Albanians of more than infant age, is DMP. Attached to the security units are tribunals. They are empowered to try and execute citizens on the spot. Keeping terrified a total national population about equal to that of the Bronx, however, has always made the tribunals highly mobile. Inadequate deliveries of meat and grain are usually a signal for DMP teams to turn up and mete out justice. In northern Albania in the town of Ibale on a spanking spring morning, DMP squads roared into the square. Shehu, who resembles closely a Hollywood version of a Balkan assassin, stepped out of a command car. The local party authorities already had violators lined up in the square. The townspeople, under guard, were also spectators at the scene. Shehu addressed the little crowd. Shehu, pointing at the unfortunate victims, denounced them as scum and jackals.

Then, he whipped out a pistol. He shot one man in the head and emptied his pistol indiscriminately into the other prisoners. Without another look, he ordered the security to finish the job. Eight were hanged from trees. Before he left the town, Shehu warned that he might turn up in civilian clothes, in uniform or in disguise. He would be all-seeing, he warned, and nobody could ever escape his "justice." The source for the grisly episode is the Albanian party which circulated the description in an appeal for added vigilance and increased production in the country.

Attacked by the Yugoslavs for uncivilized conduct, Hoxha ordered Tito's remaining diplomats out of Albania. All the other satellites maintained some form of diplomatic relationship as on-the-spot eyes and ears. The Albanian party felt it had to go the bloc one better. After which Hoxha and Shehu rushed to Moscow to be received by Stalin. They had a shopping list which they pleaded had to be met by Soviet generosity.

When the party one-two punch returned to Tirana, there was no mention of the help Albania required. Hoxha held up two eucalyptus seedlings in pots for onlookers to admire. They were, he announced importantly, the personal gifts of Stalin. The stricken nation, the most backward in all Europe for centuries, has not changed much since the death of Stalin. It writhes in the grip of an administration almost unparalleled in cruelty in modern times. Its rule by sheer terror may well account today for the regime's support of Communist China.

CHAPTER | 10

THE satellite states were taking a leaf from the practice in Russia. Prominent, usually old-time Communists, were under constant examination by purge doctors. The patients invariably died of the treatment. Their mass liquidation was accompanied by waves of arrests.

The gulf between the have-nots—the ordinary citizens—and the party aristocrats grew wider daily. Soviet plans for industry and agriculture, complete with built-in mistakes recognized years before in Moscow, were ruthlessly applied. Satellite rulers deliberately compelled their own people to endure the hardships caused by mismanagement in the U.S.S.R. If a plan called for setting up a steel plant, up went the factory, even if there was no coking coal. This happened in Hungary. The coking coal was finally bought at great cost. Standards of living fell more sharply. Grumbling was forbidden by authority. It led to seizing opportunities of desperation to escape. Sadder in some cases was the suspicion cast by neighbor upon neighbor.

Some people, thinking it might help them, informed. There were even instances when children taunted others because they imitated their elders into seeing who talked loudest in praise of the regime. Little Mila Broz was a victim of the schoolboy game. On a winter afternoon when the snow lay thick on the evergreens in the hills above Racice, 100 miles northwest of Prague, nine-year-old Mila came home from the village school in tears. His forehead was gashed and bleeding. That was not the reason he cried. Mila was at an age when most American boys want to be either cowboys or space cadets. Mila had an ambition, too. He wanted to be a Russian guerrilla because the Russians were "brave and courageous." He wanted to fight against the Americans because they were "cowardly and capitalistic." Strange things are taught in Communist schools.

But at school that winter day, Mila's schoolmates made him an American in their game of guerrilla warfare. There were no special rules for the game. Youngsters did not take a toy gun, point it, cluck the tongue like a pistol shot and say, "You're dead," as in the American game of cowboys and Indians. The "Russians" just picked up rocks and threw them at the "Americans," then took "prisoners" of the faint or the "wounded." Mila had been hit by a rock the size of a baseball. After the game was over, he left the battlefield and returned home, where his father was busy mending shoes. Ladislav Broz, a thin, wiry man of middle age with friendly blue eyes and a great shock of curly hair, looked up from his cobbler's bench. He went to the kitchen sink. Taking a towel, the father drew his boy close to him and wiped the blood from his forehead.

"They made me an American," the child sobbed. "The Americans are cowards and that is why I was hurt because I was a coward."

The father remained silent. He knew all about the game. Czech children had been urged to play it ever since the Communists seized power. In class, children were taught that the Russians were the bravest people in the world and that the Americans were cowards and bullies. It seemed natural, under high-power circumstances like that, for a boy of nine to want to be a Russian.

"But it isn't really true about the Americans," the father finally said, "It isn't true at all."

Ladislav Broz had to be both father and mother to his son. His wife had died when Mila was just beginning to walk. As he dabbed at his boy's forehead, Ladislav went on gently: "Son, you were too small to remember the Americans. They were once here in Czechoslovakia. They were kind and friendly. When we had very little, they helped us. They are not cowards or bullies. Most people are not. Governments, maybe; not most people. It's hard for you to understand."

"It must be true," Mila rejoined. "They told us so in school. It must be true. What do you know about it?"

Ladislav Broz remembered how life had been before the Communists came. It was worth thinking about some more, he decided. As the weeks stretched into an early spring and thaw melted snow in the hills, Ladislav Broz scrimped and saved for a present for his boy. It was a present that the father hoped could have a profound influence on Mila's life. The gift was part of the father's plan to counter regime teaching with another, and more logical, voice of authority. Before supper one evening Ladislav gave his gift to his son. It was a small crystal set with earphones. Not much to look at but Mila swelled with pride. He was the only boy in Racice with a radio of his own even if it was a crystal set. Ladislav soon showed his son how to pick up programs from faraway places. He got the Czech language programs from the British Broadcasting Company, London, and the Voice of America relayed from New York. He spent hours at the earphones. His father bought him a second-hand clarinet on which Mila picked out new songs he heard on the frowned-on foreign broadcasts. From news and feature programs, over which he puzzled, Mila heard other things about the Russians and what they were doing to people. Gradually, Mila drifted away from the circle of the guerrilla game.

In school, Mila began to see and to tell his father how expert the teachers were in making good Communists rather than good students. Valesova gave good grades, he noted, to boys and girls proficient in Russian and party doctrine and inferior grades to others. Then Valesova organized a group of pioneers. Members were given chocolate and favored treatment and promised summer holidays in a camp. Mila and his friend, Jindra, did not join. Their reports suffered for it. But they had organized Doubting Thomases among the children against Juri and his favored group. When the young and impressionable pioneers carried tales about other children, Mila and Jindra caught them outside school and beat them up. Word got to Valesova. She called in Ladislav Broz and, eyes blazing with anger, she said the boy could only have learned such bad ways at home. It had to be corrected, she warned, and dismissed the father.

Ladislav went home, walking in deep thought. He decided by the time he reached his little cottage that the time had come for the final part of the plan to escape to the West. He took Irene and Mila into his confidence. Together, they prepared for flight. On a bright and brisk April day, Mila went to see his friend Jindra, for the last time. He gave Jindra his marbles, the broken skis, his clarinet and his most prized possession, the crystal set. Jindra could give them back, said Mila, when the Broz family returned from seeing relatives in Prague. It was for safekeeping that he gave them to Jindra, said Mila. The same night Ladislav Broz and his two children set out on foot toward the German border. They took with them only the clothes on their backs and what they could carry in three knapsacks. The promised land was West Germany and Ladislav Broz thought how ironic the little family's predicament was. They had never cared for any kind of German but this was a real emergency.

Averaging a little more than ten miles a day, they walked 160 miles across Czechoslovakia. Generally travelling after dark, the family slept during daylight in woods or barns. They ate sparingly of bread and sausage. A couple of times they stole eggs and a few hens. Only at the West German border were they in any real danger, but they took care and had lots of luck. Roving Communist border patrols with dogs picked up their trail in a fringe of woods along a stream at the border. The soldiers, however, couldn't see the Broz family. Ladislav, Mila and Irene slipped across the frontier under cover of the noise made by the guards crashing through the underbrush. The next day I spoke to them. A child like Mila had a special insight into life. The boy who hoped so desperately to become a Russian on a snowy day wanted in the spring to become an engineer—British, French or American. It didn't matter, so long as it was in the West. Radio engineering, he said, might attract him most. He already knew, he observed gravely, about crystal sets.

There was no need, however, to tune in secretly on any kind of set when the news that Stalin had died in 1953 was disseminated grimly from Moscow. At once, Soviet Europe presented in the ruling apparatus a dumfounded stance. Everything that had gone before, the coups and the plots, were all carried out in Stalin's name for him and the perversity called "people's democracy," which was not democratic nor concerned with the people. The proconsuls of the bloc, who catapulted into power with active Soviet support fell back on the only contingency plan they could understand. Arrests were stepped up, repression of mounting protests were rudely stifled.

Plans were carried out in Stalin's name as if he were still alive, inexorably, inefficiently, and above all, inhumanly. So sweetly ingrained had Stalin's name become to the satellite regimes that political prisoners were not even permitted to ask why there were demonstrations spontaneously called for set hours in the streets outside their jails. "We didn't know at first what all the fuss was," a Rumanian journalist friend of mine who spent years in prison, told me after his release. "By peeking out of a cell fronting on the street, while others hid us from the turnkeys, we could read signs. Then, we knew. For us, Stalin dead or alive, didn't make any difference."

But the regimes became panic-stricken. They were all exhorted from Moscow to remain loyal, unchanged, and absolutely firm at home. They followed the script by putting still more pressure on their people. One outcome, as the world knows from eyewitness reports, was the revolt of the subjugated people of East Berlin. Horrified, the world that likes to call itself free watched Soviet tanks mow down German workers who went on strike. The new Eisenhower administration in America watched and was horrified, too, but it had promised self-determination in the nature of a slogan described as "rollback." The revolt in East Berlin soon showed up the pious, do-nothing intentions of rollbackers. Days before the monumental drama unfolded in East Berlin, the beginning of revolution against Soviet tyranny exploded in Czechoslovakia.

Never before had such a thing happened in Soviet Europe. Outraged Czech workers rioted through the streets and in factories of Pilsen. They hoisted the Stars and Stripes in a dozen places. Shouting, "United States come back!" crowds trampled on pictures of Stalin and Gottwald. Bouquets were placed ceremoniously at the roads, where in 1945, Gen. George Patton's victorious armor crunched. Angry, embittered Czechs, so highly regarded as trustworthy by Soviet and Communist theoreticians, sabotaged machinery at the vast Skoda Works. It had been turning out arms for Russia and for the Soviet bloc. Afterwards, the schedule was resumed.

It was at Pilsen, that the first crack appeared so wide in the Kremlin column. Because no Westerner could get into the city to see mass manifestations of self-determination and because the Berlin uprising followed so closely, the world knows little of the historic episode. A few Pilsen demonstrators, who escaped, told precisely what happened a few days after their town was in flames. In their own words, I took down what they said. Last names are meaningless in the report. All of them had been workers and they worked hard. Take Olga, fortyish, dumpy and dedicated to her husband. She had had 4,000 Czech crowns, her life savings. It was not a great sum, but, month by month, she had put aside a few crowns by skipping lunch, which cost eighteen crowns, in the Skoda canteen. For lunch, she had rationed herself to two slices of bread, except for Mondays, when she sometimes had a sliver of roast pork left over from Sunday. It was the one day workers there could afford meat. Thrift showed in the pallor on Olga's face.

Jan, her husband, did not know about this little treasure. It was to be a surprise. Olga was going to give her husband his first vacation since 1938, fifteen years before. Suddenly, the treasure was wiped out. The Communist regime, stabilizing a mass standard of poverty, revalued the currency. There also was young Jiri, age twenty, who saved enough for a bicycle. That was gone. Vaclav and Marie had saved for curtains and winter clothes for their son, Peter. These, too, were gone. Stony-faced, the little group from Pilsen sat over coffee mugs telling what happened to them, to their friends. What follows is their report. In such a case you rarely ask questions. All you do is listen because it was not your own experience. One of the men lit a cigarette and began through clouds of smoke:

"We were all at Vaclav's two-room flat that Saturday afternoon. We still wore our overalls, and on that day we were so depressed that we had not even washed off the dirt from the factory. In one horrible minute, the government wiped out all our savings. The crown was devalued. Each person was allowed to convert only 300 crowns. For his 300 crowns, he would be given sixty new crowns. If savings were more than 300 crowns, the money was frozen. The government would give back only one new crown for every fifty old crowns over 300. Olga's 4,000 crowns became worth a fine 134 new crowns. On that Saturday all our little dreams were wiped away. The government which had been saying all these years that it was the friend of the worker now ordered every family to the special exchange offices. We had to declare savings and simply have these savings stolen. Stealing from a workingman is a terrible thing to do.

"Late that afternoon, we all went as ordered and passed other dreary processions, almost like funerals, all the way. Then we had to stand in a queue for hours while the bureaucrats questioned everybody. The temper of the people in the queues was fierce. Even some of the Communist cell leaders at Skoda Works, called the Lenin Works for home reasons, were raving and raging against the government like the rest of us. Some women were crying and the men were trying to comfort them. They were calling the government leaders every name under the sun.

"There was one man—the only one—in our queue who spoke hopefully of the reform and how it would work for everybody's benefit. But we guessed he was a police agent. When you live long enough under such a system you get an instinct for agents. That night none of us slept much. It was very hard to talk at home. You become naturally careful. In our lifetime we have lived under Nazi armies, Soviet armies and the Americans; later Czechs and Czech Communists. The Americans liberated us and we danced in the streets. They stayed with us for a few months. Some of our girls married Americans. On the road to Prague, outside our town, you would have seen a little monument to the Americans. It said the Americans stopped there because they were ordered to stop. The Communists took it down. Everyone in Pilsen remembers, anyway. Some of our people went to jail because they hid American flags they kept. We always kept making new ones and finding old ones. Nobody knew when we would use them again or if we would use them at all. We just kept them.

"As we sat around the combination living-room-bedroom-dining room that Saturday night, we looked at each other silently. The children around were noisy and nervous. They sensed that something was wrong. We didn't talk much. We all remembered the boy who told his teacher that his father talked to the chimney every night. The police found a radio set in the chimney. The father was taken away. Nobody has ever seen him again. We don't talk much, even to each other, about politics.

"We were all worn out. Everybody in Pilsen is always tired. The wives and husbands work to make ends meet. The Communist management is always increasing production quotas. Life is like trying to walk on the assembly belts in the factory. Our officials always tell us, though, that we are much better off than anyone else in the 'socialist' world. If that is so, God have pity on the others.

"We never have anything to show for our work. Good food, clothes and furniture are very expensive. It is hard to even get a decent glass of beer. That's for export. On Sunday we don't go to the Cesky (Czech Woods) because police stop you and ask why and where you are going with a basket. It's almost impossible to get to a football game any more. You have to save up five kilos of paper or rags or metal for your admission. Some people have connections in the Party. They manage to get tickets. Before the war, before the Nazis came, we knew a better life. We could go out Sundays to the country or buy a good sausage and beer cheap and listen to the band play near the statue of old Thomas Masaryk.

"Nowadays, by the time Saturday afternoon comes around we are happy to crawl into our beds for a little extra sleep. We sleep like exhausted animals. What else can we do? Yet they tell us we are so much more advanced and so much better off. We have our one big meal a week on Sunday. This is usually our national dish—roast pork, dumplings and sauerkraut. It's almost impossible to get fresh fruit and vegetables. They exist on the farms but we don't know what happens between the farm and here. Often we hear from relatives working in warehouses that food comes to them already rotting.

"On the Saturday we talk about, the women were so excited they even forgot to go out and buy the pork for dinner. None of the adults slept much. We were angry, very angry. It seemed we could not stand the strain any more. It was all unbearable. It is hard to imagine what our lives can be like. We don't get to see our children and wives very much. We often have to work different shifts from our wives. We never know on our day off if we will be called to volunteer work on a farm and have to listen to self-criticism and Communist lectures. That is supposed to be educational for a worker. You always make sure you have a little food with you on such a volunteer's job. They often forget to give us any. After work, we come home and in our own homes we are careful not to talk too freely. Someone frequently shows up with a card from the Labor office. He is supposed to be a worker from the provinces. You get a special sense of smell. You smell the man as a police agent, just hunting around.

"We somehow manage to get along because everyone wants to live. But all the Communists have given us has been shortages, threats and promises and talk, talk, talk. Even if you were a stranger or a foreigner, you would have known that something was different about Pilsen that Sunday, May 31, 1953. There were all the old familiar things that distinguish our city—the sweet, strong almost overpowering smell of malt and mash that is always in the air from the big breweries. Trams clattered along the narrow streets in the center of the city. There was a football game that day at the stadium. A crowd went but didn't have much heart for it. The main reason most of them went was because they already turned in their scrap paper and metal earlier in the week. They thought they might as well use the tickets. Normally, Pilsen is football-mad. Our big team, the Skoda Works team, played out of town and was beaten two-to-one. Any other time this would have been big news on the late-afternoon radio broadcasts and everybody would talk about it. But tonight nobody cared.

"There were not many people on the streets and the movie houses were almost deserted. There were only some Russian movies and two Hungarian movies playing anyway. We never get to see Western movies except once in a long time, when movie houses need money. Then they double the price and sometimes triple them and show some Western cowboy movie or a crime movie. It's supposed to be typical of the way Americans live. That's the Party excuse for allowing it to be shown. But when "Hamlet" was shown in southwest Czechoslovakia, people made the trip all the way from Prague to see it. On this Sunday night, that will live in everyone's memories in Pilsen, the streets seemed tense and deserted. Even those of us who go to work on the six o'clock shift at the Skoda plant did not go to bed early. When we did, we did not sleep very well. On Monday morning when we got up at 4:30 to get to the 6 o'clock shift, it was raining and cold. Some of us even wore heavy underwear under our overalls. We used to wear street clothes to the factory to change there into overalls and a cap called a "cepice," which is a combination cloth and leather cap.

"Women wear the same clothes as men on the job. There are about 4,000 women working at the Skoda plant. Most of them get up earlier than the men to take their children to the government kindergarten, where they stay all day. The children hear about Communism, of course, about as soon as they are able to talk. They also wear uniforms of blue denim with white stripes and white shirts. Some women hardly get to know their own children. When the mothers take the children to kindergarten in the morning, the babies are half-asleep. They are half-asleep again when they are picked up in the evening. The children were irritated in those hectic days. When we came out on the streets in the morning, we sensed something very different. It was easy to see. Big, white-washed slogans were on many buildings: "U.S. Come Back. Robbery is the Russian Paradise."

"In the gray light of the spring morning, we could already hear shouting. Workers had already joined in small groups on their way to work and were singing old Czech songs. A blind man could have stood on the streets and known that trouble was coming—very big trouble. The uniformed police already were out in emergency numbers. They dress in blue uniforms with red shoulder boards. They look like pictures of Russian police we have seen. Our police usually travel in pairs, wherever they go, armed with pistols and submachine guns. Already, this morning, they were out in fours. There are about 30,000 workers at the Skoda plant and half of them work on the six o'clock shift. Skoda is the heart of Pilsen, almost a city within a city. It is a great arsenal with its own railway lines, emergency power systems, streets and canteens. It was damaged by Allied bombers during the war. All the damage has been repaired. The workers' houses which surround the steel plant have either not been repaired or patched up very badly. Most of us go to work past the main gate which has huge steel doors. Now that the Communists have taken over, our cards are checked for security every morning before we punch the time clock.

"We suppose that this security is necessary from the standpoint of the regime. Skoda is the largest plant of its kind in central-eastern Europe. It makes jeeps, tanks, marine engines, gas compressors and turbines, pressure chambers and schnorkel devices, artillery, shatter-proof glass and high-tension drills. Skoda is one of the most important links in the whole Communist industrial network. That is what people who lecture to us have said. From the main gate, the streets were packed for two blocks that morning we talk about. Most of the workers coming off a night shift which begins at ten and ends at six were hanging around. We heard rumors that some of the lathes in the artillery section had been sabotaged. Everybody was shouting something. It was slogans or nasty remarks.

"The workers were pushing and nobody knew whether to go to work or not. On the main gate, somebody had planted an American flag. People pointed to it. The rioting was beginning in a real way. But the police just stood by. Later, we heard they had orders not to interfere with the demonstration. The confusion, the pushing, the shouting and the anger went on all day. Each of us saw some of it and was caught in it. A riot as big as that is like war: Each man sees and knows only what is in his own sector. Consider what Vaclav saw."

Vaclav: "When I got to the factory gates I met someone who I always thought was a big Communist. He works in the automotive assembly line. He grabbed me by the collar and said, 'You're coming with us.' I asked where, and he said, 'To the Town Hall. We'll burn all the records of the currency reform.' He said if we burned all the records, we could all change some more money. As we were talking, we saw some people pushing and shoving inside the gates. We could not tell who was fighting. Then I caught sight of my wife with some other women. She was waving a small American flag, my wife! We had never talked much about America, she and I. She had been so careful in talking even to me that I thought she might be on her way to become a Communist. A lifetime of relations change in such a situation. I thought, well, we lost our savings but we found each other again.

"By now, I just seemed to be pushed along by the crowd. It must have been an hour later we arrived at the Town Hall Square. The big pictures of Stalin and Gottwald had been taken down and later I saw pieces of them in the streets. There were police in the upstairs windows. They did not seem to want to do anything. Some of the crowd already had gone into the building. I could see smoke coming out of the windows where they were burning papers. A man in overalls got up in a window and shouted over and over, 'Remember Masaryk.' I was pushed along to the front of the crowd. I looked up and saw some workers hang out a big American flag from a second-floor window facing the square. Then some people began to shout, 'To the Masaryk statue.' Our women pushed to get to the statue first. Our women are pretty strong. They have to be. They do hard work. They stoke furnaces for steel and they carry heavy loads. We sang songs at the Masaryk statue. People hung up Czech and American flags around the statue. But Karel, here, had another part."

Karel: "It took us about forty-five minutes to walk to the Town Hall from the Skoda plant. By tram it takes around twenty minutes. But the crowd was so great and the streets so narrow that it took us some time to get into the center of town. Before I left with a group—we were all swept along together as if caught in a storm—we ran through the turbine section. Some men threw dirt and things into the machinery. Our workers know their business. The older ones are old hands at sabotage. They manufactured many dud bombs for the Nazis. Sabotage is easy for skilled men. The Communists also know how skilled. We wrecked a railway once to protest. In other sections of the factory I don't know what happened except what I heard. I heard that workers did what we did in the turbine section. All of us were looking for Dr. Frantisek Brabec, chairman of the factory enterprises. We wanted to see how this professor type, who looks as if he always worries, would take this. We call him Tovarich Nikto, which means Comrade Nobody.

"'How will Comrade Nobody like these production norms,' workers yelled as they attacked the factory. It was like music, hearing your friends unafraid shout that way. Listen to Ladislav. He saw something worse, for all of us."

Ladislav: "I was in the rear of the crowd in front of the Town Hall. Police reinforcements were coming toward us. I heard shouts of warning. I turned around and a woman of the secret police had her pistol aimed at us. She fired. I will never forget the screams of the man hit. The people rushed toward the police-woman. They killed her with their bare hands. They fought the army and police and militia that came rushing on us. They took away rifles and broke them in the street. Somebody shouted for us to disperse. Soldiers fired and bullets banged off the Town Hall. The soldiers fired over and, then, into the crowd.

"We were too many. All of Pilsen seemed to be there, the whole 200,000 of us. Finally, we broke up into groups. Tanks were coming into town. They went up and down and also over people. We retreated and got to our homes. Shooting went on. On my way home, I saw patches of blood and torn clothing in the streets. I also saw bodies. Dead soldiers, dead civilians. Children cried. They wandered in the streets looking for the mamas and fathers. Bigger children showed fantastic nerve. I saw some boys lift a tank officer who was standing on the hatch of his tank and drag him away. You know the tank fired anyway even at the officer.

"The radio went on and the loudspeakers in town carried the voice of our President, Zapotocky. He is an old Communist. He denounced saboteurs of the nation. He said they were encouraged by American agents to take the country over. Believe me there were no American agents. I don't know what we would have done if there had been. We were just Czechs, fed up with robbery and tyranny.

"The men and women who fled Pilsen were not around, of course, when the might of the regime massed to restore its own version of order. Arrests were made arbitrarily. Victims were shipped out under heavy guard. The regime promised the people of the city that it would not rest until the 'seeds of sabotage' were destroyed for all time. Threats and denunciation poured out on the radio as soap operas do in other untroubled, affluent lands."

"How can you destroy the seeds," asked Vaclav, "if you, as the regime, plant them yourself. They haven't learned that wild flowers always grow. You cannot raise people in a guarded hothouse."

Two weeks after Czechoslovakia's Communist regime smashed the Pilsen workers, East Berlin went to the barricades. East German tanks and police could not, or would not, cope with the aroused workers. Then the Soviet Army and its tanks rolled through the streets. Men and boys pelted armor with rocks. That was their only weapon, but their real arsenal lay in courage and the knowledge that the regime forced upon them was afraid of the people it pretended to rule. East Germans didn't know about the Pilsen riots. Still in a state of shock after the outside world looked on helplessly as the Soviet Union smashed their demonstration, refugees from East Berlin listened wonderingly to accounts of the Skoda revolt.

"We think of ourselves, naturally," a building worker said. "That comes first. It's a human thing to think. When you hear that others, far away, do the same thing, you know you are absolutely right. Being right doesn't always help you, does it?"

Across the line, in shattered East Berlin, Soviet tanks roamed restlessly trying to prove with their presence that outraged workers were wrong. Under their protecting guns, Communist slogans were hung again on walls. The walls, however, seemed now to be hollow on the inside.

CHAPTER | 11

W ITH Stalin dead a new leadership—called collec-
tive—was in the business of trying to run the Soviet world. Between the
death of Stalin and formation of collective leadership, Lavrenti Beria was
executed. His security apparatus, which extended into the very marrow
of Eastern Europe, found itself on a separate purge list. The police system
Beria installed was only shaken up, not changed. Communists, who had
stayed silent and frightened under the old terror, brought it up to date.
The police surveillance of life introduced new and tough agents of power.
Veterans, who enjoyed the bitter fruits of the Beria operations on the
anatomy of foreign states, began to disappear.

"The whole horrible system hasn't meant anything to us," a veteran
Polish ex-Communist said with a shrug in Warsaw. "For these people at
the top, for the police, it is just that today you pull my fingernails; tomorrow, I might pull yours. This is a process that goes on all the time. It
isn't nice, because it isn't really human. The real people get nothing from
it but more heartache."

As purges and liquidations widened, the former interrogators began to turn up in the West, running for their lives. What they told of the methods used in the recent past was blood-curdling enough. It may also have been useful in learning, from inquisitors, why they did it. They personally were not responsible, almost all who got away declared. It was, in a manner of speaking, Beria who had done it. The same theme was echoed in the Soviet Union. Beria, out of the way, was a great name to blame. There were new names to be gilded, fresh or revised slogans and even promises of bold programs to be enacted. All the names and virtually all the slogans had at one time or another been intertwined with Stalin and Beria.

Consider what was supposed to be the new Soviet list. There was Georgi Malenkov, pudgy righthand man for years to Stalin. Then V. M. Molotov, on and off Prime Minister or Foreign Minister. Nikita Khrushchev, who made his name liquidating resistance in the Ukraine particularly after World War II, was itching to fill Stalin's shoes. With him on the way up to the Soviet summit strode goateed Nikolai Bulganin. They had been part of the system for all the years of their party careers. None had any intention of letting the party's power wither away. That went not only for the Soviet Union, but the satellite system of occupation in Eastern Europe. To help keep Eastern Europe safe for Soviet power, a new security boss was introduced.

His name was Ivan Serov and he had been a high officer, a security general, under Beria. He took his orders now from the collective leadership. That was the difference. Some would say a big difference. East Europeans, who lived under Serov's entrenchment program, would argue about the nuance. Serov brooked no opposition, no criticism of the way the Soviet Union did things. His police system was no longer beholden to him. A difference in technique. It was beholden to the men who led the Soviet Union and to the party. Inside Soviet Europe, regime officials and anti-regime people soon learned about Serov if they hadn't known before.

"I was present at a sort of select meeting of high government people," a Hungarian writer told me. "Serov came in to speak. It was short. 'Nothing has changed where you are concerned,' was what Serov said. He also said, 'I will, without pity, crush anyone who lifts a little finger against order here.' I remember that so well."

The Hungarian intellectual had only vaguely heard the name Serov before. Most East Europeans had some first-hand knowledge of him. So did people in the Soviet Union. His name had been affixed to the infamous "Serov Plan" for the deportation and liquidation of officials and intellectuals in the Baltic States in 1940. During the war, Serov's name struck terror into every community he appeared. With him, Serov brought special security units. They depopulated areas, forcibly transferred people and liquidated minorities which under the Soviet constitution were guaranteed protection. He also was bitterly anti-Semitic. In a rage at the crush of reporters around Khrushchev and Bulganin years later, Serov snarled, as he tried to push people back:

"I know who all you damned Jews are. Don't come near us."

There was in the group one Jew. Accuracy, however, meant little to Serov. His orders were to keep people in line. He knew only one way of doing it. His whole experience had been acquired in the Soviet secret police. Serov's rise to police eminence was due to Beria. Yet he was the product of the security system empowered by the new Soviet leadership to show that the satellite system in Europe would undergo no change. The Communist parties would remain paramount. They, however, would sponsor what looked like new and hopeful measures to satisfy people-at-large. Malenkov came out first with a brisk program that was hailed as a sop to all have-nots. It was popularly known as "consumer goods." People would get more for themselves and production would henceforth be balanced. Human needs were for the first time, across the board, officially recognized in Eastern Europe.

It gave rise to a slogan, hailed by parties as the "new course." In Hungary, for example, Imre Nagy was returned to power from oblivion. He kept harping on the "new course" that would bring Hungarians more to eat, more to wear and better places in which to live. Nothing was said, though, about talking more freely, thinking aloud more liberally or even of travelling, say, Westwards. The vaunted "new course" and Malenkov at the top didn't last long. He was demoted and so were Nagy and East European Communists who thought they finally had to make concessions to the human frailties of their nations. When that little honeymoon transition was shattered, increase in attempted escapes from Soviet Europe shot up. The carrot-and-the-stick was replaced by the pistol of appointed authority. In a resort town in Czechoslovakia, a ten-year-old boy was a horror-stricken witness to old procedures. His father, overjoyed at the prospects of a change, talked about how really bad things were before.

He told some glum but silent party members in the hotel in which they all worked that they should change with the times.

Although the Czechoslovak regime officially played the "new course" very cautiously, men like the hotel workers were imprudent in their optimism. Once again belt-tightening and additional lip-tightening became the official fashion; known optimists were given the treatment. On a Saturday, in this incident, the little boy came to the hotel to walk home after work with his father. Some of the party men decided to teach the man a lesson in front of his son. Show who was boss, so to speak. An elevator operator yelled to his colleague, walking downstairs with his son, that the lift was stuck between floors. He asked the man to crawl into the elevator and operate the controls. The contrived joke was to keep the victim locked in the lift until he recanted and begged for release.

The unfortunate man started to crawl into the elevator. He went in, from a prone position, backwards. While his head and waist were still outside, the regular lift-man pushed the button. The victim was immediately crushed to death before his son. Nobody was punished for the crime. It was meant as a joke, the hotel committee said. Something went wrong. Besides, the dead man had been an enemy of the state. Why punish, therefore, a loyal citizen who slipped up. The widow, having heard the story from her little boy who began to stammer badly after the scene of his father's cruel death, made up her mind to flee. Bundling her son and herself in layers of clothes, the fugitives secreted themselves in a refrigerator car bound for Vienna.

"Yes, we could have frozen to death," said the mourning widow later. "It wouldn't have been worse than what happened to my husband. We had a chance. He never did."

A chance for controlled hope was held out in Soviet Europe, after the "new course" was abandoned. Some of the concomitant features of the short-lived program were continued for internal and external use. The road to "liberalization," which Tito dispassionately referred to as "normalization," got some steam. Khrushchev and his collective comrades also began making approaches of conciliation to Tito. There was plenty of disagreement among Soviet European Communists about trying to make things up with Yugoslav Communists. Some were franker than other discouraged Party officials about where it would all end. In Bucharest little Josif Chishinevski, Moscow-trained and a member of the Rumanian Politburo, had open doubts about the wisdom of any reconciliation with Tito. We sat together in the lobby of the Grand Assembly Hotel. The chairs were of stuffed green leather. Chisinevschi was on his best behavior with an outsider. He pressed soda water flavored with a bit of jam, into my hands. Chisinevschi was a teetotaller.

"Tito is poisonous to any Communist structure," said Chisinevschi. "He was, to my mind, properly expelled. I saw him when he was in Bucharest years ago. A little Balkan Goering. That's all he is. Anyway, it would cause tremendous confusion, unnecessary confusion, to bring him back as a wronged comrade."

Chisinevschi's own Rumanian party was already in a merry-go-round state. The most powerful Communist woman in the world, Ana Pauker, had been dismissed as Foreign Minister and kicked out of the party. She had been accused of both left-and-right-wing deviation. Nobody would talk about her. I asked Petre Constantinescu-Iasi about Pauker's plight. A sallow, thin man who once lived in Paris, Constantinescu-Iasi was one of a handful of pre-war Rumanian Communists. He also tried to show foreigners that he hadn't lost any of his old boulevardier habits. If you check those, French police will produce a dossier showing that Constantinescu-Iasi had a record as a pimp in Paris. He rejected the charge, claiming it was a reactionary plot against him. In any case, Constantinescu-Iasi had always been most courtly to Pauker. So interested in advancing the image of Pauker was Constantinescu-Iasi that he once tried to ingratiate himself with a French diplomat who was talking to me.

"You may have heard, monsieur," Constantinescu-Iasi said, "that Mme. Pauker is reported to have been the mistress of Maurice Thorez. When they were both in Moscow, of course."

"No Frenchman, monsieur, not even a French Communist would have such bad taste in women," retorted the diplomat.

Once Pauker was expelled from the party, Constantinescu-Iasi tried to convince associates that he had been keeping a watchful eye on her. When Pauker had been disgraced I asked him about her. He replied, I thought, facetiously, "Pauker was a very bad person. You had to watch your step with her. She made tremendous mistakes. She was probably even a Titoist."

Tito probably would have been the first to deny it. To his regime, as an accredited diplomat, however, went one of Pauker's female aides. She complained bitterly because the Yugoslavs watched her. So did her Rumanian Embassy colleagues. She was sent to Belgrade to do party penance. For the public records her name was Christine Luca, although she had been born Markeson. Mme. Luca, a strawberry blonde, thought that the love we talk about was strictly a bourgeois opiate. She managed, nevertheless, to fall in love with a Yugoslav. Her remarks, like those of her superiors of the time, were well-known to Tito and his entourage. They paid no attention to them at least on the surface.

For a Communist, Tito was inaugurating several firsts. Besides his break with the Soviet Union, he began to travel outside the Communist sphere. He was the first Communist leader anywhere to become keenly interested in the emergence of new nations. Tito's advance man was his heir-apparent, Milovan Djilas, brooding and tousle-haired revolutionary firebrand. Djilas, sturdily with Tito on the break, felt that Yugoslavia needed wider scope, and it was he who shaped Yugoslav relations with India.

"Our political future is with countries like India," he told me after a trip to New Delhi.

Other Yugoslav Communists, suspicious at venturing into such vast and unknown political fields as the uncommitted world, were highly dubious. Djilas was a reckless man. Hadn't he also written a series of articles in "Borba," the party paper? Djilas, after being impressed and made humble again by the grinding poverty he saw in Asia, fell back on his original party asceticism. He lashed out at well-gowned wives of big bureaucrats, at their uppity manners and their perquisites. Djilas shook up the party with his violent words.

His sponsor, Tito, defended him at the time: Djilas was a man of moods. Besides, his ideas about broadening Yugoslavia's perspective were sound. The high-life of the party personalities, reflected Tito, should be toned down a little. It was a little, for everyone but Tito. Nobody dared mention the diamond ring he wore or the pearl stickpin in his necktie, his many homes and fancy clothing.

Then Tito secretly married a much younger, and quite attractive wife. Her name had been Jovanka Budisavljevic. She might have been an American.

Jovanka, thirty-three years younger than her husband, was a child when her father, Mike, went to the U.S. as a laborer. He tried his hand in Chicago, San Francisco and other big cities. The depression was too much for him and he went back home. At sixteen, Jovanka was plunged into Communist partisan work. She learned how to use firearms and grenades. In 1944, Jovanka met Tito. They shook hands, the marshal and the girl private. By 1945, Jovanka was a lieutenant in political affairs. She was transferred to Tito's secretariat. Between the secretariat job and the secret marriage—Tito's third and Jovanka's first—seven years of world upheaval stretched. It seemed to have given Tito an Indian summer insight into romance. He was a grandfather twice over and recently divorced.

When Sir Anthony Eden, also divorced and then British Foreign Minister, appeared in Belgrade with a new wife, Tito's secret was out. It came in an invitation to the diplomatic set which read: "Marshal Josip Broz and Mme. Jovanka Broz Tito cordially invite. . . ." The time between the marriage and Jovanka's formal coming out had been spent in putting a polish on the Junoesque brunette.

At a glittering summer ceremony, Tito signed a Balkan Pact. It brought him into a defense-mutual aid society that had as Yugoslavia's allies republican but authoritarian Turkey and royalist Greece. The era of good feeling between Tito and King Paul of Greece became the wonder of the Balkans. It also led orthodox Communists in Soviet Europe to confirm their views that Tito was an apostate in every way. They didn't say so publicly because Khrushchev was walking a careful tightrope into reestablishing links with Tito. In amazingly quick time, Tito and Jovanka of the dazzling toothpaste smile, fell into the real sport of kings. They ultimately traded visits with King Paul and Queen Frederika. Some of the ladies in the Yugoslav hierarchy saw to it that Jovanka didn't make any mistakes. She didn't fail them. Leaving a white-tie reception early one night, some of us asked what she planned to do next. "Study for my high-school examinations," Mme. Tito replied, smilingly. "You will pass with honors," assured a Communist lady-in-waiting. Jovanka didn't have to worry.

The casual encounter with the Edens went on to much more formal affairs, bigger trips and more lavish costuming for noteworthy visitors. Tito had by now become very public-relations-minded for his own brand of what the world called "national Communism." He also wanted to show he had no prejudices against other kings. To Yugoslavia, Tito invited Haile Selassie, Emperor of Ethiopia. It was a gala occasion. Yugoslavia was at odds still with Italy over Trieste. That was his anti-Western thorn of the moment. Ethiopia had been the first victim of Italian Fascism. So Haile Selassie was invited, and accepted, to come in midsummer to Yugoslavia. It turned the regime inside out. Ethiopian court protocol is quite strict. Tailcoats and long gowns are very much de rigueur for presentation to the Emperor.

Yugoslavia's operas and theaters were emptied of their tailcoats. For the top men, new ones were bought in Rome and Paris. Several in London, too. One official I know also was put in charge of buying proper gowns and materials for the ex-partisan ladies. His wife went with him. They bought some Paris originals and plunging necklines in Rome. For lesser-party wives, silks and velvets were purchased to be made in Belgrade as dresses. One awesome hitch developed in the mass seamstress trade. A few ladies, trying out their finery, discovered that their slip and brassière shoulder straps showed. Off went the harassed purchasing agent and his wife on another foray into the West. They bought a whole consignment of strapless bras. If you think it's easy to fit buxom, full-breasted ladies on a catch-as-catch-can basis, my acquaintance's hectic experiences caused him genuine nervous prostration.

"There was plenty of grumbling," he told me later. "You expect that. But one woman was so furious about her strapless bra, which fitted badly, that she threatened to have me arrested. I didn't think she was fooling. Her husband is an important police official."

Making the trial runs from the airport into Belgrade before Haile Selassie arrived was a bigger test of endurance than his appearance. The road was rutted and full of potholes. Shantytowns lined the swampy land near the shoulders of the road. The town of Novi Belgrade, begun as a mighty show of Yugoslav socialism, lay derelict on the line of march. It had been abandoned while the regime concentrated on more immediate economic problems. Nothing in the bleak area had been painted in about a generation except the slogans to Tito. The need to impress Haile Selassie induced many quick changes. Paint was daubed over buildings. Some of the uglier marshland was drained. Roads were mended. Finally, on the memorable day, great crowds lined the route to welcome Haile Selassie. They held Ethiopian and Yugoslav flags. Cheers were prearranged. When the doughty little Emperor appeared, a great cry went up: "Long Live the Comrade Czar." Haile Selassie seemed highly pleased.

Meeting all types of high-ranking people from the far-flung corners of the world from then on became Tito's regular habit. It was another first for him, his closest collaborators used to be fond of telling me. Long after, Khrushchev began to follow the trail already blazed by Tito. Guest-books in London, Paris and New Delhi, to mention a few, had Tito's name inscribed in them before those of Khrushchev and his travelling companion, Bulganin. At home, Tito, through his party analysts, went through a domestic reform. He received generous assistance from the United States. He had delivered to Yugoslavia large quantities of wheat, cotton and oil. They were desperately needed to maintain the slenderized economy of Yugoslavia. Khrushchev, while talking normalization possibilities with Tito, still kept the economic blockade in force. The Russians relented to permit a few deliveries to go through but it was of no consequence to the Yugoslav economy.

American aid and credits from the West—Tito had also recognized West Germany—shored up the near-ruinous impact of the Soviet-sponsored blockade and some of the internal Communist plans that underwent radical surgery. Taking help from America, as the Yugoslavs told our negotiators, did not mean they would change their social system. It would remain as Communist as ever. We approved. As long as Tito went his independent way and stayed out of the Soviet bloc, the Russian regime had more to fear than we did. The premise was probably a correct one to follow. Tito and his party would not willingly permit another system to erode their positions. They had defied Stalin for trying to dictate to them. The Yugoslav Communists, in effect, said they would do their own dictating and make their own terms at home or wherever they could gain influence. After considerable inner-party discussion, Tito also decided to accept American military aid.

This sent Soviet Europe into a frenzy of recrimination. Tito was taking arms from the founder of NATO. Therefore, the charges raged against him, that he was secretly in league with the Western alliance. The accusations were totally unfounded. Tito got the help on his own terms— to remain what he was. The charges from other Communists hurt more orthodox Yugoslav Communist beliefs. They hankered, even in their support of Tito at the break with Stalin, to try and be more accommodating with outside comrades. It was unnatural, they felt, to get so cozy with the West, particularly Americans. Quite a few also saw in some home-made reforms Tito instituted the beginnings of the disintegration of their own society. Tito had dissolved collectivization of the land. It didn't work. In the Yugoslav state of isolation and dependence for so much of its existence on the peasants, Tito ordered farms to go back to farmers, not party planners. The peasants had to meet certain quotas. They also were given more incentive to do it. Cash, kind and driblets of consumer goods went out to them. More important than any other factor was the psychological one in working one's own land. It was easy to see in a swing I made through Serbian and Croatian farm districts soon after de-collectivization.

In south Serbia where the habit of owning your farm has passed through generations of peasants and survived centuries of Turkish occupation, people were pointedly pleased. Near a thatched village, I sat around an outdoor bench with some of the peasants. A son of the district, an acquaintance of mine, brought me to the corn-growing belt from Belgrade. The peasants greeted the young man pleasantly. One turned to his father, a huge man in traditional leather-thonged, upturned sandals and homespun on his massive torso.

"Shall we tell your boy that you've always been a private farmer?" he demanded with a throaty chuckle.

"He always knew it," the father roared back.

He brought out a crock and a glass jar. In the earthenware crock was home-made slivovitz, a plum brandy as customary in Eastern Europe as coffee on the stove is on American farms. The jar held curled paprikas. Above us, under the eaves of the hand-hewn porch hung long necklaces of paprikas left to dry. They're supposed to be good for seasoning and they also are about as sharp as Mexican peppers. In that part of the world, you bite a paprika. Your eyes probably will tear because it's so strong. Then you knock back the slivovitz out of glasses shaped like little bottles.

"The American wants to know how we like being de-collectivized," the father told his peasant cronies.

A young man, about as old as my acquaintance from Belgrade but sporting the fierce black mustaches of the Serbian peasant, held his glass out for another drink. It was getting towards evening. Bells on cattle tinkled. They plodded on sun-baked dirt roads, sending out puffs of reddish dust. There was lots of clay in the district, a peasant explained, seeing me watch the end of a day's farm work. Barefoot women, hoes on shoulders, strode by us calling good-evening. They wore kerchiefs around their heads and long home-spun dresses under which swirls of petticoats peeped. Barefoot and bronzed boys and girls ran after barking dogs or chased trundling horse-drawn wagons. The crop fields looked pretty good to a fairly untrained in-the-country perspective of mine. Corn even looked almost as high as a peasant's eye.

"Not so good," said the father, presiding over the slivovitz. "Too dry. Not enough rain. Better than last year."

Why? They were still in collectives the year before, explained the son a little lugubriously. If they didn't care for collectives—I noticed peasants in mirthful agreement—they still needed to pool their land into bigger farms. That was the son's argument and he got an argument right back.

"When we need bigger farms, we'll do it," declared the young mustachioed peasant. "What did your collectives do? Your fine plans didn't have enough, did they? We won't work for a plan made by someone who learned about farmland in books. We can make our own plans. There have been co-operatives here ever since your great-grandfather's time. Even the Turks didn't bother us. They knew better."

Our host commanded us to stop bickering. Women came along and spread an embroidered white tablecloth. I felt the cloth and scrutinized it carefully. It took a couple of years to make, my acquaintance from Belgrade said, before I could ask.

"These people, and I know them well, are convinced they can do most anything themselves," he added with a wry grin. "You know how they bucked the kolkhoz system. I guess they really won that fight for good." Kolkhoz had been an important Russian word Tito used in the early days of shaping his federated republic of workers and peasants. Pressure, expulsion from the land and "administrative methods"—police terror, in Communist countries—only made the Yugoslav peasants more intransigent. The regime tried to collectivize but it could not collect from the peasant.

"We hid things from the party commissioner," the peasant father revealed in front of his son, a party member in Belgrade. "He couldn't get a tenth of what he called for. We buried things we needed. We also killed animals. Remember, my boy, you ate beef right here. You didn't ask how we had it. You knew."

Tito's activists also knew. They were powerless to act to show their might. Taking outside aid and credits, they also had to produce something in the factories and on the land to prove the superiority of their regime, independent of Soviet Europe, over the nearby satellite states. Stories, appearing in East European papers, pooh-poohed Yugoslav claims.

Appearance of the Workers' Councils in Yugoslavia were savagely assailed. Bulgar, Rumanian, Hungarian and Czechoslovak party big-shots called the councils revisionist, anarchistic or, sometimes, an adaptation of capitalist practice. On the outside, the councils seemed like genuine reform. They were supposed to accept direct participation from the workers. The step seemed like real liberalization, as well as the profit-sharing plan appeared.

It was a bold and imaginative idea had it not been carried out by a Communist party looking over its frontiers nervously to see what the doctrinal reaction might be. As a result, Tito's trusted party members ran the councils, every bit as doggedly as they planned other grandiose enterprises in the past. Some emboldened workers in the bigger towns thought prematurely that the councils were creations for workers to be heard and advised. They were slapped down hard by crusty comrades in charge of councils. The advertised freedom to give the workers direct voice in the councils was Communist folk-lore. What bothered and bewildered Soviet European Communist ideologists was the very idea of such liberties and direct consultation. Workers' councils have in practice always been opposed to airing workers' grievances. A few strikes and demonstrative protests that flashed through the Yugoslav economy have always been quickly quelled and promptly condemned by party officials responsible for trying to make councils meet objectives.

Meeting a goal is as much a fetish in Tito's Yugoslavia as it has been elsewhere in Communist-directed states. The Yugoslav party, naturally, wanted to show that it was building and producing more and better its way than the so-called "Stalinist" elements in the satellites. It never relaxed the dogmatic grip on the sinews of the economy. Top men, as they did in Soviet Europe, always came out on top. Their shares were much more equal than a trained worker's. Cars, trips, good housing and foreign currency were all available to them. This was not at all different from the development of corruption among the managerial group through the entire Communist system.

A factory manager and his staff of supposed experts would leave for a trip Westwards. They were on a fact-finding, credit-seeking tour. In Vienna, West Germany, Paris, London and Rome they drank at the most expensive nightclubs, ate high-priced food, bought presents for friends and relations and had a real high life. It didn't take long for quite a few to start private bank accounts in the West. They deposited hard currency, which belonged to the state. Bringing the new-fangled capitalists from a socialist state like Yugoslavia to book took a lot of doing. Quite a few were veteran party members and had been partisans. Exposing their corruption would expose a cynical rottenness in the apparatus. Tito's own standard of living might be brought into question. But it was questioned and criticized by a most unexpected source.

Milovan Djilas, agitator and revolutionary, had become thoroughly disgusted by what he knew first-hand was the life and living of his upper-class comrades. The whole revolution he so militantly supported, all his career in prison, on the battlefield and in government, soured in what he saw and knew was practice. He was not one to compromise when he was an ardent Communist. When his own philosophy withered away from that of the Yugoslav party, Djilas obstinately refused to compromise, too. He hadn't openly used the phrase, "New Class" as yet. But what he said about it before he finally went to jail shocked the party and the party's fearful apprehension of what satellite European Communists would say about Communists who let a prominent critic get away with it. When Djilas, in 1953, published his scathing articles on money and favoritism inside the party, he was applauded in the country. He didn't even spare the actress wife of a general. She was pretty but a mediocrity on stage or in the films. She couldn't have played in the movies if she hadn't enjoyed such protection from on high. This case that Djilas cited, among others, struck a very sensitive and responsive chord among the people. They knew how they were living and here a very prominent Communist was telling them how they were being exploited by people who once promised full equality.

Because he had been so close to Tito and had stood defiantly with him against Stalin, the Yugoslav dictator protected Djilas. Other high party officials, indignant over Djilas's exposure of them, demanded that a lesson be made of him. They demurred when Tito told them to subside. Djilas, he explained, was rash and he boiled over too quickly. It would be better to keep Djilas fully occupied with missions to new countries and with the examination of fresh international problems. Djilas carried out his missions faithfully but he burned even more bitterly over the class injustices he saw in the party's domain.

In the intervening period from his published explosions, Djilas came to believe that it was high time for the Yugoslav party to democratize itself and the country fully. He talked to comrades earnestly about the idea.

One of the more radical suggestions he proposed was for a second party, perhaps at first loyal opposition and socialist in structure. The proposal drew considerable inner-council attention. There were some men, including some very close to Tito, who thought Djilas had a sound platform. There were many others, in the majority, who saw in Djilas a deadly enemy. He was an apostate in an already heretical Communist community. Two apostasies could not be tolerated. So the Yugoslav central committee firmly believed. If allowed to remain in force, Djilas's own heresy would prevail. What would happen, then, to the party and its privileged? The party decided to act. The situation had become too urgent to brook a delay. Tito was in India on his first Asian trip for which Djilas had already laid the groundwork. All the anti-Djilas views were presented frantically to Tito abroad. During those hurly-burly days, the party drew into its own shell and tried to keep the fight private. It was impossible to do because Djilas would not keep quiet about it. As an old, underground fighter and ex-political prisoner, he had contempt for police methods tried on his person. Ranged alongside of him, solidly on Djilas's side, was Vlado Dedijer. By sharing Djilas's most important views, the big and brawny Dedijer added an irritant to the shock already convulsing the party. Vlado had been a valiant partisan fighter. His wife was killed by the Germans and he had been grievously wounded.

In party affairs, Dedijer was an important man. He was well-known in the West and appeared often at the United Nations to represent Yugoslavia. For some time Vlado ran the central committee's foreign affairs cadre. His second wife, Vere, had produced four splendid children. She is a beautiful Slovene blonde, as slim and striking as a fashion model. To top it all, Vlado was internationally famous as Tito's biographer. The book, published throughout the world in dozens of languages, made about a million dollars. Royalties were deposited in a fund for a memorial hospital to Vlado's first wife.

Standing before party peers beside Djilas meant, in a way, much more to Dedijer and his family than judgment on Djilas did. Although Djilas had a second wife, impeccably loyal to him, and a little son, Dedijer had a family about four times the size. Not only were there Vere and the children, but his mother, the indomitable Milice, already a diabetic. Then there was his brother, Steve, then head of the Yugoslav atomic energy agency by way of Princeton, the U.S. Eighty-second Airborne Division and Vlado's high standing in the party. Friends of Vlado and their families were deeply involved. Their loyalties and livings were at stake. As a party reject, Vlado stood to lose a villa, a car, a paying career and to remain untouchable in local political and social society. He didn't even know if he could ever scrape together enough money to feed and lodge his family in the future. At school, his small children would be exposed to the gibes of teachers and little, activist schoolmates. True, it also in microcosm was Djilas's dilemma. But Djilas had that many less to worry about and he always has cherished political martyrdom. At first he even resented Vlado's voluntary support which was unsolicited. Djilas seemed to want to go it all alone against the wrath of the party. In private and in public, however, Dedijer stood up for Djilas and his right to criticize and make radical suggestions for a Communist-shaped society.

Djilas, to whom Vlado Dedijer always had been a close personal friend, accepted the support in the end with some magnanimity. While both men suffered humiliating deprivations and Djilas, his old pre-war jail, I have always felt that Dedijer's wife was the great heroine in the tragedy. Flung out of their villa, with the most slender of resources, the whole family installed itself near what is today Belgrade's new bridge. It was a slum tenement by anyone's standards. But Vere kept the house going, the children somehow fed and the apartment immaculate. She also kept Dedijer's morale at a high, no-surrender pitch. Vlado found just how far the party's elite had, indeed, separated itself from contact with the people. Suddenly, he had to use public transport.

"From the end of the war I always had a car," he remarked ruefully to me. "Getting into a tram or a bus was a new experience. I saw and heard how the other half—I should say big majority—lived. It was not pretty to see nor complimentary to hear what they said."

Djilas had already said it so that the party leadership staged a high-level inquisition against him. He had accused the Communists, of whom he had been a leading member, of shifting control and profit to their own social class. Communist parties, he declared, not only controlled their nationalized means of production but they reserved for themselves the lion's share of the income. It was the Twentieth Century's most modern technique for man's exploitation by man. The declaration fell like a monstrous cacophony on Titoist ears. Once more they came to grips with stark heresy. Hadn't they been renegades themselves and dared to rebel? Then, the temerity of a Djilas had to be eliminated. The Titoist party, in its clamor for self-preservation, was clinging to its own version of party orthodoxy or heterodoxy.

When confronting its own, the party seeks to observe scrupulous "socialist" justice. Tito's one-time chef de cabinet, Joza Vilfan, was the on-the-line authority for this observation. Djilas was not only a menace to authority that regarded itself as thoroughly embedded, but he was a terrible embarrassment. Only traitorous pro-Soviet Cominformists, who sought to overthrow Tito with alien force, were liquidated. Djilas preached an anti-Communist gospel now but he did not in any way suggest rebellion or a political coup d'état. The party's sense of legality was stretched taut. In an impassioned speech, Vlado Dedijer begged that Djilas not only be spared but permitted his rights to speak in the future. The revolution in Yugoslavia, Vlado appealed, must not be permitted to devour its children.

The party, in its supreme omniscience, went by the Communist book in approaching Djilas. He could—and should—recant, party elders told Djilas. That would be repudiation of everything he said in recent years and all the reforms he advocated. It also meant apology to the new class which insisted it had not changed since the pulsating days of partisan warfare. A confession of guilt by Djilas, which would have been circulated throughout Yugoslavia and hammered hard in all other Communist countries, was the best way out for the party. All Communists are supposed to understand confession of sins, even by prominent personalities. Djilas's dark features darkened deeper at the orthodox offer. Instead, he urged the party to change its outlook, its ways and therefore, its future. A veteran in the upper brackets was almost apoplectic with rage at Djilas's defiance. He started lobbying for the whole "socialist" book of law to be thrown at Djilas. The prominent party man in question is something of a dullard, regarded amusedly by many of his comrades. He is highly orthodox in his views but implacably faithful to Tito and whatever he says. His name is Petar Stambolic, boss of the party in Serbia. Stambolic's claim to national fame almost wrecked a Communist Party congress. When there were calls for declarations from the floor, a delegate rose, pointed a trembling finger at Stambolic and shouted: "Comrades, that man stole my wife!"

When the rollcall came, only Vlado Dedijer in the central committee stood with Djilas. They were both stripped of office and cast out of the party. Prison sentences fixed in advance, were suspended by a court. Djilas and Dedijer were warned that any anti-state activity would lift the suspensions and land them in prison. For a Communist regime, the sentences were rather mild. Death was the usual penalty for deviation on such a high level in Soviet Europe. Tito is supposed to have decided on the lighter sentences. His regime tried to play it both ways, East and West. For Communists in the satellites, there had been harsh punishment. The names, Djilas and Dedijer, were prominent. Where the West was concerned, the explanation attempted to prove that while Djilas's and Dedijer's behavior was unpardonable, Tito' regime was different from others. It was, as the cases showed, strictly a Communist one. But it was not Sovietized. Thus, the two men had their lives spared. They were even, so to say, free.

Neither was free to search for employment in Yugoslavia. Vlado could try to scrape together painfully written book reviews his Socialist friends outside asked him to do. The Dedijer family budgeted itself on $1 a day for food. You can get tired of beans a couple of times daily. Vlado would steadfastly refuse offers of any foreign help. Djilas was in a better position. His wife, Stephanie, kept her job in a bank. The Djilases had an income of sorts. Perplexed at first, Soviet Europe commented ironically on how wishy-washy the Yugoslav Communists had been. Then it, overnight, pretended that nothing had ever happened, nor that there ever was a Djilas or a Dedijer. Khrushchev was trying to work a radical change in his relations with Tito. Soviet Europe was to shut up and fall in line.

CHAPTER | 12

By 1955 Soviet satellites grudgingly heeded the pressure for change. The tyrant Stalin had been dead two years. There had already been some basic changes in the Soviet Union. Still, the proconsuls in Eastern Europe were cautious. What was good for Russia was good for them—up to a point. They proceeded slowly as they measured and directed the amount of thaw permitted in their countries. An easy way, indeed the most useful stratagem for them, was to permit an occasional American to visit.

The United States had not had relations with Bulgaria for five years. I was the first American to enter the country since the break and the first American reporter in six years. My visa was a stamped piece of copy paper, to which my photograph was attached, giving my nationality, age and place of birth. Americans were still formally forbidden to enter Bulgaria.

Red Wolf, a country cousin of Red Bear, ruled that tormented, troubled land in its forced drive towards Sovietization. Red Wolf was the loose translation of the name of Vulko Chervenkov, the hulking, shock-haired Communist boss of Bulgaria. Chervenkov resented the name but it stuck.

Under his unswerving allegiance to Moscow, the small but strategically placed nation had been cast completely in the image of the Soviet Union. Today Bulgaria is the most sovietized of all the satellite nations. From the mausoleum entombing the remains of Georgi Dimitrov in a plaza that is a miniature of Moscow's Red Square to the highest degree of collectivization outside Russia, Bulgaria trod in lockstep towards the promised land.

Bulgaria is an agrarian nation, and its farm problems are the same as Russia's. Production is off, peasants are alternatively wooed and threatened. At the end of the war, Bulgaria was in roughly the same position as Russia at the time of the revolution. A measure of industrialization was ruthlessly and quickly carried out. The result has been some industry where none before existed. Electrification was one of the main programs. It has been carried out in part. Yet there are regular power cuts and failures that plunge even Sofia, the capital, into darkness.

To entrench itself, the Communist Party, backed by the presence of the Red Army, destroyed the opposition. Then it purged itself repeatedly. Jails and detention camps were filled to overflowing. The Communists have since disbanded the camps and released many prisoners from jail. They feel confident of their ability to retain power and they have had ten years in which to raise a new generation. There was—and is—fire in the ashes of that generation.

Because of Bulgaria's strategic position—common frontiers with Greece, Turkey and Yugoslavia, plus a long coastline on the Black Sea—Moscow was determined to make this country safe for Soviet policy.

It succeeded, according to its own power lights, pretty well. Stabilized poverty and standardized misery are the rules. This was a country where nylon stockings cost $30 a pair, if any good; otherwise you picked up cheaper ones at $5. You could buy a little radio for $150 or you could listen to the government-operated loudspeaker system for free. White rolls were expensive delicacies to be munched slowly. Russian-made automobiles were available, of course. But the cheapest cost the equivalent of $5,000. If you had a job paying the good wage of $100 a month, your family might be able to afford meat once a week. Rents were low but

1. Aftermath of War, 1945. Total defeat and total poverty in the dismal wreckage of Berlin.

2. Belgrade, 1955. Khrushchev, Gromyko, Bulganin and Mikoyan arrive for a warm and friendly visit with Tito.

3. LEFT. Tito and Milovan Djilas, 1953. When they were still Nos. 1 and 2 in the Yugoslav party hierarchy.

4. Tito with his third and present wife, Jovanka, enjoy the regal life.

5. Once Tito's closest friends and advisers, Djilas, Dedijer, Micunovic and Kardelj (left to right), confer at a U.N. session in 1949.

6. Former Bulgarian Communist leaders, now all dead, Kostov (executed as a Titoist), Dimitrov and Kolarov.

7. The "Comrade-King Michael" of Rumania speaking to Parliament in 1946 under the fond gaze of Groza.

8. Ana Pauker and Marshal Voroshilov when they brought Dimitrov's body back to his widow (left) in Sofia from Russia.

9. Khrushchev publicly hailing the Soviet pro-consul in Rumania, Gheorghe Gheorghiu-dej, Communist party leader in 1960.

10. Bucharest, 1957: The Workers' Guard march to commemorate the 13th Anniversary of the "liberation" of Rumánia.

11. Rumania, 1946: Guns before uniforms. Communist-recruited demonstrators supplied with weapons from a central depot to assist with "elections."

12. Budapest, 1956: During the Hungarian fight for freedom marchers stream across uprooted cobblestoned streets defying orders to disperse.

13. Budapest, 1956: Soviet troops, led by a tough political officer, stop at a main street. They said: "We return as brothers."

14. ABOVE. Hungary, 1956. Girls like these fired carbines as well as carried flags.

15. RIGHT. Hungary, 1956: Funeral for group of Freedom Fighters killed by the hated "Avos." The photographer, Jean-Pierre Pedrazzini of *Paris Match* was later mortally wounded.

LEFT. "Mr. Five-by-Five," Matyas Rakosi for years Communist boss of Hungary.

Josef Cardinal Mindszenty, who fought against Communist domination, was imprisoned, released briefly during the 1956 revolt and lives today in the American Legation.

18. Hungarian Freedom Fighters sack a book shop filled with Soviet and party literature.

19. Life goes on amid the ruins of Warsaw.

20. Demonstrators in Poznan, Poland carry flag, dipped in the blood of a Pole, felled by police bullets.

21. Wladyslaw Gomulka, Polish Communist leader. He was jailed in Stalinist times but released in October, 1956, to calm a gathering Polish storm of discontent.

22. Stefan, Cardinal Wyszynski. A prince of the church and a Polish patriot. His uneasy co-existence with Gomulka maintains discipline in Poland, an influence the Communists resent.

23. Ill-fated son of a great father: Jan Masaryk, Foreign Minister of Czechoslovakia. He fell, jumped or was pushed through a window to his death after Communist putsch.

24. Czechoslovakia: Moment of Triumph. February 22, 1948, Communist leader Klement Gottwald, acclaims the party's take-over of the country.

25. Czechoslovakia: Hour of Disaster. President Eduard Benes, after the Communist coup d'etat, acknowledges the new cabinet of Gottwald. Benes retired shortly thereafter and died a broken man.

26. The West German Federal Republic's austere Chancellor, Konrad Adenauer with his No. 1 political competitor, Mayor Willy Brandt.

27. During the Berlin Airlift 1948-49, the late Mayor of West Berlin, Ernst Reuter, listens to Berliners and their plight.

28. This photo has become world famous. Soviet tanks summoned to quell rioting workers in East Berlin run into defiance. Only rocks against armor but it told the story.

29. Khrushchev to the party's rescue. The Soviet strongman welcomed by goat-bearded Walther Ulbricht, East German Communist leader, and puppet Premier, Otto Grotewohl.

30. New Communist "Workers' Militia" in East Germany.   31. NEXT PAGE. East Berlin, 1961.

FÜR FRIEDEN UND SOZIALISMUS –
Jeder eine gute Tat für unsere
gemeinsame sozialistische Sache!

housing was short. Besides, there couldn't be fewer than two people in a room.

Shortly after the war there was no night life. The ban has been eased a little since, but gaiety wouldn't conform with the gravity of the program to "build socialism." Some jazz was played in a couple of restaurants and dance places in Sofia were always jammed. Peace, the population was instructed and indoctrinated, happens to be a monopoly of the Soviet Union. To keep the peace, the young men and women of the country must "fight" for it. Americans were depicted as A-bomb throwers and variations of exploiters and worse. To maintain proper vigilance against recrudescence of "capitalist" ideas, youth organizations had been banded into "sport groups." They spent spare hours in target-practice, in parachute-jumping and guerrilla training. Mothers, producing huge families, are usually recognized as exemplary socialist workers. They get medals and subsidies. Birth control is out anyway because nobody can afford to buy any birth control devices.

In 1950 the United States broke diplomatic relations with Bulgaria. Our last minister was declared persona non grata. It was the culmination of ever-increasing Communist pressure on Westerners and their association with the local people. It would be idle to speculate why the Bulgars gave me a visa. I had been a friend of Nikola Petkov, the courageous agrarian leader, who was executed in 1947 by the Communists. Petkov's executioner, Georgi Dimitrov, lies in state today as Bulgaria's own Lenin, and an eerie greenish light illuminates his mausoleum but it wouldn't be healthy to visit Mr. Petkov's grave if you could find it.

In Bulgaria, I was received with an attitude that can best be described as correct for a totalitarian state. Twice, the first two days, I was detained for taking photos, once outside the Dimitrov mausoleum and once outside the new opera. It didn't happen again. I had been assured that I was "free" to go around where I liked, talk to whom I wanted and maybe even interview Red Wolf and his associates. But when I asked to see a farm collective, I was taken to a "wine cooperative." To make amends, I was the first Westerner permitted into the forbidden industrial area of Dimitrovo, about twenty miles from Sofia. I also was permitted to visit a textile mill, where worker after worker came up to me "spontaneously," shook hands solemnly and chanted, "We want peace." I never got to see any ranking official and could not freely roam around Bulgaria. Maybe the tip-off was that I entered the country by train from Yugoslavia.

A couple of Bulgars were in the same compartment with me. We had been chatting in English. Aboard climbed Bulgarian customs police and soldiers. There were about four of them to each passenger. Traffic is very light between Bulgaria and points west. The Bulgars were shunted into other compartments. The guards missed nothing in their search for contraband. They looked behind curtains, unscrewed light bulbs, even tore up seats. Then they started on the baggage of their countrymen. Mine got only a perfunctory check. All told, customs and security checks took two hours for five passengers. From one Bulgar the copies of the French edition of "Vogue," and other non-Communist papers and magazines were confiscated.

Bulgaria's capital, Sofia, as a town was never very much to look at. It had the atmosphere and rich odors of an overgrown Balkan village, dominated by a couple of striking Orthodox churches and a shapeless royal palace. All had been changing, I found.

New buildings faithful to the Russian monolithic model were under construction. The main streets, renamed to include "Russky Boulevard" among others, always were swept clean and watered down with hoses. Sidewalks off the main drags buckled and in power failures you could easily break a leg. But cleaners dutifully made their appointed rounds, using brooms and dustpans to sweep up refuse.

There was far less traffic than in 1946. Most of the automobiles are, even today, official cars, with side-curtains so you can't see the occupants. At the crossroads between the Square of September Ninth (commemorating the Soviet "liberation" in 1944) where Dimitrov's mausoleum merges with Russky Boulevard, I took a count of the traffic one day. In fifteen minutes I counted eleven automobiles. Nine were official cars; two others belonged to diplomats. The cop on duty went through his paces as smartly as Russia's military policemen. Some other busy streets have girl police on duty. They took their jobs very seriously. One of them kept spinning on her little wooden platform out of range of my camera. In exasperation, she waved her baton at me. Maybe it was a friendly gesture.

About one adult in three wore a uniform, or so it seemed. There were the police, army and associated branches, students and party organization members. The uniforms were a complete adaptation from the Russian. If you stood a Bulgar soldier next to a Russian you couldn't tell the difference. Uniformity was the style in fashion. Most children were placed in government-run nurseries if they were too young for school. Wives and husbands must work to earn enough for basic living costs. That hasn't changed, of course. Children are well cared for by the state in more ways than one. They are well and warmly clad, by local standards; and well fed. They are indocrinated thoroughly for a least four to six hours a day. It was true then and remains so.

Except for the varying new categories of the new aristocracy-party officialdom—shabbiness prevailed in dress. Women in town usually had lipstick, although it cost at least $1.50 per tube. Face powder was generally way out of reach—from $3 to $10 a box. Men don't shave too regularly and it could be because a blade cost around 30 cents. An ordinary toothbrush was $1.75. Toilet soap ran from 35 cents to $1.15. The people, generally friendly, were not as suspicious as Russians I've encountered in the last sixteen years. Every Western-made automobile usually attracted large crowds, arguing its merits. Bulgars I talked to without an interpreter at my side were curious about my clothes and cigarets. Some of them said they had relatives in the States. It was rare that any took off against the government. The police, you see, were everywhere. I had constant companions, trailing me on foot the first few days. Perhaps they got tired. At any rate, a blue Chevrolet paced me leisurely during the remainder of my stay.

Next to the evening promenade, the opera and theater remain the favorite forms of entertainment. They are heavily subsidized by the state and tickets are cheap. Performances, when they're not propaganda pieces, are quite well done. Movies are almost uniformly Soviet or productions from other comradely states. The themes run to a boy and girl falling in love at the time they discover the unbearable bliss of a tractor. Heavies are "reactionaries" made up to look like the East European version of Americans. Normally, night life is confined to the home. Restaurants, even the cheapest, are ludicrously expensive. The tiny fleet of taxis is generally for foreigners. Taxi fares are in keeping with the rest of life. The cheapest ride is about $1.50.

Everywhere you went in public places and shops you were reminded of the affinity between Red Wolf and Red Bear in a composite of Big Brother. Plaster and bronze busts of Georgi Dimitrov adorned windows. Even when you went to buy bread, Lenin, Stalin and Dimitrov were looking down on you. They were flanked by photos and paintings of Bulganin and Chervenkov—now by Khrushchev and Zhivkov. The Communist government went a little slow on replacing Malenkov. Unlike most other satellites, the Communist hierarchy of Bulgaria had been ultra-cautious. So it was that Malenkov stared across the lounge in the Hotel Bulgaria at Lenin until mid-March. Then overnight, the photo disappeared and Bulganin adorned the wall. Later, Khrushchev landed on the same spot.

Churches were open and there is supposed to be freedom of worship. A diplomat inquired after what he claimed were abuses. The responsible minister told him to return in four hours. Punctually the diplomat appeared. In the minister's office were the heads of all the churches.

"Is there freedom of religion?" asked the minister.

The churchmen nodded.

"You see," said the minister to the diplomat, "your information, as usual, is incorrect."

"We are," said another Bulgarian in a burst of frankness, "an extension of the Soviet Union. The government likes it that way. The people will become accustomed to it. We have already had more than ten years. There is nothing you can do about it unless you want to go to war. So, we will continue to build 'socialism.'"

The tragedy of his logic is that he probably believed it.

Keeping the folks down on the farm will linger as a big Communist headache. And making them work and produce on the collectives is another. To solve these problems the strong men in Bulgaria's government were dedicated.

When the Communists took over in September, 1944, as they now boldly and proudly admit, Bulgaria was about 90 percent agrarian. Even with the imposition of some industry the ratio between farm and factory is still at least a two-thirds balance for agriculture. Proportionately there had always been more farm cooperatives in Bulgaria than perhaps anywhere else in Europe. It was a country of small farmers and few great estates and landed gentry. In Bulgaria's development, modeled ever so closely to that of the Soviet Union, collectivization was pushed hard. Today, nearly all arable land is collectivized. The result is that all the mistakes, difficulties and mismanagement in Russian agriculture are endemic in Bulgaria. When Nikita Khrushchev told the Supreme Soviet that Russian agriculture was in poor shape, Bulgars echoed the same line a few weeks later. A mournful admission, indeed, for a country that had always been a food surplus area despite previous exploitation and governmental avarice.

Bulgar regime fixers handed down an edict that was intended to drive people back to the farms. Nobody could visit the five big cities in Bulgaria for more than a week without special government dispensation. All men and women who were not registered as permanent residents of the urban areas in the summer of 1952 must get back to the farm. They went out to farms, as ordered. Then, they doubled back to town as fast as they could. How, in a little country, can you arrest a few hundred thousand people at a time? Chervenkov and his comrades, including Zhivkov, promised farmers about 30 cents more a day net pay—they average about $25 a month besides food and housing—plus a kilogram daily of grain and 600 grams of corn. To exhort them to produce more and work harder, the Communists managed to induce some associates of the late Nikola Petkov to recant their opposition. These retreads, who saw the error of their ways in jail, emerged to attempt to influence the peasants to adopt the government's program. They hailed the Communist collectivization and general projects for the country as the "true" successor of the program initiated by Alexander Stamboulisky. Before he was brutally murdered in the early twenties, Stamboulisky had been premier and was one of the most farsighted agrarian leaders to come to power in Europe. By rewriting local history, the Communists seek to show that Stamboulisky linked arms with them. Nothing could be farther from the truth. He distrusted them and they sabotaged him. To encourage peasant support, however, the regime still finds it necessary to hold up Stamboulisky as the Communists' proper predecessor. That line produced the release of some of Petkov's old associates, who had been years ago charged with usurping the Communist consolidation of power.

Since the emphasis in this, the most Sovietized of all the satellites, is on agriculture, I asked to visit a collective. I wanted to see, I said, a mechanized farm and talk to the peasants. As an old tenement hand, I am not an agricultural expert. But I have seen a few farms in my time and can distinguish between a tractor and a horse. After lots of sparring and stalling, the great day came. "Permission" had at last been granted me to visit a "cooperative." Accompanied by a translator, a friendly chap very loyal to his government, we drove in a government car southwards. From the big agricultural city of Plovdiv, which seemed more opulent than Sofia, we headed to a collective district.

Over secondary roads and past hovels interspersed with some new cottage-type farmhouses of red brick, we jounced to our destination. I noticed vineyards. But I couldn't see any stretch of ploughed fields. How come? I asked. Here, I was told, is a "wine cooperative." I asked for a farm, I reminded gently. A shrug. "It's a cooperative, isn't it?" was the reply. Off we went and found Ilya Gatev, representative of the local Communist committee. He, in turn, dug up Boyan Golatev, a vineyard expert, who studied the trade years ago in the Rhine Valley.

What about having a look at the mechanical wine presses, I asked. The workers aren't here, was the reply. Can I look at the machinery, I asked? The workers aren't here, again the reply. Can you show the mechanical installations, I persisted? The workers aren't here was the response. I got the idea and gave up. But Mr. Gatev, who has a relative living on West 102d Street in New York, is a proper host. We went together to visit the barns. I patted a couple of horses. Some of the workmen in the barns, seemingly neat and efficient, came up to greet me. They didn't, as did factory workers, shake hands with the slogan, "Peace, Mister." They shook hands and went back to work.

Mr. Gatev told me that this "cooperative" over-fulfilled its quota. He mentioned some percentage since it is a violation of state secrets to say how much is produced. He also informed me that 1,400 families have now joined the "coop." Only twenty, he said, were out of it. He claimed cooperative members earned around $100 a month—which didn't gibe with other official figures. They cultivate vineyards over 7,500 acres, said Mr. Gatev, and all workers were organized in brigades of forty to fifty each. There were, he said, 2,000 hands in all. Horses patted, barn workers greeted, we went off to quaff some of the local produce.

There was no mention again of the mechanized processes. Mr. Gatev did ask, though, that I photograph the four trucks parked near the stables as well as the five dozen or so horse-drawn wagons. We sat on a terrace overlooking the valley. It was a rather spectacular view. We talked. Mr. Gatev told me how houses were sprouting like the new harvest of grapes. The peasants are, he said, delighted with their work. Why, they even store their share of wine in the mysterious mechanized wine center. During the winter months, when slack time hangs heavy, they draw their wine. One peasant family visits another. Everybody drinks his neighbor's wine.

"They eat, drink and talk politics," said Mr. Gatev enthusiastically. "It's really high life," he added, with fervor.

I thought back to regime speeches; to acknowledgment of the manifold failures in agriculture and the new edict to get reluctant Bulgars back to the land. It certainly was, I told Mr. Gatev, a high life—for Mr. Gatev.

Brainwashing and public repentance became as much a part of Communist life as production quotas. Sins committed against established authority are acknowledged by intoning "mea culpa" to the accompaniment of triumphal trumpeting in the controlled press and radio. Yet it has been the mission of Bulgaria to retread some of the sinners for implementation of national policy. They are even sent on speaking tours around the country to whip up fervor for the government. In a manner of speaking, they are revivalists who have seen the light. Now they are trying to convince other sinners that the Communists are the true believers.

I was probably the first Westerner ever permitted to interview such retreads in a Communist country. Two former peasant leaders, once close associates of the late Nikola Petkov, talked to me—with government permission of course. They each had spent years in custody. Today they have well-paid jobs and utter public statements urging their former peasant adherents to follow them toward the promised Communist goals. Their "rehabilitation" was as planned as is the government's economy. Emphasis is on agriculture in this agrarian land. The peasants aren't coming across as the Communists want. What better emotional way, then, to encourage them than to have ex-opposition leaders say they were wrong?

That was the Communist government's patent plan. How successful it was remains pure speculation. The Communists, to make the whole idea a little more palatable, even revived the "Fatherland Front" and dumped a puppet Agrarian Party with the retreads into the organization. Lean, graying Assen Pavlov, a former minister of agriculture and close colleague of Mr. Petkov, gave me his reasons why. So did chunky, red-haired Peter Serbinsky, formerly chairman of the anti-Communist Agrarian Youth Organization. Mr. Pavlov had been in prison five years after fighting the hopeless battle against establishment of total Communist rule. Mr. Serbinsky was in a detention camp—a "preventive" measure, he called it—and was for a year under strict supervision in his home village. When I was last in Bulgaria, I had seen both men in action. They then had the courage of their convictions, which required lots of guts in those days. They were unflaggingly loyal to Mr. Petkov and they were all bitterly anti-Nazi, anti-monarchy. Their records made Communist attacks on them seem futile.

I sat in Mr. Pavlov's office, on the fourth floor of a building near the center of town. There was an interpreter along. Mr. Pavlov was well-dressed by local standards. His desk shone with a high polish. It was bare but for a calendar. Mr. Pavlov was now the director of a branch in the government perfume monopoly. Bulgarian Attar of Roses is, of course, world famous. Mr. Pavlov chatted quietly. His complexion was darker than I had remembered. It may have been sun-tanned, although pallor from confinement is difficult to erase during a few months' "liberty." A well-travelled, well-educated man, Mr. Pavlov answered questions. He said that he had been "convinced" while in jail that the Communists were carrying out the policy of Stamboulisky.

Never had he been beaten, said Mr. Pavlov. Never had there been any arduous questioning. He could read in the prison library, receive visitors, get food packages, attend political lectures and have all the exercise he required. His recital could sound logical, if utterly unimpassioned. He used all the proper phrases: "The Communists are the camp of peace. We are building socialism."

I reminded Mr. Pavlov that the type of charges leveled in a Communist court against the defendant was viewed in quite a different light in Western society. Did he, therefore, believe that he was guilty of espionage for the Anglo-Americans? Not quite, he said, but there were others in his party who were guilty. And he, Mr. Pavlov, had been associated with them. Therefore, guilty. Mr. Pavlov paused, then, wetting his lips, and offered a decanter of slivovitz. He poured a glass for each of the three of us, barely tasting his. He liked only the aroma, he explained. Did Mr. Pavlov genuinely believe, I asked, that Nikola Petkov was a traitor? Hands in lap, Mr. Pavlov studied his fingers behind the desk. I couldn't see how steady they were. Head tilted downwards, the reply came softly but reverberated around the room.

"Undoubtedly."

There was silence for at least twenty seconds. Mr. Pavlov seemd a little bemused. He recovered himself to add that Petkov had betrayed the cause of Stamboulisky and had become a tool of reaction. The record, it seemed to me, had been struck ever so briefly. Then it went back into the groove.

Serbinsky, a son of the soil, was so loquacious and wanted to make an impression so badly that even the interpreter had to cut him short. He was back at a desk in the old Agrarian Union building. He had been taken into the fold, he said proudly, as if nothing had ever happened. He was most grateful, he said. Had I read any of his recent declarations and speeches around the country? There was eagerness in his question and hope that something complimentary might be said in reply. He accepted willingly, however, mere acknowledgment that I had read some of his speeches. He had "volunteered," said Mr. Serbinsky, to stump the country to tell his fellow peasants that he had been wrong, that they should follow the example of the government, that they must work hard and be faithful to collectivization and the five-year plans.

Was his arrest justified? I asked. It was necessary, replied Mr. Serbinsky, as "a preventive measure." The government couldn't take any chances he explained eagerly on what action he might pursue before he found the truth. Did he believe that Mr. Petkov was a traitor, I asked? Mr. Serbinsky's torrent of conversation trickled momentarily into a dry bed.

"He was," he said. Then the stream gathered force again. "Petkov betrayed the policy of Stamboulisky and the interests of the peasants."

Mr. Serbinsky warmed to his theme and went on belaboring Petkov and his "treachery." I wasn't listening, though. I thought back to the time that Petkov had been condemned and Harry Truman, Clement Attlee and Ernie Bevin said that Nikola Petkov had been one of the greatest democrats of his time. This Western eulogy was banned by decree. The same no-look, no-talk spirit is extended to important monuments of Communist accomplishment. The unseen enemy may want to know, is given as cause for secrecy. Take a visit I made to the biggest Bulgar industrial complex.

Dimitrova East is a forbidden city. No strange rites echo through the halls nor are sacrifices offered to indomitable gods in the ancient, grisly and romantic sense. Great chimneys belch smoke and the clangor of cranes rasps above the hissing of acetylene torches. Inside the red brick buildings, men and women in coveralls stoke furnaces and red-hot metal bars jounce along assembly belts. Except to the coveralled inhabitants and the impassive men who supervise, Lenin-style caps pulled down over foreheads, this is a city of mystery, surrounded by barbed wire. It's banned to foreigners and forbidden to all but the inmates. This is the Lenin Steel Works at whose forges the state worships because it is industry, the first of its kind in Bulgar history. It is mysterious and forbidden because a Communist state is jealous of its production capabilities and suspicious of the alien's inquisitiveness.

Industry is new and its technicians are neophytes and the state is pleased and proud and scared of its machines. They must wonder, as did the men who ruled the Soviet Union in the first industrialization stages, how mastery could be achieved over the machines. So, Dimitrovo East, named after Georgi Dimitrov and part of a sprawling industrial complex still building, is a forbidden city.

And I was the first Westerner, I was told, permitted to tour what the authorities would show me of the plant and its facilities. This was different from the textile mill I had visited earlier, 100 or so miles from here. There shock-workers, "Heroes of Socialist Labor," and brigade leaders greeted me at every turn with cries of "peace," demanding to know if the U.S. wanted "peace." Here there were no spontaneous greetings for my benefit. It seemed as if they were primarily intent on impressing a citizen of the greatest industrial power in the world that they could operate lathes and machines and turn out steel. My interpreter and I came here from Sofia, twenty-odd miles away. We had a pass and were admitted to the offices of the administrative director. He was Dimo Stoichev, a large man with a moon face and a walrus mustache. He had been a Communist for many years.

No, he said a little sadly, there weren't any "Heroes of Socialist Labor" in the steel works yet. It had only been finished in 1953 and it would be years before the rest of the program could be completed. Around the conference table in his office, Mr. Stoichev answered some questions, evaded others and refused to discuss a few. When I asked how many people were employed, he pursed his lips in silence. That kind of information is secret. He talked about quotas, always using percentages, never figures. The Lenin Works, he said, had passed its quotas by twenty-five percent, whatever that meant. As he talked I noticed a magazine on the table, published in Chinese characters. I wondered if Mr. Stoichev could understand the magazine and if the percentages he quoted to me were about as incomprehensible to him as they were to me. The best technicians, he said, earned as much as $200 a month. The scale ran down to about $100 a month. The plant complex had its own housing and stores. Prices were about the same as in Sofia. I could understand why the young people were coming here from the farms. At least they could earn more money to buy the few consumer goods they yearned for.

Rain slanted across the concrete street strips as we left his office to visit an installation. The streets had been hastily laid down. They were buckling and inundated with several inches of rain water. Mr. Stoichev paused in the downpour to show me a magnetic crane lifting huge chunks of scrap metal piled 30 or so feet high. In the building we visited, I stood

on a platform, flanked by technical experts and looked down on the loading and packing processes. The machinery, down to the nuts and bolts,
was all Soviet-manufactured. It bore the imprint of "C.C.C.P." (U.S.S.R.
in the Cyrillic alphabet). Soviet technicians, Mr. Stoichev explained,
helped install the machinery and set up the steel works. Bulgar technicians
had been trained in the Soviet Union preparatory to the establishment of
the Lenin Works. Then, they trained other steel workers who were recruited from all Bulgaria. It reminded me of a football talent scout hunting around the country to recruit the best human raw material. But the
Lenin works are the showpiece and the only steel industry of any consequence in Bulgaria.

I saw young women operate the mechanism for the cranes and run the
most delicate phases of the production end. If married, their husbands
worked at the plant, too. But the state was very solicitous of husband-wife
relations, Mr. Stoichev explained.

"We always try to keep them on the same shift," he said.

It's an eight-hour day, six days a week, and the plant runs full blast
twenty-four hours daily. I talked to a twenty-year-old girl, Eleanora
Stanienierova, who operated the levers that send steel bars towards the
cooling process. She said she came down two years before from a farm to
learn the trade. Her husband, Ivan, had been an electrician and knew
something about machinery. Eleanora asked how American girls found
working in steel plants. Looking at her gloved hands, I said I didn't know
that any ever did except in an emergency like the last war. Mr. Stoichev
took me over to one of the furnaces where the heat was so glaring that
it could be approached only with smoked glasses. Two of the workers
tossed in a couple of logs, probably to make it glow a little more for the
visitor. My guide assured me they used coal, too.

As we wandered over the building, I noticed huge collections of steel
strips, piled near the assembly belts. Inferior manufacture, Mr. Stoichev
said. They would be reduced to scrap and made over. How large, I asked
him, was this plant. I had forgotten, for the moment, his Communist
vigilance. He wouldn't talk about it. I volunteered that, by American
standards, the works would be found in an industrial town of medium
population. Mr. Stoichev didn't answer. What was the steel used for, I
asked? Building materials, was the terse reply. What did they manufacture in other buildings around the industrial complex? Steel, was the
answer, just steel.

In silence we walked down the overflowing streets, water sloshing over our shoes, past the sentry box. I noticed a few strips of rags hanging limply on the barbed wire. Solemnly Mr. Stoichev accompanied us to our automobile and gravely shook hands with me. As we drove past the barbed wire, I could see him striding past the sentry box, Lenin-cap pulled down, heading for another building that I hadn't entered. The forbidden city was under wraps again.

The way the country was run, Bulgaria's Communist counsellors, if so prompted, could demand incorporation into the Soviet Union. It was a thought, Communists elsewhere told me, that often came to them. Bulgaria, another republic of the U.S.S.R. By attaching a little piece of real estate, meaning a strip of Rumania to the north, Bulgaria would be mountain-by-valley against the Soviet Union. That's one outstanding problem, if the decision ever arose, about adding this nation to Russia's empire. The other, of course, is the Bulgar people. Chances are, however, that the problem will not be pondered for a long time, if ever. By retaining the façade of a national entity, Bulgaria can maneuver within the strategic enclave of Greece, Yugoslavia and Turkey. It can send out diplomats and trade missions to countries with which it has relations. Communist control inside the country is assured, Soviet European politicians tell each other, and the opportunities for shaking that rigid grip, or even developing a form of "Titoism," are virtually nil. They say so, but they are not crackingly confident. Therefore, it is to the Russians' advantage to permit the fable of independence to remain with the Communist government of Bulgaria.

What, I asked myself and others, are the possibilities of Bulgaria wrenching away from the Red Bear's embrace? The conclusion I reached was that a lot depended on us, but still more on Bulgars themselves. Short of war, Bulgaria cannot in the present context of power relationship be detached from Soviet Europe. The Bulgars, however, can by their own forms of protest, frequently only inaction, make their displeasure known over the years. Bulgaria's new generation, raised and indoctrinated since September, 1944, balked and was forcibly fed Moscow doctrine.

Their opposition, as far as anyone knows, is leaderless. The Titoist opposition has been cut down at the head, with Traicho Kostov, at the gallows. Nevertheless, whenever the regime experiments with a little relaxation, the demand for more is so great that terror is forthwith used to smother the small ventilator.

The worst offenders to the regime are the young intellectuals, who should have come of age and service to the state by now. Among the peasants exists probably the steadiest dissatisfaction. The government admits it. It is not cohesive nor is it organized. The voice of protest in the countryside in Bulgaria is a combination of defiance and discontent against Communist collectivization policy. To prove its power and devotion to doctrine, the Communists do things to peasants in Bulgaria that youngsters remember when they grow up. Villages that held out against collectives are sealed off by troops. Peasants can neither enter nor leave. Isolated and starved into submission, they sign. They submit, but they remember. That is something long-time emigrés don't understand.

Emigrés and their leaflets have little impact on the country. Bulgars, quite like other subjugated people, seem to resent someone sitting safely and comfortably, telling them to resist. It doesn't go down. The most militant opponent of the Communists, Nikola Petkov, lives in men's minds. He is dead but his image isn't. Nor are his hopes. As a latter-day martyr, Petkov's name always will remain. He stayed and died. Communist security can throttle a person. His messages do not, necessarily, die with him. They are transferred from one generation to the next. In the transfer, those inherited hopes grow bigger, more tempting, and more embarrassing questions to the ruling regime are raised. I think I have a little idea why. A Bulgar newspaper man, released in a general amnesty, turned up near my hotel. Beside him was a nearly grown boy. The journalist stared at me, took the boy by the arm and they crossed the street. I don't blame them.

An act of supreme courage occurred when I went to the railroad to get my train. It was early in the morning, but crowds were out to see people off to the border town. The same boy who had walked across the street with the newspaperman entered my compartment. He had a tiny vial of rose perfume that he handed me.

"You may not remember," he said. "I was the little boy Petkov took when my father disappeared. We do not forget."

He shook my hand, slipped into the crowd outside and hustled to the outdoor buffet. There he joined my old journalist friend. They nodded. We did not wave.

CHAPTER | 13

AUSTRIA, once a great Danube empire, had been truncated after World War I and then driven into "anschluss" with the Nazis. It wanted fervently to end the post-World War II occupation. As years rolled by, Austrians could see for themselves how the successor states of the old empire had become satellites of Russia. In mid-war, however, the Allied powers all declared in Moscow that Austria would certainly be restored to its between-the-wars boundaries. First, it had to undergo four-power military occupation. That was to remind the Austrians that they had been part of the Third Reich.

Unlike Germany, the Russians never seriously threatened to partition Austria and Vienna. It could easily have been done. There has been speculation as to why it wasn't. The Russians have never given any explanation. It might have been that Austria started with having, early in the occupation, national elections that were free. Everyone recognized the government throughout the world. It was a strange coalition, drawn together against Soviet domination. Conservatives from the People's Party and their traditional enemies, the Socialists, made common cause. Most of them, not too long before, fought each other in the streets. The Communist Party was a joke; they never had more than five percent of the vote and rather impotent in the trade unions which were strongly held and organized by Socialists.

In the speculation at static Soviet intrigue in Austria, one highly held view was that the Russians made the first mistake by permitting free elections in the whole country. They had no influence outside their own zone. As the coalition government became bold in demanding the Russians cease to meddle in local affairs, the Soviet command and Moscow retaliated with threats. They held out the dread word, "partition," but it always petered out quickly. Carving up Austria would have meant that the Russians kept for themselves the eastern zone that fronted on Czechoslovakia, Hungary and Yugoslavia. Economically, the artificial state would have been a dead loss. To the world, such a partition would have seemed cruelly bizarre. The Russians continued to forget their occasional menaces. They kept tabs on the West in Vienna and vice-versa. It was always cloak-and-dagger in Vienna on the Danube. The government, anti-Communist to the core, tried to warn its own citizens about becoming enmeshed in great power espionage nets. It didn't help much. People still got hurt, made a few fast bucks and the plots and counter-plots continued to be hatched.

Through the Marshall Plan and other large-scale credits, the Austrian economy was revived. Vienna particularly was made a shining showplace compared with the scared, have-nothing neighbors to the east. In its spiral of modest prosperity, little Austria began to daydream of becoming another Switzerland.

"It would be so nice to have none of you here except as real guests," sighed Leopold Figl over a Grinzing dinner one night. Figl was then Foreign Minister. He had for five years been Chancellor. Before that, Figl spent years in Dachau. Although he was a conservative of peasant origin, even Communists swore by his integrity. Party politics demoted him and brought to the Chancellor's chair hulking Julius Raab. He used to run the People's Party but he had been suspect a long time of having been too right-wing. It was Raab, though, who really started the work that brought off the Austrian treaty.

While the Russians were talking in all corners of the world about coexistence, they went at it more doggedly in Vienna. Soviet diplomats talked of it to Raab, Figl and their Socialist coalition partners. Khrushchev had made already his first break-through attempt to meet with President Eisenhower at the summit. Winston Churchill had been the first to make the summit suggestion but age and infirmity compelled him to step down. Sir Anthony Eden was Prime Minister. Khrushchev had to deal through Bulganin, who, naturally, was willing. There was reservation about the whole idea in the United States, led by Secretary of State John Foster Dulles. Until the Russians showed in deed a more amicable turn of East-West relations, he said, it was useless to talk of a summit conference. For years there had been great power negotiations over Austria. They always drifted off into hot air and dashed hopes.

The Austrians heard from the Russians in Vienna and Moscow that Khrushchev favored rather quickly an Austrian settlement, a treaty, after ten years of occupation. They should not be snickered at for thinking that the treaty at long last unleashed a chain of events of moving significance in all Eastern Europe. The Austrian treaty was the first Soviet move to go from Stalin to Khrushchev policy in the outside world. Veteran Bolshevik V. M. Molotov, still Soviet Foreign Minister, was opposed to an Austrian treaty. Over his protests, an Austrian delegation of experts headed by Raab rushed to Moscow. They made a deal, which mortgaged for some years to follow, Austrian income. This was especially true in oil production. Austria's oil fields are among the most lucrative in Europe for their size.

In return for the mortgage, the Russians also said Austrian governments must be strictly neutral. Their hearts could be with the West but Austria must reject attachment to military and economic alliances affecting the Soviet Union. Back rushed the excited Austrian specialists. A treaty was in the bag. The West had to be consulted and briefed. We had to begin our own negotiations with the Russians on the oil memorandum. A treaty was in the offing. It was a step, calling not only for evacuation of Soviet forces but of ours, too, within six months of the treaty. Had we been opposed—and I heard some grumbling about how the Austrians pulled a fast one on us—we could not in any good faith sabotage the deal. Molotov was opposed as well but he ultimately had to put on a cordial face to sign for Moscow in Vienna.

To a world, weary of bickering and tension, this seemed in the nature of a thaw. Tito, on his first trip to Asia, wanted to be in on the transition. Khrushchev was telling the Yugoslav ambassador in Moscow how nice it would be for him to be invited to visit Yugoslavia. Summitry seemed to be splitting old suspicions. On the outside, nobody really knew Khrushchev. The Yugoslavs knew something about his career but little about the man.

"He was always another one of those little bald men who worked for Stalin," a Yugoslav Communist said. "We saw him occasionally in the old days. Hardly anyone spoke to him. You dealt with Stalin."

During the height of the Stalin-Tito conflict, Khrushchev also lent his invective in the anti-Yugoslav campaign. One of the pithier Khrushchev comments of the time was that Tito was a treacherous, carnivorous hog. The thaw was setting in fast, though, so Tito started for home on his yacht, a converted minesweeper, called the "Galeb." Tito doesn't care to travel on airplanes.

By the time he got back to the comradely coasts of Yugoslavia, Britain, France, the United States and the Soviet Union were agreed in principle to hold a summit conference in Geneva. Dulles' demands for deeds would be shown positively in the Soviet Union agreeing to a treaty making Austria Europe's new neutral. Afterwards there would be an East-West summit. Khrushchev, through the guided missives of Bulganin, would get to meet the big men of the West. Only a few dissenting voices that mattered were raised against high-level, hastily improvised conferences. Dulles quieted American dissenters who feared Eisenhower was not up to such an encounter. Everything would be all right, asserted Dulles, because he would be present.

Men experienced in national tragedies had a deeper, more somber warning to issue. Salvador de Madariaga said that conferring with Khrushchev and Bulganin would mark acceptance by the West of an Eastern Europe under the Soviet heel. De Madariaga pointed out that a summit meeting could end the hopes of peoples in satellite states for outside support. This, he declared, was the most immoral and hypocritical phase of summitry. He was absolutely right. Khrushchev referred for years after to the meeting he had with Eisenhower on the sparkling shores of Lake Geneva as evidence that the West forgot all about Soviet Europe. When Ike, at the summit, tentatively raised the subject of East Europe, it was Bulganin who angrily said the Russians wouldn't listen to anything about it. Khrushchev heartily approved. Not another word on that score was mentioned again.

Before this historic scene was set Tito was showing the world he would not be an also-ran in the world's eye. The invitation Khrushchev asked for bluntly was referred to the Yugoslav Mr. Big, fresh from his consultations in India and Burma. A new international vista had opened in front of Tito. Non-alignment rang in his ears like a siren song. Neutrals, as he learned on his tour, dealt with all political societies. Self-determination was a mystique with them and Tito claimed proudly that he set Yugoslavia on self-determination by saying no to Stalin. Thus Tito said yes to Khrushchev. The invitation was announced and Communist propaganda reverberated through Eastern Europe.

"The satellites are going absolutely crazy about this invitation," chortled a high Yugoslav official. "They dare not oppose it. But what can they say about us now? Khrushchev is coming to apologize to Tito."

Khrushchev's visit to Belgrade was called many things. Alarmists saw him being trapped into returning to the old "socialist" fold led by Moscow. Doctrinaire Yugoslav Communists always hoped there would be this reconciliation. They were fish out of water with the West and felt like capitalist pilot fish at that. Yugoslavs themselves wondered openly where they would find themselves. They openly liked attachments with the West and appearance of Westerners at their resorts and Western fashions which other parties denounced and tried to prohibit. The few weeks between the signing of the Austrian treaty, Khrushchev's arrival in Yugoslavia and the summit were a political version of "Hellzapoppin'." Only the Austrians knew what to expect in advance. They got it.

In the baroque Belvedere Palace, set in a jewel of a green midtown park, the Foreign Ministers representing the United States, Britain, France and the Soviet Union signed the Austrian Treaty. It was called a State Treaty because Austria was treated officially as a "liberated" country with reservations. The reserve had been maintained in occupation of the country. Austrians celebrated their new status in the world somewhat soberly. Ten years of occupation, backed by seven years of Nazi rule, made people a little limp. Molotov, eyes opaque behind pince-nez, clinked glasses of Austrian wine with Dulles. It might have been a post-signing sour note, considering the quality of Austrian wine. Both men pretended to be of good cheer, saying they would meet again shortly in Geneva.

The bounciest enthusiam was reflected in Vienna's Palace of Emperors. At Schoenbrunn, where the Austrian government celebrated its totally sovereign arrival in the world, Yugoslav guests were asking everyone around how they assessed the impending arrival of Khrushchev in Belgrade. The event was only a matter of hours away and vast preparations were made to spread the red carpet all over Yugoslavia for their guests. It was made plural because although Khrushchev was first secretary of the Soviet party and therefore most important, Bulganin held the position of Prime Minister. Communists are precisely protocol-conscious even when they know where the power reposes. Long before the Bulganin-Khrushchev two-motored Ilyushin circled Belgrade, the powder-blue uniformed Praetorian honor guard of Tito was at the airport. Diplomats, in striped pants or black suits, depending on their politics, were lined up on one side. Diagonally across, reporters stared at them. There was no communication. Photographers shifted restlessly in an isolated enclave.

Yugoslav and Soviet security mingled with everyone. Russian plainclothes men were easily distinguishable. They all wore grayish gabardine coats, floppy fedoras and wide-bottomed dark trousers. It wasn't so easy for them to spot Yugoslav security. The UDBA men of Rankovitch looked like most other people at the airport. They were smartly dressed, usually in dark Italian-styled suits. Many even wore Italian-type moccasins. Just before the Soviet planes came overhead, the Yugoslav Politburo appeared. They nodded all around and took up their places at a spot away from all of us. Mosa Pjade kept his neck craned to the sky to see the Russian planes he said were promised back in 1943. The roar of an expensive motor on the ground distracted everyone's attention.

Into the airport swept Tito, in his marshal's uniform. He came in a convertible Rolls-Royce with the top down. The car of kings and captains of industry he got to know and like on a visit to London. His honor guard, towering above him, smartly saluted the ruler of Yugoslavia. The timing was perfect. Over Belgrade swept the Ilyushins bearing the Soviet guests. They were escorted, ceremonially, by Yugoslav jet fighters made in the United States. The jets had been delivered to Tito's air force under military aid agreements with Washington. All the pilots had been checked out by American flying specialists.

As the Khrushchev-Bulganin Ilyushin taxied up to the waiting reception lines, Tito strode briskly to the mobile stairway on which the Russians were to make their descent. Ground to a halt, the silvery main plane opened a hatch and out popped Khrushchev first. He was followed by Bulganin. Few present at the airport had ever seen Khrushchev before.

Hands outstretched, the spring sun shining on his bald pate, he bounced down the stairs. All eyes were on Tito. Expressionless, he offered a stiff, right hand over which Khrushchev's pudgy hands went in greeting. Joviality exuded from Khrushchev. His side-kick, Bulganin, shook hands genially around and stood a respectful pace behind Khrushchev. Yugoslav eyes, excepting Tito's, swivelled again to the plane. They were looking for Molotov. He didn't come. Molotov had been against the visit from the start. Not once did he ever recant what he had said about Tito. Neither before, then or after. His absence didn't seem to put a shadow on Khrushchev's radiance. Mikoyan was smilingly evident instead. They were introduced to Tito's immediate entourage. The photographers, penned up, were also let loose. They chased the main protagonists, Tito walking with his affected military gait and Khrushchev alongside, bouncing on the balls of his feet.

Photographers shouted at them to walk a little more slowly. Eyes on the honor guard, Tito never slackened his gait. Khrushchev did, hastened to recover and catch up with his Yugoslav host. Photographers jostled. A Soviet photographer who elbowed Jim Pringle never recovered that day.

Pringle, an Associated Press camera man who had been in wars and riots all over the world, calmly backhanded the unsuspecting Russian. But he backhanded him with the side of his own camera. Pringle took the picture of Khrushchev the Russian tried to get and never glanced at the fallen photographer. Diplomats, though, audibly gasped at the scene. It set the frenetic tone of the visit that followed in and outside Belgrade. Escorted by Tito, Khrushchev got through the honor guard ceremonial. The guardsmen, all six-footers, shouted a welcome after presenting arms to Khrushchev. He beamed, said thanks, and headed for a microphone he noticed on the way to the honor guard.

Settling spectacles on his nose, Khrushchev read a prepared speech. Tito, who speaks excellent Russian, listened quietly. His eyes were hooded and he didn't move a muscle. Within half-a-minute, Khrushchev's theme was clear. It was all Beria's fault, the whole Soviet-Yugoslav break. There was no mention of Stalin. Khrushchev did, indeed, apologize for all that had gone before: Soviet behavior towards Tito, the economic blockade and the bad name that had been given Yugoslavia in the Soviet world. Obviously, it didn't sound good enough to Tito. When he finished, Khrushchev beckoned Tito invitingly to the microphone. Tito shook his head and turned to his car. Khrushchev rushed after him. He said something. Tito introduced him and Bulganin to the waiting diplomatic corps. Then Tito led the way to the Rolls-Royce, Bulganin padding behind.

The two Russians squeezed in on either side of Tito. Security cars fore and aft, the cavalcade to Belgrade streamed past the marshland shanty-towns, the gaping buildings of Novi Belgrade to what a Yugoslav called, with satisfaction, "a correct reception." There were crowds and banners. Children also waved Soviet and Yugoslav paper flags. The applause was modulated. Cries of "long live Tito" rang out. They drowned out any cheers for the Russians.

"Just enough," observed a contented Yugoslav journalist as the hosts and visitors prepared for meals, receptions, toasts and tours. "We will see how all this goes later on."

Khrushchev, in public appearances, evoked the grisly memory of Beria. It met a stony silence. He began to dwell more, then, on future Yugoslav-Soviet understanding than on the recent past still unhealed. Tito, smoking cigarettes in a holder, was the correct and sophisticated host. In his toasts, he always emphasized Yugoslav independence and the achievements made by Yugoslav Communists under the Yugoslav party. For his own concerned doctrinaires, he also spoke glowingly of the achievements of the "people of socialism" in the Soviet Union. The Russians did not mention the Djilas case to Tito. Their journalists, as political instruments of the party, talked about it in a puzzled and lengthy manner to Yugoslav and foreign colleagues. It was very strange, they thought, that someone who was such an obvious traitor to them as Djilas got off so easily. Yugoslavs generally retorted that this was better than spilling blood and in any case, the Russians had better mind their own business. The Russians shut up—for the time being but only on that count.

Khrushchev, Bulganin, Mikoyan and their camp followers finally began their tour of Yugoslavia. They went west. That is where Tito's regime can show off by far the most highly developed parts of the country. Comparatively, when the new regime took over after the war, western Yugoslavia was more highly advanced than any other area. In addition, new factories had sprung up where technical knowledge could be more easily found and where production and distribution were easiest. It was a part of Yugoslavia to which the Tito Communists could point and claim as their own achievement.

Khrushchev took an active interest in cornfields he passed in Croatia.

There, farms are rather neat and orderly. He also saw some state farms, commented on the high quality of agriculture he saw there but kept mum about other farms. They were de-collectivized. Khrushchev, in an aside, said that he saw a future only in collective labor, be it on farms or factories. Publicly, he annoyed some leaders of workers' councils in plants around Zagreb, the steamy, old-Austrian provincial-style capital of Croatia. He congratulated workers for turning out what seemed to him splendid objects of production. On workers' councils, he was most condescending. They had long ago been tried in the U.S.S.R., he observed, but weren't good enough in practice. Anyway, he said in a conciliatory way, each country should develop as it thought best. Communist-governed nations, he meant. Yugoslav party activists challenged him on the philosophy of councils. There was no booing, of course. Treatment was to be "absolutely correct," on Tito's orders.

Wherever the Russians challenged Titoist doctrine, though, Yugoslav Communists had been instructed to defend it energetically. Khrushchev abruptly broke off from any implied public criticism of Yugoslav methods. Instead, he extolled Soviet proficiency and slyly referred to the emotional appeal of Russian-Yugoslav solidarity against the common German enemy of the war. He declared wherever it was opportune that "socialism" would triumph. With this, the Yugoslav Communists had no quarrel at all.

In a back-breaking tour, that had the UDBA uniformed and plain-clothes details strung out over western Yugoslavia, Khrushchev and his party went diligently through sight-seeing and meetings with peasants and workers assembled to see them. Tito had gone off to his private island home at Brioni, where he rested until his guests arrived.

Italy possessed the island until capitulation. Tito took it over as rightfully Yugoslav and as the spoils of war. The weather almost always was benevolently mild. Hotels on the island, guarded by Tito's special sea police, were in fairly good shape. There was also a big villa fronting on the sea. It was refurbished and new, semi-tropical plants and foliage were added from the house to the edge of the sparkling sea. Tito had begun to stock the island with tame deer and with a private zoo. Birds and animals presented to him, beginning with his first trip to Asia, were given special preserves in Brioni. A poor boy, turned immeasurably wealthy, might have dreamed of Brioni as a place in which to relax.

Guests stayed at the hotels, accessible immediately after landing. To get to Tito's villa, special guests were taken by motor launch to a private, guarded landing. They didn't have to walk through good roads and pleasantly shaded spots to enter the villa grounds. It was a long walk. Khrushchev and Bulganin didn't have to walk if they didn't want the exercise. They showed up in old-fashioned, brightly polished landaus and fiacres. No cars are permitted on the island except for Tito's special out-door island rig. This is an open-air, carriage-style car which he delights in driving. Photographers were summoned from Pula, whooshed in motor-boats to Brioni, where they could snap the scene. In floppy panamas and open shirts, Khrushchev and Bulganin waved from seats behind Tito, the driver, showing them around his estate.

Thereupon, photographers and all outsiders were shooed away from the grounds. Into the villa, with awnings discreetly drawn, Tito and his comrades faced Khrushchev, Bulganin, Mikoyan and their specialists for Communist business at hand. Some of the conversation which emerged was astounding even for Yugoslav party ears. Everyone drank and ate sparingly. Talk was the most sought-after meat and drink. I was later told by a Yugoslav present that Tito asked Khrushchev about Communists, international and Soviet, he had once known intimately in Moscow. How, Tito asked, as an example, is Dmitri doing? Khrushchev would look at Tito and reply, "Dead." Another name. "Dead." Still others, known to virtually every one present in the room. A shrug from Khrushchev and the one-word answer: "Dead."

"Even to hard men of experience," my informant reported pensively, "it all sounded pretty spooky."

Not so macabre were the arguments between the Russians and the Yugoslavs. They went round in circles, using dogmatic and power doctrine on each other. Khrushchev wanted bygones to be bygones. The economic blockade of Yugoslavia would end and the Soviet bloc would make amends, he promised. More vital, he shrewdly asserted as one Communist to other Communists, were the interests of what these parties like to call the struggle and the interests of the working class. Khrushchev proposed that Tito should rejoin the movement—meaning return to the Moscow fold and the Soviet orbit. Yugoslavia, under this term of reference, would be free to develop her own road to socialism. Recognition of the primacy of Moscow was more vital than ever to counteract imperialist intrigue.

It was a powerful ideological lever that Khrushchev wielded on Com-munist Yugoslavs. Stalin was dead; there were changes busting out all over in the Soviet system. What would be more natural for Communists, even heretics, than to return to the mother church after the bad saint was smeared and the injured asked to forgive. For the first time, too, the Yugoslavs had advance insight into the preparations Khrushchev was making for the Twentieth Soviet Party Congress. He was going to tell the Communist world, he confidentially imparted, just how Stalin had almost wrecked all interested parties.

"We were as free as birds under this Khrushchev formula and the way he presented it," a Titoist trouble-shooter in trade union affairs afterwards said. "But someone, maybe it was Tito himself, said that birds always were naked."

The Yugoslavs, led by Tito, argued back. They had experienced isolation and subsequently the delightful and heady aroma of being very special in the world. Their counsel was solicited by new nations on how to deal with the Russians. The thought of being an independent Communist state and being uncommitted either to the West or the East blocs appealed to Tito. Yugoslavia could have the best of three worlds: Credits from the Soviet Union and the West, plus great moral credit and influence in Asia and Africa. That didn't appeal at all to Khrushchev. Then and there, in Brioni, he said he didn't believe anyone or anything could really be neutral when the chips were down. The great; private debate raged and was carried over on the return to Belgrade.

Gala wind-up receptions were offered by Tito, the host, and Khrushchev, the star guest. In between, they argued the outcome—the document that was to seal Khrushchev's visit as a penitent and Tito's recognition of the change in Soviet leadership and outlook. It came to be known as the Belgrade Declaration and has ever after been a paper the Yugoslavs wave under the Soviet nose. Most important in the Belgrade Declaration was the Yugoslav reiteration, agreed to by Khrushchev, that Tito would not rejoin the bloc. On his part, Tito recognized the supposedly great work for world peace and peoples' relief on which the Soviet Union was embarked. Yugoslavia was again a recognized "socialist country"—something shorn from them by Stalin. It was something Soviet Europe's leaders had to readjust in their minds and it was extremely difficult. Tito had achieved an armistice with Khrushchev but there was conditional ideological Soviet surrender.

Khrushchev had by no means abjectly acquiesced. He still was opposed by a suspicious Tito, glorying in his own worldwide acclaim. Becoming a member of the Soviet bloc would have made him a super-Gheorghiu-dej, or Bierut, but still a satellite personality. It was not for Tito. Re-buffed, Khrushchev never relaxed trying to draw Tito step by step further into his own bloc plans and controls. In Belgrade and then in Moscow, Khrushchev never gave a sign of any disappointment. Reconciliation had been achieved, he thundered. That, in itself, was a mighty defeat for re-action. So Khrushchev declared and turned the conclusion of his Yugoslav visit into a bizarre celebration.

In a roomy, ornate office building in downtown Belgrade turned over to the Russians for the occasion, Khrushchev gave his goodbye party. This was the return for Tito's mammoth reception in the old White Palace over which the Yugoslav red-starred flag flew. For his party, Khru-shchev flew in magnificent folk dancers, renowned musicians and great delicacies and drink.

It was a humid, heavy night. Summer penetrated earlier that year into heaving Belgrade. The jammed rooms kept a collective eye on one salon, reserved for the Russians and their highest Yugoslav guests. Outside that room, Soviet and Yugoslav security watched each other stonily. They stood between each other, or sat on chairs facing one another. Reporters, especially those from the West, strolled in and out and peeked in on the salon of honor. On his feet, Khrushchev proposed vodka toasts. Tito sat beside him, with Jovanka on his left. "Mir!" Khrushchev pronounced the Russian word for peace and drained the glass. Tito toyed with a glass of white wine. He used the same glass for hours. As soon as he finished his toast, a white-jacketed waiter at Khrushchev's elbow, filled the glass with vodka. The performance went on for a long time except for short breaks for imported entertainment and Khrushchev's meeting some foreign dip-lomats.

At one point, he shook hands with the veteran and highly able James Riddleberger, the U.S. Ambassador. Flushed with his speech and a bit incoherent, Khrushchev told Riddleberger that he knew nothing of real work. Riddleberger retorted that he knew more about how a working man made out than Khrushchev did. He had been a farm worker and a brick-layer, said Riddleberger. His more recent experience than Khrushchev's with work-to-live made him more aware of how working people felt, ex-plained the American ambassador. Khrushchev began to growl angrily, choked it off and said it was nice to exchange views with the representa-tive of the United States. Then he went back to drinking toasts to Tito and eternal Yugoslav-Soviet friendship. Khrushchev got roaring drunk.

From that drunk scene, which I witnessed a nose-breadth's length from Khrushchev, came a sadly distorted picture to the Western world. The Soviet No. 1 was plastered as any muzhik could ever be on a week-end. He apparently felt no cause to be reserved. It had been a very tense time. Moreover, it was his party and the Yugoslavs were considered comrades again—up to a point. To regard Khrushchev as a sodden buffoon was a terrible error in judgment. A tough and veteran Yugoslav apparatus official remarked sagely as Khrushchev stumbled out of the salon of honor in the wee hours of the morning, "Probably his first drunk in a long time. He never made first secretary of the party by getting into that condition. If he had been usually drunk, he would have been dead."

For that night, Khrushchev was simply dead drunk. He bounced off the door sill and stumbled towards the packed, waiting group of foreigners hanging on to the stairway down which he had to descend. Eyes glazed, Bulganin staggered after Khrushchev. Next to Khrushchev hovered Mikoyan. His gait was uneven but he looked alert. Tito followed closely. He had a cigarette in a miniature pipe-holder. His dinner jacket was immaculate and he presented a totally prepossessing picture to the world. When Khrushchev said something in Russian, Tito translated it into the English he had begun to learn a couple of years before. It was a good public relations stunt.

At the stairwell, an American reporter stuck his hand out and asked Khrushchev a question. Khrushchev grabbed the outstretched hand to avoid falling down the stairs. My wife was caught between the two men. A German reporter asked about Khrushchev's feelings towards the Germans. "I don't fear the devil himself," was Khrushchev's snorting reply. Frank Kelley of the *New York Herald Tribune* asked him then to give visas to American reporters to go to the Soviet Union if he wasn't afraid of the devil. "Come and see us," replied Khrushchev. On the strength of the remark, some of us got visas promptly. But Mikoyan was becoming impatient on the stairway. "Let's go, Nikita Sergeevich," Mikoyan kept saying, tugging at Khrushchev's jacket sleeves. Reluctantly, Khrushchev left off arguing with reporters and was helped down the stairs. Before he got into a waiting car, he tried to embrace Yugoslavs saying goodbye. Not Tito, though, who stood watching him with his hands stuffed in his tuxedo pockets. When Khrushchev tried to kiss a Yugoslav woman, she ducked. His kiss landed on the mustache of a bewildered official. The photograph was taken but killed by Yugoslav brass.

Next morning, farewells were said at the airport. Back in uniform, Tito looked fresh. Khrushchev seemed pale and had the hangover gravity of a man who kept tasting the night before. His party and he flew off to Moscow. The world, particularly the Soviet-led world, began to post-mortem the visit. In Belgrade the Yugoslavs were busy assuring the apprehensive West that they hadn't changed but Khrushchev had. Theirs, in sum, remained the orthodoxy of heterodoxy. To other faithful satellite regimes the visit and the Belgrade Declaration seemed much more radical. They were openly confused and highly suspicious of any new two-way arrangements with Tito.

I went into Czechoslovakia soon after Khrushchev returned to Moscow. It was the first time since the Associated Press' Bill Oatis had been sentenced to jail that an American reporter was allowed to travel for any spell inside the country. Oatis was thrown in prison four years before. Returning to Czechoslovakia was a shock for me. I saw it as a kind of Paradise Lost. The Czechoslovak regime thought about similar possibilities but where Khrushchev's mission to Tito impinged on the men who ruled in Prague. Over and over I asked the key ideological question: "Do you now think that Yugoslavia is a socialist state?" The answers from Communists were interesting and frank because they represented a strictly dogmatic point of view. Most Czech Communists said "no," that they didn't think Tito was building a socialist state or regime. Others were undecided. They were not sure what it all meant but they didn't think Yugoslavia was developing a socialist society. If, however, Khrushchev believed it was useful to be on good terms with Tito, they'd go along.

There was, then, no "new look" for internal Czechoslovakia. Of all the European satellites, Czechoslovakia had been the last to be taken over. But its Communist regime was the bloodiest of all the satellites. It devoured its own leadership and rewrote history. Stalin was dead but his hand lay heavily on the country. His massive, ninety-two-foot statue, towered above the golden spires of beautiful Prague. After finishing the eye-sore monument, the sculptor committed suicide. Czechs spoke softly in Prague, were polite but didn't want to talk to foreigners too much. Thomas Garrigue Masaryk had become, by state edict, a bad name not to be mentioned in public. His dead son was studiously ignored in any public notice. So were the riots that had blazed in Pilsen. Conformity with regime demands was laid down as the rule of law and life.

There was plenty of basic food, more than in any other Soviet European country. The Czechs had always been much more advanced. Outside staples, prices were very high. To a wandering tourist they might seem cheap, equated between the special dollar rate and the Czech crown. The real gauge of the cost of living is how much work it takes to buy food and clothing. When I returned that time, it required one week's work to buy a pair of shoes. Fresh meat had become a treat. It was ridiculously high to buy. In the mayor's office in Prague, a party worker explained why meat was priced that way.

"There's too big a demand for meat," he said earnestly. "You know, everyone thinks he ought to have meat for supper."

Farmers and peasants had another explanation. The regime was speeding up collectivization. Walking around a collective farm, I asked a curious farmer, who stopped a tractor, how he liked the system. He looked around, saw that the rest of the party was out of earshot and replied: "I plant many things. Sometimes nothing ever grows again when I plant. Lots of other people do the same." He waved his hand and gunned the tractor down the fields. Farmers demonstrated against collectivization publicly, at first. The regime went after them ruthlessly. Arrests and executions throttled demonstrations. Doing what came naturally after centuries of foreign rule led the Czechoslovaks into passive resistance. Farms didn't flower according to plan. Neither did plants produce the way quotas were set.

The party, always on the lookout to show the way to the rest of satellite Europe, tried to keep the drive up. Figures were falsified, according to occasional party revelation. People were punished but they were generally non-party. A new generation was being raised, indoctrinated in the Sovietized way of life. Parents and children alike were cautious. It was a national trait, a Czech long ago told me. That was the best way in which to survive any catastrophe, or occupation. On the outside, life seemed to embody enforced drabness and a calculated listless quality. Old friends were usually happy to see you. Their greeting was again cordial and cautious. They could manage to make ends meet if husband and wife worked. Few would say any more in public to you. They looked around to scan the sidewalk if you met them.

A writer friend, now dead, summed it up best. He had just finished telling me that you could not buy Franz Kafka's books in Czechoslovakia. They were bootlegged and the party would be rough on an intellectual caught with an unauthorized copy of Kafka. For that matter, the classic, "Good Soldier Schweik," had been disapproved for sale. The book, set in Austro-Hungarian imperial army days of World War I showed how deliberate passive resistance could foul up a system.

"You manage to live," explained my friend. "The human being has a strong survival sense. Tourists can come and say that everything looks normal. They don't see people being beaten by police in the streets. They don't see people dying of hunger in the alleys. The shops have things to sell—if you can afford them. The foreign visitor wonders where the abnormality is, where is the Communist ogre. He can't see it so he wonders about all he's heard. As a casual visitor, you do not see factory meetings where people are denounced. You do not hear the party censor lecturing you on what you have written. You do not see people taken to jail and sentenced. Fear you do not see unless you live with it. I have just finished a Russian book. Strongly disapproved here, by the way. I fully agree with the title, 'Not By Bread Alone.' Communists will never understand its full spiritual title."

Unrelieved drabness in life, even for a full dinner pail, also was the mark of regime direction in Hungary. Five-by-five Rakosi had been back in the saddle gain, directing Hungary after the short-lived "new course" of Imre Nagy. The Khrushchev visit to Yugoslavia, virtually on the frontiers, didn't change ruling Hungarian Communist feelings towards Tito. It took another year before the official line on Yugoslavia softened. Khrushchev, in the interim, never brought pressure to bear on either Czechoslovakia or Hungary directly to correct their stances.

In Budapest, the time when every girl seemed to look like Zsa Zsa Gabor and every woman like Mama Gabor was a thing which the regime denounced as the "vicious past." Girls worked in the "New Hungary." You saw them on the scaffoldings of buildings, or heaving loads into factory stockpiles. Of all Soviet Europe, however, Magyar women tried hardest to keep their identity. It was most difficult and expensive. They spent precious money for lipstick and Western fashion magazines went the rounds until they were in tatters. In the new factories, women wore overalls, but they changed to dresses as soon as they got home.

The material may have been shoddy but the styles had nothing of Moscow in them. They also felt good. Among the younger people, sullen silence prevailed. It was broken only when they got together to hear themselves talk about what was wrong that they became animated. There also were a growing group of don't-give-a-damn youngsters. They spent their time thinking up ways of outwitting the regime.

In the Hungarian Writers' Club one night, I was getting a sour rundown of youth, censorship and top party blindness from a celebrated author. He later personally ignited the spark disturbing many intellectuals on the eve of revolution.

"There must be a way to decent, socialist justice," he exploded. "Something must happen quickly to expose the miscarriage of legality in the past. It must be done. Otherwise, I don't know. . . ."

A few months later, Khrushchev electrified the Communist cadres of the world with his anti-Stalin charges at the Twentieth Party Congress. The accusations exposed Stalin's tyranny. They also laid open the fraud perpetrated on millions forced to accept planned deception and the revolution of terror that went with it. "Khrushchev had his reasons for what he said about Stalin," a Polish Communist told me. "He doesn't know what he really has done. Ours is a party on borrowed time. But Stalin made the party. What next?"

CHAPTER | 14

THROUGHOUT Eastern Europe in the early 1950's, hope for change began to burst in the most vital places. Workers, students, peasants and the ruling parties were encouraged, or rocked by the feverish inside reforms advocated by the new management in the Soviet Union. The sight of Red Army units withdrawing from Austria to terminate Soviet occupation in Europe's new neutral, inspired great expectations. Communists holding power doubted the wisdom of the evacuation but kept mum. Bulganin and Khrushchev—especially Khrushchev because in Communist-ruled countries people learn fast that the first secretary of the party is Mister Big—seemed to symbolize change from stabilized poverty and tenacious terror. What the change meant nobody could really say. Nor was anyone prepared to plan serious surgery to alter existing conditions. Basically, they knew something was inherently wrong with the system. The people were impatient and their authorities were dismayed and frightened.

In consternation, satellite regimes began to let up a little on their people. They thought of it as planned retreat to prepared positions. The Russian example was followed, loosely and in bewilderment. Political prisoners slowly trickled out of stony jails. Intellectuals, who in fear spoke for so long in whispers, removed their silencers. Voices in the satellite stretches began to be heard. They were not the voices of the top Communist Establishment. Installed in power and maintained by survival in the perpetual purge, party bureaucrats abhorred gradualism as a sign of weakness. It was found only, they insisted, in old bourgeois so-called liberal thought. Now, they were under pressure to enter into gradualism. The controlled let-up in the Soviet Union suggested such a technique to copy.

Soviet Europe was vastly different from the U.S.S.R. It was a factor Khrushchev has never realized and which Communists abroad generally refuse to recognize. As it was at the creation of satellite Europe so now were Soviet reforms imposed to create a new look forward. They boomeranged because Eastern Europeans were alien people and the imposed system was intolerable. The wind of Soviet change soon turned into an uncontrollable tornado. Nowhere was the changed mood and the confused regime better portrayed than in the popular feeling that surged through Poland. Now, in 1956, after some years of absence, I was back again in Warsaw. My very first night there showed how seriously Poles wanted to reform conditions on their own.

The little bachelor attic apartment was jammed but nobody cared. There were teen-agers and youngsters in their early twenties. Some had on blue jeans. They overflowed from the sofas and chairs on to the floor. All were devotedly intent. This was no party meeting; no indoctrination lecture. The kids sipped Cokes for the first time in their lives or beer from cans as the strains of "Rhythm in Blues" filled the apartment. Then came Ol' Satchmo and Artie Shaw. That record player was oven hot. The kids were swaying and beating time. "Like it?" an American voice inquired. "How wonderful," a girl murmured in reply.

I believe that little jam session was symptomatic of the ferment and the bitterness; the craving for a whiff of the West and the inner demand for more relaxation, more freedom, that had been sparked by the death of Stalin. The jazz incident was remarkable because these kids trooped over to the apartment of a young American. They were members of a jazz club. One had written a letter to the American Embassy, asking if any records were available. I was in their clubroom talking to the members when the young American entered. He said the letter had been turned over to him because he had a jazz collection. If some would like to hear the records, they were welcome. When would it be convenient for them? Right now, they chorused. How many? Maybe 10,000, but there was no room. How about a couple of dozen? Okay.

In this spirit, Poland was vastly different from any of the other Communist regimes. On the highest levels, the party ruled. It had no intention of permitting change. But the Communist leaders were rocked by the criticism that washed over the country once the floodgates were unlocked. When Stalin died, the people had a chance to cry out. So massive was the volume of protest that the governing leaders became alarmed. The criticism, some of them declaimed, had assumed "an anti-state, anti-Russian" complexion. Police powers were diminished, just how far no Westerner could tell then with accuracy. Fear of terror was pretty well gone, though. Several times I walked on the campus of Warsaw University, stopping a student to talk. Obviously I was a foreigner.

Yet they talked freely. The discussions I had on all levels—officials, peasants, students and writers—were franker than any I have ever known in Eastern Europe. When I asked officials whether they were going to try to rescind the spate of criticism, the complaints they had heard, the answer was:

"We try to be realistic. You can't take back what you've given. That does not mean, however, that the 'socialist' state and our alliance with the Soviet Union are going to be changed."

The point is the ruling groups felt compelled to alter the former slavish devotion to comradely duty without affecting the embracing association with the Soviet Union. Quite frankly, many will tell you, they didn't know just where they were heading or how it could be done. Some called the rosy atmosphere, "the new revolution." They wanted reforms—big ones.

Penury had been fastened on the Polish state and people by a regime that used strict copy-cat methods of Russian plans and ideas. Having a contact meant buying cloth or food, under the table; or even staying away from a job while drawing a salary. Government cars were openly hailed in the streets and people in a hurry paid fares. Goods and influence were bought and sold across a counter like slabs of beef. The rottenness of the system was stablized in fear of the secret police. Little attention was paid to Soviet troops, actually mobile occupation forces, stationed on Polish soil. The Soviet Marshal Rokossovsky continued as

Minister of Defense for Poland. Jokes about him began to circulate openly.

"How do you become a Pole?" one of the stories went. "You leave Russia, under Soviet sponsorship."

Rokossovsky stayed in his post, Poles told each other bitingly, because he didn't want to return to Moscow. Bad as their conditions had become, they were better than anything in the Soviet Union. That was another reason, Polish wit insisted, that the Russians had to name their alliance against NATO, the "Warsaw Pact." Not even a satellite government, Poles observed, would dare join something named directly for Moscow.

"Warsaw gives this fraud of an alliance a tone of respectability," a young and disillusioned poet told a couple of us. "A Polish name still means something special."

So did the Roman Catholic Church in Poland. Roman Catholicism remained the prevalent religion. Cardinal Wyszyński had been removed by police to a retreat. It didn't help the regime. His name was always on Polish lips. You could hear it in churches which were open. The Communists didn't dare challenge the Poles by closing down churches. On Sundays, they were filled to overflowing. It was, and remains, the only Communist-governed country where I have seen men in uniform attend church services.

"We, by no means," a Central Committee member told me ruefully, "have a classless society."

George Orwell and his "1984" were discussed in print recently in Poland. The article appeared under the title "1984 and 1956" in, of all places, the Communist Party newspaper "Trybuna Ludu." This was a pretty lengthy take-out on Orwellian forecasts for the future. To an astonished public, though, for the first time in the Communist world, Orwell and his vocabulary were analyzed. There were the words, like "double-think" and "newspeak." They were the products of a dying, sick mind, the article huffily declaimed. But Orwell's language was exposed in public. I talked the Orwell article over with a young man I met by chance at the theater. Like most young men and women there, he was easily approachable, even by a foreigner. And like so many young Poles, he was eager to talk. Tadeusz was twenty-two. He had lost his father and nearly all his relatives during the war. His mother was hopelessly crippled by the Germans. As a youngster, Tadeusz saw embattled, desperate men chop down Nazi troops and he watched the occupiers mow down Poles by the hundreds.

"In a way it was exciting for a child to see all those horrible events," recalled Tadeusz. "But you always thought it would have to be better one day. After the war, when Warsaw was in ruins," he continued, "they came and said we would start to build socialism. It sounded fine to me.

"We were told that life had to be difficult because Poland was in such a dreadful state after the war. This I accepted. I was going to school, was fed and learned all about Marx, Lenin and Stalin.

"In school I was, I suppose, a real militant. I told my comrades how lucky we were. Here we were being clothed and fed and going to school. Our worries were over I believed. I scolded schoolmates who were critical of some things. I also reported some of the worst critics to my teachers.

"Friends in school would come to me and tell me about their fathers, uncles and sisters who were sent to jail. Police came at night and took them away. They were enemies of the state.

"I tried to answer their questions. They must believe, I told them, that somewhere their accused fathers and relatives had gone astray. I quoted remarks of our leaders, of Stalin. Oh, I was glib and I knew so many answers.

"You know," observed Tadeusz, "I never thought that I'd even talk to an American, especially an American who said he detested socialism, or what you call Communism. The Americans were the enemy at large. This I also believed devotedly.

"In school so many of my comrades would say to me: 'Tadeusz, how can you ignore what is going on? If we or our elders raise our eyebrows and somebody think it's wrong, we are in trouble.'

"I told them to kill that type of talk. Yes, useful word, 'kill,' no matter how it's used. My comrades always deferred to me. Now, I know why they did. They were afraid of me and afraid of what I could do to them. I was a militant.

"The day I heard that Stalin died, I wept. I don't even remember weeping for my father. I walked the streets that night. The loss, I felt, was a personal one. I kept telling myself that I would build socialism as Stalin wanted. This was my way of praying, of going to church as others do for divine guidance.

"I plunged into youth activity, exhausted myself in party work. But everything began to tumble fast after that. One after another. My school comrades were grumbling about conditions. Now I couldn't even shut them up by saying, 'Kill that talk.' Kruschchev and Bulganin went to see

Tito. Tito, the mortal enemy of Stalin and the people. There could be other roads to socialism, they said.

"Finally we heard about Stalin's terrible mistakes and how he had wronged so many, how he had murdered. For days I could not go to school. If it was so, that Stalin wronged people, murdered them, then so had I, in my way.

"Criticism of our government, of our socialist programs came like a storm. I heard things I could hardly believe existed in people's minds. This was treason.

"I am trying to forget all I learned. I'm asked to believe that we are now going the right way. Who is telling me? The people who used to teach me that Stalin was showing the right way.

"No, it will not work for me. I believed. You cannot ever believe like that twice in a lifetime. This is for me the 1984 in 1956."

Tadeusz shook hands and walked away, up the street called Nowy Swiat (New World) and out of sight.

There was a blazingly hot afternoon some days later. An eerie shade was cast in twisted patterns from shards of buildings and mounds of rubble piled high. I picked my way through the path past the wreckage. In a circular area, hidden from the view of the main drags, loomed a synagogue. Behind it were a couple of sagging two-story houses. This survived systematic Nazi destruction of Warsaw's Jewish community life —perhaps the most compact in all Europe. A few old men were in the synagogue. They were waiting for prayers to begin. Had the synagogue been rebuilt after the war? No, it survived, miraculously.

An SS officer used the synagogue as a storehouse. The SS officer didn't order the edifice to be put to the torch. Maybe, one old man reflected, maybe he had some Jewish blood in his veins. Maybe, another replied sarcastically, he didn't have time to burn the synagogue.

"Anyway, it's standing here," said the first oldster. "It's all we have left of what was before. Except for The Monument." His voice capitalized and underscored the two words.

The Monument is a fairly short walk from the synagogue. Apartment houses are going up, but acres of powdery rubble stretch before you. This is where the Ghetto began, where hundreds of thousands of Jews were slaughtered by the Nazis. All that was left undone was forgetfulness to sow salt in the vacant lots. Here's The Monument then. It's a simple black slab, with Polish and Hebrew inscriptions. Faces of the suffering are etched with arms upraised and expressions of desperation.

This, graphically, is the story of the slaughter of Warsaw's 300,000 Jews, of Poland's 3,000,000 Jews. A wilted floral wreath lies at the base of the memorial. You stare around at the houses going up on one side and the sea of powdery rubble on the other.

"Let's walk away from here," my companion said. He was a chunky little man, who somehow managed to live through the war years in Warsaw. His children, wife, relatives are all dead. How did they die? Does it really matter how?

"The Monument," he said as we walked back more briskly than we had arrived, "is our tombstone. It is the tombstone for the mass grave of the Jews in Poland."

There aren't many Jews left in Poland. Estimates go between 60,000 and 80,000. Nobody can accurately get up a roll-call. Many of the survivors here still use their Polish pseudonyms, taken during the war. About 6,000 remain in Warsaw. There is no longer a ghetto.

How many remaining Jews would like to leave the country? Emigration to Israel was beginning and I asked the question at random of five Jews. They told me without exception: "About ninety percent of us. The remainder prefer to stay."

"Anti-Semitism is prohibited by law, as you probably know," one Jew told me. "But you cannot outlaw what is in people's minds and emotions. Anti-Semitism is still here in Poland, still strong. It is strange, isn't it, for a people who suffered so much as did the Jews from the Nazis."

Through the years that Communism was consolidating itself in power here, some Jews were leading executors of policy. They were singled out by the rank-and-file citizenry as the apostles of oppression. Jews and Communists became synonymous in Poland. When the ax of anti-Stalinism fell, old hands in the security and police agencies were booted out, arrested and condemned. It was a popular move, though, particularly when Jews were the victims. Before going to bed one night, I wandered down to what passes for a combination bar-snake-pit-dance floor. At the bar I ordered a vodka and mineral water on the side. I sipped the vodka and a lean young man about thirty nudged me. Was I a foreigner? Yes, American, I replied and went back to sipping my vodka. My chance bar acquaintance was well along in vodka. He wanted to talk. He spoke some German.

"I'm a real Communist, American," he said. "I've been an officer. I fought, fought pretty well. Here are my cards."

"Things got a little dirty for a while," he added. "It was the Jews. They tried to keep us down, tried to keep us, the real Polish Communists, down. It's a good thing we got rid of Berman [Jakub Berman, No. 2 man in the party only recently demoted]. We'll get rid of lots more. *Juden nichts gut.*"

The phrase, spat out as it was, stopped me cold for a minute. I thought briefly about The Monument, the tombstone of Poland's Jews.

Nearly everyone in the hotel lobby did a double-take. They stared at two men in uniform. Some of the foreigners were puzzled. The Poles, from their expressions were downright furious. The men in uniform were East German officers, part of the existing army allied through the Warsaw Pact to Poland. Obviously, they were not masters of tact. The uniforms they wore rolled back the years for every Pole in that lobby, tore them back to the bitter days of Nazi subjugation, the execution squads and the wasteland that was made of Warsaw. The uniforms, you see, weren't much different from the ones in those times.

Cheeks reddened, necks stiff, the East German officers entered the elevator. They descended later in civilian clothes. Although the official line is that the "German Democratic Republic" has taken its place among the countries of "socialism," there is scarcely a Pole, officially or unofficially, who privately buys the program. They are frightened stiff of Germany, East, West, or united. Ghastly memories of wartime and the human slaughterhouse that was Auschwitz are only part of the story. The Russians, who partitioned Poland with Hitler in 1939, again took over eastern Poland in 1945. To compensate for the territorial loss, the Russians gave the Poles former German provinces. Today these are loosely lumped together on the "Oder-Neisse" line and are called ironically "Recovered Territories.

For years the Russians have been trying to obtain recognition from the Western powers of the territorial transfers. They haven't obtained it, nor have they stopped trying. The Poles, squeezed between the Soviet Union and Germany, are constantly fearful of a deal the Russians might make at their expense again.

Fight, you ask. It might be suicide, they agree, but fight the measure they would. The fact remains that the Soviet Union has it within its power to unite Germany and to tempt the Germans with the sugar-coating and aspiration of the "Recovered Territories." All powers affected, as well as the Poles and Germans, know it. Every suggestion from the West that old East Prussia and other areas now under Polish rule are lost and must be so recognized are eagerly seized upon by Polish officialdom. Similarly, Soviet defense of the present frontiers are welcomed by the regime.

Millions of Poles have been resettled in ex-German areas. Polish prisoners, after years in Soviet labor camps, also have been installed in the territories. The vast majority of Germans who lived in the provinces have long since fled to Germany. At present the Polish government also is repatriating to East and West Germany those few remaining ethnic Germans who no longer want to help "build socialism."

Psychologically, it will take the Communists a long time to convince the average Pole that the "Recovered Territories" are part of his future. The Government has qualms about that itself. No proclamation is going to change a Pole's views on what he considers belongs to his country.

In a grimy, crowded train, a young man and his girl couldn't take their eyes off the pocket book lying face down on the tiny table.

"Look it over," I said, giving them the book.

It was a copy of Thoreau's "Walden"—most satisfying reading, I find, for visitors in Eastern Europe. The youngsters thumbed a page or two politely. They seemed a little disappointed.

"We thought it might be a detective story," said the girl.

A whodunit is worth its weight in zlotys and it takes an awful lot of local currency to make anything seem substantial. Raymond Chandler, Erle Stanley Gardener and Agatha Christie are being translated. The biggest seller once in Poland was a derring-do whodunit entitled: "The Bad Ones." Hemingway is being translated; so are Steinbeck and modern American poets. The dreary literary diet of hand-picked "progressive" American writers started being supplemented. It's rich fare for those so starved so long. British newspapers, notably the *Times* of London and the *Guardian*, were put on sale at hotels for foreigners. They became available at a couple of large newspaper and book shops. French and American papers published in Paris were added. You can't find that anywhere else in Soviet Europe.

These were only random ramifications of what Polish pro-party and non-party people called "our revolution." It was sparked by the young intellectuals and youth generally. They raised an articulate voice that demanded action, relaxation—and, dread word: "Freedom." Their elders were generally apathetic. They had been through too much, deceived too often and misused too frequently to really think they could get a square deal.

When the government took off the wraps it didn't realize what it was getting into. The ruling spirits had been isolated too long from reality. They had forgotten or ignored, as have all Communist governments, the human factor. Anti-Stalinism must have seemed to them a safe enough valve from which pent-up steam could be released. Instead, they blew the whole boiler works, emotionally speaking. Criticism buried barbs deep in every facet of the life. Government clamps were applied too loose and late. Powerful Communist forces, alarmed by what they witnessed, demanded a complete end to the whole episode of criticism. They saw their own positions threatened. If the party can, it will channel or control criticism.

The criticisms and outspoken denunciations that first flared and flamed in Poland were not a super-Machiavellian technique to deceive us. Top party leaders sternly demanded a reassessment. They could not, they warned, tolerate an upsurge against the alliance with the Soviet Union. Encouraging this criticism along with relaxation of rigid discipline, and liberalization of thought, one would think should be part of Western foreign policy. We need not think that by helping the kids who stick their necks out and criticize we are clasping a Communist government to our bosom.

One of our most loudly proclaimed declarations of foreign policy in recent years was the "rollback," authored by the late John Foster Dulles. It was a cruel piece of deception.

"Where did the people of East Berlin get in June, 1953?" a Polish student at Warsaw University asked me. "They rioted and rebelled. They could no longer stand the conditions. What happened? They got rolled back by the Russians. They'll try again. Usually when nobody expects it. Great powers can never make a deal with people. They act usually like they feel."

At the summit conference in Geneva in 1955 between President Eisenhower and Khrushchev, Eisenhower started to speak of the Soviet satellites. He was told to keep his mind on his own business by the Russians at the conference table. He mumbled about inequality and retreated from Soviet Europe.

"In a way that fixed things," a Polish youth leader told me when he talked about the summit of a year earlier. "It proved to us you didn't understand what had gone on or what was now going on. Maybe you didn't want to come to grips with the whole problem.

"We know, I think, what realism in politics is supposed to mean. History has been very unkind to my country. We often blame you. Everyone looks for an out. We will always blame you. We should blame ourselves, too. We don't have a national patience in Poland. We are capable of almost anything, any time."

The intense young man was certainly gripped with the prescience of the pent-up fury of his countrymen. The next afternoon, a few hours' drive from Warsaw, Poznan—Poland's fifth city—exploded in a protest heard around the world. It was June, 1956. Workers from the near-by Zispo factory downed their tools. They swarmed out of the factory, sweeping aside horror-stricken party floor managers with their cries: "Bread and liberty." Into town went the workers in overalls and hand-me-down clothing. They carried Polish flags and hastily scrawled signs, demanding, in effect, a decent life. It was as genuinely a spontaneous a demonstration as was ever seen in a Communist-governed country. The protest march also was designed to catch the eye of the world. An international fair had just opened in downtown Poznan and many foreign visitors had flocked there for the first time in years.

Local authorities were powerless to do more than call out all available police and notify the government in Warsaw. In the streets of Poznan, the police tried to disperse the workers. Warning shots were fired overhead. Armored cars rolled up. Workers shouted: "Poles do not shoot Poles." Police officers hesitated. Suddenly shots rang out, thudding into the massed demonstrators. Some fell, dead and wounded. A flag was dipped into the blood of the fallen and borne high. Workers marched and shouted, wresting arms from confused, frightened and ashamed policemen.

Top government men rushed to Poznan, including the loyal Soviet collabator, Premier Cyrankiewicz. Naturally, he saw an "enemy" hand behind the demonstration. Naked pate glistening with perspiration, Cyrankiewicz warned that the state would not hesitate to smite any opposition that stood in its way. Police and army units, meanwhile, ringed the city and the topsy-turvy factory from which bread and freedom demands had gone out. But the regime, sensing the defiant mood of the city and fearing its chain reaction across Poland, backed off its iron-fisted ultimatum. There would be, promised Cyrankiewicz, an investigation into the wrongs felt so bitterly by striking workers. It was a strike, too, one must understand.

A strike, virtually unknown in Soviet Europe, which had experienced uprisings and death before. Walkouts were something new.

Foreign reporters drove, hell-bent, for Poznan. Police roadblocks held them up, usually only for a quick check. Apparently, they radioed on ahead. It was progressively easier to move through the armed cordons. I found out later from an associate of Cyrankiewicz that some of his advisers argued that foreign correspondents be permitted into Poznan. Some already were there for the fair. Keeping others out would only make matters worse, the government was warned. They entered a tense city, already wearing black to mourn heroic dead. Police and army guards sensed the tension. Their knuckles were white on the weapons they held.

Relatives, with pinched expressions or openly weeping, went through the mortuary. They held back tears and kept voices pitched low when they slipped softly through hospital wards. A twenty-three-year-old boy, a young groom, was being comforted by his ashen-faced bride. They had been married a fortnight before. His right arm was bound up in bandages but dirt and blood were caked on his forehead.

"It can never be the same," he said in a voice so filled with passion that it carried through the corridor. "They can kill us all. One after another. Some day, we will get them—all of them."

In Warsaw, I heard a totally disillusioned woman, a veteran Communist, tell her husband to prepare for the worst. He was a life-long Communist, a powerful man in the party.

"You can smash these people," she told her husband. "You can make a new jail out of this country. They will still get us, in the end. When the people come to get us, I ask only one thing of you: Please try to behave with dignity."

He clapped a cap on his head and stalked out. She turned to my companion, a newspaperman well-known in the U.S., and asked for a cigarette.

"The Polish people know," said our hostess. "Why shouldn't you?"

CHAPTER | 15

I n early 1956, before the Poznan uprising, a fresh wind of hope and change blew over the plains of Hungary. Defiance in Poland, limited as it was, was a symbol of triumph against the Russians. It toned up the pulsating blood stream of restless, impatient and frustrated Hungarians. In October, workers, intellectuals and peasants saw a means for their own deliverance. All that summer, their feverish activity had sparked debate that led to frenzied reshuffling of the government and party apparatus. The squat, implacable Rakosi had been removed for Erno Geroe, himself a party product made in Moscow.

To still the disturbing rumbles in other parts of Soviet Europe, Khrushchev strove to drape the mantle of reform on Geroe. On a hurry-up trip to the Crimea in early summer where he had persuaded Tito to go with him, Khrushchev sought to show Geroe as an independent. He arranged to have Geroe (by chance) meet Tito on a walk. Trapped, Tito was furious. He was vain enough to believe he could aid Khrushchev in a comradely way

in all Eastern Europe and the Soviet Union. The sudden appearance of
Geroe raised Tito's defenses and suspicions. He had been duped. Moreover, he always had been deeply contemptuous of Geroe's fainthearted-
ness and lack of imagination.

On a wooded slope above the Crimean strand, there stood Geroe, all
smiles, with hand outstretched. Khrushchev, clucking happily, remarked
that it was a most amazing coincidence. Bygones should be bygones, he
added. They all had a lot to talk about. Eyes blazing with anger, Tito
wheeled and strode briskly back, accompanied by Rankovitch, a Vice-
Premier and the Yugoslav operational security chief. The sight of Khrushchev padding as fast as he could go, with Geroe puffing behind him, in
Tito's wake, didn't amuse the Yugoslavs.

They resolutely called their little party together, began to pack and
prepare to leave. Geroe hung around in the park outside the villa, staring
at yellow roses while Khrushchev talked pleadingly with Tito. Khrushchev
probably never will forget the lengths to which he went to bring Tito
around. Tito's services were desperately required, declared Khrushchev,
to put out fires flickering in Eastern Europe. The clincher was simple. Tito,
after all, was a Communist. Could he bear to see other Communist
societies, whose leaders he may have despised, go up in flames. His Yugoslavia might be caught up in the forest fire, too. Changes were needed,
of course. Tito could help. How? By inviting Geroe to come to Belgrade
on an official visit. Tito thought about it for a while, as Khrushchev joined
Geroe in the garden. Soon Tito summoned Khrushchev. Quite a change
for Khrushchev. Tito agreed, but reluctantly.

He had some demands to make first. Hungarians, like the late Laszlo
Rajk, executed as a Titoist, must be publicly rehabilitated. Others, long in
Hungarian jails for Titoism, must be released immediately. Khrushchev
relieved, agreed. Geroe would undertake all those commitments. Geroe
nodded. Tito flew back to Yugoslavia to consult his party aides. Geroe,
following the Soviet assent to Tito's demands, released the broken men
who had been caught up in the party purges. He also ordered rehabilitation of Rajk. "Nikita Sergeevich said to do it," Geroe told disbelieving
security officials. "Do it."

Just before Geroe went to Belgrade for the meeting with Tito that was
supposed to endow him with the mystique of independence and change,
Rajk was restored to regime favor, posthumously. The explanation was
that it had all been Rakosi's fault; and behind Rakosi had been Beria. Be-

fore the ceremony, Rajk's widow, Julia, was called to security headquarters. A terrible mistake had been made, she was told. As a good comrade she must try to understand. Rajk had never been guilty as charged. It was a gross distortion of "socialist legality" that liquidated him. To make amends the regime was going to have a public rehabilitation ceremony. All Mme. Rajk had to do was to make the identification of the body.

"They showed me a box of human bones," Julia Rajk told me. These were supposed to have been Rajk's remains. The widow stumbled out of the room, followed by a high police officer with a certificate she was to sign. In a state of shock, Mme Rajk signed, and the ceremony went off as planned. Some of Rajk's colleagues blinked in the light of freedom soon afterward and Geroe set off for Belgrade. While he listened to Tito, the storm broke in Poland. Khrushchev and his marshals rushed to Warsaw and the Tito-Geroe tête-à-tête was broken off.

Budapest was acclaiming Poland's stand. The Writers' Union, which for the entire summer had denounced the party's straitjacket on creativity and on the nation as a whole, demonstrated to show its solidarity with the Poles. The unionists led a procession to the statue of the Polish General Joszef Bem, who in 1848 aided the Hungarians in their revolt against Hapsburg rule. Intellectuals and workers in Budapest drafted demands for a change in the system that was fastened on the country and which ruled them. Communist rule was being directly challenged in Hungary. Geroe hastily took his leave of Tito, who must have had a pretty shrewd idea of what had been ripping through Hungary. Some of his own Hungarian-speaking activists and intellectuals had been speaking to Budapest audiences of writers, artists and workers. I had heard them urge Hungarians to demand change. What they meant was a change in the direction of Yugoslavia.

Returning from Belgrade, Geroe found Hungarians seething with resentment and with the excitement of the impending action which finally erupted in October. To his eternal infamy, Geroe claimed proudly that he gave the police orders to fire on the demonstrators. But the volleys turned the eruption into a genuine people's uprising.

It caught the West unawares and unprepared. Americans were gripped in a spiritual catalepsy and the little band of professional diplomats in our weatherbeaten legation on a street called "Freedom Square" were, to all intents and purposes, leaderless. By the time an experienced diplomat was rushed in to take charge, he had no chance even to present his credentials.

The Russians were back. Budapest became the scene of a massacre and what began as a monumental but peaceable demonstration against oppression had spread to open revolt.

The hunted became the hunters. Soviet tanks, spewing death and terror, were stalked to their own destruction. AVH men—the hated security police—fought back with machine-gun fire against the rebellion. The tanks, giant T-54s, lay down close-range barrages against Csepel Island.

Soviet tanks milled in the street. Only minutes before they fired point-blank into crowds massed in Parliament Square. The fusillade may have been the single act of butchery that led to a point of no-return. A huge crowd that had been twitting Russian soldiers from occupation garrisons in the country in a twinkling became a screaming, bleeding and infuriated rebellion. Tank flashes and fire at boxing range is a fearsome spectacle. Hungarian dead and wounded spilled and sprawled in Parliament Square. Most ran, not out of fear but with the resolve to square things immediately.

Into this concrete abbatoir came a street cleaner. With his brush, he swept up leaves. He picked his way among corpses. For them he could do nothing. The groaning wounded were too much for the old man. All he could do was put their jackets behind their heads. He did it during the wild after-the-shooting melee in the square. A Soviet officer shouted, gesticulating for him to get the hell out. The old man shuffled, trailing his brush and cart. At the edge of the square, he stooped. A bunch of flowers some girl carried an hour earlier was strewn on the ground. The old man brushed his hands on his baggy, brown uniform. He picked up the flowers. One by one, he placed them next to the fallen. He wasn't able to finish. A machine-gun burst almost cut him in half. He fell, face down, clutching the last few flowers.

Up and down the streets fist-shaking crowds came out to shout at Russians. Tankers would stare at them, frozen for a few seconds. Then shots rang out and people crumpled. You thought it was insane—fists and even some waving banners against the tanks. It was more. "Russkies go home," students catcalled. They spoke in Russian, which they had to learn at school. Paving blocks were torn up and used to build barricades.

"It's hopeless, my son," an hysterical mother screamed at her nineteen-year-old boy. "Hide!"

"There is no place to hide, mama," replied the boy. He had a rifle which a Hungarian soldier turned over to him. Beside him a teen-age girl stuck a banner in the paving blocks. There were the national colors, red, white and green but no Communist emblem. In lapels you suddenly noticed national colors, all homemade. The hammer-and-sickle was fast disappearing from public view. So were red stars. "Independence" was the cry that rose from thousands of throats as people marched, ran and dashed about the street.

Nighttime was macabre. The city electricity worked. Streets were illuminated. Soviet tanks idled below street lamps. Telephones inside Budapest also worked. I called up diplomatic missions, friends and people in the provisional regime headed now by Imre Nagy, who although a Communist was regarded as a symbol of anti-Soviet defiance. Interviews you got by entering an office or catching someone going out. Janos Kadar, drawn with anxiety, mumbled about being too busy to talk things over. He was the first secretary of the party and had hailed the "glorious Hungarian revolution."

Nagy was more placid. I talked to him three or four times during the revolt. What I remember best is his thumbnail summation of the situation: "Russians shot Hungarians. This is the most serious thing of all." He would not speak of Geroe and his crowd. They had all been bundled off to safety in Soviet armored cars by order of Anastas Mikoyan and Mikhail Suslov, who soon flew to Budapest themselves.

If they had been able to get around, they would have noticed truckloads of Hungarian soldiers called to restore some order. "What will you do with your guns?" asked their countrymen. "Give them to you," a young officer said as he ordered his unit down from the trucks to stay with a crowd. "Tell the world," workers who could not enter besieged Csepel Island urged observers. "Tell all about this mass murder."

There was plenty of spontaneity and little organization was the one thing you quickly noticed. When Soviet tanks were hammering the Killian Barracks, the old Maria Theresa thick-walled cantonment commanded by then Colonel Pal Maleter, a students' revolutionary committee had taken over a university laboratory. The undergraduates, boys and girls, guns slung over their shoulders strode in and out. In the professor's chair sat another student. He had been selected, because he had done some military service, to run that command post.

"Do Americans know what has happened?" he asked me in quite good English after I identified myself. "No, they really don't. This is 1789, not in Paris but in Budapest. Help us, if you understand revolutions at all."

That particular headquarters certainly looked as if it might have been set up for a 1789 rising. Youngsters poked heads out of windows to see what was going on, or rushed back and forth from the street with the latest news and rumors they acquired. Had a Soviet tank cruised down that street, raking windows where curious heads showed, the students revolutionary committee would have been out of action with one shell. They scarcely seemed to mind the danger. Scouts came in to report on the progress of fighting at the Killian Barracks.

"They won't surrender," a girl called out breathlessly. "We'll beat them." Then, in an undertone, "We must."

Getting to the barracks area was a strange stroll. Private and government cars, with hastily scrawled Red Cross signs, hurtled around the streets. They would stop, haul up wounded into the back seat, and careen off again. At the corner where Soviet tanks were spread out, firing into the barracks, Hungarians motioned to John MacCormac of the New York Times and me to stay put. They pointed. On the corner lay a corpse. His hand clutched a worn briefcase. He might have been fifty or so. Ducking behind some scaffolding, we could see the field of fire.

Four tanks would open fire simultaneously and then draw back. They would be replaced immediately by another rank. The same time-on-target system. MacCormac went out into the street for a better look. I had no choice but to follow. We could see how one Soviet tank, disabled, had been used by the defenders to plug a hole in the walls. At least five other tanks were charred. Bodies of Russians and Hungarians littered the street in front of the barracks.

Slipping from door to door, behind the last row of armor, we could spot some boys. We paid no attention until we realized they were trying to get at the tanks. They had no weapons. Bottles were in their hands. Along the street, directly behind the tanks half a dozen boys crawled. We watched the scene, dumfounded. From a half prone position at virtually spitball range, the boys tossed their bottles at tank treads. Molotov cocktails. One tank caught fire immediately. Another smoked. Guns swivelled in the other two. The boys stayed down. In the excitement and smoke, they apparently could not be seen. The flaming tank was finished and the crew came out of the lifted turret and scampered to the corner we had left a few minutes before. Eyewitnesses began to argue with them and shake fists in their faces. These gunners, from Asiatic Russia, seemed stunned. Not for long. The young commando squad slipped up to them, simply grabbed their sidearms and marched them off.

Occurrences like that led to the demolition of the mammoth Stalin Statue, set up in the city's center. Students and workers went out by the thousands to remove the monument. Death ricocheted in the streets but the columns moved steadily to the Stalin figure. They were drawn to it as to a symbol which must be destroyed to help wipe out one's past. Watching them struggle with the colossal statue in the eerie night bespoke their own determination. Block and tackle, hauled from a factory, went into willing hands. Cheers split the streets when the tugging started. Lines frayed and broke but nobody appeared impatient. They tried again. After what seemed like endless pulling and tugging, the statue came down. Only Stalin's concrete boots were left. A man in a faded blue beret leaped up to the pedestal. He stuck a Hungarian flag in the right boot to thunderous cheers. Then, the vast crowd hauled the statue away, down the streets filled with violence. Pieces came off the statue but nobody cared. Neither apparently did the Russians. They weren't showing their armed fist at night then.

Daylight was something else. You could count on dawn to see that below the seven hills dominating Budapest, the city lay in a smoking valley of death. On a cloudy Saturday, when couples strolled briskly for exercise along the quays of the Danube, Hungarian national flags fluttered from most windows. People made them, I was told, or had hidden some away. Across the way, on the Buda side of the river, big guns thundered in the hills.

"Russian guns," a student with an armband in national colors around a ripped windbreaker sleeve explained. "We don't have any."

"It's the kids over there," another boy shouted, pointing to the smoke haze camouflaging the hills of Buda.

The "kids" belonged to all Hungarians in Budapest. They had written a new "Red Badge of Courage," facing death afraid but determined. They were all under twenty, boys and girls in about equal numbers, maybe 200 in all. They threw up barricades of logs, interlaced with carts and abandoned cars. It was makeshift, unmilitary—and glorious.

I visited the barricades with Hungarian army officers and police, none of whom wore a red star.

"Come and join us," was the greeting of the kids.

A major pleaded with them to leave their puny stronghold.

"No, no, no," the kids cried. "We don't go until the Russians go."

"The Russians must save face," the major said helplessly.

"Let them come then," the undaunted youngsters replied. "This is war," one of them shouted grimly.

Soviet armor massed in the hills all night. From prepared positions they shelled "the kids." The matchstick barricades weren't there the next day. Many corpses were. Someone had sprinkled the bodies with lime—to prevent the stench of rotting, I was told. Hungarians made pilgrimages to the scene. Women knelt and prayed beside the fallen young. In box-like formation, Soviet tanks, armored cars and infantry carriers leveled their guns on the area.

"Haven't you killed enough?" a young woman overcome with frenzy shouted at Russian soldiers. She started to rush at them and was forcibly dragged back by sobbing bystanders. Led by Russian-speaking youngsters, hundreds of Hungarians told the Soviet soldiers what they thought of them and their system. It was the wildest street debate that has probably ever been held. Russians held the crowd off at gun-point. The crowd jeered, sneered and cat-called at them.

"Fascists are responsible," finally spoke a Soviet officer from a jeep in which a machine gun was mounted.

"Fascists," roared the crowd. "Look at us."

If you looked you saw drably dressed, tear-stained, emotion-choked men and women, boys and girls. Perhaps one out of six was past twenty-five. Suddenly, tank engines started up and jeeps began to roll. The crowd began to run as the Soviet motorized unit moved out. Heading down the hill were five T-54 tanks. Red stars on them. The gun barrel of one flashed and a shell exploded beyond the fleeing crowd. Mrs. John MacCormac, and my wife, Stiva, disappeared. We found them a half-hour later. They had been scooped up by the crowd and half-carried to safety.

"I beg your pardon," an elderly man said, tipping his hat to my wife as we started to go. He spoke rusty but careful English. "I hope that you can remember that 9,000,000 in Hungary are fighting your fight. Please, I beg your pardon." He tipped his hat again and walked off. For the first time in pulsating Eastern Europe, a prominent anti-Communist had been taken back, voluntarily, into a coalition still headed by Communists. Bela Kovacs, only recently released, was a dying man. His spirits and passion were as fresh as always.

"I want to do what I can to help my country," he said thoughtfully as his reedy arms went out to old friends. "I do not know what we shall do. It all is so bankrupt in the government. Outside, every Hungarian has hope, yes, belief. They want action."

As gently as he could, Kovacs was saying what the already desperate Nagy and his comrades felt. They, as Communists, backed the revolt after it blew the old Soviet-made order to pieces. "It took less than twenty-four hours for the apparatus to disintegrate," a sickly Geza Losonczy observed. He had come out of prison as a former Communist victim of the party purge. What he said was uppermost in the minds of Communists like Nagy and Kadar. They wanted, as Nagy hoped, to channel the uprising into a new deal for Communist initiative. The Hungarian people simply took it out of their hands. They wanted no more Communist direction of any kind.

"The revolution is a great, patriotic national movement for a free and independent nation," Nagy had solemnly declared.

Earlier, Kadar emotionally described the rebellion as the most spontaneous and genuine in history. When the Russians kept calling the revolt a "counter-revolution," Kadar's own doubts began to take form. They seemed to have coalesced when he received a little group of us in a great state of excitement. Kadar, after all, was first secretary of Hungary's Communist Party. He was in search of a party looking for its future.

"Our party must lead," he asserted when a questioner asked how he felt about the party after his long jail term and torture.

"Where is your party?" came another question.

It ended the quick interview. The same question, I was told by a Polish participant in the Soviet-bloc conference right in Budapest, was asked by an aroused Suslov. Beside him, imperturbable, Mikoyan just shook his head. Hungarians, however, didn't want anything to do with Communist parties or the Russians. They removed, often in great danger, red stars, hammers and sickle emblems and monuments to Russians. There was pride in their faces, a spring in their step and erectness in their bearing. They trod the streets as if they had shed a great and encompassing fear.

"We feel like free people," a housewife told us. "My children are the best example. I cannot tape them down in the house. They want to be with their schoolmates. Such babies against tanks."

Then there was the father with a child about six who was lifted so the lad could touch the American flag on our car. The flag had been wind-blown and wrinkled. The father, still in blue overalls, smoothed out the flag with gentle but awkward hands. It made a few Americans on the spot rather tremulous. The father smiled shyly at us.

"We are pretty mild people, we Hungarians," he said when we said hello to him. "But after all the terrible years that we had, we had to tell the world how we feel. It's really for the youngsters, for him and his older brothers."

He patted the boy on his crew-cut head and took him off to rejoin two older boys, waiting for them. They were joining vast throngs streaming in the direction of the Killian Barracks. That was the main armed stronghold, commanded by a professional, which had become Hungary's victorious Alamo. The barricade of the "kids" was gallant, and grisly. The Killian Barracks were almost in downtown Pest. People were running there as fast as they could go because the defenders had emerged. The Russians had withdrawn, but not too far. Only a few blocks from the beleaguered barracks, Soviet roadblocks forced pedestrians in other directions. I saw three girls, arm-in-arm, walk scornfully past a Soviet machine-gun emplaced on the sidewalk. They would not take a detour. It was a straight line to the Killian Barracks, the one the girls took. To Russian soldiers who thrust tommy guns, muzzle first at them and waved them towards the other side of the street, the girls paid no attention. Heads erect, they walked right to the no-man's land separating the clawed Red Army units and the barracks. Into the break made by the girls in the Soviet lines, poured thousands of Hungarians. They walked past Russian machine guns and tanks; in front of nervous infantry skirmish lines. Budapest was turning out to pay tribute to its heroes.

The story of about 1,200 defenders of the barracks has become an epic of the revolution. A rangy professional soldier turned Communist while a prisoner in World War II stood beside his embattled countrymen when the chips were down. Pal Maleter was a colonel in the Hungarian Communist army—a rapid rise for a young officer who had a second lieutenant when captured eleven years earlier. Maleter, who rallied a handful of trained soldiers, installed his forces behind the three-foot-thick walls of the barracks. With them went students, workers and a few ex-party members. Deployed in sniper positions around the barracks were youngsters, trained in para-military techniques at schools.

"Two things the Communists taught us," said a young boy no more than seventeen, face blackened by days and nights of fighting and sleeplessness. "They taught us, first, to hate. They also taught many of us to fight. Now they get the benefit of the lessons."

Up to us came a burly man of middle age. He had a snub nose and he spoke good English. His name was Geza, which is all that matters. By profession, he was a chauffeur who drove for the municipal sanitation department.

"We greet you in the name of Hungarian freedom fighters," he said.

Protecting Geza like a human screen stood a ragged company of boys and girls. Did they ever think of surrender. Geza laughed with the bitter note of a man who suddenly decided to face death day and night for nearly a week. The Russians had, he said, until midnight that night to withdraw.

"If they don't we will fight to the last man, boy and girl," he added defiantly. His comrades-in-arms clustered more closely around us. They shouted agreement with him. Proudly they brought forward a fifteen-year-old girl. She had a Russian tommy gun in her arms. Took it from a Russian soldier, a boy beside her explained approvingly.

"This child is only one of many of our girls and women who fought with us and who also died with their people," said Geza.

The streets in front of the barracks, where the signs said Ulloi Street and Calvin Place, were a shell-torn jumble of wrecked houses, burned-out tanks, dangling over-head wires, shattered vehicles and smashed bodies. Glass was knee-deep. Civilians, caught in houses near the barracks, were buried under the debris. A physician described to me how he watched, between operations from his clinic across the street from the barracks, the fighting that raged.

"The Russians went wild," he said. "They couldn't get near the barracks, so they shot up our hospital some, too."

"That was bad because some of our nurses got caught," a younger doctor, his smock stained from the operating room, continued. "We have a boy here. He was loyal to his people. He was caught sneaking away from the barracks. The Avos grabbed him. He doesn't have a tongue any more."

The unwounded from the barracks had their tongues in the right places. They put working parties to duty, clearing wreckage so there would be passageways and a clear field of fire from riflemen. Colonel Maleter came by to look over the scene. He had a cool, professional eye for detail. Where was he going? To a conference, replied Maleter.

"Politicians always talk and haggle a lot, don't they," Maleter observed bemusedly. "There is a lot of talk now. I'm supposed to present my views. I'm also supposed to be ready for anything."

Expressively, he shrugged his wide shoulders, saluted by way of saying so long and strode off. A couple of officers in uniform and two tommy-gun-bearing boys clumped behind him. The boys had been selected by their own comrades-in-arms as a combined bodyguard and honor guard for Maleter. Their personal bravery brought them the special distinction. Talking to them later provided another insight into decisions like theirs. They felt a deep responsibility and they had fought, without rest, for many days. Their first names were common enough in Hungary, Janos, nineteen and an apprentice machinist, and Zoltan, eighteen, in his first year at the university. With their homemade arms and a gun here and there, Janos and Zoltan fought in the streets before they joined the defenders of the Killian Barracks.

But these were products supposedly of a Communist generation, a new generation most fussed over by the regime and most indoctrinated—or so the Communists believed. They were both sons of workers. What made them turn, and so violently, against the regime?

"You have to go back almost to the first time we ever went to school, or even earlier," said Janos. He bit his lips between sentences. "We hardly ever saw our parents. Everyone in the family had to work just to live in a single room or maybe two rooms. The adults were always exhausted. For us, getting a suit of second-hand clothes was almost a celebration."

"There also was fear," chimed in Zoltan. "It seems that in our block every family had someone who had been arrested, or spent time in jail. We came to hate authority, the kind of authority we had to swallow even when my mother sent me to a state shop to buy bread. We learned how to hate people who watched you suspiciously when you talked to a friend in whispers."

"When I went to my own factory. I listened with such surprise to the discontent of older workers," said Janos. "At first, I was afraid. You shouldn't talk that way, I thought. Pretty soon, you got fed up yourself. You got fed up with slogans, with false promises and with threats to do better or else.

"The Russians call us fascists or counter-revolutionaries," he went on and the bitterness showed in his blazing, black eyes. "How do they account that almost everyone in Communist youth organizations, like myself, fought against them. No matter what they do, Communism is really finished in Hungary."

"It catches on like a fire," Zoltan added, speaking of the revolt. "You know that somehow you must be in it. It's like a fire that begins in dry grass in a park. Before you know, it is a forest fire. That is a way I see to explain it all."

A little boy, all of eleven years old, had been found by his frenzied mother near the barracks. Older children couldn't drive him out from their sniper positions. Luminous eyes in a face so haggard for one so young peered intently. All he wore over faded blue coveralls, cut down to size for him, was an old sweater. Little Lajos was the youngest revolutionary I ever met. He flung gasoline bottles at Russian tanks, from close up. He was the son of a worker father and a worker mother. His father had once been a Socialist and gone along when his party merged with the Communists in the regrouped Hungarian Workers' Party. When Lajos entered elementary school it had been a momentous day.

"A teacher told us," he recalled, "that we were all sons and daughters of the workers. The teacher said we should be very proud. We were building a great socialism in Hungary.

"A strange thing happened a little while later. Our teacher called one of our good comrades in front of the room. 'Look at him,' she said. 'His father is an enemy of the state, an enemy of socialism. Try to correct him —our friend—if you can.'"

Lajos said he asked his father about his school friend and the other boy's disgraced father.

"My father took me in his arms," continued Lajos. "It was the first time he did that, I guess, since I was a baby. I just finished telling my father how some of us went with our friend to his house. The mother was crying. The father, neighbors said, was in jail. I will never forget what my father told me.

"'Lajos, help your little friend by being his friend,' my father said. 'Never mind what your teacher says. Your own father tells you to do that.'

"My father, I noticed, did not sleep very much. He worked very hard. But something always bothered him. I remember him saying in a loud voice in our apartment, 'How much longer can human beings stand this? Everyone is afraid. My mother used to say we must hope that better times will come. She told him too, to keep his voice down.

"Then, when I was about nine, two men came to our flat. My father was eating some bread and a little salami for his supper. The men asked his name; my father gave it. 'Come with us,' the men said. They never took off their gabardine coats. New coats. My father kissed me. He kissed my mother who began to cry.

"I was eleven years old when I saw my father the next time. He looked like a very old man. My mother had been working but we had very bad times. I saw that all my father's teeth in the front were missing. I asked how. 'They knocked them out,' he said. Afterwards, my father would tell me how the government had lied to us, the workers; that they arrested and tried to make decent people look like the worst criminals.

"When the demonstrations began, we all asked questions about them. My father became a new man. He was up day and night. He told me, when I asked, 'We will have justice after all.' Then one night—just the other night—he came home. 'The Russians are shooting at us,' he said. 'They have come to murder the people. This is the end.' I never saw my father again. He is dead, killed by a tank.

"Some of my friends called for me. There was no school. We could hear loud booms. Russian tanks, said my friends. We talked and all of us told how our fathers had gone away. 'Where do you think our fathers went?' one boy asked. 'They fight the Russians, don't you know,' said another.

"We went out in the streets. We saw many of our young men. They carried guns. We followed them. They tried to chase us home. We stayed behind them. They turned over cars and even trolleycars. They were waiting for something. We lay down in the street, too. Someone yelled: 'Here they come.' It was Russians and tanks. Somebody noticed us. 'My God,' he shouted, 'where can we hide these kids?' It was too late. They told us to lie flat. I was very, very scared. So were my friends. We lay on the ground, close to each other.

"After a while, you get less scared. We got enough courage to ask our young men to let us help. Our own fathers, we told them, were also fighting the Russians. If we walked out, we said, the Russians would probably shoot us. There was shooting all over as a Freedom Fighter with my friends that day."

Lajos' mother, grief-stricken, tugged at her boy and said they had better get along. The boy, his hand in his mother's hand, and a rifle slung on his small back, was a little reluctant. He shook hands, all around. "Do you think," he asked gravely, "that we were brave enough?"

The whole world, outside the Communist bloc thought so. Even the Russians answered grudgingly, temporarily, yes. The shock troops and armor they sent against Budapest slowly withdrew from battle-rocked streets. It was, thought the Hungarians, victory for them. Imre Nagy, in an emotional broadcast, said a Russian withdrawal had been agreed upon at the conference table. In sullen silence, Hungarians ignored a dawn-to-dusk curfew to watch Soviet vehicles, troop carriers and tanks roll over the bridges. There was jubilation in the coalition government.

"They'll all be out," enthused Geza Losonczy.

"You mean we hope that they'll all be out," Maleter, now a general and Minister of Defense, observed sourly.

We were standing in the dully illuminated second-floor corridor of the Parliament. Reflections of the electric lamps cast off spread-eagle figures on the stained glass windows. New Hungarian government figures were busy talking to each other—and to anyone who questioned them. They were excited and exhilarated. The two big topics on all Hungarian official tongues were the release and return to Budapest of Joszef Cardinal Mindszenty and the need to make the new government's authority operate inside the capital.

Among other visitors I went to the Cardinal's residence and shook hands with him. He appeared in good health. On his head he wore a red skull cap. A red, white and green Hungarian national cockade peeped from a buttonhole. Outside, two tanks, with Hungarian insignia, commanded approaches to the Cardinal's eighteenth-century palace. Soldiers on the roof kept watch on the streets below.

Questions popped at the Cardinal. The laconic answers, occasionally had to be repeated. They were drowned out by rifle and machine gun fire that rattled and burst not far away. The Cardinal had been liberated from a house fifty kilometers from Budapest where a detail of Communist security police, including four women, kept him under constant surveillance. It was seven years that he had been in custody. The night before, Hungarian soldiers swooped down on the house. Taken by surprise, the police detail surrendered without protest. The Cardinal stayed overnight at a barracks to which he had been brought in a small passenger car. The next morning, escorted by soldiers in uniform, Cardinal Mindszenty returned to his residence.

"I must inform myself about the situation," said Mindszenty. "I have been in prison a long time."

As two soldiers passed the group talking to the Cardinal, he smiled and told them: "You are good Hungarian boys." The smile fled when Hungarians began to describe to him the situation inside Budapest. "There has been tremendous sacrifice," said Mindszenty slowly. "Now, there must be as great a sacrifice to building a national discipline." There were quick nods, yes, from the Hungarians around him. They all thought they had Budapest and, therefore, the country. The Russians, some even said, would leave soon. Politicians began to think in terms of bringing the revolution under their terms of understandable order.

Although the spirit of uprising still burned, self-discipline was pretty much the rule. Looting was expressly forbidden. I saw two Freedom Fighters tack up a notice on a grocery whose windows had been shattered. "If anything has been taken, notify the municipal authority at once," the sign read. Communist Party headquarters had been sacked. That was during the fighting. Villas of party higher-ups had been raided. Taking souvenirs was prohibited. A group of girls who ironically held up lacy lingerie from one Communist's house, was sternly told to put it back for a later inventory.

"Of course, some things must have been taken or looted," Bela Kovacs said. "Even angels lose a sense of proportion in situations like the one we have here. These poor people behaved well, on the whole."

That was also true, at least in my view, when the AVO was told to surrender. Many holed themselves up in a fortified building. They synthesized the hatred Hungarians held for the whole Communist regime. Russian book shops they would sack, and burn the propaganda merchandise in the main streets. Instead of holding on to Communist membership rolls, Hungarians threw them into bonfires. Prisoners they turned out of jails. It was liberation for anyone who may have felt the sting of the old Communist regime.

The police who had served the regime were looked at differently and wrathfully. At Kossuth Square, opposite Parliament, an AVO agent was recognized by workers. "Kill him, kill him!" they shouted, grabbing the frightened man. One of the captors roughly seized the policeman's wallet. From it he took a card in a plastic case. The man's identity and affiliation were on the card. Someone swung at the AVO man. Others interfered.

"Let's have real order," a man in a torn military overcoat shouted. "Let's try not to do what these bastards did to us."

The crowd roared agreement although there were nasty grumbles. Off went the AVO officer under an escort. His comrades, who barricaded themselves in their headquarters, weren't giving up. Revolutionaries tried to storm the building. They were mowed down. Finally, out of side entrances, the security men tried to break out.

"Don't take any prisoners," a youngster screamed.

A great cheer suddenly went up and people who had been taking cover swarmed into the open. Shots still came from the building. People paid no attention. The besiegers had forced their way into the secret police headquarters. Once tough secret policemen and officers whose word could a few days ago mean life or death headed panic-stricken for the entrance. Determined, gun-toting revolutionaries stopped them. Eyes wild with fright, AVO men tried to run through the armed avengers at the doorway. They were shot down on the pavement. Others, still in police uniform, stopped in their tracks. They argued.

"We are not guilty," one said.

"Why do you still keep a gun?" demanded a Freedom Fighter, ripping the policeman's gun from his holster.

For a few minutes, the trapped secret policemen and their hunters argued in the street. The police officers maintained their innocence.

"Ask them why they stayed on their jobs." a girl demanded.

"We couldn't do anything else," stuttered an AVO officer.

"They were the best kept and they were the most brutal," a boy still wearing a student's cap roared. "Forget the talk and get rid of them."

The police group was marched to the nearest building wall. Their knees sagged. A couple stumbled and fell on all fours at the wall. Guns, only three or four feet away, pointed directly at the police. Not a gun wavered. "Fire!" a man in the front rank commanded. Hands above their faces, as if they meant to ward off point-blank bullets, the AVOs fell before their executioners. Everyone concerned was Hungarian.

"Death is always unpleasant when it is violent. It is more unpleasant to die because your people say you betrayed them," a man just behind me said. He was fearfully fatigued. His face and eyes showed how tired he was. He carried a small satchel.

"They want you, doctor," a boy shouted as he rushed up. "They want you to help somebody inside."

The doctor nodded and followed the boy. He didn't ask, I thought later, who it was who needed help.

CHAPTER | 16

THE very atmosphere changed in Budapest. It was almost as visible as the mist that rose from the Danube. Mirage-like, it was the shimmering image of a free Hungary. In the streets, patrols wearing national colors as armbands solemnly made their rounds. Hungarians thought they had shaken hands with destiny.

"They are ours," a mother showed her little daughter a passing patrol near Parliament.

The little girl blew a kiss and waved. "Ours" and "theirs" were very special words. Children knew immediately what they meant. Russians had evacuated main arteries and strategic points they had held in the besieged city. Hungarians believed they were free. Hadn't Nagy and Kadar told them on the radio they would try to make Hungary neutral? Just like Austria, Hungarians thought, and their minds turned on what the change would bring them. Hungarians believed that they had won their fight.

With their own eyes, they saw the withdrawing Soviet troops. Moreover, Nagy promised free elections. It was a dream, but hadn't it been realized miraculously and completely?

"Hope, not reality—certainly not now," was the terse comment of General Pal Maleter. "They still surround the airport and they have reinforcements coming in. Take a look for yourself."

In the wooded slopes of Buda, looking straight down on the city, Soviet armor was parked. Tanks and tank crews were different. The markings and unit numbers were different. Motorized infantry ate stolidly on the roadside. Theirs were different numbers than the ones we noted during the fighting. You couldn't get near the airport. Soviet road-blocks kept you from getting in or out. Driving in a car, a Chevrolet, out through Soviet lines into the country seemed a joyride. The little American flag sticker on the windshield brought out clapping little crowds. Every round of applause reverberated as a sound of shame to the touring listener. Sometimes the Russians stopped the car. The questions were the same. Who were we? What did we want? Whispered roadside conferences and then a wave to get moving. All the way to the common Soviet-Hungarian border, the traffic was one way. It was Russian, troop-filled and armor-bearing, heading towards the place we left—Budapest.

The ride was instructive. Nagy and his aides told us that the conference with Mikoyan and Suslov had been successful. They wanted to retain certain bases in Hungary. Nagy said no, it couldn't even be a matter of negotiation any more. Hungary only wanted to be left alone and neutral to bind up her wounds. Mikoyan and Suslov left saying they understood. Watching the trucks, tanks and soldiers move in from the East, you could grasp the difference in language. The Soviet negotiators understood, in their fashion. Battered Budapest was getting a little free time, just a few days. Maleter doggedly briefed the government on what he knew. It was there to see, on the highways and at the airport.

"Negotiation with the Russians always is very hard and very complicated," Nagy told him one evening.

"Surrounding you with a big build-up in force is not negotiation," Maleter told me after a conference.

The government was negotiating in Budapest with Russians left on the spot. They ran the usual table of organization: diplomats, military officers and security men. Between conferences, the Russians took precautions. Wandering along a quay on the Danube, John MacCormac and I noticed a river boat, with a crowd moving up the gangplank. We went to the mooring. It was a Czechoslovak boat, with its steam up. The passengers were Russians. Some men had books under their arms. Women held on to their children. One little girl clutched a yellow-brown teddy bear. We asked a quayside boatman where the cruise was headed.

"Cruise?" he looked up at us, a leathery face impassive. "This boat is going to Bratislava."

Bratislava is the capital of Slovakia, on the Danube. The boat was packed with people. An evacuation was in process. The Russians must be getting ready for something drastic. We talked to Losonczy that night. Worn-out, he managed a thin chortle. We sounded, he said, like Maleter: All skepticism. There were more talks going on with the Russians. They looked good. So good, as a matter of fact, that Nagy himself would hold a press conference the following evening for the press of the world.

In the semi-darkened streets leading to Parliament, the press conference was held. Nagy did not turn up. Neither did Losonczy. None of us ever saw Maleter again. Old Zoltan Tildy, retreaded in the coalition, said he was sorry, that he would take over for Nagy at the press conference. Nagy had something urgent to attend to.

"What about Kadar?" somebody asked Tildy. "Why shouldn't he be here?"

"We can't find him," replied Tildy, helplessly.

The press conference was anticlimactic. Tildy tried to answer questions. Uneasiness and bickering broke out in the conference room. Nothing is more disheartening than the spectacle of journalists quarrelling with each other and with the person answering questions. Leaving Parliament Square, Hungarian national patrols could be seen, silhouetted from street lamps against the building line.

"Poor kids," an Englishman said feelingly.

At our hotel, a graduate student with an escort of two armed, young revolutionaries got hold of us.

"Something's very wrong," he said. "We can't find Maleter."

"Maybe he is busy at some meeting," was the reply.

"Never like this," said the student, fiddling nervously with rimless spectacles he held in his hands. "There always is someone we can reach. Not tonight. Besides, if you go over, you can hear their stuff moving down from the hills."

He was referring to Soviet tanks. Post-intervention jitters, he was told nervously. A little sleep might help. The boy shook his head dubiously and left the hotel lobby. It was after 1 A.M., Nov. 4, a Sunday. We went up to our bedrooms and stretched out. Shoes off only, for most of us. A little later, the boom of artillery echoed in the hills, the usual night's sound effects.

Pounding on the bedroom door was not usual. That was human and there was an excited voice that went with the knock. A Hungarian friend, father of a boy who escaped to the West a few years back, stood outside.

"They're coming back," he said in anguish. "They will stay."

We calmed him down. He lived on the Buda side. The noise of rumbling tanks woke him up. The whole neighborhood come to life, he said. Russians in trucks and Russian tanks were on the move. Fire from Freedom Fighter roadblocks delayed them briefly. The old man crossed another bridge and came to the hotel. In his frenzy, he knew no other sanctuary.

"Poor Hungary," he muttered, almost to himself.

"Nagy is speaking on the radio," a hotel porter shouted at us.

That was Nagy's last time on the radio. He spoke of Soviet treachery and Hungary's determination to defend itself. The government, he told the world, was at its post. The world was not. Just as at a Sunday dawn nearly fifteen years before aggressors struck at Pearl Harbor, so did Russians launch themselves on Budapest and the rest of Hungary. Reducing Budapest, however, was the main Soviet objective. There was the heart and soul of revolution. The missing Kadar had turned up on their side while Nagy, also a Communist, stayed with his countrymen. The name Kadar became a post-war synonym of the wartime Quisling. Kadar's treachery was even worse. He had praised the revolution against Soviet occupation.

Over the beleaguered city droned Soviet planes, dropping leaflets. On the ground, Soviet tanks and motorized infantry crunched over leaderless, but fight-to-the-death revolutionaries. The heroic Killian Barracks became a real, no-survivors Alamo. There was not even a Pal Maleter left to lead. The Russians had made sure, by first luring the revolutionary government into thinking negotiation was possible, of setting up conditions where their own armed might was guaranteed victory. Leaflets that fluttered to the ground told Hungarians that the Russians were coming as "liberating selfless brothers." The Russian military commander spoke out of the other side of the Soviet mouth. He would measure military rule, General

Grebennik told Budapest, "in accordance with the laws of war." In other words, Soviet military occupation had formally been announced.

Inside the United States and other Western legations, confusion, embarrassment and frustration ran rampant. Cardinal Mindszenty strode the corridors of the American legation, his lips moving in prayer. He was permitted to stay. A member of the Nagy government was told, regretfully, by our diplomats that he had to leave. No sanctuary for him. Orders from Washington. He shrugged, shook hands with some of us.

"I'm interested in my own safety, naturally," he said. "But there is more at issue than me. Will the Americans never understand?"

Apparently not. Back home we were winding up a national election campaign. Patrick Hillings, a Republican Congressman from California and a member of his party's ironically-named "Truth Squad," said the uprising in Hungary was the greatest example of the success of Eisenhower's foreign policy. Nothing could have been farther from the truth.

"The Hungarian revolution was carried out with the blood of Hungarians," Professor Istvan Bibo, a member of the Nagy government, said. "Nobody helped us. That is our tragedy and the tragedy of the West."

Into Budapest the Russians swept as conquerors. Their reinforced armor stormed through the streets, smashing down pitiful little obstacles thrown in their path. Heavy-caliber guns beat a steady obbligato of death on all armed opposition. Boys died, rifle against tank. Frenzied Soviet troops also swept through houses, looting, pillaging and raping. The macabre atmosphere that shrouded Budapest was made more nightmarish by the fact that telephones mainly continued to function. A Freedom Fighter told us, as he emerged from a pay telephone booth, how he tried to telephone his wife every hour.

"She just told me that the Russians are searching our apartment house now," he said desperately. "I told her to barricade the door with the chifforobe. She is so young and I love her so much."

In the streets, youngsters tried to go back to their pavement guerrilla warfare. Their Molotov cocktails were running low. They bloodied Soviet might again but it overwhelmed them. I saw them fight and die once more in the span of a few days as others did. At the time many of us foreigners described what we saw and heard. The efforts, sparked by strong emotion, are insignificant compared with the diary of a seventeen-year-old boy. It was written partly in pencil, partly in ink, in a ruled lesson-book. He gave me the tattered copybook to keep when total Soviet occupation of Budapest was nearing completion. His name for these purposes will be Ferenc Szabo. He told me, quite calmly, that he had no intention of surrendering. His copybook is a diary of death that no outsider could read without feeling ashamed.

Its scrawled text reads:

"Sunday, 4 November—Mist from the Danube got us wetter than usual. It was early Sunday morning. We had talked about the Russkies getting out. There were reports they were talking to Maleter. Some of us thought it was the end of the Russians. We were happy for a while. Our group had about 180 at the start. We lost friends. Some were dead. Some were wounded. We could count about 140 now.

"We had been uneasy. Why, if the talks were going well for us, were Russian reinforcements coming in? All of us had talked about the new Hungary. We all knew each other. We had been at school and played together. Only the other day we all became soldiers together. While we talked, we also looked over places we defended and would defend again. We were on duty. In crisis, you are always on duty.

"Someone noticed that we had plenty of gasoline in cans to throw at Russian tanks. But he also called attention that we didn't have enough bottles. We were even using little medicine bottles by that time to have a good supply. One of the older university students was sort of our military commander. He had done his military service. But from our first fighting we learned what to do when Russian tanks came into our street. Cellars held ammunition we needed. Most of the stuff was behind barricades. It was most convenient that way. We didn't have much food, just mostly bread. Everyone had been too excited to eat much. I thought how my mother used to complain when I had less than eight hours sleep. I wondered if I really had that much all week.

"We tried to see that the younger kids got some sleep. We tried to send them home. They wouldn't go. I was finished checking guns and ammunition among my friends. A girl we had listening to a portable radio ran out. She yelled: 'The Russians are coming. Our people have been tricked.'

"We all looked at her. I think everyone knew in a way this would happen. You feel things. Someone cursed. Then he apologized to the girl. We sent couriers around buildings telling old people and women with children to get out fast. Very few of them went. Then we got our guns and bottles ready. There were almost enough rifles and tommyguns for one out of three. We were well armed. We had to ration our grenades. We waited quietly. We knew we didn't have long to wait. We heard them coming over bridges and main streets. They made a lot of noise. They opened up. We knew they'd be at us soon. About 7:40 there was firing down the line about 150 meters from my position. Our Soviet comrades were back to finish their jobs of murdering.

"I prayed that I would get at least six. Strange prayer. It was a long time since I prayed. You don't get to pray in the Young Communist Organization. Then they opened up on us. Some of my friends and I were behind burnt-out trucks and a wrecked Russian armored car. We crouched and waited. From windows our people were pouring bottles wildly and firing shots. I saw boys down the lines, screaming with their wounds. We had one practical nurse. She said she was and she could wrap a bandage around someone without crying.

"Then we got it. The Russians were shooting wild. They shot at windows mainly. Houses were their targets—at first. One of my comrades got behind a tank. He climbed up to the top. He waited until the tank finished firing and went back down the street. When the turret on the tank opened, he dropped a grenade in it. Then the other Russian tanks saw what happened. They killed him. We were luckier with another tank. It cost us five comrades but finally we got a tank. We could run it because some of the boys had a little experience in military training. We put a crew in and our tank went with the Russians. It shot suddenly at other tanks. It got one and stopped another. The Russians were confused and scared. They began to shoot at each other and ours. After about an hour, we lost our tank. But we put at least four of theirs out of commission.

"Our rifles and tommyguns weren't much help except when there was infantry against us. We could handle them. Finally the Russians gave up on infantry. Naturally the tanks ran right over our positions. We learned to crouch and hide and tried to come up behind them. Every time a bottle was thrown or a shot fired, the Russians put their tanks together and shelled the spots; five, ten or twenty tanks at a time. All morning and all afternoon it went. From our 140, we had thirty-five dead and about fifty hurt. Very bad. We couldn't do anything with the wounded. The Russians shot Red Cross cars. We tried a system with ropes and pulleys to get the wounded from house to house. They were also shot.

"All the wounded who could use a weapon stayed. Nobody left. Nobody deserted. There were enough guns left for everyone who could use one. When it got dark the Russians stayed away. They shelled us from safe distances for them. They were afraid we would get to them in the dark spots. This Sunday night we counted our weapons and ammunition. Some of us went out to get what guns and ammunition we could from dead Russians. In looking around, on patrol, we used those guns against looters. They were Russians who broke into shops. They would have said we were responsible for looting. We used up a lot of ammunition to prevent them looting.

"Those are bad military tactics. But we aren't really soldiers. Our rations this night were some bread. We saved the rest of the bread for morning. Before it got too light. We had to scold two boys who slipped out at night and went home. They came back but they had gone to tell their parents they were all right.

"Monday, 5 November—We are less than half of yesterday. We decided to keep the wounded who could still use guns in fixed spots. The rest of us would run around to different places. That would make it seem we were more than we were. Some of us had read about this in a book somewhere. They are coming now. The first tank pushes through the barrier we put up during the night. [The remainder of the Monday account was noted afterwards.] The tanks didn't come with such a rush as yesterday. They were more cautious. Two of my oldest friends died from wounds during the morning. We covered them with their coats and with little flags they wore on their coats. There is no time to mourn. Nobody cries because men don't cry any more. Where is the help from the West? Doesn't the West understand? Is America more afraid than we are? We tell ourselves we must fight for ourselves. We are not many. Someone must help.

"The Russians are not using so many tanks now so close together. It gets more difficult for us. We see what they are doing. The Russians are making a big ring round us. Then they will make the ring smaller. Then it will become a few rings. It will be a miracle if any of us survive. It's better to fight than to surrender. We ran out of medicine. Not even iodine now. There are two bottles of brandy we ration for our wounded. We are now twenty-seven able to fight. Worse than ever.

"One of our fellows had an idea we rejected. He thought if we could stand some of our corpses in places where they would show, the Russians would think we had many more people. It was something he once saw in the movies. We said no. It would dishonor our brave dead. At least we taught the Russians to respect us as fighters. Twenty-seven freedom fighters left and they have sent, by counting, at least thirty-five tanks against us. An old lady who tried to bring us bread was shot almost as she reached my barricade. One boy crawled out and dragged her in. It was too late. We placed our little national flag in her hands. May she rest in peace. At night the Russians went a few streets away. We couldn't afford any more patrols to go after them. We decided that half our remaining people would be in cellars and the rest hidden behind burned tanks and barricades. Somebody sort of laughed and said we even had reserve forces.

"Tuesday, 6 November—It's very strange. We all slept when we had two hours' rest. We are very tired. But none of us is hungry. Most haven't eaten in around twenty-four hours. You get to lose your appetite. The Russians are coming a little earlier this morning. Until now they had waited for pretty full daylight. I suppose they realize there are very few of us left. [As previously, subsequent notes on the day were made after the fighting subsided.] The tanks didn't come as close as the first two days. They parked and just shot and shot. Three of our boys and one girl tried to crawl to them. We kept up all the fire we could over their heads. One boy and the girl made a tank. They each had a grenade. They threw them each at the tank treads. The tank stopped running. When the tankers came out to look at what went on, we got them. The girl managed to get back to us. She had bullets in her. The tanks seemed to get infuriated. They rushed up the street. They shelled and shot. Houses came down. Two of our boys were trapped in a house that collapsed.

"Now we were just about twenty. But we only had enough ammunition at 1500 hours for five guns. Then we decided to get out and try to join other Freedom Fighters. We didn't have much of a terrible decision to make about our wounded. They, wherever they could, remained fighting and were killed. Those who were unable to continue died because they couldn't reach medical care. A few were huddled in cellars. One of our boys carried the wounded girl who knocked out the tank. We kept in the cellars until dark. Then we went from one cellar to another. That was to prevent us from getting caught coming out of a cellar we defended.

"We only lost one boy. He thought he saw a Russian tank in the ruins. He fired and the tanks let go. Maybe it was deliberate of him. There was so much noise and shooting that the rest of us got away. We made it through the streets for about a thousand meters to join another force. We added nearly 20 effective men to them. They had enough ammunition for perhaps another day. They also had some bread which they naturally shared with us. Some of us thought we might shave. One of our friends had a razor. Curious thing to think about. As a rule we shave at our age twice a week at most. Somebody explained that we were just thinking about dying as cleanly as possible."

The detailed diary ends with the notation of that night. The next dawn these boys joined in a big resistance pocket on the Buda side of the Danube. When I last saw him, skinny in someone else's greatcoat that was belted with a cartridge container, he had only a simple request:

"Please tell the West not to believe any lies that we looted or stole. They [the Russians and their puppet Communists] will spread such propaganda. Please do not believe such lies. My comrades and I ask only that you tell what you have seen and heard. We fought for our freedom and we fought alone. Some day you perhaps will realize what we have tried to do."

A gentle giant in spiritual stature was Professor Bibo. He refused to leave his office at Parliament. Soviet tanks and troops had already invested the building. Bibo, by telephone, kept in touch with reporters he knew. He called us at various legations and gave precise details on what he could see from the window. His office door was barricaded with desks but he refused to leave as Nagy and many others did to seek refuge.

"They are at the door, my door," Bibo said over the telephone. "It is goodbye to the Hungarian revolution—this time."

Nagy and his party, including some writers, fled to the Yugoslav Embassy. The telephone lines operated there, too. I talked to Yugoslav newspapermen at frequent intervals. They would not say who was being given shelter except that they were "unexpected guests." Julia Rajk was among the guests who the Yugoslavs claimed at the time simply showed up at the door. All Western legations had guests, as well. They were mainly journalists and a few students who wandered in from Western Europe. The students came into Budapest between the first and second Soviet interventions, looking for kicks. They should have been kicked right back to their schools. The only foreign students I had ever heard about from Freedom Fighters who fought with the Hungarians were Polish students.

When the Russians uncoiled their second intervention, the thrill-seeking students lit out for their diplomatic missions for sanctuary and stayed there.

They were far more fortunate than Hungarian students—or workers— or any young Hungarian for that matter. Trucks, guarded by Soviet soldiers and some re-formed AVO units, rolled down Budapest streets to the West Station. The open vehicles were jammed with standing young men and some girls. They were sternly silent until troops began to unload them roughly. "Don't touch me," a girl shouted at a security officer who pushed her into another group for speed. "Long Live Free Hungary," cried others to tongue-tied bystanders. Into railroad cars, boxcars and second-class carriages, the human truck consignments were delivered.

This was the beginning of the deportation of young Hungarians to the Soviet Union. For a couple of days you could see Communist police and Soviet security detachments hunt their quarry in the houses and streets of Budapest. They were bundled off the streets, after being hailed, into trucks that followed the scent. I didn't notice any prisoner cry. Some cheeks were wet but there was no weeping. The sound of soughing sobs came from the watching crowds, powerless to rush the guarded trucks.

"They are taking everything away from us," a middle-aged woman in black cried out. "Look, they even take away our children."

"We can watch, if we want to," bitterly remarked a father, holding two little girls by either hand. "This is meant for us to watch."

To match the terror in mass deportations, the Kadar regime, at General Grebennik's behest, began meting out sentences in kangaroo courts. Hungarian prisoners, separated from deportees, were taken to jail just over the river on the Buda side. They appeared before drumhead courts. Sentences of death by firing squad were ruthlessly carried out. The victims were denounced as "traitors" or "counter-revolutionaries." Nothing was left to chance in imposing iron occupation in Budapest. Nagy and his comrades found that out soon enough. The Yugoslavs had been promised a safe conduct for the refugee charges in their embassy. Nobody really can say today whether the Yugoslavs decided to wash their hands of Nagy and his comrades and entered into a cynical deal with the Russians. Tito, who first supported the Hungarian revolution, approved of the second Soviet intervention. His regime, patently worried that Titoist reform might be swept away as quickly as the whole Communist superstructure, wanted a strictly hands-off situation.

The neutral country promised Nagy and his group was Rumania, deep in the vise of the Soviet Union. A Yugoslav friend of mine who watched them leave said he was appalled at what he saw. "They were all arrested practically within calling distance of our embassy," he told me later. Smaller people, the rank-and-file, had already begun to flee the country by the tens of thousands. On the Austrian border barbed-wire entanglements and minefields, removed only a short time before the revolution, were still wide open. It's a big frontier and families rushed pell-mell for the border areas. They evaded main roads and pushed through forests and lakes. Under the brilliant moon illuminating the desolate Hungarian plain thousands of Hungarians were in flight westwards.

I had just left Budapest by car with a Soviet permit to get out via the main highway. Being held up by eleven roadblocks on a three-hour trip was no hardship, compared with what refugees were going through. If you didn't stop soon enough, shots were fired at your car. Rolling again, the little American flag still attracted waves from village windows. Each wave made you slide farther down in your seat. But you couldn't really find a place to hide. It was the only time in my life I had ever been ashamed that I was an American. At the little border station of Hegyeshalom, Soviet officers were on duty with a couple of self-conscious Hungarian guards. They did nothing but stand around. The Russians looked the car over. "You can go," an officer said. "Have a good trip." On the brow of a little hill above him, I noticed, a Soviet tank was parked, its gun muzzle deflected to command the customs post.

At that point, even the Russians didn't have enough guns to plug up gaping holes in the border. Soviet patrols stalked fleeing refugees. Oblivious of freezing winds, men, women and children straggled up to the Austrian frontier. For a few days the Russians only sought to prevent them from reaching canals and the Neusiedlersee, a great reed-filled lake between Austria and Hungary. So a human game of hounds and hares was enacted nightly near the border. Refugees, almost naked, hid among the reeds. Then, when the sounds of marauding patrols grew faint, they'd strike out for what they hoped would be Austrian territory.

The frost-enveloped plains stretching eastward were deathly still. Tracer bullets occasionally stabbed the night. Sometimes they were varied with star-shells that burst far overhead and made the ground underneath blindingly brilliant. The still plains actually pulsated. There was a little cry, suddenly, or a whimper. From the lake wraith-like forms rose in the reeds, asking; "Austria?" Austrian students prowled the border stretches, trying to reach injured and badly frightened refugees. The actual frontier was crossed and re-crossed so often those nights that nobody ever thought to keep count. What mattered was to help a Hungarian. Some bad ones got through, of course. "We'll worry about that later," an Austrian Red Cross worker said, picking a numbed boy out of an icy canal.

How long, I asked a Hungarian who led a group to safety, did he think the exodus could last?

"As long as we have feet on which to walk," he replied. "Later it will take wits and great bravery. It will go on as long as the Russians are in Hungary."

He removed his sweater and swaddled it around a child weeping in its mother's arms. In his shirtsleeves, he headed into the icy wind for a truck. Then he swivelled abruptly, waved to us and returned on the run. "Forgive me," he said. "I forgot for a moment. All our thanks. We do not intentionally forget our manners." Nor did they forget, in the main, people they left behind in Hungary. One man I met went back. He had just brought his wife and two children to safety. His brother, a New York sweater manufacturer, found the little family in Vienna. But the man who went back, was troubled. He had left two brothers—one of them a paralytic—a sister and their children in Hungary. Going to the border didn't help the uneasy man. His relatives were not among the outpouring of refugees. In the deathly darkness of the frontier, the man embraced his brother from New York. Then he bolted into no-man's land to re-enter Hungary.

For three days and nights, the New York manufacturer, who made good long before as an immigrant, was beside himself with grief. But then the brother turned up at the frontier with the entire family. There were fifteen of them—including children aged from thirteen months to twelve years. He managed a mass exodus by putting his crippled brother on a make-shift litter. Into the bargain, the determined escape artist brought out nine other persons, neighbors. He had a total of twenty-four following him blindly but faithfully. Relays took turns carrying the paralytic over the border in a tortuous route laid out by the man who went back to save his people. He went unarmed and alone. Another man, Janos Kadar, also had returned to Budapest. He came with Russian tanks to save Hungary for the Soviet Union. I can still remember though, an earlier Kadar broadcast:

"We can safely say that the ideological and organizational leaders who sponsored this uprising were recruited from Hungarian Communist writers, journalists, university students, youth of the Petofi Circle, thousands and thousands of workers and peasants and veteran fighters. We are proud that you honestly stood your ground in the armed uprising and in leading it. You were permeated with true patriotism."

These are Kadar's words, on the record. Three days after he broadcast his thanks to Hungary's fighters for freedom, Kadar betrayed his country and his countrymen. Their fate is bound up in the moving, desperate appeal of a young Hungarian poet, who wrote:

> *What will happen to us?*
> *Is there no freedom but in the grave?*
> *No answer. There is only blood*
> *And the tears of the mourning. . . .*

Kadar abhorred poetry. It was too unrealistic, he claimed.

CHAPTER | 17

JUSTICE was not the outstanding characteristic in the turbulent lands of Soviet Europe after the cataclysm of the Hungarian revolution. Except for Poland, where many intellectuals and disillusioned party members, the youth and the Catholics sympathized with Hungary, restoring Communist order immediately was the only justice under the law. Turmoil and dissatisfaction sent tremors through hitherto solid party organizations. Tito, the heretic, was quick to show that he remained the indomitable Communist master of Yugoslavia.

Tito had ambitions to see that a pro-Yugoslav regime came out of the Hungarian uprising. He and his party underestimated the extent of anti-Communist feeling that would emerge in Budapest. He was, as a Yugoslav Communist told me later, alarmed about the possibilities of a non-Communist Hungary. Although he had disapproved strongly the first Soviet intervention in Budapest as provocative, he approved the second one as necessary to the overall Communist cause. To show how much he approved, Tito had Milovan Djilas hauled before a court.

When Hungary exploded, Djilas noted that it was the natural reaction of people fed up with deceit and terror. His articles had appeared in the West, mocking the Soviet system and the hollowness of Communist regimes in Eastern Europe. Later, Djilas' book, "The New Class," exposed the self-perpetuation of party bureaucracy and its ruthless exploitation of the people. It even became a black-market best-seller in Yugoslavia and brought up to $15 a copy. Djilas' deviation was too much even for the Yugoslav hierarchy. The party had to prove that it was still in control. Djilas was sentenced to three years in prison, which was certainly better than being shot. Tito could thus tell the world, especially Socialists in Western Europe and Asia, that he was being lenient and at the same time maintaining his position as a Communist bulwark.

Off went Djilas to the forbidding prison in Sremska Mitrovica, about fifty miles from Belgrade. By design or coincidence he was locked up in the same concrete cell in which Royalist Yugoslav authorities imprisoned him before the war. Dedijer never wavered in his support of Djilas. However he hadn't written anything inflammatory so he was spared prison. But work was not available to him in Belgrade and official isolation was enforced in a day-and-night UDBA watch over his apartment. His letters were opened and all his telephone conversations were tapped.

Yugoslav police became even more vigilant as strong anti-Communist noises reverberated in near-by satellites. In Bulgaria peasants demonstrated their intense dislike of forced collectivization. Writers and journalists complained of having to submit to blinkered party hacks who served as censors without ever having put down a creative idea on paper themselves. They were quickly turned out of jobs, arrested or threatened with loss of position. Police and army units smashed peasant demonstrations and the country withdrew into a sullen silence.

It was more difficult in Rumania. A large Hungarian minority in Transylvania demonstrated in provincial streets in heartfelt sympathy with Hungarian revolutionaries. In the schools, Rumanians forgot their traditional antagonism and stood shoulder-to-shoulder with Hungary.

"I had never seen Rumanians get along so well with Hungarians before," a Rumanian playwright said in Bucharest.

That sort of camaraderie was quickly smashed. Rumanian army shock troops and detachments of the "Securitate," renamed from the Siguranza, patrolled trouble spots. Students were expelled from universities, doctors were interchanged between the western and eastern parts of the country, and peasants were compelled to bring in deliveries under the eyes of the security units. Troublemakers, who had been vocal during the hectic days of the Hungarian revolution, were arrested. A friend of mine released from a long prison sentence recently told me how lines of new prisoners shuffled into cells. In time, through the prison communication system—pounding on walls in jail Morse or by writing messages on the bottom of mess kits with soap and a spoon—older prisoners learned there had been a revolution in Hungary and that Rumania was badly shaken.

Of all Soviet Europe however, Poland shook worst and longest. Gomulka, for a Communist, was running scared. He had scheduled elections to uphold his return to power and had exiled party die-hards who had fought his policies. Cardinal Wyszyński had been released from jail and was back in Warsaw. A strange compact was worked out for co-existence of Gomulka's Communism and the Cardinal's church.

"The church got more here in Poland than it has had for fifty years in France," Wladyslaw Bienkowski, then Minister of Education, told me. He had been so pro-Gomulka that he, too, had been thrown in jail. Unrepentant party enemies, like Jakub Berman and Hillary Minc, called Bienkowski a "revisionist." It is one of the worst, if not the most opprobrious, label to apply to a Communist where the doctrine rules.

But students in Warsaw and the big cities like Krakow revelled in calling themselves revisionists. Writers, poets and intellectuals at large poured out their innermost souls. They spoke without fear of being arrested. Poles began to straggle out of jails, their sentences terminated. Their stories of torture and the subnormal life of prison aroused already inflamed popular feeling. Students rioted in the streets, grappled with police and sacked Communist Party headquarters. Demands of "Russky, Go Home," were shouted and smeared on walls of the garrison town at Lignice. The Red Army in Poland had its big base there.

Soviet technicians, the most noticeable ones in the government apparatus, had already been sent home at the behest of Gomulka. Most prominent of all was Marshal Konstantin Rokossovsky. Stalin had assigned him to Warsaw after the war, ignoring Polish feelings. By Soviet order, Rokossovsky became a Polish citizen, Minister of Defense and a member of the Politburo. When the Russians created the Warsaw Pact, as a military answer to NATO, Rokossovsky was Moscow's military agent on the spot.

Gradualism, exercised by the party, could not meet increased Polish enmity. To stem the tide of rage, the Polish central committee met with the released Gomulka. Its apprehensive membership was about to confer party leadership on the slender, humorless Communist who had been jailed as the closest Polish equivalent to a Titoist.

Polish bureaucrats who attended the meeting remember seeing from the windows crowds surge through the streets, shouting the Poznan slogan: "Bread and liberty." In the midst of a party debate, in which the standfast Stalinist element of the party exchanged recrimination with the call for a quick change in political approach, came word that the Russians were flying into Warsaw. It was tense in the emotion-charged committee room. Stand-patters, participants in the meeting have told me, looked pleased. Khrushchev, Bulganin, Mikoyan and Red Army marshals were storming in to try and check the re-emergence of Gomulka as head of the Polish party. They rushed into the plenary session, which cut its debate to see Khrushchev, contorted with rage, point to Gomulka contemptuously and say: "Who is this bastard who sleeps with his mother?"

The story of the pell-mell rush into Warsaw was described to me by a veteran Polish Communist, a member of the central committee, who attended the wild meeting. He told me about it in the setting of a café which overlooked a square, where thousands of young people were milling and the police stood on corners to watch in bewilderment. The demonstrators were yelling: "Remember Hungary." Their shouts almost drowned out my acquaintance's conversation. He leaned close to me and we must have looked like two nineteenth-century conspirators. The red light atop the Palace of Culture, Stalin's gift to Warsaw, started to shine. Poles were accustomed to saying that the best place from which to see the palace was on the roof. Why? Then, you couldn't see the building.

"Khrushchev couldn't see how a shift to Gomulka would be anything but harmful to the Soviet Union and Eastern Europe," my central committee informant continued. "We were in a fantastic state but so were the Russians. They had been met by Polish security, who escorted them to us. These were Poles and they had orders to be strictly neutral on the Polish side of the border. I don't think anyone knew what he was doing or how it would all turn out.

"The people who seemed to know what they were doing were our army officers. I have been told by very good and informed friends that when Soviet tanks started to move on Warsaw in conjunction with Khrushchev's dropping out of the sky, our tanks moved, too. For miles, they went along towards Warsaw, their guns facing each other. It must have been some sight. Then both columns stopped. I suppose the Red Army was waiting for orders from Rokossovsky. I never heard that his orders—if he tried to give any—were obeyed at the time by Polish units. He had alerted the military to move on Warsaw.

"Khrushchev was so angry I thought he would drop dead of a heart attack on the floor. He had just insulted Gomulka, who walked away from him. Rokossovsky, in a marshal's uniform, was pale as he approached Khrushchev. Khrushchev turned on Rokossovsky. 'You're not a marshal,' he shouted. 'You're a horse's ass.'"

Rokossovsky's political career was terminated there and then. He later left Warsaw quietly for Moscow and a job in the Ministry of Defense. Khrushchev, in his spur-of-the-moment decision to face down the embattled Polish Communists, found himself literally trapped. All he could do was to accept the switch to Gomulka. Frazzled tempers got a quick rewiring job. Khrushchev warned he did not want to see the change as a move towards liquidating the Polish party and the satellite regime. He gestured towards the clamoring crowds outside. Gomulka coldly assured him that he, too, was a strict Communist. He would not preside over the party's liquidation. Khrushchev said he would see Gomulka in Moscow. The Russians hastily departed Warsaw without ceremony.

Later in Moscow, as a member of the Polish party has since told me, Gomulka made it up with Khrushchev. The country was in terrible shape, Gomulka was reported to have said. He would repair it with drastic reforms and party personnel changes. But the Communist Party would remain supreme. In a black, post-Hungary mood, Khrushchev accepted.

In stating his case, Gomulka reminded Khrushchev of the area left in a vacuum after his own speech to the Twentieth Party Congress. At a going-away reception, a sturdy figure in a Soviet marshal's scarlet-striped uniform passed the time of day pleasantly with Gomulka. It was Marshal Georgi Zhukov, restored to favor in the Khrushchev regime.

"I am still confused what you want to do in Poland," Zhukov told Gomulka with a smile as he fingered his glass. "I'll tell you one thing not to do—don't ever even suggest you will leave the Warsaw Pact."

Gomulka, a Communist, never had any such idea. He returned to Poland, determined to try and make his anti-Communist countrymen devote themselves to building a better "socialist society." He made a pact with the Catholic church, providing for religious instruction during school hours. As a Communist he also instituted a fresh land reform. Gomulka de-collectivized. Peasants who wanted to leave could. Collectives in Poland quickly became an old-fashioned and despised left-over from earlier Communist times. For all effective purposes, farm collectives were abandoned.

Clipping police powers, without trimming authority, was an immediate Gomulka preoccupation. A Communist regime, a minority, had to depend upon police security to perpetuate itself. Yet the feeling in Poland against excesses was boundless. Even a drunk being hauled in by the police could call out, as some did: "The police are beating the people." In a twinkling an angry crowd would mass and maul the police mercilessly. The arrested man would vanish into the throng.

Top security men of the past were arrested. Officials who had interrogated and tortured prisoners, including party members, were sent to jail to await trial. Their downfall was exuberantly reported in the press, including the party newspaper, "Trybuna Ludu." A strange glut on the manpower market began to appear in Warsaw—unemployed former police. They had been in the lower echelons of state security and were flung out for past associations. Some banded together and tried to open espresso coffee bars. They couldn't get any customers except other out-of-work cops. Other jobs were closed to them, for the time being. Some got so hard up they talked about forming a union through which to air their grievances. It got nowhere but a Polish friend of mine took me to where the former cops hung out. I bought a drink for one, after my friend left. "Just to be seen with them is a black eye," he apologized.

The ex-cop complaining to me said he thought the state owed him a decent job. He had, he said, learned two foreign languages to make himself a good security agent. He was a long-time member of the party and still a good Communist. Did he ever torture people? (You could ask questions like that in post-October Poland.) No, said the former agent. That wasn't his job. He arrested Poles as an operational officer for the UB, the internal security division. It was with nostalgia that he spoke of his past work. He had the luxury of living in overcrowded, under-housed Warsaw in two rooms, plus his own bathroom. His pay was three times the salary of a skilled worker. Moreover, he had access to special canteens and commissaries. The change wiped it all out, he said. Didn't he realize that he was committing crimes, as Gomulka's revamped regime declared, against his own people?

"We used to be told that we were only doing our duty, protecting 'socialism,' " he replied. "Now they say they are protecting 'socialism' another way. It makes you dizzy to think about it."

It made outsiders dizzy to read the reports every day about inquiries into earlier mass arrests, phony espionage cases and brutalities visited upon UB victims. The former security man felt himself the injured party. I told a friend of mine about it the same night. He had fought valiantly in the anti-Nazi underground. The story of the UB man provoked only a two-word reply. Translated it means the same in English: "Drop dead." My friend spent five years in a UB jail. Like most Poles, he wanted speedy change. Writers and ex-party members, intoxicated with amazingly free expression in a Communist-ruled country, began to urge speedy dissolution of the interlocking apparatus of control. So overwhelming did their demands seem to Premier Cyrankiewicz that he sharply rebuked a group with whom he dined.

"Some of you have been party men," he lectured sternly. "Ours is a Communist Party. What you are asking for is a political Sweden. You will not get it. The party will remain supreme."

Poles got another sharp reminder of supremacy re-established. In the midst of a feverish campaign to draw a near-unanimous vote for Gomulka, Communist China slipped into the affairs of Eastern Europe. On a swing through the Soviet bloc, Chou En-lai, Prime Minister of Red China, turned up in Warsaw. This was a highly unusual comrade-to-comrade appearance on the eve of any Communist elections. Chou dashed some popular Polish party hopes that he would support its demand for changes.

"We hoped that Chou would plant some of Mao Tse-tung's hundred flowers in Poland," said a Polish theoretician sadly. "All he did was to twist off the buds of our own hope."

A young Polish intellectual saw Chou's demand to make the party invulnerable and the bloc more monolithic than ever as a Chinese view of a small province. "What do 27,000,000 Poles really mean to China?" he asked. "They have more people in one county than we have in the whole country. We are romantics, always." Romanticism gave Gomulka an overwhelming vote in the election. It was the Communist single list—no opposition. The difference, as a sop to reformers, was the opportunity to strike out names of candidates for office. Before Poles went to the ballot boxes, Gomulka gave them a national warning to vote all the way for his "road to socialism" or face the liquidation of Poland. The leaden threat hung heavily, declared Gomulka, that Poland could disappear from the map of Europe. He got a big turnout, in which Cardinal Wyszyński also cast a ballot.

At the beginning, it was not so great a victory. In the country, the party was mainly in the hands of anti-Gomulka Communists. They believed, and said so, that a little relaxation was the most dangerous thing the party faced in an up-hill fight. They opposed directives from Warsaw and fought planning as devised by Gomulka. To them, Gomulka's "Polish road" was a detour to oblivion. In their opposition, they forgot one thing he told Khrushchev: "I am a Communist." Confusion, politically, and chaos, economically, were the first products of Gomulka's new tenure of office. The country was desperately short of everything. Plain food for people was inadequate.

"We will have to ask the United States to assist with some surplus so we can eat and avoid catastrophe," was the way a senior Foreign Office official broke the first news that the recast Polish regime was looking to Washington for help. Why not Moscow? The Russians were putting in a food and consumer-goods pipeline to ease post-revolution conditions in Hungary. Polish Communists said Khrushchev could only give them a little, very little. The U.S. agreed to send over wheat, flour, beans and later more material assistance. It opened a door to the Polish people again. They were elated and overly optimistic by what American assistance could mean to them. In the end, too many believed in their excitement that Gomulka would find a solution in a pro-American point of view. Most of them didn't think twice about their soaring hopes. They talked about how free Poland had become and how much freer it was going to be. That called for little extra celebrations. On every level of society Poles turned to the vodka bottle. It was the one sure way to find relaxation and surcease from life around you. Students, on week-ends, drafted bottle parties. Tickets to the theater, movies, opera were strictly limited in supply. A bottle, even a shared one, was easy to get. Drowning frustrations and sorrow became an alarming national habit. Gomulka, the teetotaler, tried with little success to stop the drinking.

Overt anti-Semitism returned and the party was in the forefront in drumming up racial hatred in a country that had seen its Jews slaughtered by the Germans. Conservatives—in Polish politics a term applied to

Stalinists—accused Jews of forcing the change to Gomulka and to reforms. In the party over which Gomulka tried to establish his control, his
efforts were ascribed to Jewish "revisionists." Up to a point, that was
true. Many of the disillusioned were Jews. Anti-Semitic outrages, including the beating of victims in the streets, returned to Warsaw for a
while.

Secretly, the Polish regime began to work out a system of Jewish
emigration with the government of Israel. There was only a handful of
Jews left in Poland, but Poles, including a sizable number of Jews, were
being repatriated by agreement from the Soviet Union. These were Polish
citizens, stranded as prisoners or deportees in the U.S.S.R. One of them
was of especial significance. For these purposes, we'll call him Josef
Nowak. He is slight of build, would be around seventy today, and looks
like a sawed-off version of Trotsky. As a matter of fact, he had known
Trotsky and the entire Soviet hierarchy, beginning with Lenin. At an
early age this little man was an important agent of the Comintern. He
worked in Asia and then headed up the apparatus in the Middle East.
His work caught the eye of Dimitrov, who asked for him to help in
Germany. Nowak spent a long time in Germany with the Communist
Party. As a Soviet citizen, he left Berlin on New Year's Day, 1934.

"When I crossed into the Soviet Union, in 1934, I began twenty-three
years in prison," said Nowak. "I was brought before a summary court
immediately, charged with working for the Nazis and sent off to prison."

He had been caught up in the permanent purge, said Nowak. His sentence, at various times, was changed to death. He knew all the angles
in fighting before his tribunals for his life and used them. In death cells
he used to hear other victims taken out and shot. He escaped because of
his experience with the system. During the war, he was moved from
camp to camp. He survived, he guessed, because he didn't need much to
eat. On a 1957 summer afternoon twenty-three years after his arrest,
the commandant of a camp in northern Asia called him to his office
and told Nowak he was a free man. The astounded inmate was handed a
first-class railway ticket and a suit of clothes.

"Of course, like everyone else, I knew there had been a change at the
top in the Soviet regime," recalled Nowak. "I figured it meant little to
me. These, I thought, were new tactics. But I had no choice, I took the
train to Moscow. Two men—security men—met me at the station. They
knew the passenger car number. They were polite. They took me in a

big car to a fine Moscow hotel. I had a suite; me, who had been living on filthy straw for twenty-three years. They said they would call for me the next day. I was alone in Moscow."

Nowak said he recalled looking out of the window, watching the crowds and the traffic. There was a large bowl of fresh fruit in each room. He circled the fruit. "I hadn't eaten any for twenty-three years," Nowak said. "Oranges and apples looked exciting. I didn't want to touch them. That was for later." He went out the door but returned to the ante- room. "I put an apple in my pocket," he said. Then he walked around Moscow, the Moscow he had known well many years before.

"I walked for hours," he continued. "Late at night, I went back to my suite. I didn't eat any supper. I was too excited. Besides, I had all that fruit. I had finished my apple on Red Square."

Nowak didn't sleep all night. He looked out of the hotel windows, and every few minutes strayed near the fruit bowl. "I did a strange thing," he remembered. "I think I bit into each piece of fruit, at least once." The security men called for him in the morning. Nowak went quietly with them. He firmly believed, he said, that this was the new treatment to rub out old political prisoners. They came to a big building he hadn't known before. His escorts showed him into an anteroom with leather chairs and two secretaries behind mahogany desks.

"I thought it was the Khrushchev version of Lubianka Prison," added Nowak. "I waited only a few minutes."

The door to a big office was flung open. A small, dark man with a gray-black mustache rushed to Nowak and embraced him. "Comrade Nowak, how wonderful to see you," said the host. "Comrade, what a terrible wrong has been done to you. Come inside and talk to me now."

It was Anastas Mikoyan. In the office that looked to Nowak as big as a skating rink with sofas and big chairs and two desks, Mikoyan said that the old Polish Comintern hand needed a vacation right away.

"Go to the Crimea," Mikoyan urged. "I'll arrange for a villa right away. When you're rested, come back and talk. There are big jobs waiting for someone like you. What terrible mistakes have been done—and to you."

Nowak said he felt giddy. "I had been in jail twenty-three years and relived my life every day in prison," he told me. "I thought deeply about the system. Years ago, I had rejected it. Still in jail, of course. What I knew that I had done and what I saw done in the prisons to thousands convinced me of one thing: There was no feeling for humanity in it. There never would be, no matter what new men in power said."

Mikoyan kept chattering. Nowak, silent, was thinking. He kept his gaze fixed past Mikoyan on a bowl of fresh fruit. "I had to make up my mind fast," declared Nowak. "I decided to ask to go back for a while to Warsaw, my native town. Once I had family there. I wanted to see who was left."

He told Mikoyan he wanted to do that and then might come back to Moscow some time later. A little disappointed, Mikoyan agreed. Off went Nowak to Warsaw.

"I left the day that Molotov and the others with him were thrown out by Khrushchev as anti-party people. It seemed that political life for big party members hadn't changed a bit while I was all those years in jail."

In Warsaw, Nowak learned quickly that only a daughter survived. She long ago had emigrated to a non-Communist country. He got in touch with her and received an ecstatic letter, begging him to visit her and her husband and children. "My own grandchildren," said Nowak. "I applied for a passport to go and visit. I have it here." He patted his breast pocket. When would he be returning to Warsaw? Nowak looked at me gravely. We were sitting in a little park, watching people hurry home from work in crammed busses.

"I have had a chance to look around, to talk and to talk party affairs," replied Nowak. "The system cannot change. It can pretend relaxation. Even make a few concessions. But it is built on false foundations. Power, not people, matters. I know. When I leave, I will not come back. There is only tragedy here."

I have never, unfortunately, seen Nowak again. He is well, I hear, and with his grandchildren. The tragedy he foresaw in Poland burst out all over in a series of telling explosions. In Lodz, the great textile city, I saw transport workers go out on strike. They paralyzed the city and army and police units surrounded key points in and around Lodz. "We cannot stand living like this any more," a woman worker at the carbarns on a street appropriately named Tramwayova, explained passionately. "We work for nothing; bread and scraps. We live worse than animals. Gomulka, the trade union says, has troubles. I know what they are. They are Poles, us."

Strikes spread all over Poland and ground the sputtering economy to a halt. Gomulka demanded that people go back to work. He asserted that he would re-establish party authority in the country no matter what it cost. Intellectuals, who called themselves the "enraged," recoiled. Gomulka began to muzzle them. Veteran party officials who clamored for his head earlier started to applaud the return to "administrative order." The party was showing its teeth again and the refurbished police were biting again. When students demonstrated police charged them, flailing with clubs and making arrests. Where had Gomulka's reform taken Poland?

"We advanced five steps and we have just lost four," a well known writer and apologist for Gomulka, said. "The party could not vanish. Let's keep what we have. It's better than any place else in Eastern Europe."

By that yardstick of coexistence, Poland's status was better in the area of free speech, but in the matter of food and clothing it lagged behind Yugoslavia. When Gomulka reached out in the country to show he was an unregenerate Communist, faithful to the Soviet Union, Tito was locked in ideological combat with Khrushchev once more. When the Yugoslavs asked where promised Soviet credits were, Khrushchev said they would remain unavailable until Tito rejoined the Soviet Europe. An angry Tito retorted he would not become part of the Soviet bloc, under any conditions. Now, he was "uncommitted" and wanted neutral leaders in Africa and Asia to help him neutralize the heat generated by both great blocs in the East and West. What was more, Yugoslavs contended, the economic development in their state was much more beneficial to the people than could be claimed by any other Eastern European country. American and Western aid helped make it so, it was true, but that was not a point that was stressed.

Yugoslavs were eating more and could buy more than anywhere in Soviet Europe but Czechoslovakia. Tito's Government was the first Communist regime to make installment buying a national practice. The Soviet bloc sneered at the idea. It was typical of Tito, the propaganda line ran, to use a capitalist device to get consumer goods to the people. (Later on, the Soviet Union led satellite Europe into installment buying.) Radios, some Yugoslav-made refrigerators, furniture and even potatoes and coal were available on the installment plan.

People signed up, putting down ten or twenty percent of the price of the article. They gave their offices or enterprises as references. The practice, with the opening of American-style supermarkets first shown at trade fairs, took immediate hold. So much so that the installment planners ran into a normal credit headache—deadbeats. In Yugoslavia, it sometimes went the regular bad debt collection system one better. Customers would leave jobs and buy things on the installment plan, using new offices as reference. When the bill collector got close, they moved. A number moved from town to town, especially if they had special technical skills. The bill-skipping dodge came to an end when debtors just took off, escaping into near-by Italy or Austria. They were lumped with other "economic refugees." The runaway system became known in Yugoslavia as pay now, flee later. Every summer since 1957, 18,000 to 20,000 Yugoslavs have escaped. The frontier with the West is pretty wide open for booming tourist seasons. Another big contrast, Titoists say proudly, to the sealed borders of some neighbors. They shrug off escapes.

"Let them go if they want to," a Yugoslav security official told me. "We could keep people in the country if we wanted it badly enough."

"Outside, we believe we can make a better future for ourselves," young Yugoslav refugees have explained their escapes. "We don't want to stay where we are forever. You don't advance."

"Compared with earlier years, it's much better now," an artist who studied in France said. "Writers have trouble. The party reads words closely. They don't seem to be interested in art so we do what we like. Talking is something people usually do with friends."

Djilas was not regarded as even a friendly enemy by the regime. From his prison cell, he was brought out to a courtroom close by. Another seven years was tacked on to his sentence for "hostile propaganda." His rheumatism wasn't helped in the unheated cell. But he was getting something to read by now: Yugoslav party papers. In them he could note that Marshal Zhukov had come on a state visit. It was soon after the Russians launched their first sputnik in 1957. Zhukov, I remember, walked around his reception benevolently. His answers to sputnik questions breathed confidence in Soviet technology.

"We are a very great country," he said to me. "Americans don't give us enough credit."

Khrushchev apparently did not think that Zhukov should be getting all the credit. Russians and Yugoslavs, during the Zhukov visit, spoke rather glowingly of how Marshal Zhukov made it possible for Khrushchev to beat off the attack on him by the Politburo group that was itself defeated. They talked about Zhukov sending out military planes to bring back Central Committee members to stand in support of Khrushchev. Zhukov seemed to have become a personality of stature. He conducted himself with brimming confidence. When he left Belgrade for a longish visit to Albania, Yugoslav Communists were puzzled and annoyed. Hoxha and Shehu were as shrill and violent, as in Stalin's day, in attacking them. Albania was no place for Zhukov to go, said Yugoslav party officials, if there were to be at least correct government-to-government relations. They were angrier than ever when Zhukov returned from Albania to Moscow and was abruptly dismissed by Khrushchev.

"What an insult to us," exclaimed a ranking party bureaucrat in Belgrade. "Sending us someone who is on his way out."

Tito also was highly exercised that when he recognized Communist East Germany, Chancellor Adenauer immediately broke relations with him. The Yugoslavs had been warned. Still, they felt they should have the same treatment as the Russians, who recognize both West and East Germany. Adenauer's doctrine of no-recognition, except for Russia, held firm. Yugoslav Communists prefer East Germany because, bad as conditions are there, it still has Communists. The doctrinaire mystique is hard to break. East Germans treated Yugoslav diplomats abominably. They hauled them off trains, followed them and searched them. Propaganda was vitriolically anti-Tito. The Yugoslavs answered back sharply but nonetheless stayed in East Berlin.

Such was not the case of a Communist intellectual much admired by Yugoslavs. Alfred Kantorowicz did leave East Berlin. He did not simply say that his god failed. What he declared was that ideas and thinking have to stand nakedly against the brutal power of the Soviet system. Those same ideas and creative human qualities, he added, were submerged but they had not drowned.

He said, "I can no longer refuse to recognize that I myself have contributed my tiny part towards the very thing I meant to fight against—lawlessness, exploitation of the workers, the spiritual enslavement of the intelligentsia and the arbitrary rule of an unworthy clique who defile the concept of socialism as once the Nazis defied the name of Germany.

"I could no longer close my eyes to the almost legendary lesson that where we believed we were fighting for freedom and against Fascist barbarism. Fascism and barbarism had arisen again behind us, in word, deed and spirit. We aimed in our struggle at the rule of the people and found ourselves enmeshed in the dictatorship of the party officials.

"The People's Chamber (Volkskammer) was a chamber of party officials; the people's welfare, the welfare of party officials; the people's factories were factories in which the workers lost the basic rights for which they struggled and suffered for a century."

Soviet policy towards Eastern Europe, declared Kantorowicz, was a total failure. It was bankrupt and could never become solvent. "Man's hopes were never considered in the planning or the power," concluded Kantorowicz after he joined the ordinary East Germans' flight to the West.

Other Communists in East Germany who saw the Soviet mission fail dismally also fled. Traitors or weaklings, Ulbricht sneered at them. They had a place to go—from East Berlin to West Berlin. Such access to the outside struck a spark of envy in Soviet bloc countries deeper in Soviet Europe. It was quite noticeable in Rumania, badly shaken up after the Hungarian uprising.

On another return tour there, I found that the regime doggedly preserved all the grim and monotonous features of the Stalin regime. It was a sign-painter's paradise. Shops, public buildings and public transportation displayed posters chanting loyalty to the party, to Moscow and to Soviet protection. Loudspeakers in communities carried the government radio. Nothing else. Party officials, artists and intellectuals lived well by local standards. I used to stand in a shop and watch the imported goods counter. Textiles that cost a worker half-a-month's pay were snapped up by men and women who had cars waiting outside. They were called "Tovarich Ion" by salesgirls but they were not tovariches to the bleak-looking men and women who somberly watched them buy.

In a restaurant once well known for its beef a Rumanian writer sent back our inedible burnt offering. We went out and had a meal in a noisy tavern; bits of lamb, pickled tomatoes, gritty wine, all very expensive. The writer, a man who had known and suffered police rule under the prewar regime, had only this remark to utter: "We eat much better than the public."

But the public was permitted the pleasure of a day off on gala occasions. They had to march in demonstrations when they didn't have to go to work. They turned out, very quietly, when the Rumanian regime met Janos Kadar at the railroad station. Kadar, the symbol of the East European quisling, was a "dear guest." Gheorghiu-dej embraced him, I noticed, and kissed his cheeks heartily. It was a good state show. The crowds at the station cheered on command and quickly fell silent again.

There was a much different atmosphere a little later at a party congress in Yugoslavia. Before attentive Yugoslav ex-partisans, Tito told the world for the first time that Communist China believed in the inevitability of world war—between Communist and capitalist states. It was wrong of Mao to say so and he was incorrect, thundered Tito. What was almost as bad, he paused for emphasis, was for the Soviet Union to demand Yugoslavia's return to the bloc or to walk in Communist darkness. Anyone threatening Yugoslavia would get measure for measure back in defiance. The Chinese were wrong in their view, said Tito, as was Khrushchev in his. The partisans cheered. They sang, "Tito, we will always be faithful to you." Ideologically, Tito was taking on not one but two Soviet Goliaths.

CHAPTER | 18

CLEANING up the mess in the Communist Party and inside Poland is Wladyslaw Gomulka's biggest job. At best, he will be only partly successful. He may patch up the party. But his runaway country will balk, jump the track and even sit down in the middle of Gomulka's dearly beloved "road to Socialism." The Poles, embittered again because they thought Gomulka would somehow lead them away from the Soviet Union, are busy making their country as unpredictable as possible.

"Just don't take Poland out of the Warsaw Pact," Marshal Georgi Zhukov told Gomulka. That was when Gomulka was still feeling his way to placating a suspicious Khrushchev. Zhukov was still a high man on the Soviet bloc totem pole and spoke with an armored voice. He didn't care about Gomulka's problems, or even of Poland's. Khrushchev knew more and cared a lot. In the turbulent post-Hungary days, Khrushchev got an eye-opening report on what happened in the heart of downtown Warsaw.

There a faceless pile of gray masonry sprawls along most of one street. This is the vault of Poland's political hierarchy, the Central Committee headquarters of the Communist Party. In its steamy auditorium, a few months after the Hungarian uprising, Wladyslaw Gomulka, first secretary of the party, rose and angrily resolved another crisis in the endless cycle of emergencies riddling Poland.

Gomulka's program of cautious relaxation inside the country, and his church policy, were under savage attack. Embittered veteran party officials—Stalinists, their opponents called them—were seeing their life's work and their entrenched positions threatened. They demanded abandonment of cooperation with the Roman Catholic Church. The only way out, they clamored, was to reaffirm total primacy of Moscow.

By sheer coincidence, at virtually that moment, the man who more than anyone else symbolizes their fury and fear knelt in the Vatican to receive his red hat as a Cardinal. Stefan Cardinal Wyszyński, Primate of Roman Catholic Poland, was three years late receiving his hat from Pope Pius XII. He had been in prison without trial, after having been made a Cardinal and Prince Primate. Now, not only could Cardinal Wyszinski feel free to travel to the Vatican, he could also return to Poland, safe in the conviction that there were no changes in the unique agreement made with him by an atheist, Comrade Gomulka. The Roman Church is supreme in Polish spiritual affairs.

Indeed, as a realist, Gomulka could brook no alteration of the astounding concordat that restored the church's control over its flock. The pact also reintroduced into Poland universal religious instruction in the nation's schools. These are utterly unparalleled concessions in a Communist-ruled country. But the boiling ferment in Poland also is unprecedented.

Poland is living on the razor's edge. The tragedy of Hungary was that it never inched its way to the edge. It just exploded. Hungary, say the Poles, was at one minute after twelve. In Poland the clock is held at two minutes to twelve. That's the margin of time placed in the hands of the twin symbols of authority in Poland, the Cardinal and the Comrade. Discontent rumbles constantly beneath the surface. Frequently it erupts in a village or in a large community.

Each in his own way, but essentially together and uneasily, Comrade Gomulka and Cardinal Wyszyński strive to beat out the fires that flame and lick their way towards the dynamite. A grisly bloodbath would not be the only consequence of national explosion in a Poland cut off from outside. It could trigger a chain reaction in turbulent East Germany. As World War II began in Poland, so might World War III blast through the wreckage of a Poland that went over the edge and was suppressed by Soviet Power. This factor is perhaps the key to the sullen Soviet acceptance of dual control over the country by the Cardinal and the Comrade. Gomulka, in the turbulent years that followed the "Polish October," has made his peace with Khrushchev. By national Communist standards, it is for Gomulka a peace with honor. He must, however, always prove to his powerful ally in Moscow that the Communist Party can control Poland.

To that end, Gomulka often probes church influence. The Cardinal, who holds the balance of influence over the average Pole, defies the state whenever the regime talks of practising anti-clericalism. Wyszyński does not believe in the permanence of Communist rule; Gomulka does. The church in Poland has far more divisions than the regime can ever muster. They are armed with fervor and deep disbelief in their temporal rulers. Their spiritual leader warns them against outright conflict. The last thing he wants is an uncontrolled showdown between the Polish people alone and Soviet might. That attitude does not prevent Poles from protesting. They are past masters at making complaints felt. Poles go on strike, customarily outlawed in Communist-run nations.

"The regime says industry is owned by the people," an ex-soldier told his co-workers at the automobile plant assembling Russian cars under license as "Warszawas." "Fine. If something you own is bad, you show you don't like it. We don't like conditions, pay and the way this factory works. Out we go. Strike."

Party officials plead with strikers. They warn them to work more and harder. Otherwise, the reedy standard of living goes down some more, the regime warns. You fix it, enraged and impatient workers retort. Students immediately hear about the trouble. Having been temporarily silenced and turned back by police in street demonstrations, they keep schools and parents in a turmoil of discontent by word of mouth.

"In this country, you have what amounts to a daily trial of strength between the people and the government," an economic planner remarked to me in an interview.

Just that morning the news had spread about workers in a southern Polish city blowing their tops at the administration and security. They wanted to build a church and had obtained materials. The party in the district said, no. Besides, self-important officials sent police to stop work on the church. It was being done in the workers' own spare time. Better, said a party administrator, to use the extra time at the factory.

When police details tried to stop construction at the new church, workers rained bricks on them. Then they piled down from the scaffolding, were joined by their women and children, and chased the police back to headquarters. There, they laid siege to the police building. Heads were broken and community life became chaotic.

"You couldn't argue with them," a Polish reporter described the rioters. "All you had to do was promise that they could build their church without interference."

The same flaming spirit rests behind Polish determination to turn out by the tens of thousands for pilgrimages to church festivals. They will take over all highways leading to the shrine at Czestahowa. Not an irreligious remark dare be uttered. The faithful pray and chant, "Mary, Queen of Poland."

"Why can't we get crowds like that?" Gomulka demanded angrily of his highest ranking party associates. "Where are our slogans? Why are they missing?"

Nobody replied, in a straight way, to Gomulka. I was told by a participant in the meeting that everyone there figured the party secretary knew why. He was badly upset as he is each time there is an overt demonstration for something besides a regime project. Gomulka remains a brass-bound Communist. Make no mistake about that. In his way, he also is a realist. The Communist regime was installed in Poland by the Red Army. The Polish party's original leadership was liquidated by Stalin in 1938. There never was a Red revolution in the sense that these occurred in China and Yugoslavia. A centuries-old Polish history of being anti-Russian drove resentment of an alien regime even deeper into the Polish national character. The Communist Party was a comparative handful when it set up shop under the sponsorship of the Red Army.

For ten years the Russians tried to penetrate every branch of Polish life. Russians, who overnight took Polish citizenship, were installed in the apparatus of government, the military, schools and the dread security police. Remember they had even established a counter-church movement, called "Pax," headed by a prewar leader of the Polish Fascist movement. When the chips were down, however, when Khrushchev and his collective comrades saw the possibilities of Soviet hegemony washed away in the restoration of Gomulka, a decade of Soviet rule had paid no dividends whatsoever.

National revulsion reached such proportions at the time that Gomulka, released from years of prison and then house detention, was the Communist Party secretary without any party to speak of. What exists in the substantive manner of a party in Poland today is a skeletal apparatus. This is the self-perpetuating machinery whose members have a vested interest in trying to continue things as they were. Gomulka does not control the apparatus. The old bureaucrats still do. They do not dare make any frontal assaults on Gomulka. They strive to isolate him to their own views. Gomulka is not a Tito, nor is he forged in the prewar Moscow mold. He is unique in that he resents old-time Polish Communists and members who demand headlong reform.

Gomulka's own program is something of a Communist catch-all, run through by insistence on Poland's right to conduct her own domestic affairs. There are no illusions in this program that Poland can bolt from the main line of Soviet foreign policy. Geography thwarts that goal, Gomulka keeps telling Poles. But the Poles made no secret of their feeling for the Hungarians. They raised money, medicines and food parcels from their own meager resources to help Hungary. In no uncertain terms did they state their contempt for Janos Kadar and their praise for the revolutionaries. Officially, that theme has undergone outsized alteration. Kadar is acceptable to Gomulka; Tito is a pariah and Khrushchev is a big father figure. Disillusioned party members are reviled as "revisionists," a dangerous and dirty word in the Communist vocabulary.

Gomulka would not succumb for a long time to Soviet pressure to say that the explosion in Hungary was a "counter-revolution." He shifted ground when the Chinese Communists, during a visit by Chou En-lai, were regarded as Communist reformers by the Polish party. The pro-Gomulka Poles looked to Peiping for comfort and ideological surcease. They seized, like poor relations at a family banquet, on Mao Tse-tung's secret speeches emphasizing "one hundred different flowers in the garden." When the Chinese became violent, dogmatic and warlike, Gomulka made up with Khrushchev.

The party, Gomulka insists, must remain pre-eminent as the governing organ of society. Then, he also emphasizes the need for de-collectivization, a complete break with Soviet iron rule. Privately run small businesses and shops also are approved by Gomulka. There are basic reforms, important in their way, but far from enough to clear up the fantastic economic mess bequeathed Gomulka by his predecessors.

What did the Russians and their ultra-loyal agents do to make such a shambles in Poland? Here are a few eye-filling items of exploitation over the years:

Between 8,000,000 and 11,000,000 tons of Polish coal was sold annually to Russia at less than half the world market price. Frequent deliveries also were made that were credited only to the cost of Soviet "liberation" of Poland. Although the Soviet Union sounds off regularly about its support for Poland's retaining of former German provinces, the Russians stripped the areas of machinery. Removing machinery was justified as reparations from the vanquished enemy. According to terms at Potsdam, the Poles were entitled to fifteen percent of Russia's total reparations from Germany. No tangible evidence exists that this was ever fulfilled. Between the loss of reparations and the mouse-trap play on forced export of coal to the U.S.S.R., the Poles lost around $2,000,000,000. None of the highly publicized loans and credits from Moscow came within striking distance of this total.

For a long time, until Gomulka regulated a status-of-forces agreement over the Soviet divisions stationed in Poland, plus the use of port facilities, the Polish regime defrayed a large slice of those costs.

"One cannot plan human consciousness," Gomulka told his party comrades and the Polish nation at large when he returned to power.

It was a staggering admission for a veteran Communist to make, but it was in tune with the feeling of the Poles. The Russians had tried, in their own image and with all the mistakes they had themselves committed, to impose a planned economy of their own in Poland. The result was huge capital investment for industrialization which the country's shattered postwar economy could not support. It also led to collectivization and resulting defiant refusal of the peasants to conform or produce. Living conditions, deplorable in the main, led to theft from the state enterprises and factories as an added source of income. Life in Poland became life without hope, without incentive, limping along on fear and terror.

How can he retread the national economy, which gets worse? There has been a shift in the sale of coal, the country's biggest natural asset. The Poles are selling to the West at world market prices. They no longer, by Soviet decree, haul coal to other "People's Democracies" and the Soviet Union for beans. They are cutting back on megalomaniacal capital investment projects. The reduction, however, is resulting in unemployment. For the immediate future, Gomulka seeks loans and credits to help keep himself and his government afloat. As ordinary living becomes tougher, Poles get more restive. Sparks begin to fly. The mood grows a little more desperate, plunging finally into a mold of utter cynicism and frustration. This feeling heads, then, towards the point of no return. In all the usual debate in Washington over whether to offer Gomulka's government credits or surplus farm products, that factor apparently was never openly cited.

Obviously, credits will help a Communist regime. They also will seep down, in the form of food and employment in textile mills, to the people we say we want to assist. It has taken us lots of soul-searching to come up with an answer as the Polish economy has passed into what one knowledgeable local described to me as "controlled chaos."

Such a situation must also have been uppermost to Gomulka when he recently received a delegation of young Poles. They were disappointed, they told him, that he was curbing various reforms. Among them they cited a crackdown on the press, denunciation of "revisionism," which hit at reformers in the party, back-tracking on the activity of workers' councils and alteration of the public stand on the revolution in Hungary.

Gomulka, according to the story, paced the room as he listened to the impassioned outbursts of the young men and women. He suddenly stopped before a window and leveled a finger at the streets of Warsaw below.

"What do you want to do?" he demanded. "Rebuild Warsaw every ten or fifteen years?"

There was silence for a moment. One of the kids spoke up.

"Remember, Comrade Gomulka," he said, "people like us were responsible for bringing you back. If you lose our good will you lose everything. When you rebuild, you must rebuild lives and futures."

The story faithfully reflects Poland today.

When the Cardinal and the Comrade were restored to public favor and power in Poland, a diehard Moscow-trained Communist remarked bitterly: "So now we will be run by two jailbirds."

What he didn't grasp, nor have his comrades, is that victims of political prison wear a badge of honor in the eyes of most Poles. Because they were both victimized by the rule of terror, a firm bond of practical understanding links Cardinal Wyszyński and Comrade Gomulka. Each man was technically at the pinnacle of his office when police struck. Gomulka was party secretary, but implacable in his opposition to further Soviet encroachment. The Cardinal was Prince Primate, but defied verdicts of the state sentencing priests as spies. Years of prison and isolation seem to have left them both with a common belief: Poland must somehow survive. They have contradictory ideas except on the objective of survival.

When the rush for a change in regime threatened to become a stampede in 1956, Gomulka's opportunity was imminent. Negotiating with comrades who not too long before had denounced him as Enemy No. 1, Gomulka insisted that Wyszyński be released to return to his clerical office and responsibilities. Friends of Gomulka went to the monastery where the Cardinal had been transferred from prison. The Prince Primate's thinning blond hair.was graying, but his will and thought had not been dented. He demanded, as a condition, that all imprisoned bishops and priests be released. It was fulfilled. A similar demand had been made by Gomulka on behalf of other political prisoners, many his associates. Gomulka's conditions also were carried out. Right from the start the Cardinal and the Comrade went after the secret police. They broke its back. Police methods would return but they would be questioned. As a start the Cardinal and the Comrade appealed to the country.

Gomulka spoke eloquently about past abuses. He asked Poland to remain calm, to return to work and try to remedy the country's economic catastrophe. As a Communist and party secretary, he addressed the people. As a symbol of defiance of the Russians, as a Pole, Gomulka became a hero. Up stepped Cardinal Wyszyński separately, from the calm restraint of his episocopal palace.

"Poles know how to die wonderfully," the Cardinal said. "But, my children, it is necessary that Poles know how to work wonderfully. One dies only once and becomes famous quickly. But one lives in difficulties, in pain, in suffering, in sorrow, for many years, and this is the greater heroism in the present time."

He had returned, the Cardinal said, as the shepherd of his flock. The flock had not scattered; indeed, it had become more tightly knit than ever. It was a piercingly accurate observation. Always in Polish history, in times of stress and persecution, Poles sought relief in prayer at their churches. Even during the worst days of terror, the regime never dared close churches or forbid masses. Poles, as had their forebears, jammed churches on Sundays and flocked to pray. Each in his own way, the Cardinal and the Comrade urged their countrymen away from thoughts of violence. Through the force of their collective influence, they reduced the fevered tempers of the people. It wasn't easy then, and it keeps becoming more difficult. Once the Cardinal was roused from sleep late at night. A group of youngsters had taken it into their heads to demonstrate. They also were planning to demonstrate around the Soviet Embassy. An incident like that could explode the bomb ticking away in Poland. Away went the Cardinal to the crowd. He spoke feelingly and persuasively. The youngsters dispersed.

In an old car, chauffeur-driven, the Cardinal has made the rounds of nearly every diocese in Poland since his return to Warsaw. Everywhere he appeals for tranquility and orderly life. Too superficially, some Westerners have characterized Wyszyński's cooperation with the Comrade as "collaboration." Nothing could be further from the truth. Although the spectacle of a Cardinal as a pillar of a Communist dictatorship—even this type with such deep differences—is extraordinary. Remember what Cardinal Wyszyński has obtained from this regime. Complete restoration of Church control over its flock and reintroduction of religious instruction in the schools are concessions yielded by this Communist government.

Not even, as Gomulka pointed out, do such concessions from the state to the Church exist in Britain, France and the United States. Priests and qualified laity conduct religious training two hours weekly in all the primary and secondary schools. After the age of eighteen instruction is an hour a week in the higher institutions. Hard-core Communists see in religious instruction more than a present threat in their campaign to win the new generation. The Church, they clamor, will win the long-range struggle for Polish youth. These party diehards try to press the Church on schools, then when opposition wells up, they recede hastily. Above the age of twelve the party did not command the obedience of the youth anyway. The failure may well have provoked Gomulka to retort to his critics in the party that there must be a form of "coexistence," not political war, between Church and state.

Some strange reactions have resulted from the newly restored religious instruction in schools. Children of Communists who do not attend church classes with schoolmates are beaten frequently. Their parents today cry out: "discrimination." So a few schools have been established where only children of non-believers attend. The relative handful of Protestant and Jewish children also have become targets of such scorn as can only be administered by the unblinking cruelty of children. Non-Catholic parents in many cases resort to the path of least resistance. Their children simply take religious instruction. Jews who survived the extermination camps and sought to assimilate as Poles even under assumed names suddenly find their lives totally exposed when the religious instruction issue arises and they tell their children to refrain from special classes.

After Gomulka was restored as first party secretary, he defied the Russians and established his regime's right to manage domestic Polish affairs. Many freshets of hope dried up as many reforms were abandoned or altered. Party control has been tightened in government and press censorship again is exercised—not as harshly as in Stalinist times, but screws can still be turned. The one reform that remains generally untouched is the policy towards the church. Within that frame of reference, the patriotic Cardinal and the patriotic Comrade find room for maneuver and the cooperation of survival.

Old-line Polish Catholicism took little interest in contemporary social problems. As a young priest, Wyszyński realized that more than charity would be required to retain the allegiance of a rapidly developing working class. He studies Catholic social work in the West and became its leading exponent in Poland. In between, trying to apply these techniques at home, he also wrote the Catholic answer to Communism and fought with his social doctrine the Soviet myth that found favor among some Polish intellectuals. The Nazi invasion stoked the flames of Wyszyński's passionate Polish patriotism. Like Gomulka, he was associated with the underground. Neither man sought to flee, either to Moscow or Rome. War's end found them both in a shattered nation, each rising rapidly. Gomulka became an important Communist Party official. Tough and inflexible in doctrinaire matters, he resented the "Moscow imports," the Soviet-trained janissaries brought back by the Red Army to run Poland. Gomulka encountered stormy weather from the beginning.

So did Wyszyński, by this time a bishop. The Communist regime centered the main fury of its attack on the Church. The devotion of Catholic Poles created a built-in resistance to party indoctrination. Destroying the influence of the Church and clipping clerical activity became a mainspring of the Communist campaign to consolidate its power. As a vigorous man, still young—in his forties—Wyszyński led the Church defense with his sound grounding in social doctrine. Some of Wyszyński's Church associates, unalterably opposed to any shift in techniques or tactics, caustically referred to him as the "Red Bishop." Wyszyński never compromised on any of the essential issues of Church doctrine or his Polish patriotism. Soon he found himself pitted against the Communist-rigged Church organization, "Pax." An old admirer of Hitler, Boleslaw Piasecki, got Soviet blessing and cash to compete for the devotion of the faithful against Wyszyński.

In complete violation of an earlier agreement with the Church, the Polish Stalinist regime snapped off remnants of religious instruction in the schools. Catholic charitable activities were closed down. Into Piasecki's hands flowed the biggest monopoly revenues enjoyed by any individual in Soviet Europe. All sales of Catholic literature, Bibles, devotional articles and charity enterprises were entrusted to Piasecki. In return, he organized "peace priests" and "patriot priests," who followed the party line as Moscow called it. At the best estimates, Piasecki managed to entice about 300 to 350 priests into his organization. Most of them were sent to do penance after Wyszyński returned to the episcopate. Some were excommunicated.

Piasecki had—and still has—other sources of ready cash. He has vast interests in quarries and in fishing boats. His organization exists despite the concordat between Gomulka and Wyszyński. It is fairly efficient in terms of organization and it pays its employes better than virtually any other type of business in Poland.

The Cardinal, by one declaration, could chop Pax to pieces. He has not yet done so. Why, then, does Gomulka's regime continue to tolerate it after his agreement with the Cardinal? As a Communist who believes firmly that in the long run his ideology might yet force the retreat of Catholicism, Gomulka is not too unhappy over a situation where the Church could be drained of some strength by a rival organization.

Pax got going into really high gear after Gomulka was bounced from his party post and Wyszyński denounced the state's campaign against the Church. Battle was joined. Two days after Wyszyński wrote an open letter assailing the relevance of government action against any member of the Church hierarchy he was arrested. That was the fall of 1953. Stalin was dead six months. The Polish Communist regime, its economy in tatters and its hold on the country maintained only by terror, increased terrorism.

Resentment shifted into open rebellion in Poznan. It was barely contained. The Russians became nervously itchy. Rebellion rumbled ominously all summer. Word got out that Gomulka had been released. Yet there was no sign of him in public life. Churches were filled to overflowing as Poles prayed and begged divine guidance for the next phase. The season of October revolution, 1956, opened in Eastern Europe. It was kicked off in Poland and exploded in Hungary. The Poles were more fortunate, in the sense that they didn't die heroically and uselessly. To save their skins and the party apparatus, the repudiated regime called Gomulka back to service. The Russians tried to intervene, in the most classic imperialist sense. Gomulka held fast at that moment of decision. He accelerated his negotiations with Cardinal Wyszyński. In that time of crisis and since, neither man ever met the other. They have dealt through intermediaries. Each returned, respectively, to temporal or spiritual power, and has conducted himself as a man of the people according to his own lights.

The Cardinal retains his habits of austere living, a genial informality and indefatigable, dedicated work. Comrade Gomulka, unlike so many of his comrades, lives in a cramped tenement apartment. He has few close friends and a passion for work. His wife, a Jewess, is the woman he knew as a neighborhood girl. When Gomulka faced his first real test in the 1957 elections, Cardinal Wyszyński came to the rescue. These were elections, Communist-style, with an exception. There were far more choices than ever before. Gomulka warned on the eve of elections that striking out names of candidates he favored might well eliminate Poland from the map of Europe. The Cardinal's office issued a simple statement. It merely said that Sunday masses had been so arranged as not to conflict with the duty of the citizen to vote. Gomulka was overwhelmingly endorsed, his first and probably last popular endorsement.

With all the shifts and tortuous alterations Gomulka's regime takes in trying to stake out a life of its own in Soviet Europe, the principle on which the Comrade pledges cooperation with the Cardinal was cited in Wyszyński's first sermon after his release. Poles must learn how to live, not to die, for their country. This gets more difficult every day.

CHAPTER 19

STANISLAW, as a case history, is a stubborn peasant of middle age. He had just come down to Warsaw from his farm in old East Prussia to visit relatives for the first time in more than ten years. The wrinkled letter he held in his thick fingers was written in German, a language Stanislaw doesn't understand.

He had been born, as generations of his family before him, in eastern Poland. His home had been in the Polish territory partitioned by the Russians when they divided the country with Hitler in 1939. After the war, the Soviet Union kept and incorporated the area. Stanislaw, with thousands of his compatriots, left the land of his fathers so he could remain Polish. He was resettled in East Prussia, on a farm vacated by Germans who fled westward. They, too, uprooted themselves from land their families tilled and on which they lived for centuries. The letter had been sent from West Germany. It was written by the son of the German peasant in whose house Stanislaw lived and whose land Stanislaw worked.

How Stanislaw's name had been obtained, nobody knew. Anyway, the letter was specifically addressed to Stanislaw. It was brief and to the point.

"I have heard that you are living on my farm," the writer noted. "It always was a good farm. It provided us with a decent living. Take good care of the farm and our house. We will come back. We will settle accounts after we have seen the condition of our farm."

The letter was signed, "respectfully," in the traditional German business manner. To Stanislaw, normally a phlegmatic man, it meant uncertainty for the future, a world of doubt about the present and the painful imagery of things past when he tore himself away from the old farm and began life anew. Stanislaw's life again became a life of boundary shifts when he looked at the letter. Stanislaw is only one of millions whose lives reflect the agony of displacement, rebuilding homes and jobs. His experiences, terminating in the letter from Germany, show up one of Poland's main problems: her geography. Stanislaw's farm is in the area taken by the Russians from Germany and given the Poles as compensation for eastern Poland absorbed by the Soviet Union. It is commonly called, in the diplomatic trade, the "Oder-Neisse," or the line separating the former German provinces from Germany today.

The Polish regime has continued to call it the "Recovered Territories." None of the Western powers has ever accepted, or recognized, the territorial adjustment. Today, the Russians are more aggressive than ever to wring this recognition from the West. In Western Germany, "the lost lands" engender bitter feeling and are frequently exploited by professional politicians for votes among the millions of refugees settled now in the Federal Republic. Any way you look at it, newly resettled provinces represent potential conflict, appeal to nationalism on either side, and plenty of trouble.

"Poland not only has to readjust her own road to socialism," a Communist official remarked, "she has to do it under the most burdensome geographic conditions."

If anything, he was underplaying the burden. Resettling Poles from the East had a second beginning. Families that fled before the Nazi invasion into the Soviet slice of Poland have been coming home again, to Poland, that is. Many, particularly those originally from western Poland, were sent summarily to forced labor camps or dispersed over the vast stretches of Siberia and Asiatic Russia.

A trip to the Polish-Soviet border or down to Warsaw's railroad station some night to catch a repatriation train is a depressing experience. When the train pulls in, nobody alights to tread joyously on Polish soil. There are few tears. Almost everyone is in a state of shock, or so it seems.

"Am I happy to be back in Poland?" a man of fifty-five repeated my question. "I have been thinking about it for so long that it is kind of a dream. I should be laughing and happy. I can't laugh. It's hard even to talk."

He was a carpenter for sixteen years in the Soviet Union. An old grandmother—she thought maybe she was around eighty-five—held her granddaughter in her arms.

"I am with all my children and my grandchildren," she said slowly. "For me this is all that matters. We go from one place to another place. We move; we move too much. Too many different places, too many different people. We get very tired. Pray to God it will be different for her."

Getting agreement for repatriation of Polish nationals from the Soviet Union takes a bit of doing. It had been going on, sparsely and piecemeal for a few years. Gomulka, after he took over and in his subsequent trips to Moscow, succeeded in exacting a steady stream of Polish repatriates from the Russians. It is a mixed blessing. How to acclimate the returnees, where to settle them and how to find employment for them are the problems with which Polish officialdom must grapple. The only area that makes sense in which to relocate repatriates would be the "recovered territories." Many of the returned Poles are not peasants. They would be useless on the land. Readjustment to industry, to cut back capital investment, makes jobs hard to come by. Housing is pitifully short.

After you have been down to meet a few of these trains, you notice groups and families a little apart from the other repatriates. They seem even more solemn than the average. You go over to them, perhaps the third or fourth time out, out of sheer curiosity. They are Jews who were Polish citizens. They are Jews who were for years ghettoized by Soviet decree in labor camps, or in central Asian villages. Of all the uncertain people who return to Poland, or who have been resettled in former German provinces, they are the most bewildered. They don't want to stay in Poland, to try and rebuild a life. They want to leave, to emigrate to Israel.

"In my immediate family, there were about forty of us," a gaunt man who looked fifteen years older than his age, thirty-five, said. "You can talk about trying not to live in the past. That is easier if you aren't walking around every day in the cemetery. There are five of us left. We were luckier than most of them."

This was a more tragically philosophical explanation than many others. Outspoken anti-Semitism, the fear it engenders in any Eastern European Jew, is the main reason that repatriated Jews want out. Although Gomulka has sought to combat anti-Semitism, he isn't getting very far in checking it. At the ninth plenary session of the Communist Central Committee, he even heard his opponents in the party denounce reformists as "Zionists and cosmopolites."

Anti-Gomulka party members and anti-Communist Poles resort to large-scale Jew-baiting, for quite different reasons. It adds up, in the last analysis, to anti-Semitism. Police point to the disproportionate number of Jews who held high party places in the regime for about ten years after the war. Police excesses are ascribed to Jews because security was run by ranking Communists like Jakub Berman. Therefore, in the emotional reaction, Jews are the scapegoats. Hard-core Communists, inflexibly cast in Stalin's techniques, accuse Jews in the party of having led the country to open anti-Sovietism and to reforms that at best are non-Communist and, at worst, anti-Communist.

Nobody knows what part of Poland's prewar Jewish population of 3,500,000 remains. In any event it's small. About 3,000,000 were slaughtered by the Nazis. After the war thousands fled to Palestine via the underground before Israel was created. Thousands of others never emerged from Siberian and central Asian camps. A rough guess leaves about 60,000 in Poland, including Jews returned as repatriates from the Soviet Union. About 30,000 have been permitted to emigrate. Among the first batches of repatriated Jews, some were relocated in the "recovered territories." They had scarcely been installed in houses or apartments when Jews who had gone out there a few years before told them they were leaving or would try to get out as emigrants.

In schools, students were beaten up. In villages, lonely Jews found themselves boycotted socially and reviled specifically. Not long ago, a brawl that blew up into a political demonstration also lashed out at Jews. A passerby was badly injured. He looked Jewish, one of the rioters told police. It turned out that he wasn't. Even in Warsaw, anti-Semitic incidents occur. On Sunday afternoons a group of young men took to terrorizing some of the most popular restaurants. They would burst in, shouting: "We're looking for Jews." Someone would be beaten. It's a lot more isolated though, if a Jew is living somewhere in the "Recovered Territories." Because of the overpowering impact of fear quite a few have taken to banding together in their own ghettos. They live in the same house, go out together and never mingle with any other Poles.

"It is' a form of self-protection," one of them explained. "You feel that when there are some people with the same interests together all the time, you can escape harm or fear. It really doesn't work. The only thing is to leave forever."

Another people besides the Jews have grievances and frustrations. These are the scattered Germans who stayed behind the East Prussia and Silesia when the provinces were handed to the Poles by the Soviet Union. An agreement, negotiated painfully between West Germany and the Polish government, provides for repatriation of Germans to the Federal Republic. Few Poles considered Germans even as second-class citizens. Except for official protestations, there is little conviction generally that Germans remaining within Poland's boundaries today would become sound and loyal citizens. Too much remembrance of German things past, visited on Poland, and the German yearning for the Teutonic life not the Slav, carve an unbridgeable gorge. As a matter of facing up to reality, the Poles signed an agreement to repatriate Germans willing to leave. Around 15,000 left for West Germany after the agreement.

German eyes on those lost provinces haunt Poles almost as much as their own brooding, burning enmity of the Russians. They don't talk much of the territory absorbed by the Russians, Communist or anti-Communist Poles. Great cities like Lwow and Vilna, Russian now, are mentioned in sad nostalgia. It's outright defiance when you talk about the possibilities of yielding ex-German provinces to Germany. One of the motivating factors for Gomulka's cooperation with Cardinal Wyszyński is the Church's loyalty for Poland's Western frontiers. Ties of co-religionists do not for a moment reduce the span of bad feeling between Catholic Pole, inside the "Recovered Territories" and Catholic German, on the outside mourning for return to his "lost lands." Under Poland's circumstances today, there is little opportunity to stir gently and have a non-combustible melting pot. Instead there are all the elements—resettled Poles, dislocated Germans and wandering Jews—for a cauldron. Molten lead frequently pours out of that kettle.

"We haven't enough problems," an exasperated writer exclaimed. "Poland has to have majority and minority problems, too." He was right, except that none of them are minor. All he had to do was follow the crowd one evening. Warsaw's depressing, ramshackle railroad station was alive with human activity. Nobody was getting on a train. They were all waiting for one to depart. Hours before Cardinal Wyszyński left for Rome the station was jammed. Straight from work or their homes streamed wellwishers. Most of them were young workers.

As the Cardinal made his way through packed humanity, freshly baked cakes and flowers were pressed on him. "May he live a hundred years," welled up from thousands of throats. Married couples held their babies for a glimpse of the Cardinal. Then, they sang: "God Bless Catholic Poland." A twenty-three-year-old university student, not especially religious, who accompanied me to the station stared thoughtfully at the milling, joyous crowd.

"There it is," he observed. "A really genuine demonstration."

For a student, it was still another sight of reality torn from the few remaining veils of indoctrination. The young generation of Poland, the postwar boys and girls, have just about abandoned any trust in the system that tried to make them its crusaders of the present and the future. Talk to them and you find a penetrating awareness of the criminal faults of the past. Don't even ask. They'll tell you without traces of fear how they resent the system today. The frustration of their years of development, the revelations of Stalin's megalomania and their own endless penury have left them with dangerously little faith in the present. They scarcely consider the future.

"We want to be people, just ordinary human beings," a nineteen-year-old girl told me one evening at a university jazz club. "We want to live like people. We don't want to live dangerously. But we do."

Boys and girls growing up today were born in the disaster of World War II. They lived in ruins and alongside memories of inhuman slaughter practised by the Nazis. Each year they saw their own kind executed or expire through malnutrition or torture. Just about every youngster walking the streets of Poland today has a story of deep, personal disaster. From the time of birth, they have been living dangerously. Risks, therefore, become a quality of normalcy. Keeping calm and resolute in the face of peril is like it used to be scrounging for a meal.

Polish youth to whom I have talked in many visits are in a continuous state of ferment. To them, virtually anything Western is good. It isn't simply a question of why it may be better. First, it isn't Russian. Then, it isn't Communist. Usually, they equate Russian and Communist. In defiance they often go to extremes. Existentialism, surrealism, bitter satire and utter disbelief mark the youngsters in the universities. Their newspapers and periodicals, in the vanguard of demands for reform, have been muted from above, by the party authority they today ignore. So the youngsters feel another betrayal. Wladyslaw Gomulka, they say, is retreating from the dramatic days of 1956, from reforms they want to push further. Gomulka soon recognized the incompatibility of ferment in the country with the position of the party. If the voices of discontent hammering at the very existence of the party threatened to sweep the party away, measures had to be taken. He took them. The newspapers that had been belaboring the Russians openly, the intellectuals who were sneering at the disintegration of the party and the youngsters demanding more freedom of expression and movement were all checked.

"What they all forget," a Communist official told me in his office, "is that you cannot have the party as the ruling organization in the country and denounce it at the same time. This is not Sweden or England."

Embittered intellectuals lapsed into sullen silence under the restrictions. Party members, having experienced the unaccustomed delight of criticizing, found themselves denounced for "revisionism." Students, workers and young peasants fell back in surprise. The political realities of a Communist regime, even this one with such contradictions, was not about to abdicate. After the first shock passed, the youngsters returned to the attack, boiled up the ferment anew and began again to live as dangerously as before.

In the universities they mock the hard-core party instructors. For relaxation, they head for their jazz clubs. There they have the strangest jam sessions ever known. Between Dixieland and rock 'n' roll these kids talk openly about how they hate the Russians, how things must change and how they don't care about the consequences. Youngsters attending school don't drink hard. They are talking tough and they are talking turmoil.

"We've had enough," they tell you.

Communist youth organizations, reupholstered, have little impact. Meetings are rarely compulsory, so almost nobody goes. But call a meeting where a classmate, just returned from Hungary, relates his experiences and you'll get an overflow audience.

Recently, a youngster who had been an exchange student in Budapest came home. The first thing he did was to ask his comrades to meet with him. Word spread rapidly and friends of friends turned up to listen. The lad talked of the revolution, of the Soviet intervention and the subsequent repression.

"He called the Russians gangsters, murderers and barbarians," one of the students who attended the session said later. "He called the present regime in Hungary hired killers. You know, when he finished, if someone had said, 'Let's go and burn down the Russian Embassy,' I think we would have done it."

In Szczecin (formerly Stettin) one winter's night, a brawl began in the streets. The cops, known as the militia, hauled in a few young men. They had gotten drunk on vodka. In custody, the brawlers shouted as they were being led to the police station, "Police are beating us." In a matter of minutes, a non-political fracas roared into a frenzy of mass disorder. It lasted for hours, resulting in about 100 arrests. The Soviet consulate was sacked. Such incidents are what sharpen the razor's edge in Poland. Suppose, as one Polish official told me, the headquarters of the Soviet garrison were assaulted in the same way. What would happen? Red Army sentries would probably fire into the crowd. Then? He shrugged and spread his hands across his throat and closed them in a vise.

Preventing its people, especially young, from exploding is probably the regime's paramount security problem today. But just yell cop, any place. Chances are almost certain that the police will be surrounded by a crowd, mauled and then a riot will spill over the streets. These emotions have their ups and downs. On the upgrade, they rip like a collective shock treatment. It happened just that way on a recent trip to Poland. At a garrison town, some young men, factory and farm workers, had a hassle. Militiamen came on the run to take them to headquarters. The kids, under escort, screamed they were being manhandled by the cops. Like a roaring flood, the townsfolk sprang to their rescue. The police were overwhelmed. Then, soldiers from the garrison joined with the crowd in venting their anger on police authority. They all stormed police headquarters. It took reinforcements of two battalions of troops, summoned from outside to quell these riots.

Among young peasants, fervent in religious faith and unshakably opposed to collectivization and Communist doctrine, the party apparatus has virtually no influence now that fear of police is largely gone. Gomulka's opponents charge that because of his de-collectivization and mixed-up

Communist doctrine the party apparatus has virtually no influence now. Opponents claim that the de-collectivization program led to rampant anarchy and capitalism in the country. They were thinking about situations like this: District party leaders in the country hold meetings. Many of them were never even farmers. They had been assigned, with all the emoluments of the party bureaucracy within the state, to supervise agricultural production. Few of them knew a tractor from a haying machine.

In the Marxist book, though, the line on farming was laid down. They followed it to the letter. The result was chaos and great shortages in a nation of farm surplus. By seeking to provide incentives to farmers, particularly young ones, by de-collectivization, Gomulka indulged in a calculated risk. Young peasants are allowed to buy land, as a gesture of cautious confidence. Suspicious of governmental authority by nature, they also try to show district party officialdom what they think of it. When meetings are called, peasants pack the meeting. About a tenth, at best, of the people showing up are or have been party members. But they stand up and tell the party officials what to do and how to do it, or else.

All the old, phony slogans that played a tune like "A Tractor for Two on the Old Collective" have been abandoned. If a party official, still firm in his conviction of rule by authority, sings out the old-type encouragement, he is chased right out of the fields.

"The anti-Gomulka party people think they can turn the clock back to the old collectivization measures," a Gomulka supporter in the hierarchy said. "The new generation of peasants, if anything, are more opposed to those ideas than even the old ones. If we should try the old pressures again, nobody knows what would happen. Nobody would raise anything. We are not about to starve the millions Stalin did."

Rumblings of discontent that echo in coal fields for lack of consumer goods, housing and the overall low standard of living reverberate right back in the wheat fields. Parents and blood relations on the farm react sympathetically to the plight of their kin in the factory and the mine.

Chain reactions are then fired off from factory to the plant in the next city right among industrial workers who with their families have lived in cities for generations. Almost invariably, young workers, products of postwar training, take the lead as they did in Poznan or the tramway workers strike later in Lodz.

In a steaming car barn a work-worn, middle-aged woman held an empty tear-gas canister and voiced strike demands that would be familiar to workers in the Western world: more money and better conditions.

The woman, a streetcar conductor, was one of more than 2,500 transport workers out on a strike that gripped the attention of turbulent, Communist-ruled Poland.

As I listened to her list the complaints, some of her fellow workers wept, some shouted encouragement. The empty canister the woman held was from one of the tear gas shells lobbed at the strikers by police early in the walkout.

The strike, which kept trolleys in their sheds and buses in garages, was partly countered by the local administration, which pressed Army and factory trucks and tractors into service on makeshift schedules.

Demands of the strikers seem pitifully modest by Western standards. But the standard of living in Poland is extremely low and there is little sign of anything better in the immediate future.

What the workers sought was a raise of about 3 cents an hour. For a work-week of nearly sixty hours, they have been earning slightly more than $50 a month, at the official tourist rate of exchange for the zloty. If they worked a forty-hour week take-home pay would be around $25. Overtime is their only way out, the strikers say. The raise sought by the strikers would net another $7 a month, big money when all basic necessities are so scarce and expensive.

I have talked not only with the strikers but also with the editor of the local Communist paper and the Communist secretary of the city council. All agreed on one point—that tear gas was used.

The strikers said about forty of their number were arrested when those in one car barn tried to make contact by truck with another car barn. Rank-and-file strikers also said they were held back by police with fixed bayonets when they tried to approach the offices where a meeting between the strike committee and government officials was going on.

"Our women were in the first ranks," a striker said, "when the militia kept us back. We sang a patriotic song."

The song was "Rota," an old Polish folk song. The opening verse is: "We will not part with the land in which we were born."

The cops broke up the singing by donning gas masks and firing tear gas. The strikers said at least four workers were in the hospital and many others were suffering bruises and minor gas burns.

The strikers displayed notes from the transport director warning them to start operating the trolleys and buses immediately or face dismissal. They also said their families were warned about unstipulated consequences.

Many strikers brought their families with them to the car barns, to maintain round-the-clock vigil to keep all public transport idle. The strikers swore they would not return to work unless their conditions were met.

A strike here of meat workers earlier in the month won only minor concessions.

The transport strikers are aware of the difficulties facing Wladylsaw Gomulka in solving the country's severe economic problems. But, they say, "Gomulka has his headaches and we have ours."

A younger brother behind a plow in eastern Poland knows pretty accurately the difficulties of his married sister in Poznan. That's why flash sympathy demonstrations rip across the country and bedevil state security. Even today police and security agencies are at a loss to provide explanations for these far-flung demonstrations, seemingly unrelated to the cause 500 miles away.

Riots in Poland are not directed against the person of Gomulka. They foment against the grotesque conditions that are left for Gomulka to administer.

"We are not just tired, we are fed up with working for the next generation the Communists want. It will never be here." Those were the words of a young machinist.

"Forget the promises. We want something today; we never had a past as children. We want something in the present." That's how an undergraduate in his last year at Warsaw's university spoke up.

Gomulka isn't only in search of a party. He has to find his way to Poland's lost and inflamed generation. As a Communist he cannot make the grade as you can hear in most places. In a crowded little coffee house I entered everyone babbled. Political talk—in Poland they call it "discussion"—was as thick as the smoke that curled up from two dozen cigarettes. People in the café were indulging in the favorite national pastime, indoors and out: conversation and complaints.

Two young writers, chairs backed against a surrealistic mermaid daubed on the wall, said they were fed up. Wladyslaw Gomulka, Communist Party leader, had intellectuals like them wrong. Why? Instead of taking the high road to bigger and better reforms, he was being too cautious, too much of a Communist. Gomulka was also acting like a man on a tightrope, balancing this faction today, that one tomorrow. Then he was always looking over his shoulder eastwards, to see how the Russians reacted.

They wanted more boldness, the disgruntled young men said. Did they have anyone else in mind for Gomulka's job?

"There isn't anyone else," they replied instantly.

That's just the point. No matter how deeply disappointment, fancied or real, bites into a Pole's attitude towards Gomulka today, there is not a successor nor a replacement around who can spark as much confidence as Poland's party secretary.

It is not ideologically fashionable to talk of Gomulka's program as national communism. Doctrine doesn't admit to such a condition. Gomulka talks instead about the "Polish road to socialism." What it means to an outsider is the Western concept of national communism. Tito, in Yugoslavia, by defying Stalin, set up the first blueprint of a separate Communist road free of Soviet directions. It was dictatorial, but not from the outside.

Conditions for Tito's behavior pattern were quite different from the shambles handed to Gomulka. Remember, in equating Gomulka's task and Tito's role in the Communist world, there also is a world of difference between them. What Gomulka strives for is a wide measure of domestic sovereignty, uncluttered and unfettered if possible by Russian interference. He cannot afford to offend the Russians by setting off on an independent foreign policy. If the Poles can manage their own internal affairs and obtain grudging Soviet recognition of this fact as a matter of custom, a new form of domestic rather than national communism will have been created.

Gomulka has two strikes on him, which Tito didn't have, besides Poland's terrible geographic location. Within the Polish Communist Party, which Gomulka as a Communist is sworn to uphold, exists a powerful opposition wing. They are as reluctant to accept Gomulka's program as most Poles are to submit to Communist doctrine. If Gomulka cleans them out, he doesn't have much of a party left. Step by step, Gomulka is trying to make over the party machinery to conform with his ideas. On the way, he has even abandoned many leading voices for more drastic reform. Gomulka's method of operation began as two steps forward, then retreat one backwards. Now, it goes in circles. It's a balancing act that mystifies most Westerners, infuriates the young and bold and keeps Soviet suspicions running madly up and down like a temperature chart. The important thing to bear in mind about Gomulka's operative procedural method is that it has been successful so far. He has staved off disaster and emerged with a bloodless victory for greater domestic sovereignty. It is only the first phase of a long campaign. Along his Polish road to "socialism," Gomulka compromised or rejected outright quite a few principles his supporters demanded.

Totting up the balance sheet, though, other assets remain untouched besides Gomulka's sliding-scale cooperation with the Church. His agricultural policy, de-collectivization which liquidated in a short time about two-thirds of the country's collectives, is almost unaltered. And, perhaps, the most effective psychological concession is always present in everyday bickering and griping about Gomulka's shortcomings. Fear and the midnight knock on the door have been pretty well eliminated from Polish life and living. In Western society, this may not seem so tremendous a concession but don't forget Poland is still ruled by a Communist Party, teetering for five years on the precipice of no-return.

Without outside aid the Poles cannot have a revolution that would leave them in one piece. It's a matter of survival. As a result, in the expression of a Polish university professor searching for the proper English word, "Poland evolutes." The process is being slowed down but the people's resolve to remain anti-Communist picks up speed.

Gomulka pruned the apparatus of government of virtually all the Russians who had been deliberately planted in the administration. Getting rid of them may sound easy, but it wasn't, for two reasons: First the Russians, nervous and trigger-happy over Hungary, suspected it was a move to take Poland out of the Communist orbit. Next, Russians had penetrated to many key and sensitive posts in government and they had to be replaced with competent and trustworthy Poles, not simply successors who may have been too long under Russian thumbs.

Gomulka, under the gun so to speak, went ahead and made the changes. Old Communist associates, jailed with him or because of him, stepped right into posts freshly vacated by Soviet appointees. From jails, too, returned non-party and anti-party officers. Men who served in the Home Army, the strongest underground force during the Nazi occupation, were rehabilitated. They were given jobs and a fair number were taken back, generally with promotions, into the military. A few hold responsible staff positions in the air force. They are closely watched. The biggest clean-up was in the state apparatus. In the party machinery, which Gomulka has said he wants to remove as a state within a state, his problems and opposition linger. How can you have a Communist Party without Communists? So, Gomulka does what comes naturally. He tries to create Communists. In turn, they create problems. They are totally undependable. That point was brought home to me more strongly than ever when I talked to two university students in Warsaw. One had just been warned to refrain from anti-Marxist comments in class. The other got a similar warning a week earlier. They took leave of me and each other with this remark in English:

"See you later, deviator."

We must deviate from our hidebound, do-nothing past, too.

CHAPTER | 20

KHRUSHCHEV has never swerved from his deeply rooted, fanatical belief in the superiority of the Soviet system. The consolidation and extension of the system was carried out ruthlessly in Soviet Europe after the great shocks recorded in Poland and Hungry. The technique varied but the objective was the same: rule by the Soviet Union and its Communist lackeys. Symbols of opposition, captive within the bloc, were liquidated pitilessly, secretly and silently. Indignation on the outside and helpless anger on the inside did not deter Khrushchev from his appointed task—that of being a supra-national undertaker.

Leading anti-Soviet, but Communist, figures of the Hungarian revolution were executed. Imre Nagy, Pal Maleter, Geza Losconczy and Miklos Gimes were put to death in Rumania, where they had been sent under Soviet guard. The Russians would have the world believe that the Hungarians they arrested after promising Tito safe conduct for the victims, went to Rumania voluntarily. A cold-blooded announcement revealed the liquidations. In Hungary, Kadar would no longer have to fret about the physical presence of a ranking party oppositionist. Nagy would be a skeleton in the Communist closet. He would have to take his place, however, in a long line. A Soviet diplomat in Belgrade with whom I argued about the executions reached a contemptuous conclusion for the evil end which the prisoners met.

"They lost their misplaced fight," he declared. "Nagy, Maleter and the others went on the wrong side. They knew better but they stopped being real Communists. Their execution is really a small thing. People get excited for a little while, only. They forget, in time."

He was wrong, because people do not forget. They always remember names for what they tried to do against overwhelming odds. Communists and non-Communists alike who fought the Soviet Union in the Hungarian uprising are never forgotten. I recall not long ago when mourners knelt and murmured prayers, beneath the vault of the great cathedral that is St. Stephen's in Vienna. A choir, refugees from the twilight land across the border, raised their voices in the magnificent crescendo of Mozart's "Requiem." It was a mass for the dead, simple in its majesty and overpowering in its humility. It was intoned for the souls of men who long ago had strayed from religion, but who in an hour of supreme crisis kept faith with their countrymen.

The mass was specifically for the memories of men who had been Communists—for Nagy, Maleter and others whose names were not worldknown. But the nameless ones are important, too. Once they had been dedicated young Communists—the intellectual avant-garde of a whole generation. They had been responsible for lighting the great flames that leaped up and consumed the rotten timbers of Soviet-constructed foundations. For several years before the revolution in Budapest, these men were motivated by a single, obsessive passion. They were determined to tell the truth and thereby achieve political and spiritual freedom. It was this passion after a once-morbid dedication to the party and the Soviet Union that enabled them to endure prison, ostracism, threats and torture.

They were murdered but their ideas live. Men may be buried in unmarked graves, as were the captives in Rumania, but their exposure to terror, deceit and intellectual castration still stalks Soviet Europe and its party proconsuls. Nikita Khrushchev himself tried to pretend everything in Hungary was going his way. He went, in a bold and prepared propaganda show, to Budapest. It was his way of showing that he was not afraid and that the uprising was really a bad but passing dream. Khrushchev showed himself to crowds assembled under the eye of Soviet security forces. In the workers' stronghold, Csepel Island, Khrushchev belittled the revolution and praised Kadar. What he didn't notice, or avoided noticing, was the stream of workers who walked out on him. Far from being scared, asserted Khrushchev, he was confident. The repression and the terror that had gone before his visit, guaranteed a non-violent reaction to Khrushchev's appearance in Budapest.

"You will remember that he did not come here in 1956," a Hungarian writer, an elderly man, remarked to me in Budapest, "The men who did the dirty work for him came—in armored cars and tanks."

Khrushchev's comrade-to-comrade whistle-stopping in Budapest kept him away from two spots of particular significance to Hungarians. In the blasted block where the Killian Barracks, Budapest's Alamo, once stood, an apartment house project was going up fast. It was intended to make locals forget the stand made there a few years before by a few hundred Hungarians against the might of the Red Army. When I walked by, I noticed that people sometimes stopped and stared. They looked briefly at slogans, hailing Kadar's achievements. In the few minutes in which I wandered around, I saw that a few passers-by spat in the street.

They could not do that and get away with it on the other side of the river, where you can walk down to the weatherstained quays of Buda.

Tommygunners patrolled, in day and night shifts, a long, low-slung building. People who stopped were ordered, with the jab of a thumb and the flick of a gun muzzle, to move along. This is the prison at Foe Utca. Kadar kept kangaroo courts in overtime session there to hand down sentences. Many met death by firing squad. Others were handed long terms in prison. The victims, overwhelmingly, were all young. Some older and more prominent men became known locally as the "imprisoned intellectuals." They were writers, like Tibor Deri and Gyula Hay, to whom the regime once pointed with pride while denying that there had been any stultification of the Hungarian genius. These men had been sent to prison for supporting the revolution and for refusing to have anything to do with the Kadar version of a Soviet government in exile.

Kadar's attempts at stabilizing Communist conditions of power were somewhat tragically comic. The apparatus of rule was transplanted directly from the Soviet Union. It all had to be revamped. How could there be a successor regime of any ruling quality in the light of the disappearance, in emergency conditions, of the old in a matter of hours? Kadar keeps spending his time trying to make it seem durable and palatable. He even sought to retread a Communist-Social Democratic alliance by bringing into his government Gyorgy Marosan. With the opportunistic Szakasits, Marosan was a renegade Socialist. In conversation, he always made speeches of devotion to the Soviet Union. Marosan, for public appearances, believed in the old-style religious behaviour of the party. That meant a cloth cap and an open-necked shirt to match his fire and brimstone oratory for solidarity with the Communist party.

"The government is absolutely determined to restore order in the schools and to maintain discipline under all circumstances," declared Marosan to a captive audience of parents and teachers.

"The power and strength of our state cannot be defined," he told me once. "People must obey because they must believe."

Not the imprisoned intellectuals. They steadfastly shunned offers to be placed back in society as good as new. All that was required of them was some public support for Kadar. They stayed in jail, some growing older more infirm, and some just sicker. In the outside world a campaign to release the intellectuals got under way with great names leading the lists. There were, among others, T. S. Eliot and Jean-Paul Sartre. They got a world hearing, wherever creative thought is held in esteem and a talent for words is regarded as a fine art. In time, the imprisoned intellectuals were released. Where Kadar is concerned, they have all remained mum. They are also all in Hungary, where they studiously shun a unique apologist for the Kadar regime.

He is Noel Field, once a specialist in the United States State Department and later enmeshed in war-time intrigue, particularly where Communists were concerned. Descendant of an old Quaker family, Noel Field was erratic in thought and habit. Czechoslavakia's Communists threw him in jail on charges of espionage. His architect brother, Hermann, went looking for Noel and also landed in prison. He was arrested in Warsaw on his way to board a plane to Prague.

When the regulated thaw in Soviet Europe became policy, both Fields were released. The Polish regime, with apologies and a large cash compensation, asked Hermann Field to go. First he went to England and then returned to the United States, where he lives quietly today. Noel chose to live in Communist-governed Hungary. He went there with his German-born wife, Herta, who keeps foreign visitors away from their villa by the simple expedient of slamming the door in their faces. English and German translation are, according to a telephone talk with Noel, their means of livelihood. They apparently are not fluent in Hungarian. The drawback didn't prevent the Fields from having a good house, normally reserved for the party or its elite new class. During the revolution, the Fields hid. They returned with the re-entry of Kadar and the Russians and have remained ever since.

"Noel Field used to tell us about how terrible conditions were in America," a refugee Hungarian scientist recalled of his meetings with the Fields. "He always told us how free we were here. We couldn't take Field seriously. Everyone knows what our frontiers are like."

Getting out had always been easier in another cornerstone of Soviet Europe. Up north, near the Brandenburg Gate, refugees could cross from Communist East Berlin to West Berlin for the price of a five-cent subway ride. For years they took full advantage of the chance to shuttle to a new life. About one in five persons in the Soviet Zone of Germany rode the subway west—and stayed there. Some of them were East Berliners, fed up with a life of empty promises, bare larders and coercion. Most refugees were Germans from the zone. They included physicians, teachers, engineers, technical specialists of all kinds, farmers who resisted collectivization and workers.

The regime they fled calls itself, through Soviet fiat, the German Democratic Republic. It is neither democratic, nor a republic and German only in language. Through all political vicissitudes and upheavals, Walther Ulbricht remains the Communist in charge. In continuity he is the Mikoyan of Communist Germany, surviving all changes. When Khrushchev rolled back bitter opposition in Hungary and dictated his own form of coexistence within the Soviet bloc with Gomulka, he set his sights on East Germany. This was an unruly, unwilling and uneasy satellite in Soviet Europe. It compared miserably with West Germany, which was prosperously booming and seemed to many uncomfortably powerful.

The West German mark became the most coveted of the world's currencies. Their goods were on display in all the world's markets. Countries that like to call themselves uncommitted in Asia and Africa eagerly went to buy from the overflowing counters of the West German economy. In the Western community of nations, the Federal Republic took its place as a powerful and respected, if not particularly loved, member of NATO. Its Chancellor, the starchy and unflinching Dr. Konrad Adenauer, became a symbol of West German eminence in the world, synonymous with a stern, anti-Communist posture. Old and unbending though he may be, nobody, East or West, ever seriously tried to equate Adenauer with Ulbricht. Neither did they ever make the comparison between East and West Germany. There simply was no comparison.

Khrushchev militantly set out to show the world that there should be not only an equation between the two but a favorable comparison. It was no coincidence, an important Communist in Soviet Europe told me that Khrushchev went out to make East Germany an equal before the world only a few months after Hungary's Communist rebels had been liquidated. There were, to be sure, many other factors and compulsions. But Khrushchev seems to have felt that in Eastern Europe, the removal from the scene of Nagy, Maleter and others finished off rebellious spirits in party structures of Soviet Europe. He thereupon issued his unilateral declaration in November, 1958. Khrushchev declared he wanted recognition for East Germany, that West Berlin had to become a free and neutral city and that he would sign a separate treaty with Ulbricht if the West refused to accept his proposals.

First result of Khrushchev's declaration was a swift rise in the escape rate to West Berlin. That exit hatch had been kept open although the machinery to seal it off always existed. Why it was left open so many years always will remain a matter of some guesswork in the Soviet world. An explanation given to me by Polish Communists once was that closing off East from West Berlin bothered the status-seeking ambitions of Khrushchev. It would have been, they said, prima facie admission to the world that an escape-proof cage was required to keep the East Zone intact. Khrushchev, according to them, dallied as long as he dared.

His status symbol ambition of super-power co-equality with us made Khrushchev slow to create an international boundary in the city. But he was up against it in the massive drain on East Germany's manpower. Between 1950 and 1960 about 3,300,000 fed-up people fled to the West. The mangled, mismanaged economy threatened not only the ramshackle foundations of the Communist German state but all Soviet Europe. Something drastic and dramatic had to be done. It was not enough to offer the East German regime a contract, in the form of a separate treaty. Action, was Ulbricht's demand, or else Khrushchev could be held accountable in the thoughts and eyes of the world's Communists.

This exposition still seems to me the most logical explanation of why

Khrushchev went into the kind of delayed-action he sponsored in Berlin last summer.

It was the do-it-yourself method. But Khrushchev's impinged directly on Western positions, contracted with the Russians as a result of a wartime alliance. As the leader of the West's alliance of nations, the United States was the logical target for Khrushchev's unilateralism. Berlin was under the gun, so to speak, but it was up to American prestige, power and wisdom to reject unilateral proposals.

Had Ulbricht been a devout man, he would have said that Khrushchev's offer was heaven-sent. For him, it was just as good, coming as it did from Mr. Big in the U.S.S.R. Forcing recognition of his discredited regime on the world suited Ulbricht's concept of Communist militancy. His grandiose plans for catching up with West Germany on a head-to-head basis of production and well-being began to flop soon after it was launched. To distract attention from other internal matters, Ulbricht embarked on a hurry-up collectivization scheme. Activists, backed by Volkspolizei (People's Police) worked on peasants individually and collectively. They used the collective form to show their victims how easy it would be for them to fall in line.

Peasants, despite their loathing for the regime, tried to stay on their land. Many tried to the very end of their resources. Jail, mixed with judicious threats, sent tens of thousands packing in flight, across the sector into West Berlin. One old man, his son at his side trying to comfort him, described to some of us at one of the West Berlin refugee centers, the psychological squeeze used on him.

"For a week, Communists from the town party organization came to my farm," said the old man, his eyes dull with fatigue. "They spoke to me in the fields. I must join, they said. No, I replied. They followed me into my house. Join, they said. No, I answered.

"I couldn't sleep. They wouldn't let me until I agreed. Even when they went away, I could not doze off. I thought of what they wanted. I stopped going into the fields. I stayed in bed. Better to kill me, I told them. They said I had no choice. I would join in a collective. I even turned my face to the wall when I was in bed. They still talked. I was the last of our family on the farm, you know. My son and grandchildren went away some time ago. They would not stand it."

The son reassuringly patted his father, who was inconsolable. The old man kept mumbling: "They wouldn't even let me die on my own farm."

Ulbricht wanted to show that his regime achieved as nearly 100 percent collectivization as it could in the shortest possible time. It was supposed to represent a red star of excellence for special effort. Not only did the farm economy falter and then go to the verge of collapse but manpower dried up in the countryside. Old men just didn't fade away from their farms. Young people, between sixteen and twenty-five, fled in droves. Among them were many trained agronomists. The regime expected that because they were sons of workers and peasants, specialists would remain loyal and grateful to the Communist state.

Mayor Willy Brandt of West Berlin stood at Tempelhof Airport, watching huge passenger planes laden with refugees climb above the tenement chimney pots girdling the field.

Brandt, wide of chest, has a big heart and a brain to match. Western newspaper men got to know him in Berlin just after the war. He was in a Norwegian officer's uniform then. The world has already often heard how Brandt, the lifelong Social Democrat, fought bravely in the anti-Nazi underground. His position today is unique. He probably is the only mayor in the world with an international policy. Part of it may be due to his stature as German national leader of the Socialists and the opposition spokesman to Adenauer. The other part is that Brandt is in the forefront of the present-day Battle for Berlin.

"The Communists will never understand what motivates a man to take off, to leave his life behind," Brandt said one time as he waited to see the Western foreign ministers in Geneva. "They try in all possible ways to keep people in their grasp. Property, hostages and jobs are some of the means they use. Some they may want badly, they even try to lure back or kidnap. They will never learn, I believe, that you cannot use people who are fenced in all the time."

His theory was translated into a joke by cautious Czechoslovaks on my last visit to Prague. Soviet technology was being praised lavishly in theatrical skits, the newspapers and radio. No expense was spared to hammer home what Communists could do with sputniks and luniks. The story that Czechs loved to tell trusted friends and intimate family was about going to the moon. "But do you think we could get to Vienna?" they would ask at the end.

By car, the trip from Prague normally is a little over four hours. That

type of trip, however, is not usual. At the frontier you can see watchtowers in the fields. Armed patrols with great police dogs check the
border districts. They examine incoming as well as outgoing trains, down
to the steel rods lacing the undercarriage of each car. The long train
examination, nearly three hours, exasperated an Asian friend of mine.
He had spent a fair amount of time on business in Prague. He asked the
police, "Who do you think would be foolish enough to want to sneak
into this country?"

In his anger, the Asian traveller was oversimplifying the problem.
Nevertheless, he put his finger on a peculiar Czech Communist trait—
smugness. It annoys the Poles to the north, who are anti-Czech generally,
when they speak of Czechoslovak regime policies. "Nothing can be more
orthodox and middle class," I've heard Polish Communists say bitterly,
"than a Communist Party made up of middle-class minds. That is what
you have in Czechoslovakia." Or, the dirty digs Yugoslavs take in their
on-again, off-again ideological quarrels with the Czechoslovak party.
"The Czechs," the Yugoslavs have said scornfully, "are horrified by the
sight of blood—especially their own."

Purges in the Czechoslovak party, however, were more bloody and
grislier than elsewhere in Soviet Europe. The regime also has been very
careful to keep liquidated Communists in the grave and not to re-
habilitate their names. None of the militant fervor of the true believer
is reflected in the Czechoslovak role as an ideological monitor. It is a
job that must be done, like that of a cop walking his beat. A good cop
gets promoted, for diligence if not brilliance. Czechoslovakia's regime has
been strictly orthodox. Khrushchev's Twentieth Party Congress revelations left the theoreticians unmoved in Prague. They glanced backwards
hastily at the explosion in Pilsen, and decided it was better to avoid
rattling old skeletons.

Much more useful, the party points with pride, is the Czech pioneer
trailblazing in Asia and Africa. The country's technicians and physicians
are the best in Eastern Europe. You can find, as I did, Czech engineers
and doctors working in West Africa or Southeast Asia. There are other
East Europeans as well. Most regimes in the underdeveloped parts of the
world prefer Czechs when they have East Europeans even to Russians.
I asked a West African minister why he felt that way. "They are so efficient on the job, like other Europeans we know about," he replied. Tito's
Yuogslavs have an extra explanation. The Czechs, they say bitingly,

served the interests of the Austrians in underdeveloped Eastern Europe for 300 years. Therefore, conclude the Yugoslavs, it is perfectly natural for Czechs to follow in the format to whatever power they are politically attached today.

Day in and out the regime makes it perfectly clear that the handbook it follows is published in Moscow. A hard-headed, inflexible man named Antonin Novotny is today both head of the party and president of the republic. The two big posts are a reward to Novotny for services rendered. During the Hungarian revolution, Novotny mobilized elite party units and sent them across the border. Theirs was a cynical mission, strikebreaking in factories paralyzed by walkouts after the last full Soviet intervention in Budapest. The Czech party is determined to try and keep everything submissive and orderly on their comradely frontiers. The sight of a Communist-ruled satellite, seemingly safe, sound and a-glow with activity, is a great beacon for other Communists.

It accounts for a great flow of on-the-cuff tourism in Czechoslovakia. Touring delegations are perhaps the greatest invisible, deductible item in Soviet Europe. A trip to the West for a conference, cultural exchange or academic get-togethers is a real prize. But money usually changes hands and there is a cash outlay. Not within the bloc, however. A member of a delegation gets free transportation, free hotel, free meals, gifts and pocket money. For a died-in-the-wool Communist, going to Czechoslovakia is a dreamed-of tour. He can see factories and farms, castles and combines. The fact that they all existed long before the party seized power is inconsequential. Czechoslovakia is the showplace of Eastern Europe. A good party man from another satellite state can dine out and lecture for some time when he gets home on what he saw and heard on his trip to Czechoslovakia. A delegation lives it up well anywhere it lands in Eastern Europe. The Czech party has the procedure down to a nicely regulated art.

Foreign delegates are met at the airport or railroad station. Every visitor usually gets a bouquet. Speeches of welcome and thanks are given and returned. Depending on the delegations' importance, buses or chauffeured cars are at their disposal. Hotel rooms are among the best the state can offer. Party newspapers of their own country are in every delegate's room. The official visitor gets a code number from the local escort, who invariably speaks the language of the delegation. All checks in the dining room are signed with the number. I have known some bored businessmen who noted a code number from the next table. They signed their own checks with the code. The bills went through. Conscience-stricken, these outsiders later confessed to the manager. He told them to think nothing of it. They had been good customers. Bookkeeping would become too complicated now to try and separate their checks from that of the actual delegation.

In a way, this method is on the house. It comes out of the toil, however, of Czech workers and peasants. Where the Pole might easily make loud and sneering remarks about an expense-paid tour by a visiting delegation, the Czech usually turns inward, to himself, and keeps quiet. The average writer waits until the party today approves of something a little more daring in expression than the past. It is a foreign product. Then, the local talent feels safe enough to follow the leader. The purges served, a writer told me matter-of-factly, as a lesson. Czechs learned how to lie low and try to roll with angry regime retaliation. A working couple eat better than anyone else in Eastern Europe. They seem, in Prague, to be eating all the time. There may be more food shops in Prague than in any city that size in Europe.

Cafés, restaurants and pastry stores flank the shops. Open-air stands that sell little fat sausages with a thick slice of black bread on the side, have plenty of customers. Eating is a compulsive habit in Czechoslovakia. It keeps your mind on your stomach and out of trouble. In the towns today, Czechs are trying to prove to their no-nonsense Communist regime that they can live by bread alone. It is a deceptive, dissembling habit. The government always looks for protective coloration concealing political radishes—red on the outside and white on the inside. Periodic arrests, therefore, result and the party newspapers warn the public to be vigilant. The townsfolk munch a little more and quietly do their work. No more, no less, as an old friend told me blankly over the rim of a coffee cup in a Prague Automat. It may not be an inspiring example of derring-do to an outsider. The regime, constantly suspicious, is kept guessing about what Czechs really think in the towns.

In the country, it's quite different. Your urban eyes can immediately size up the fact that something is wrong. Collective farms are untidy. Compare them with the small private plot the peasant is permitted to keep and you see the difference. It is the same with collectives in the Ukraine which I've seen, to Communist collective speed-up programs in Soviet Europe. Czechoslovakia's Communists, eager to show that they are first next to the U.S.S.R., embarked on headlong collectivization. The results, in Slovakia where there had been traditionally surplus farm products, were total deficits. Slovaks can by their detractors be called backward, overly clerical-minded and blindly obstinate. They have never been accused of laziness or of being bad farmers.

Collectivization in Slovakia produced have-not farm conditions. The Czech regime had to go outside to buy grain and barter for agricultural commodities to feed the towns. They also had to bring food into the countryside for peasants whose crops failed miserably under the plan. Peasants can normally take care of themselves even under drastic regime supervision. It was more difficult for Slovaks. They carried their enmity on their faces and in their work. Arrests, special fines and even deprivation of the family cow in a private plot, brought resisting Slovak farmers to sub-normal conditions for them. Pressure and threats, however, have not succeeded in making a thriving garden of Czechoslovak collectivized agriculture.

"After forty years, the Soviet Union has not solved the problem," a serious-minded Communist farm commissar explained to me. "It will come in time and it will come to us, too."

The staggering system of queues had come, presumably to stay, in Czechoslovakia as in all Eastern Europe. Men and women line up at groceries today, wait their turn and then buy one item at a time. Attendants in food shops wait on customers with harrassed but taciturn expressions. They wear white smocks, like hospital attendants. That is to emphasize the regime demand for a show of outward cleanliness. Go into the slaughterhouses, however, and you'll see something very different. It's a gory business, of course, but certain standards are demanded in the Communist-deprecated West. Quotas, not standards, are more vital in Communist supply plans. Meat is stacked, unrefrigerated, for consignment to trains or trucks. Flies swarm on entrails, trodden underfoot. This was a slaughterhouse near Prague I visited. One of the more advanced of its kind in Soviet Europe, so to speak.

"When you get meat, get it out," was the rejoinder I got from an overburdened assistant director at the meat-chopping center.

His was one way of looking at the job in hand and how it had to be implemented. Personal service carries no incentive. You do so much and you get so much. Overtime is for special shock workers. They are even uncertain except for propaganda stunts at present whether they will receive the promised bonuses. So you find men who may be trained for their jobs, checking in on time and leaving by the watch, too. Eastern Europe has built up a society of the most expert clock-watchers in the world. They can down their tools, leave the job and be out in record time. A mechanic who came out to fill my gasoline tank on a main road to Prague said it was lucky for me that I came when I did. He would be going off in ten minutes, he said. How about his replacement? If the other man got to the garage on time, fine. If not, there wouldn't be someone for a while. In silence, he filled my tank, took the coupons I previously bought at the bank and looked mockingly at the automobile.

"You have just bought the most expensive gasoline in the world," he said. "Your car will never be the same. You will hear knocks in the engine you never imagined. Come again. Thank you."

He was right. Short, fitful explosions burst through the carburetor within fifty miles. With a companion, I tried to see what was wrong. We stopped at a bad place, from local police standards. Stretched in the fields around us were huge transmitters. They were jammers, built at great cost and requiring expensive maintenance, by the Czech regime to stop broadcasts beamed on Czechoslovakia from the West. As we tinkered, a patrol car drew up. We couldn't stay around the area, a uniformed man said. Fine, we replied; tow us into town. They did. It was the first time Soviet European policemen had ever helped me.

Police anywhere are rarely admired. In a police state, they are universally hated. All are associated with the feared midnight-knock-on-the-door in Eastern Europe. Persons who receive the slightest favor from a policeman are regarded with suspicion by their neighbors.

Through years of bitter experience, Milovan Djilas' wife, Stephanie, became convinced of the bad omen of police. That's why she thought that an UDBA suggestion that her husband might soon be released was provocation. Should the suggestion be spread and even published, it might do Djilas harm. People get to think that way after living in the Communist-governed society. Only after she was summoned to high security authorities and told to collect her husband from jail, did Stephanie Djilas believe that the news was true. Still, she held it back from those foreigners she knew. Djilas came out, on a suspended sentence which can always be reinvoked. It was about a year after Vlado Dedijer had been permitted to take up an academic post with his family in Britain. Release of the two men was, ranking Yugoslav Communists have told me, the personal decision of Tito. I was in Belgrade on the night Djilas was released, at dinner with Asian and African diplomats. They seemed delighted with the news. Djilas had made contacts and lasting liaison for the Tito regime with uncommitted, underdeveloped nations. Many neutrals never hesitated, while visiting Yugoslavia, to see Dedijer and to ask why Djilas was still in jail.

Ulbricht wouldn't give you a hearing in East Germany on men and women he jailed, many of them dissident intellectuals. His regime has for years turned itself inside out to court Asians and Africans. The courtship has sharply defined limitations that can be summed up in one warning phrase: Be friends but don't meddle into East German internal affairs. Tito had also spent time, money and infinite patience building up contacts with Asians and Africans. Yet he heard sometimes impassively, occasionally impassionedly, new nations' appeals to release men like Djilas and Dedijer. His regime presented the confidence of entrenchment while Ulbricht's has always wavered between cruel, public repression and a desperate quest for international recognition. The men who could have been like Djilas in East Germany are either dead or locked away in squalid jails for a long time.

Djilas' name was widely known and Asian and African politicians and intellectuals were keenly interested in his personalized struggle for self-development. His refurbished interest in a form of social democracy intrigued many. Djilas' overpowering energy and fighting past as a Communist obsessed the imagination of others. The protests he raised against the new class in Communist society evoked sympathy in socialist-minded, but democratically inclined neutrals. Djilas, to them, suffered and fought for his convictions. Therefore, he must be accorded subjective self-determination. The same people who pleaded for Djilas also began to lose a blind spot they had for years on self-determination elsewhere in Communist Europe. Until very recently, you could not strike a spark of real sympathetic interest for the plight of the East Germans. They were unfortunate people, Asio-African neutrals often explained to me, but there was no practical solution for them. Mass flights of East Germans perturbed the world's uncommitted countries. But, in any case, they thought, it was a European problem that the East and West blocs had to settle among themselves.

Their worries took real form, however, and their mystique about self-determination became more expressive after Khrushchev stuck to his proposals for Berlin and a separate treaty with East Germany. The meeting in Vienna between President John F. Kennedy and Khrushchev sounded alarm bells in neutrals' ears. This was no longer a European problem, but one in which the whole world had a stake, including them. The dread possibilities of war over Berlin struck the first premonitory note in the consciousness of many Asians and Africans. That made the crisis all-important to them. On an intellectual plane they grasped for a compromise of ambivalence. Those with European experience ask, plaintively, what can really be done to honor the inherent right of self-determination. At home, their policy-making peers declare that demanding self-determination for a territory like East Germany is asking for the moon. It is, admittedly, a double-standard. In short, the Russians won't listen to such reason. Somehow, we will. Asian-African consciences began to get bruised when they were fully exposed to Berlin. It was a human, not a political, feeling. Those of them on the spot started taking notice of ordinary people leaving everything behind to seek refuge in the West. Most sophisticated Asians and Africans, no matter what their views, have had first-hand experience with refugees. Long and hopeless-looking lines of men and women in quest of a haven ring a familiar bell with them.

In many respects, I was more interested in observing their early reactions in East and West Berlin to flight traffic. For the first time, Asians and Africans from uncommitted countries were asking refugees why they found it so necessary to run away from Communist East Germany. The answers, simple, direct and absolutely forthright, have struck home in the mind, where it matters most to the higher-up Asian and African self-determination. A refugee factory worker, holding a five-year-old girl with one hand and an eight-year-old boy by the other, spoke tellingly about the reasons why to an Indian.

"I want to work and work hard," he said. "I don't want force to be used to make me or my family do something. I am a human being, like you. Don't you understand?"

My Indian acquaintance said he did. He looked away from the refugee family and straight down the street. The signs read: "You are now entering the Democratic Sector." The refugee family had just come from there, where the Communist world begins.

CHAPTER | 21

.

I T was August, 1961, and the sooty haze hanging over Berlin lifted unevenly, that midsummer's Sunday dawn. To anyone who cared to look, it revealed that the latest Battle of Berlin had been joined. A man-made wall of brick, concrete and barbed-wire split the city as an international frontier. It made the signs pointing eastwards to the "Democratic Sectors" of Berlin a total mockery.

At the wall, East German policemen kept their countrymen at a distance. Hoses that could sweep water under high pressure in a trajectory had nozzles trained on stunned crowds in both East and West Berlin. Tenements were bricked up to the first floor if they stood by the wall. The demarcation line that broke a city into halves with boundaries and checkpoints extended to house numbers, too. A tenement in East Berlin could have its front entrance on West Berlin pavement but now it was forbidden to use that entrance.

The wall, built with the approval of the Warsaw Pact members, isolated

East from West Berlin. The Soviet Union and members of the Warsaw bloc announced that the wall was justified. Politically and physically it meant that Khrushchev took the drastic step of forcibly dividing a city with a wall of terror. It was a fact, cried the German Communists triumphantly, and the West would have to recognize man-made facts.

There will, of course, be negotiations and perhaps even uneasy settlements. Recognizing East Germany because it is supposed to be a fact may, indeed, be part of an accommodation. But the problem of a great and sprawling city divided by barriers defies solution. Khrushchev once referred to Berlin as "abnormal." He was right.

In East Berlin, people had to stop running for freedom. Tanks, armed soldiers and roving police patrols choked off mass escapes. In a matter of hours, beginning August 13, 1961, concrete and mortar slabs were raised to crush all spirits. This was done just after Khrushchev had promised that a Soviet millennium was at hand.

The feat of a second Soviet astronaut, Major Titov, was still being hailed in Russia's Europe. Man might whirl through outer space but East Germans had been driven backwards in time to the Dark Ages. There was a wall to keep them sealed inside and to still their protests. It had been the Communist world from which they sought relief. All late spring and early summer, the total escapes rose steadily. Escapees increased from an average of 4,000 a week in June to 1,700 a day until that fateful August week-end. They still come, naturally, when they see a chance to escape, but it's a desperate trickle.

The life-and-death escapes today created bitter code names among shaken Berliners. They talk about the 100-meter special hurdles race— that is for sprinting to a low point in the wall and leaping over the barbed wire. Or, many have begun to mention the semi-submerged, all-weather swim—meaning swimming, half-under-water, from the East Berlin bank of a canal to the Western bank. Doing it submerged lengthens your chances. East German police fire at you as you swim. The Communist regime awarded one policeman a medal for killing a swimmer. He was, as the announcement declared, vigilant.

One of the most active codes refers to the world's highest pole vault. Actually, it often means death in the afternoon. Desperate men and women take to the roof tops. They cannot walk out their front doors because the entrances have been walled up. Stretched outside the street, on the other side of the wall, are safety nets. If escapees can shake loose from police on the roofs, they jump. Often, they miss. Towards dusk one day, an old lady wriggled out of the restraining grasp of two policemen. She jumped and landed safely. Cheers of relief went up. The wispy grandmother shook her head sadly at the wellwishers crowding around her.

"We're human beings, too," she cried. "But take a good look at the zoo they put us in."

She pointed at the wall. Reinforced with barbed wire, the barrier reached as far as anybody could see. Below the wall, extra precautions had been taken. Near some sections of the wall, areas of uprooted cobblestones, called commonly on both sides of Berlin "the dead zone," had been created as extra insurance against people getting out. The same stringent precautions were taken in the country along the 800-odd mile frontier separating East and West Germany.

Fencing in the green belt is physically harder because of its size, but actually it is much easier to guard. Berlin is the symbol—pulsating, frustrating and packed with potential dynamite. But East Germany is as uneasy, depressed and repressed as is East Berlin. We tend to forget that more than 16,000,000 men, women and children are contained in other towns and on the farms in East Germany. They, too, are East Germans who would like to live normal lives. Even in the wide open spaces, their plight is basically no different from the sealed-in East Berliner. In some ways, it's tougher.

Consider, briefly, an episode in human determination of sixteen families. All told, they comprised fifty-five people, from peasant elders to infants. Under the protective camouflage of a dark night, they made up one of the strangest and most desperate convoys that ever set out on a perilous journey. Their goal was Duderstadt, a little West German farming community of which you probably never heard. To get to Duderstadt the convoy had to move silently across fields and pass through the beetle-black Thuringian forest.

Four generations were in the mass escape. The oldest ones' lives spanned some turbulent history. Some were even around as youngsters when the first unified German state was in its infancy. These were very plain people yet they risked everything they ever knew: farms on which generations had worked and lived, their own lives and the futures of the just-born. In their own village, they had been forcibly collectivized. Stubbornly they resisted collectivization measures. They'd outlast and outwit the plan, they told each other, just as millions of others comforted themselves elsewhere. But they remained on the land.

"These were our homes," a middle-aged farmer remarked sadly. "We don't understand very much about politics. This one has authority or that one. You do what you can to keep out of trouble. We do know one thing—our land."

When the wall loomed in East Berlin, regime authority did not forget the land. Police surveyed farms near the green belt on the frontier. They took inventory of livestock, houses, fields and farmers. The police ordered the peasants to get ready to be evacuated. A defense-in-depth on the farmland frontier would be built. Families lost their last illusions with the curt command to be ready to evacuate. They consulted with each other. Finally, sixteen families, a quarter of the village's population, decided there was no longer a future and that they should try to escape.

Paths were found through the fields and the thick forest. Men and boys dragged out the largest wagon they could find. A team of trained draft horses, hoofs wrapped in sacks for silence, was hitched up. Thick rubber tires went on the wheels. Around the sides of the wagon, mattresses and blankets were hung as protection against bullets.

To prevent anyone on foot in the convoy from going astray in the darkness, the rest of the party roped itself together. Then they all set out on the long journey. They made it, and today they are in search of a future. Their fellow-villagers aren't. The village has been evacuated and declared a "dead zone."

"No man, no trouble," was how a runaway peasant summed it up in his thick local dialect.

It's a policy, in effect, of planned humiliation. We recoil at the degrading acts which force people to take desperate measures for flight. Berlin, however, is the place where we rivet our attention. The rationale is simple since we seem always to seize on over-simplification. Too bad about the East Germans. They are swallowed up and reluctantly we have to turn away from them. Besides, Europeans in Western and Soviet Europe have sharp and embittered memories of Germans. Why go into unnecessary risks to help East Germans? they ask. The answer to many, is that human dignity is still worth rescuing and protecting.

West Berlin has drawn the concentration of our planners to the exclusion of East Germany. President Kennedy has staked the honor and resources of the U.S. on keeping West Berlin free. We have, after all, every right to be there. We concentrate on West Berlin and on West Germany. Neither active Soviet menace nor sly blockade can alter our promises or our determination. So we swear and enter with the Russians into the international hot-rod game of "chicken." Between maneuvers both sides claim they are prepared to negotiate.

But the Russians are not prepared to negotiate about the same things on the same level. There may well be a settlement but it won't settle human aspirations or reduce the wall or even permit peasants to plough fields which happen to be near a border. We send big names to West Berlin to show that we are unafraid to face up to another Battle for Berlin if our rights to be there are abused. It seems to me it is highly egoistic of us to think that way. On the other side of that wretched wall people are maltreated all the time. Down that long 800-mile green border, they also suffer. But nobody seems to hear, or perhaps they pretend that what cannot be heard is not happening.

I spoke to a young GI after the wall stood malevolently between the halves of Berlin. He was from the Midwest, a youngster barely out of his teens. His father, too, had been in Berlin after the war as an occupation soldier. The boy was upset. His lean face was wrinkled in puzzlement as he lit my cigarette. "It's real lousy over there," he said jabbing a thumb in the general direction of the Brandenburg Gate. "Been there, mister? People shouldn't be so miserable. If they want to get out, let them out. I can't figure their system out. But it can't be much good."

He had not developed any solutions but at least he was aware. The young GI was very much different from an old friend, a highly educated, well-travelled American. He was on a cultural mission. His thoughts were studiously selective and sophisticated. It was not simply an issue of Berlin, he observed. It went further, perhaps wider than we have permitted ourselves to believe.

"The Russians are trying to force us to recognize not only this odious satellite regime in East Germany but their permanent control over Eastern Europe," he said. His well-tended fingers drummed thoughtfully on the gleaming cloth of the dinner table.

"How do you prevent it?" he asked in his monologue. "Try and get all Germany reunified and neutralized. Demand at the same time the wider neutralization of all Eastern Europe. You satisfy self-determination. You satisfy Russian worries about security and the potential of West Germany. Will the Russians accept? Who knows? You must keep trying, keep thinking in more imaginative and bolder patterns. Sooner or later it will make an impact on non-aligned countries in the United Nations. Where else can they hear it?"

He was, at least, a thinking American, even if you disagreed with him. I put his thesis to an Asian friend who had crisscrossed in and out of East Berlin with me. It had quite a lot of merit, the Asian acquaintance thought. "But it's a long and drawn-out business," he observed. "You can't expect it overnight. Too many Americans believe it can be done quickly, or should be done that way, like a flat business deal. Try it on the other side and you'll see."

Over in East Berlin there is a Soviet diplomat I knew years before in Vienna who claims to be "practical and realistic." A neutral, reunified Germany? "You won't buy that," he said. "Nor will we accept this neutralization for Eastern Europe you mention. Why should we? We will not willingly change their social system. What you call a crisis on Berlin is easily settled. Recognize the East German government. I assure you that it's too late to change their social system, too."

His last point gets some private support from many important West Germans. A divided Germany is in the world to stay for a long time, a veteran West German official told me as we drove slowly past the Soviet war memorial inside Berlin's western sectors.

Why don't politicians say so and make their people aware of it?

"Nobody in politics would dare talk about it to voters," he replied. "I wouldn't be in office one day if I did. We're all for reunification. How do you think it can be done? You talk about super-neutralization for all Central and Eastern Europe. Examine it from this side. What happens to NATO? The Common Market? Let's also take a hard look, in terms of votes. Sure, East German votes will be anti-Communist in a very big way. But they won't go to Adenauer's party. The Christian Democrats could be a permanent minority. I don't see it happening. I'm a politician."

For him, it was a power matter brought right down to an election-district level. A tough go-getter, he was in the booming community that is today West Germany. An official American viewed the pressures of power on a higher plane. The big picture, so to speak. He had been blooded in years of international bureaucracy and in countless across-the-table negotiations with the Russians.

"Whether you like it or not," he said, "we are gaited to try and protect a status quo. The Russians took Eastern Europe with military force. They stayed there. We can flagellate ourselves all we like on the mistakes we made and how naïve we were. We weren't there. They were. Of course, they deceived and misled us. Their regimes are miserable. We can't do anything about it without a war.

"In Berlin it's different. We have every right to be in West Berlin, legally. We are not in Eastern Europe because we permitted them to take it with force. On West Berlin we will fight if we have to. Not on Eastern Europe. The power position there is much different."

If war comes strategists admit that the Western garrisons will be lost. There are about 11,000 troops, Americans, British and French. They are very good troops, too. In case of trouble, they would have the support of 3,000 well-armed West Berlin special police backed by 10,000 uniformed cops with a pistol and a billy apiece. Taken together, it's a force of 24,000 men. They are inside West Berlin, sealed off in case of conflict just as much as the East Berliner.

On the other side of the wall, the Russians deploy a few thousand men. They are kept discreetly out of sight. Communist German security police for their truncated part of the city total 8,000. Add to that another 30,000 armed factory guards. In a fight, the morale of all these units might be uncertain. Tactically, the Russians have taken out insurance against defection in a fighting crisis. Within a thirty-mile radius of Berlin, controlling every point of communication, is a mixed Soviet-East German force of 70,000 mechanized and armored troops.

That's only the beginning. All told the Russians have around 400,000 men in East Germany. They are divided into twenty divisions, of which ten are armored and ten mechanized. Against them, striking north and east, would be a multi-nation army based in West Germany. The U.S. has about 180,000 men, Britain 50,000, France 30,000, and the Federal German Republic around eight divisions totaling 150,000. Canada, Holland and Belgium could field immediately a beefed-up four divisions. Nuclear warheads and air fleets are behind and above these statistics.

It may all sound like a risky numbers game. We talk about it constantly to reassure ourselves and our friends. So do the Russians. Everyone concerned seems to have lost sight of the biggest power imponderable, the human element. In the midst of crisis a great lament that went almost unnoticed came from a prominent Communist philosopher. In Poland, Adam Schaff said he discovered that there is an unfilled gap in Marxism. He wrote in an uneasy essay that Marxism has nothing to say about the meaning of life. Or, indeed, about the fate of the individual in the unfathomable universe around us. Schaff said that persistent questions by young Poles made him think about the vast problem of human relations. Had he bothered to ask the questions himself, he might have gotten straight answers earlier on the streets of Warsaw or from Polish peasants. Marx ignored the human element. Schaff then dares to ask whether Communism is not in danger of losing the struggle for the minds of men.

We talk in terms of men's minds, amorphously and vaguely. In the end we fall right back to the comfort of our prosperous society and on the status symbols that mean power in the world today. Americans cluck mournfully at hair-raising stories of escapes from East Berlin or mass imprisonment. Few, if any, of us have ever bothered to think what made fellow human beings do what is so rare that we think it's strange and wonderful. Frightening, too. Communists will always find a reason to show where they failed. When East Germans were still escaping in ever-growing numbers, a prominent educator cried out his perplexity.

Professor Kurt Hager spoke bitterly of the party's near-total failure to reach and penetrate the minds of young Germans. He should know better than most. Hager is head of the education department of the East German central committee. Something serious had gone wrong in the teaching process, Hager declared. The people were estranged. Instead of welcoming the system, they had gone the opposite way. He unwittingly put his finger on the focus of the disenchantment. A human personality is not as easily molded as is a plan.

"School-children and students find a contradiction between their lessons and reality," Hager concluded.

Hager made the same mistake as did his Polish comrade, Dr. Schaff. They search for a hidden persuader that would convince fresh and inquisitive generations to follow the doctrine. Instead they meet with active resistance or formal acceptance that turns to opposition in a given crisis. The principal reason for their perplexity and fear can be found in the structure of Soviet Europe. It is based on the occupation by a great power of alien territory. When the test of fire and blood explodes suddenly, as it did in Hungary, the entire façade of the foreign structure vanishes.

Yet because of power considerations the occupation is strictly enforced. Even in regimes with limited, local autonomy as in Poland, the outlook must be uniform with the East German on foreign issues and the dogmatic devotion to the Soviet Union. In background, cultural heritage and creative talent, a Hungarian has practically nothing in common with a Russian. He may even be far to the left by conviction. But he still prefers, if he can, to criticize and also to laugh at rules of conduct laid down by the party. Humor and irony are very narrowly defined in Soviet Europe. The advent of the "Soviet Man," as promised in the Twenty-second Party Congress by Khrushchev, cannot be transmuted to the East European.

In the first place, he doesn't want to be a Soviet man or woman. He hankers to be a Pole, perhaps, or a European in the sense of belonging to a world that has found the best accommodations for equality during his lifetime. After imposing their strictures on an alien society, the Russians also have left the bitter taste of inequality. It is a harsh factor of life East Europeans often discuss. Within a community hailed by the Soviet Union as equal before the world, 100,000,000 alien people do not have equality with Soviet citizens. This fact acts as the catalyst for ferment that churns up the human reactions of so many disaffected, discouraged and dismayed East Europeans. When they can stand no more, they commit the feats of self-determination at which we marvel.

Have we the right to even applaud great acts of human expression in Eastern Europe? In all the years I travelled around the western approaches to the Soviet Union, I heard of protests we made against the denial of basic human rights. Did we do anything else? Very little, outside of broadcasts in which many emigrés were telling their countrymen how bad things were at home. Nobody knows this better, by the way, than the average East European. He doesn't have to be told so by someone who had long ago left the country. The satellite regimes, in their all-consuming fear and suspicion, give these broadcasts more importance than they are worth. It is still an offense in many nations under Communist rule to listen to Western stations. Huge sums are spent on jamming broadcasts and keeping technical staffs on the job.

As a link with Soviet Europe, information beamed specially from the West has questionable value. You might be able to keep a man's spirits up for a while but not when it seems to be forever. There was a time when East Europeans believed fully in what we held inviolable: life, liberty and the pursuit of happiness. The strange thing is that they say this is what they believe today but that we have cut corners on our convictions. Moreover, they say bitingly, that we are reserving these rights strictly for ourselves. What they want is tangible evidence that we mean, where they are directly concerned, the same endowed human privilege.

In Warsaw and Budapest, at separate intervals, I listened to impassioned remarks about the American Negro. Being a second-class citizen, Poles and Hungarians lectured me, was unimaginably degrading. In the U.S. with all the difficulties of transition and evolution, progress was noticeable in the status of the Negro in society. There are laws to defend Negroes from discrimination. A long, rough road has to be travelled before equality is attained. Couldn't we see the same possibilities in Eastern Europe? It was a pointed but valid question, put to me by the way, by present and former Communist Party members. Never before had grudging credit been given to us in seeking an honest solution to our race problems.

But there is no succinct reply to the main question. The U.S., as a practitioner in power politics, has withdrawn from every crisis that flamed within Eastern Europe. It was the status quo we strove to protect in Europe, not people bent on achieving a status of equality. In the quest to buttress our means of keeping the status quo, we made deals with dictators and unsavory regimes. The phrase, "free world," was created and tossed around as our inherent right with which to confer membership in this particular club of nations. It is by no means our particular prerogative to gild a distasteful regime with our protection because we believe it is practical. Such a political house can stand only as long as our power permits it to exist.

So, if we really mean "free world," we have to start housecleaning in our own home. At the same time we must extend the benefits to Soviet Europe. Do we want to do it and are we capable of it? The answer rests with the Americans themselves. A clean-up job cannot be confined to one corner of the world which we call ours. The result will be some mitigation of the problem. Most of the difficulty will remain unsolved and highly dangerous—in Eastern Europe.

This is where the Soviet Union is most exposed and highly vulnerable. An occupation is based on self-protection in a war. What Americans never seem to have grasped is that we have been locked in warfare with the Soviet Union. It is deadly, no-quarter and based on the principle, in the long run, of total victory and total defeat. Tradition has conditioned us to believe that only the sound of shells and the chaos of physical conflict add up to war. Bombs haven't exploded and the Red Army hasn't come to grips with GIs. Still the war, sometimes silent and always remorseless continues. In between battle phases come armistices, known as periods of coexistence. We remain on the defensive.

By choosing to stay static we will one day soon exhaust our own ability to maintain and sponsor a Western defense community. Impatience for something more dynamic and more imaginative would sap our appeals to take care and to help pay for it. It would be an old story, repeated so often as to fall on heedless ears. Our friends would not necessarily go Red. They would probably strike out on their own to create a force between us and the Soviet bloc in Europe. The alternative then imposed on us will be withdrawal to North America.

To go over to the offensive we must put into practice what we preach about a free world. Europe, particularly Eastern Europe, is the place in which to start. It would be striking out on a genuine new frontier. Reforms on which we have embarked at home to bring equality to the Negro and to dispel the image of the "hungry American" where he subsists in squalor, must have more vigor. Similarly, modifications must be made in European regimes we have adopted as allies in the community of nations that proclaim themselves free.

But this is not a step-by-step system of progress. They should all go together along with the most decisive step of all: the people of Eastern Europe must be promised ultimate self-determination. We cannot, in honesty, condemn Soviet occupation unless we are willing to help put an end to it. My experienced and wise American acquaintance had the seeds of great vision and imagination when he spoke in Berlin about super-neutralization from the Rhine to Soviet frontiers. Such a highly complex plan is the basis of negotiation. It is not enough, however, to talk about it and to whittle away points. The Soviet Union must be shown conclusively that it is neither entitled to nor responsible for planning human lives in Eastern Europe. That is for East Europeans to determine themselves under proper conditions and assurances.

Here is where the American people will be called upon to put up or shut up. We want to negotiate for the self-determination of Eastern Europe. We don't want the area to swing over and become part of our community. The hope is that what was once Soviet Europe might live in decency and dignity as, for example, Austria. For this Americans must be prepared to risk the comfort of an affluent society and packaged praise of how fortunate we are. Spreading some of our good fortune calls for risk and sacrifice. If we mean to genuinely encourage the human factor in Soviet Europe—and I am convinced we must if only for selfish, self-survival motives—then we must take chances.

The biggest, riskiest of these is guerrilla warfare. If we set about seriously supporting clandestine operations in Soviet Europe, the Russians say it means war. Does it? Guerrilla warfare and pyschological warfare in Europe have been waged by the Soviet Union since 1945, with Greece as a classic example. The huge zone of occupation in Eastern Europe is much more fertile territory for guerrilla warfare than was Greece. Mao Tse-tung's thesis works in reverse over this ground. "Guerrillas are like fish," he said of China. "The people are the water in which the fish swim. If the temperature of the water is right, the fish multiply and flourish."

Conditions in Soviet Europe are rather like those Mao described. By supporting guerrilla activity by East Europeans we may well halt the slide towards war rather than provoke it. We also must be prepared to stake our resources and nationhood not to cold-bloodedly abandon those who revolt. Negotiation leading towards self-determination is always the objective. To speed it up and provide it would soul and meaing calls for counter-subversion.

Americans may today shrink from these awesome alternatives. I do not know. It has never been put up to them with chilling clarity. In the past Americans customarily have been freely generous with their treasure—and also with their blood. They certainly have not understood the scramble for life in Soviet Europe. Our diplomats never made it clear. The most experienced and sagacious of them stay on a plane high above human compulsions—on questions of power, potential and spheres of interest. So they were caught as open-mouthed and flat-footed as were the Russians when the Hungarian uprising nearly blew down the edifice of Soviet Europe. It was equally true of their stupefaction at the time of the East Berlin demonstrations in 1953.

Power as the status symbol today takes our minds off why people rise up in revolt or try to run away. We count our blessings in terms of steel, cars, ballistic missiles, space vehicles and assorted techniques. Nobody has paused to reason why this is so. It is, in the final analysis, to prove that we can do more materially for man than the other side can. If not, then man faces destruction. Not only have we remained on the defensive but we have been following the Soviet set of ground rules on the pattern of human behavior. It is a false thesis violated countless times by innumerable people in Soviet Europe who have rebelled or run away.

Escape is internationally recognized. We appear to have forgotten or overlooked this covenant, too. "Everyone has the right to leave any country, including his own." That's the language of the United Nations' Declaration of Human Rights. When possibilities to leave are choked off and when it is deemed a heinous crime to try flight, what good is a declaration? On the frontiers of Soviet Europe walls, barbed-wire, landmines and special patrols flourish to prevent anyone trying to leave.

It can all be seen, and Americans in Europe ought to take such a macabre sight-seeing trip at least once before they go home. I went down on a ribbon of road to Nickelsdorf, a tiny Austrian border community, just before the fifth anniversary of the Hungarian revolution. With me was an old acquaintance, a Hungarian refugee. He had been an intellectual of some note under the Communist regime.

It was a morbid trip for both of us. I had just come down from Berlin where the wall was still in the news. It was a different scene down on the Austro-Hungarian border. There, the plain was nearly noiseless. The autumn afternoon was colored a glorious russet. Fat pumpkins gleamed in the strong sun on the Austrian side. Smoke rose lazily from farmhouses and children spoke in excited whispers from apple orchards where they found the forbidden fruit that always tastes so much better. No other sounds.

We walked near barbed-wire fences. They rolled their segregating way for miles. In saw-toothed rows they protected rich earth. It was freshly churned. I'd seen that before. Fall plowing had just been finished. Mines were planted against this season's possible crop of escapees. The visit, in its way, rounded out for me the mid-Twentieth Century tale of two borders, Berlin and Hungary.

"Seeing always is believing, I suppose," said my companion. We stared at a Hungarian security officer. He had unslung field glasses and studied us from a twenty-five-foot watch tower. It didn't matter although rubbernecks have been chased away from there before with rifle fire that thudded into trees on foreign soil. The officer descended, his boots rasping on the steel ladder. He waited until a patrol of four armed men and a dog approached from a clump of trees. They all went off on a winding path that leads to a shallow canal. Hungarians used to escape that way, but no more.

"Trust does not exist between these regimes and the population," said my companion. "You do not know what it means to have authorities ask why you got a letter from abroad. Who was that foreigner who stopped you on the street? Over here, if you have money to buy a ticket to travel, that's all you need. Nobody asks a reason. It sounds so simple and terribly non-intellectual, doesn't it? I used to think so once. Ordinary people don't theorize about it. They'd do anything to get out. Yes, anything."

Today in Berlin that simple truth almost overshadows human consequences. A daily diary of death is inscribed around the wall. The cumulative brutality dulls indignation. Back at the first Battle of Berlin, under the Brandenburg Gate a policy of non-existence was begun on the ashes of extermination.

Around that monument millions of desperate men, women and children have fled. Many more millions can look at it today, from a distance. They cannot get closer. For all these people and the world-at-large, the Brandenburg Gate is now an Arch of Terror. It should have been made into an Arch of Triumph for the human race. Power, instead of reason and dignity, took over. It made nations satellites and their regimes instruments of a greater power. But people are never satellites. They are compelled to live in artificial states and societies that are satellites on earth. Beyond the Brandenburg Gate, due east, you see why it's so. It must be altered if we are to preserve the shreds of human dignity still left to us.

SEYMOUR FREIDIN

Seymour Freidin is the Executive Editor in charge
of foreign news for the New York Herald Tribune.
A born New Yorker, he has been a newspaper man
for about twenty-six years—some twenty of which
were spent as a foreign correspondent covering
Europe from London to Moscow. He has known
and talked to most of the European political public
figures on both sides of the Iron Curtain and it is
from these personal contacts plus his own sharp reporter's eye that this contemporary history has
been composed.

Index

Absenteeism, in Poland, 70
Action committees, in Czechoslovakia, 80, 86–87, 88–89, 90, 92, 99, 101
Adenauer, Konrad, 132, 298–99
  breaks with Tito, 265
African relations, and self-determination, 307–8
Agit-prop, 2, 4
A. K., 68
Albania, 39
  communization of, 143–46
  and Yugoslavia, 29, 111, 144–45
  and Zhukov visit, 265
Allied forces, in West Germany, 315
Allies, protest German rearmament, 129

American College, Sofia, 58
American Forces Network, 51
Anti-American attitudes: in Bulgaria, 179
  in Yugoslavia, 30
Anti-Communist attitudes: in Bulgaria, 253
  in Croatia, 29–30
Anti-Communists: in Czechoslovakia, 25, 78, 82, 93
  in Hungary, 27–28
  in Rumania, 63
  Serbs as, 53
  in W Europe, 20
Anti-Fa, 2, 19, 126, 129
Anti-Russian attitudes: in Hungary, 225

Anti-Russian attitude (*continued*)
  in Poland, 217–18
  in Yugoslavia, 30
Anti-Semitism: in Poland, 23–24, 215–
  16, 259–60, 283–84
  in Rumania, 63
  and Serov, 162
Anti-Stalinism, in Poland, 218
Anton of Hapsburg, 74
Antonescu, Ion, 31, 32
Apollendorf, 6, 7
Asian relations, and self-determination,
  307–8
Atomic bomb, 39, 51, 72
Attlee, Clement, 42, 93, 187
Auschwitz, 24, 216
Austria, 26, 74, 110, 319
  partition of, 192–93
  refugees to, 124, 249–50
  withdrawal of Red Army from, 209
Austrian treaty, 193–94, 196
AVH (Avos), 36, 75, 224, 231, 236–37

Balkan Pact, 166
Bases, Soviet, in Adriatic, 143
Battle of Berlin. *See* Berlin
Beirut, Boleslaw, 22–23
Belgrade, 53
Belgrade Declaration, 202, 205
Beneš, Eduard, 24, 96, 98
  attitudes of, 80–81
  and Communists, 87, 88–89, 90–93
Beria, Lavrenti: activities in Eastern
  Europe, 21, 41
  blamed, 161, 198, 199, 222
  execution of, 160
Beran, Josef Cardinal, 28, 90
Bereitschaften, 129
Berlin: Battle of, 1–19
  as center of intrigue, 126
  revolt in, 151
  and West, 127–28
  See also Brandenburg Gate, East,
    West Berlin

Berlin problem, solution to, 313–
  15
Berman, Jakub, 23, 216, 254, 283
Bessarabia, 31, 33
Bevin, Ernest, 42, 187
Bibo, Istran, 242, 247
Black markets, 138–39
  in Rumania, 64
  in Yugoslavia, 110–11
Blankenfelde, 16–17
"Blue hats," 21
Bodnaras, Emil, 33
Bohemia, 77, 99
bomb plots, in Czechoslovakia, 78, 81–
  82, 94
Books, American, in Poland, 217
Bootlegging, in Eastern Europe, 141
Boris, King, 35
Brainwashing, 185
Brandenburg Gate, 1, 2, 3, 4, 19, 126,
  127, 298, 322
Brandt, Willy, 301
Bratianu, Constantin, 34, 62
Brioni, 53
  Khruschev, 201, 202
Broz, Ladislav, 148–50
Bucharest, 31, 62
Budapest: Allied missions in, 26
  revolt in, 223–247
Bulganin, Nikolai: and Geneva confer-
  ence, 194, 195
  and Gomulka, 255
  pictures of, 181
  rise to power, 161
  travels, 168
  in Yugoslavia, 22, 197–204
Bulgaria: anti-Communism in, 253
  attitude toward West in, 58, 179
  Communist party in, 34–35
  consolidation with Russia, 190
  industry in, 187–90
  Social Democrats in, 36
  See also collectivization, Frieden
Bulgarian Agrarian Party, 73

Carol, King, 31, 74
Catholicism, Roman: in Poland, 23, 212, 254, 257, 269–70, 275, 276, 278. *See also* Wyszyński
 in Slovakia, 99
Cepicka, Alexj, 99, 101
Chervenkov, Vulko, 34, 178, 179, 181, 183
Chetniks, 22, 53, 54
Children: Czech, 155
 Greek, 122
Chinese Communists: and Albania, 143, 146
 in Poland, 258
 and Tito, 267
Chisinevschi, Josif, 164
Chou En-lai, in Poland, 258
Chrishinevski, Josif, 63
Church. *See* Catholicism
Churchill, Winston, 194
 Iron Curtain speech, 71
Clementis, Vlado, 25, 77, 99, 119
Coal, Polish, sale of, 273
Collectivization, 40
 in Bulgaria, 178, 182–84, 187
 in Czechoslovakia, 206, 304–5
 in East Germany, 300–301
 in Poland, 273, 287
 resistance to, 59–60, 253, 311–12
 in Rumania, 32
 in Yugoslavia, 30, 104, 116
 See also de-collectivization
Cominform, 78, 84, 108, 109
 Tito opposes, 114–15
Common Market, 314
Communism: in Albania, 144
 in Austria, 193
 in Bulgaria, 178–91
 and Catholic Church, 254, 269–70, 276, 277–78
 in Poland, 211, 272. *See also* Gomulka
Communist party: in Bulgaria, 34–35, 178

in Czechoslovakia, 34–35, 178
 and intellectuals, 36
 in Poland, 68, 211
Communists: in Czechoslovakia, 24–25, 304–5
 in East Germany, 87
 in Hungary, 27, 28, 46–49, 74–76, 207–8. *See also* Hungary
 and peasants, 37, 63
 in Poland, 23
 in Rumania, 31–34
 and West Berlin, 126–28
 in Yugoslavia, 22, 30, 105, 106–7, 108, 112, 183, 200
 See also anti-Communists, non-Communists
Communization: of Albania, 143–46
 of Bulgaria, 55–61
 of Czechoslovakia, 21, 72–73, 90, 99–101, 205–7
 death threats in, 120
 of E Europe, 21
 of Hungary, 26, 41–42, 44–45, 74, 207–8
 of Poland, 22–23, 42–43
 resistance to, 71
 of Rumania, 41, 63–64
 See also collectivization, industrialization
Conover, Willis, 141
Constantinescu-Iasi, Petre, 164
"Consumer goods," 162
Crime, in Eastern Europe, 36
 See also delinquency, looting, stealing
Croatia, 22
 Khruschev in, 199–200
 and Nazis, 30
 and Serbs, 29
Csepel Island, 47, 224, 225, 296
Csornoky, Viktor, 75–76
Cyrankiewicz, Joszef, 42–43
 under Gomulka, 258
 at Poznan, 219–20

Czechoslovakia: attitude toward West, 24, 151, 155
economy, 77, 206
present regime in, 302–3
Social Democrats, 43, 87–88, 89
See also collectivization, Communist party, communization, Pilsen

Dalmatian coast, and Serbs, 29
Dangulov, Sava, 65
Danube conference, 110
de Madariaga, Salvador, 195
De-collectivization: in Poland, 257, 272, 287–88, 292
in Serbia, 169–70
in Yugoslavia, 168–69, 200
Dedijer, Steve, 106, 173
Dedijer, Vladimir, 30, 50, 104, 107, 108
and Djilas, 173–74, 253
punished, 175–76
released, 306–7
and Western aid, 115
Dedinje, 53
Delinquency, juvenile, in E Europe, 139
Demonstrations: for Au, 60–61
anti-Soviet, 270–71
in Czechoslovakia, 91–92
"spontaneous," 48–59, 61, 63, 127, 128
for Wyszyński, 285
Deportation, mass, of Hungarians, 248
Deva, Lukai, 144
Devaluation, financial, in Czechoslovakia, 152
Dimitrov, Georgi, 34, 35, 57–58, 119, 181
and Petkov, 58, 73
tomb, 178, 179
Dimitrovo East, 179, 187–90
Divizion i Mbrojtjes se Popullit (DMP), 145

Djilas, Milovan, 30–31, 84, 103, 119, 133
attitude toward US, 52
criticizes regime, 172–74
in India, 165
punished, 175–76, 252–53, 264
released, 306–7
Dobrudja, 31
Dononeyeva, Maria, 13, 14, 15
Drtina, Prokop, 78, 94–95
Drunkenness, in Poland, 259
Dulles, John Foster, 194, 195, 196
and "rollback," 218

East Berlin: escapes from, 310
Soviet troops in, 315
East Berlin wall, 309–12, 322
East Germany: and Communists, 87
population of, 311
rearmament of, 128–30
recognition of, 132, 309
refugees from, 298, 299
status of, 299
and USSR, 22, 313
and Yugoslavia, 265
See also collectivization, communization
Eden, Anthony, 166, 194
Eisenhower, Dwight D., 4, 9, 12
and East Germany, 151
and Geneva conference, 195, 218
Hungarian policy of, 242
Eisler, Gerhardt, 128
Elections: in Austria, 192–93
during Groza regime, 64–66
in Hungary, 239
in Poland, 258–59, 279
Emelyanov, Vladimir, 11–12, 13, 14
Entertainment, in Bulgaria, 81
Escape, as right, 321
Escapes, mass, from East Berlin, 310–11, 316
Europe, postwar division of, 20, 38–39
See also partition

Evacuation, of East German peasants, 312

"Fatherland Front," 185
Field, Hermann, 297
Field, Noel, 297
Fierlinger, Zdenek, 43, 73, 101
  and coalition, 80, 87, 88, 89
Figl, Leopold, 193, 194
Five-Year Plan: in Bulgaria, 187
  in Yugoslavia, 115
Food supplies, in Rumania, 64
France, and Austrian treaty, 196
Free world, concept of, 318–19
Freedom Fighters, 241, 242, 247
  See also Budapest
Freidin, Seymour: and Ana Pauker, 31–32
  in Bulgaria, 60–61, 177, 179–80, 183–91
  in Czechoslovakia, 205
  in Hungary, 44–50, 239–49
  in Nickeldorf, 321–33
  in Poland, 210
  with Russian army, 2–19
  and Tadeusz, 212–14

Gatev, Ilya, 184–85
Geminder, Bedrich, 119
Geneva conference, 194–95, 196, 218
Georgecu, Teohari, 32–33
Georgiev, Kimon, 35
German army, 16
  communized, 126
German citizens: in Poland, 284
  in Rumania, 64
German Democratic Republic, 216, 298
Germany: partitioned, 280–81
  unification of, 313–14
  See also *East, West* Germany
Geroe, Ernoe, 26, 221–23, 225
Gheorgiu-dej, Gheorghe, 32, 73, 267
Gimes, Miklos, 294–95

Gomulka, Wladyslaw, 21, 23
  and anti-Semitism, 283
  and Catholic Church, 254, 257, 269–70, 274–75, 277, 278, 279, 284
  and communization, 22–23
  disgraced, 43, 69
  re-emergence, 255, 256–58, 271–72
  and reforms, 268, 272, 274, 275, 277, 286, 291–92
  and repatriation, 282
  and strikes, 262–63
  and Tito, 291
Gottwald, Klement, 25–26, 81
  and action committees, 80, 86, 88, 89, 91, 92
gradualism, 210, 255
Great Britain: attitude toward Europe, 42
  and Austrian treaty, 196
  and partisans, 22
Grebennik, General, 241–42, 248
Greece, 320
  and Balkan Pact, 166
  border closed, 121
  resistance in, 72–73
Gregor, Antonin, 99
Grotewohl, Otto, 131
Groth, John, 8–9, 11, 15, 18, 19
Groza, Petru, 33–34, 62–63, 64–65
Guerilla warfare, 320
Gypsies, in Czechoslovakia, 123–24

Hager, Kurt, 316
Haile Selassie, 166–67
Harassment, in Bulgaria, 57
Harriman, W. Averell, 62–63
Havas, Bela, 75
Hebrang, 103
Hitler, Adolf, 24, 73, 216
Hitler Jugend, 49, 126
Hitler-Stalin Pact, 13, 21, 44, 68
Hlond, August, 23
Home Army, 68, 292–93
Horthy, Admiral, 40

Hoxha, Enver, 29, 39, 143, 265
  seeks Russian assistance, 145–46
Hungarian Writers' Club, 208
Hungary: anti-Soviet revolt in, 221–
  47, 279
  attitude toward US, 229–30
  attitude toward USSR, 44–45, 295–
  96
  border zone of, 22
  Socialists in, 47, 76
  See also Kadar, Mindszenty, Nagy

India, and Yugoslavia, 165, 173
Industrialization, 40
  in Bulgaria, 178
  in Poland, 69, 273
Industry, in Bulgaria, 187–90
Inflation: in Hungary, 26, 49
  in Rumania, 64
Informing, 137–38, 147–48
Installment plan, in Yugoslavia, 263–
  64
Intellectuals, 210
  in Bulgaria, 190–91
  and Communist party, 36
  in Hungary, 295, 296, 297
  in Poland, 254, 263, 286, 290–91
International Trading Corporation (Intrac), 141–42
Iron Guard, 31
Israel, emigration to, 260, 282

Jazz: in Bulgaria, 179
  interest in, 45, 140–41
  in Poland, 210–11, 286
Jews: in Poland, 23, 214–15
  repatriation of, 282–83
Jovanovic, Arso, 83, 117

Kadar, Janos, 272, 295, 296
  in revolt, 225, 229, 238, 240
  joins Soviets, 241, 248, 250–51, 267
  stabilizes Communism, 296–97

Kangaroo courts, in Budapest, 248,
  296
Kantorowicz, Alfred, 265–66
Kardelj, Eduard, 31, 84, 117
Katyn Forest, 24
Kennedy, John F.: and East Germany,
  312–13
  meets Khruschev, 308
Kethly, Ana, 27
Khruschev, Nikita, 181, 182
  and Albania, 29
  anti-Stalin charges of, 208
  and Austrian treaty, 194
  in Budapest, 195–96
  and East Germany, 299
  and Geneva conference, 195, 218
  and Geroe, 221–22
  goal of, 294
  and Gomulka, 255–56, 268
  meets Kennedy, 308
  in Poland, 223
  rise to power, 161
  and Tito, 163, 194–95, 196
  travels, 168
  in Yugoslavia, 22, 197–205, 207
Kidric, Boris, 105
Killian Barracks, 225, 226, 230, 231,
  232, 241, 296
Konev, Marshal, 125
Kopecky, Vaclav, 78
Koralov, Vassily, 34
Kostov, Traicho, 57, 119–20, 190
Kovacs, Bela, 27–28, 48–49
  released, 228–29, 236
  seizure of, 41–42, 74
Kun, Bela, 26

Labor, in Czechoslovakia, 100
Labor camps, 281
Land reform, in Rumania, 64
Lausman, Bohumil, 87, 88
Lenin, Vladimir, 4, 104, 181
Lenin Steel Works, 187–89
Lidice, 25, 81

Living standards: in Bulgaria, 178–79, 180–81
in Czechoslovakia, 25, 206, 304, 305–6
in Eastern Europe, 135–37
in East Germany, 132–34
in Hungary, 48
in Poland, 211, 273, 288, 289
in Yugoslavia, 263–64
Looting, in Budapest, 236
Losonczy, Geza, 231, 235, 240, 294–95
Love, in Eastern Europe, 140
Lublin, 68
Lulchev, Kosta, 36
Lupescu, Magda, 31
Luxury, in Eastern Europe, 135–36
Lwow, 23, 284

MacCormac, John, 226, 239–40
Majer, Vaclav, 43, 77–78, 87, 89
Malenkov, Georgi, 161, 162, 181–82
Maleter, Pal, 225, 230, 231, 235, 239, 240, 243
death, 294–95
Malokovsky, Alexandre, 2–8, 9, 17–18, 19
Maniu, Juliu, 33, 34, 62, 64
Mao Tse-tung, 144, 258, 320
in Albania, 29
Marosan, Gyorgy, 297
Marshall Plan, 77, 193
Marx, Karl, 4, 82, 104
criticized by Schaff, 315–16
Masaryk, Dr. Alice, 96
Masaryk, Jan, 24–25, 77, 78, 90–91, 205–6
attitude toward, 79–80
and Communist takeover, 90–91, 92, 93, 94
death and funeral, 95–98
Masaryk, Thomas G., 24, 79, 80, 98, 154, 157, 205
Metaxas, John, 43

Mihai, King, 31, 32, 40–41
exiled, 73, 74
Mihailovitch, Draja, 22, 53–54
Mikolacjczyk, Stanislaw, 23
Mikoyan, Anastas, 141–42, 261–62
and Gomulka, 255
in Hungary, 225, 229, 239
in Yugoslavia, 198–204
military aid, US, to Tito, 168
Minc, Hillary, 23, 254
Mindszenty, Josef, 28, 74
in American embassy, 242
return of, 235–36
Molotov, Vyacheslav, 161, 198
and Austria, 194, 196
Monarchy, in Eastern Europe, 40–41
Montenegrins, and Tito, 30
Monument, The, Warsaw, 214–15, 216
Moravia, 77, 99
Mueller, Vincenz, 129
Munich betrayal, 24, 72, 80
Mussolini, attacks Greece, 73
MVD, 7

Nagy, Imre, 26–27, 207, 235, 238–39, 240, 241, 247, 248, 249
death, 294–95
return to power, 162, 225, 229
"National Communism," 166
See also Gomulka, Tito
Nationalism, in Eastern Europe, 317
Nationalization, in Yugoslavia, 30
NATO, 168, 212, 298, 314
Natolin group, 69
Nazis: and Russians, 21
in Yugoslavia, 30
Negro, American, interest in, 318
"New Class," 30
"New course," 162, 163
Nickelsdorf, 321–22
Ninth Army (US), contacts Russians, 4–5
Non-Communists: in Czechoslovakia, 77, 82, 86–87

Non-Communists (*continued*)
in Hungary, 27
Nosek, 90, 94, 96
Novotny, Antonin, 303
Nowak, Josef, 260–62

Oates, Bill, 205
Oder-Neisse line, 216, 281
Orwell, George, 212
Ottilinger, Margarethe, 125
OZNA, 36

Partisans: Bulgar, 60
Yugoslav, 22, 28–29, 44, 50, 72, 82,
104–5
Partition, of Poland, 23, 216–17, 280
Patrascanu, Lucretiu, 32
Pauker, Ana, 31–32, 41, 63, 164
Paul, King, 166
Pavelic, Ante, 22
Pavlov, Assen, 185–86
Pax, 68–69, 271, 277–278
Peasant resistance: to collectives, 59–
60, 104
to communism, 37, 63
to Soviets, 68
Peasants: in Bulgaria, 34–35, 56–57,
178, 191, 253
in Czechoslovakia, 99, 101, 206,
304–5
de-collectivized, 168–69
in East Germany, 300–301
in Poland, 287–88
and population shift, 38–39, 312
in Rumania, 32
"People's Democracies," 21
Petkov, Nikola, 35–36, 37, 58, 59, 179,
185, 186, 187, 191
Petrescu, Titel, 34
Piasecki, Boleslaw, 68–69, 277–78
Pilsen, 77
riots in, 151–59, 206, 302
Pjade, Mosa, 22, 31, 44, 115
and Khruschev visit, 197

and Socialism, 52
Ploughman's Front, 33
Poland: anti-Soviet demonstration in,
270–71
attitude toward Hungary, 272
attitude toward USSR, 23, 268, 271–
72, 284
economy of, 272–74
elections in, 258–59
partition of, 216
reform in, 210–11. *See also* Gomulka
riots in, 290. *See also* Poznan
security problems in, 287
Socialists in, 42
Soviet control of, 67–68
US aid to, 274
US attitude toward, 70
youth in, 285–86
See also collectivization, Commu-
nist party, strikes
Police: in Bulgaria, 35
and communization, 21
in Czechoslovakia, 78, 306. *See also*
UDBA
in Poland, 257
See also secret police
Police organizations, 36
Popular Front, in Hungary, 27, 28
Population: of Eastern Europe, 72
postwar shift, 38
Poznan, riot in, 219–20, 255, 278, 288
Prague, 77
Prejudice, religious, in Poland, 276–77
See also anti-Semitism
Propaganda: jazz as, 51
Russian, 102–4, 112, 129
Purges, 147, 161
in Czechoslovakia, 302
Pushkin, Georgi, 40

Quotas, in Yugoslavia, 171

Raab, Julius, 193, 194

Rajk, Mme. Julia, 223, 247
Rajk, Lazslo, 26, 47, 222–23
Rakosi, Matyas, 26, 28, 72, 74, 75, 207, 222
  and re-education, 46–47
  replaced, 221
  and Socialists, 46–47
Rakosi, Mrs., 27
Rankovich, Aleksander, 53, 104, 222
Rearmament. *See* East Germany
"Recovered Territories," 216, 217, 281, 283, 284
Red Army: in Bulgaria, 35, 178
  backs communization, 20–21, 22
  in East Germany, 126
  in Hungary, 74
  in Poland, 271
Red Wehrmacht, 129
Re-education, Communist, in Hungary, 46
Reform: approach to, 317
  in Bulgaria, 35
  desire for, 209
  in Poland, 210, 256–58, 286
  See also workers' councils
Refugees: Asian-African interest in, 307–8
  to Western Europe, 123, 124, 249–50, 266, 298, 299, 301
  from Yugoslavia, 264
Rehabilitation, of political deviates, 185
Reichschancellery, 98
Reiss, Istram, 27
Religion, in Bulgaria, 182
  See also Catholicism
Repatriation: of Germans, 284
  of Poles, 260–62, 282
Resettlement, of Poles, 217, 280–81
Reuter, Ernst, 127–28
Revanchism, 143
Revisionism, 274, 286
Revisionists, 254, 260, 272
Riddleberger, James, 203

Ripka, Hubert, 88
Roadblocks, in Eastern Europe, 55
Rokossovsky, Marshal, 211–12, 254, 256
"Rollback," 151, 218
Roman Catholic Church. *See* Catholicism
Roosevelt, Franklin D., 4, 8, 12
Rumania, 163–64
  anti-Semitism, 63
  and Hungary, 253
  Nagy in, 249
  postwar conditions in, 31–34
  Social Democrats in, 34
  Tito in, 73–74
  See also collectivization, Communists, communization

"Salami" techniques, 75, 76, 143
Samborsky, Anton, 13
Saxons, in Rumania, 63–64
Schaff, Adam, 315–16
secret police, 41
  in Czechoslovakia, 79
  in Poland, 211
  Russian, 21
  in Yugoslavia, 82–84, 106
  See also Beria, Serov
Securitate (Siguranza), 36, 253
self-determination, 319–20
  desire for, 317
  and world opinion, 307–8
Serbia, de-collectivization in, 169–70
Serbinsky, Mr., 186–87
Serbs, 29–30, 53
Serov, Ivan, 161–62
Shehu, Mehmut, 29, 39, 143, 145, 265
Shopping, in Eastern Europe, 136–37
Simeon, King, 35, 40
Simon, Andre, 79
Simpson, William, 4
Skoda works, 151, 153, 155, 156, 159
Slansky, Richard, 79, 100

Slansky, Rudolf, 26, 78–79, 87, 90, 119
  and Zorin, 81
Slovakia, 77, 78
  persecution of, 99–100
Slovenia, and Serbs, 29
Smallholders, 27–28, 74
SNB, 25, 36
Social Democrats: in Bulgaria, 36
  in Czechoslovakia, 43, 80, 87–88, 89
  in Hungary, 27
  in Rumania, 34
Socialist Unity Party (SED), 127
Socialists, 42, 76, 193
Sofia, 56, 178, 179, 180
Soviet bases, in Adriatic, 143
Soviet occupation: of Berlin, 2–3, 18–19, 315
  of Germany, 1–14
Soviet planning, mistakes in, 147
Soviet tanks, in Budapest, 239, 240, 241, 243, 244, 245, 246
Soviet troops, in East Berlin, 315
Sovietization. *See* communization
Spychalski, Marian, 69
Stainov, Petko, 35
Stalin, 12, 38
  and Albania, 28
  attitude toward Eastern Europe, 21
  criticized, 104, 105, 110, 208
  death of, 150–51
  pictures of, 2, 4, 7, 19, 43, 44, 181
  and Poland, 21, 68, 271
  and Tito, 21, 82–83, 119
  and Yugoslavia, 202
Stalin Statute, Budapest, 227
Stambolic, Petar, 175
Stamboulisky, Alexander, 35, 183, 186, 187
Stealing, 48, 69–70, 138, 139–40
Steinhardt, Laurence, 93–94
Stepinac, Alois Cardinal, 30
Stoichev, Dimo, 188–90
Strike: in Poland, 262–63, 270

  in Poznan, 219–20
  right to, in East Germany, 131
Sudetenland, 25, 77
Sviridov, V. P., 76
Suslov, Mikhail, 225, 229, 239
Syzinki, Stephen Cardinal, 23
Szabo, Ferenc, copybook of, 243–47
Szakasitz, Arpad, 27, 76, 97
Szczecin (Stettin), 287

Tartarescu, Gheorghe, 33
Taylor, Maxwell D., 127, 128
Technicians, Czech, 302–3
Tempelhof Airport, 18
Third Army (US), contacts Russians, 5
Tildy, Zoltan, 75, 240
Tiso, Josef, 77
Tito, Josip Broz, 31, 39
  and Albania, 145
  anti-guerilla tactics of, 121–22
  anti-Western attitudes of, 110
  assumes leadership, 28–29
  attacked by USSR, 112–119
  attitude toward US, 51–52, 72
  and Chinese Communists, 267
  vs Gomulka, 290
  defies USSR, 82–84, 102–3, 107, 263
  and Djilas, 252–53
  and East Germany, 265
  and Geroe, 221–23
  and Hungarian revolt, 248, 252
  in India, 173
  and Khruschev visit, 196, 198–203
  pictures of, 43–44, 50, 74
  re-approached by Khruschev, 163
  and Soviet agents, 22
  struggle for power, 22
  visits Rumania, 73–74
  world outlook of, 165–68
Tito, Jovanka, 165–66
Tito, Zharko, 105–6
Titov, Major, 310

Topencharov, Vladimir, 57
Torgau, 5
Tourism, in Czechoslovakia, 303–4
Transylvania, 31, 253
Tresca, Carlo, 121
Trieste, 85, 120
Truman, Harry S, 187
  and Czech crisis, 93, 94
"Trybuna Ludu," 212, 257
Turkey, and Balkan Pact, 165
Twentieth Soviet Party Congress, 202,
  208, 256, 302

UB, 36, 37, 257, 258
UDBA, 36, 116, 197, 253, 306
Uhliek, Rade, 113–14
Ulbrecht, Walther, 22, 127, 128–29,
  130–32, 266, 298, 307
  and German communization, 300–
  301
Unemployment, in Poland, 273
Union of Soviet Socialist Republics
  (USSR): area of control, 39
  and Austrian treaty, 196
  and Budapest revolt, 239, 242
  and East German negotiations, 313
  economic apparatus of, 21
  and European occupation, 316–17
  and Greece, 72–73
  and local economies, 66
  political apparatus, 21
  postwar power of, 71
  and Tito, 109, 111. *See also* Tito
  See also Communism, Communist
  entries, communization, Soviet
  entries
United Nations, and East Germany,
  314
United Nations Declaration of Human
  Rights, 321
UNNRA, 30
United States: and anti-Communists,
  20
  and Austrian treaty, 196

and Budapest revolt, 242
and Bulgaria, 179
criticized, 28, 320
curiosity about, 8, 50–51
and Czechoslovakia, 93
and Eastern Europe, 218–19, 318
and East Germany, 300, 312–13
and Poland, 70
postwar attitudes of, 39–40
and Rumania, 61, 66
and Yugoslavia, 108, 223
  See also anti-American attitudes
United States aid: to Poland, 259, 273–
  74
  to Rumania, 64–65, 66
  to Yugoslavia, 22, 30, 51–52, 111–
  12, 114–16, 168, 263
United States intelligence, 124
United States military missions, 26,
  39–40
United States, representatives in Eastern Europe, 66–67
Ustachi, 22

Vafiades, Markov, 73, 121
Van Fleet, James, 122
Vas, Zoltan, 27
Vidali, Vittorio, 120–21
Vienna, as center of intrigue, 124–26,
  193
Vilna, 123, 284
Volkspolitzei (People's Police), 129
von Einseidl, Heindrich, 130
Voroshilov, Klementi, 26, 28
Vukmanovic-Tempo, Svetozar, 121
Vyshinsky, Andrei, 33
  in Bulgaria, 35, 37
  in Rumania, 62–63

Warsaw, 67–68, 211–16
  ghetto uprising in, 23
Warsaw Pact, 212, 216, 254, 256, 268
Warsaw University, 211
Watchtowers, frontier, 122, 302

West Berlin: Allied troops in, 315
  Communists in, 126–28
West Germany: Allied forces in, 315
  boom in, 132, 298
Wittenberg, 7
Women, Soviet, in army, 6, 7, 10, 11,
  12, 13, 15
Workers' Councils, in Yugoslavia, 171,
  200
Workers' resistance, to Communism:
  in Hungary, 47–48
  in Poznan. *See* Poznan
World War II, end of, in Berlin, 1–19
Writers' Union, 223
Wyszyński, Cardinal, 28, 259, 276,
  285
  and Gomulka, 269–70, 274–75, 277,
    278, 279, 284
  released, 254
  removed, 212, 278

Xoxe, Koci, 143

Youth, in Poland, 285–86
Youth Brigades, in Yugoslavia, 50
Youth groups: in Bulgaria, 179
  in Czechoslovakia, 80
  in Hungary, 48–49
  in Poland, 286–87
Yugoslav army, 106

Yugoslavia, 21
  and Albania, 29, 111, 144–45
  attitude toward USSR, 44, 50, 82
  defies USSR, 82–84, 119
  and East Germany, 265
  and Intrac, 142
  Khruschev in, 197–205
  nationalism in, 112–13
  postwar conditions in, 28–31
  production in, 170–71
  shortages in, 115–16
  US aid to, 168
  See also Bulganin, collectivization,
    partisans, Serbs
Yugov, Anton, 58

Zahna, 14–15
Zaisser, Wilhelm, 129, 130
Zerkl, Peter, 78
Zheltov, Alexei, 125
Zhirkov, Todor, 34, 181, 183
Zhukov, Georgi: in Albania, 265
  in Germany, 12
  and Gomulka, 256, 268
  and Yugoslavia, 264–65
Zog, King, 40
Zorin, Valerian, 77
  in Czechoslovakia, 87, 93
  and Slansky, 81
Zujevic, 103